# The Conservative Party and European Integration since 1945

*The Conservative Party and European Integration since 1945* provides an up-to-date, readable and comprehensive introduction to British policy in Europe.

By exploring the schisms within the party over Europe, through primary source-based history and theoretical discourses of political science, N.J. Crowson gives the reader the best sense of understanding of how and why the Conservative party's policy attitudes to European integration have evolved. This fresh approach seeks to cast a new light on an often Anglo-centric study.

*The Conservative Party and European Integration since 1945* adopts a thematic line based around two chronological periods, 1945–75 and 1975–2006, and uses different methodological approaches. The book explores the shifting stances amongst Conservatives within an economic, political and international context as the party adjusted to the decline of Britain's world role and the loss of empire. Crowson analyses Britain's role and relationship with Europe together with the study of the Conservative Party, and deals with economic, commercial and monetary issues, successfully bridging a serious gap in any discussion of the UK's relations with the European Union and appreciation of the political world in which Conservative European policy has been framed and pursued since 1945.

This up-to-date survey book is recommended for background reading in undergraduate courses in British politics and European history.

**N.J. Crowson** is Senior Lecturer in Contemporary British History at the University of Birmingham, UK.

# Routledge Advances in European Politics

1  **Russian Messianism**
Third Rome, revolution, Communism
and after
*Peter J.S. Duncan*

2  **European Integration and the Postmodern Condition**
Governance, democracy, identity
*Peter van Ham*

3  **Nationalism in Italian Politics**
The stories of the Northern League,
1980–2000
*Damian Tambini*

4  **International Intervention in the Balkans since 1995**
*Edited by Peter Siani-Davies*

5  **Widening the European Union**
The politics of institutional change
and reform
*Edited by Bernard Steunenberg*

6  **Institutional Challenges in the European Union**
*Edited by Madeleine Hosli,
Adrian van Deemen and
Mika Widgrén*

7  **Europe Unbound**
Enlarging and reshaping the
boundaries of the European Union
*Edited by Jan Zielonka*

8  **Ethnic Cleansing in the Balkans**
Nationalism and the destruction of
tradition
*Cathie Carmichael*

9  **Democracy and Enlargement in Post-Communist Europe**
The democratisation of the general
public in fifteen Central and Eastern
European countries, 1991–1998
*Christian W. Haerpfer*

10 **Private Sector Involvement in the Euro**
The power of ideas
*Stefan Collignon and
Daniela Schwarzer*

11 **Europe**
A Nietzschean perspective
*Stefan Elbe*

12 **European Union and e-Voting**
Addressing the European
Parliament's internet voting challenge
*Edited by Alexander H. Trechsel and
Fernando Mendez*

13 **European Union Council Presidencies**
A comparative perspective
*Edited by Ole Elgström*

14 **European Governance and Supranational Institutions**
Making states comply
*Jonas Tallberg*

15 **European Union, NATO and Russia**
*Martin Smith and Graham Timmins*

16 **Business, The State and Economic Policy**
The case of Italy
*G. Grant Amyot*

17 **Europeanization and Transnational States**
Comparing Nordic central
governments
*Bengt Jacobsson, Per Lægreid and
Ove K. Pedersen*

18 **European Union Enlargement**
A comparative history
*Edited by Wolfram Kaiser and
Jürgen Elvert*

19 **Gibraltar**
British or Spanish?
*Peter Gold*

20 **Gendering Spanish Democracy**
*Monica Threlfall, Christine Cousins
and Celia Valiente*

21 **European Union Negotiations**
Processes, networks and negotiations
*Edited by Ole Elgström and
Christer Jönsson*

22 **Evaluating Euro-Mediterranean
Relations**
Stephen C. Calleya

23 **The Changing Face of European
Identity**
A seven-nation study of
(supra)national attachments
*Edited by Richard Robyn*

24 **Governing Europe**
Discourse, governmentality and
European integration
*William Walters and
Jens Henrik Haahr*

25 **Territory and Terror**
Conflicting nationalisms in the
Basque Country
*Jan Mansvelt Beck*

26 **Multilateralism, German Foreign
Policy and Central Europe**
*Claus Hofhansel*

27 **Popular Protest in East Germany**
*Gareth Dale*

28 **Germany's Foreign Policy Towards
Poland and the Czech Republic**
Ostpolitik revisted
*Karl Cordell and Stefan Wolff*

29 **Kosovo**
The politics of identity and space
*Denisa Kostovicova*

30 **The Politics of European Union
Enlargement**
Theoretical approaches
*Edited by Frank Schimmelfennig and
Ulrich Sedelmeier*

31 **Europeanizing Social Democracy?**
The rise of the Party of European
Socialists
*Simon Lightfoot*

32 **Conflict and Change in EU Budgetary
Politics**
*Johannes Lindner*

33 **Gibraltar, Identity and Empire**
*E.G. Archer*

34 **Governance Stories**
*Mark Bevir and R.A.W. Rhodes*

35 **Britain and the Balkans**
1991 until the present
*Carole Hodge*

36 **The Eastern Enlargement of the
European Union**
*John O'Brennan*

37 **Values and Principles in European
Union Foreign Policy**
*Edited by Sonia Lucarelli and
Ian Manners*

38 **European Union and the Making of a
Wider Northern Europe**
*Pami Aalto*

39 **Democracy in the European Union**
Towards the emergence of a public
sphere
*Edited by Liana Giorgi,
Ingmar Von Homeyer and
Wayne Parsons*

**40 European Union Peacebuilding and Policing**
*Michael Merlingen with Rasa Ostraukaite*

**41 The Conservative Party and European Integration since 1945**
At the heart of Europe?
*N.J. Crowson*

**42 e-Government in Europe**
Re-booting the state
*Edited by Paul G. Nixon and Vassiliki N. Koutrakou*

**43 EU Foreign and Interior Policies**
Cross-pillar politics and the social construction of sovereignty
*Stephan Stetter*

**44 Policy Transfer in European Union Governance**
Regulating the utilities
*Simon Bulmer, David Dolowitz, Peter Humphreys and Stephen Padgett*

**45 The Europeanization of National Political Parties**
Power and organizational adaptation
*Edited by Thomas Poguntke, Nicholas Aylott, Elisabeth Carter, Robert Ladrech and Kurt Richard Luther*

**46 Citizenship in Nordic Welfare States**
Dynamics of choice, duties and participation in a changing Europe
*Edited by Bjorn Hvinden and Håkan Johansson*

**47 National Parliaments within the Enlarged European Union**
From victims of integration to competitive actors?
*Edited by John O'Brennan and Tapio Raunio*

# The Conservative Party and European Integration since 1945

## At the heart of Europe?

N.J. Crowson

Routledge
Taylor & Francis Group

LONDON AND NEW YORK

First published 2007
by Routledge
2 Park Square, Milton Park, Abingdon, Oxon, OX14 4RN

Simultaneously published in the USA and Canada
by Routledge
270 Madison Ave, New York, NY 10016

*Routledge is an imprint of the Taylor & Francis Group, an informa business*

Transferred to Digital Printing 2009

© 2007 N.J. Crowson

Typeset in Times New Roman by
Taylor & Francis Books

*British Library Cataloguing in Publication Data*
A catalogue record for this book is available from the British Library

*Library of Congress Cataloging in Publication Data*
The Conservative Party and European integration since 1945: at the
   heart of Europe? / N.J. Crowson.
      p. cm. – (Routledge advances in European politics)
   Includes bibliographical references and index.
   1. Conservative Party (Great Britain) – History. 2. Europe –
   Economic integration – Great Britain – History. I. Crowson, N. J.
   JN1129.C7C66 2006
   341.24'2 – dc22                                        2006018728

ISBN10: 0–415–40022–8 (hbk)
ISBN10: 0–415–55392–X (pbk)

ISBN13: 978–0–415–40022–0 (hbk)
ISBN13: 978–0–415–55392–6 (pbk)

**To Alfred Neville Crowson**
Born 30 October 2001

# Contents

*Acknowledgements*                                                    xii

**Introduction**                                                        1

*The narrative  1*
*The historiography  4*
*Methodology  8*
*The sources  8*
*Preamble  10*

**1  Conservative moves towards Europe, 1945–75:
    'like chasing a girl'**                                            14

*The opposition years: the Council of Europe and the
    Schuman Plan  14*
*European defence and free trade areas  21*
*EEC and EFTA: at sixes and sevens  26*
*The first EEC application  28*
*Surviving the veto?  32*
*Labour's 1967 application  34*
*Third time lucky? The successful 1970 application  37*
*Renegotiation and the 1975 referendum  40*

**2  From EEC to EU, 1975–2006: 'in Europe, but
    not run by Europe'?**                                             45

*Direct elections  45*
*Thatcher's budgetary battles  47*
*Towards a single market  50*
*The European Exchange Rate Mechanism  53*
*Maastricht: 'game, set and match'?  55*
*The single currency  60*

**3    The issues and debates: 'head versus heart'**                    **71**

*Atlantic or European world power?  71*
*End of empire  76*
*Defence of Europe  78*
*Common European foreign policy  80*
*Political union and federalism  81*
*Sovereignty  83*
*'Let the people decide!' Referendum demands  89*
*Free trade versus preference  92*
*Agriculture: from an economic to a patriotic issue  94*
*The single market, monetary union and the euro  98*
*Enlargement  103*

**4    The Conservative Europeanist**                                  **105**

*Definition  105*
*The historical Europhile  106*
*The Strasbourg years  107*
*Edward Heath  108*
*The converts  109*
*The legacy of the war  110*
*Political expediency and missed chances  113*
*Reverse decline  115*
*Economics and markets  116*
*British leadership  117*
*Forums  118*

**5    Selling Europe: 'a pretty big thing to undertake'**             **127**

*The mechanics of selling  132*
*The electoral message  146*
*Electoral tactics 1997–2005  150*

**6    The Conservative sceptic: 'a confederacy of zealots
       and lurchers'?**                                                **152**

*Leadership  153*
*Parliamentary support  159*
*Activist base  165*
*Tactics  172*
*The message  179*
*The alternatives?  180*
*The Eurosceptic media  185*

**7   Conservatives in Europe: 'the concern of a private army'?     188**

*Inter-European party liaison 188*
*The Council of Europe 196*
*Members of the European Parliament 201*
*The European experience 206*
*Conservatives and the EU's institutions 209*

**Conclusion     218**

*The future? 225*

*Notes*          227
*Bibliography*   279
*Index*          293

# Acknowledgements

This book was originally conceived as a self-contained two-year project that would fit the duration of a postdoctoral fellowship held in the department of politics, Queen's University Belfast. Twelve years later, several jobs forward, and with a few other books written, this has finally reached a conclusion. Or has it? Unfortunately the ongoing contemporary relevance of 'Europe' means that it is virtually impossible to draw a line under the subject. That said, the conclusions reached in this study should hopefully inform and explain current Conservative predicaments on the subject. That will, of course, be for the reader to decide!

This project could never have been undertaken without the generous funding of the Nuffield Foundation and the British Academy. Nuffield's Small Research Grant enabled me to undertake the majority of constituency association work between 1994 and 1996; the British Academy Small Grant facilitated much of the work in the Conservative Party Archive and other miscellaneous archives. Grants such as these are the lifeline of the historian. I was also fortunate enough to secure an AHRC Study Leave grant which meant the filing cabinets of research notes and photocopies could be finally tamed and a manuscript produced. To my colleagues at Queen's, the then Institute of Contemporary British History and since 1997 the Department of Modern History, University of Birmingham, I owe a debt of gratitude for providing both intellectual stimulation and friendship. Matthew Hilton, Graeme Murdock and Corey Ross deserve particular mention.

I have incurred a debt to Stuart Ball from the very beginnings of my research days as a doctoral student. Likewise, John Ramsden, Peter Catterall, Richard Aldous, David Dutton, Bob Self, Larry Witherell, James Ellison, Piers Ludlow, Peter Marsh and Martin Alexander all deserve a mention. I must also acknowledge my many postgraduate students whom I have had to pleasure to work alongside, particularly Andrej Matayla, Philip Beswick, Matt Cole, Carl Watts, James McKay and Kieran McGovern. I must also thank David Richardson, one of my final-year dissertation undergraduates, who brought to my attention a number of documents relating to the reaction of the Macmillan government to the de Gaulle veto.

In the course of my research I have incurred numerous debts from friends, librarians, archivists and officers of Conservative associations. Although there are too many to acknowledge individually, I must acknowledge that without their help this book would never have been written. In the time that I have been researching the Conservative Party, the Conservative Party Archive (CPA) at the Bodleian Library has seen four archivists: Sarah Street, Martin Maw, Jill Davidson, and Emily Tarrant. To each of them I owe considerable thanks. The CPA would not be what it is without the assistance of Colin Harris and his 'team' in Room 132 of the Bodleian. Colin's patience, good humour and encyclopaedic knowledge (assisted by the all-important card box files) have made the experience of researching in Oxford all the more pleasant.

I would like to thanks the following for access to and permission to quote from copyright material: the President and Fellows of Magdalen College, Oxford (Dodds-Parker); Lord Sandwich (Hinchingbrooke); Lady Avon (Avon); Chris Woolgar (Thorneycroft and Tuckman); University of Leeds, Special Collections (Boyle and Legge-Bourke); Major Hugo Waterhouse (Waterhouse); House of Lords Record Office (Britain in Europe); Trustees of the Harold Macmillan Book and Archives Trust (Macmillan). The material from the Conservative Party is quoted with the permission of Sheridan Westlake, Conservative Central Office; in this respect I am also grateful to local associations who have given similar permission. Whilst every effort has been made to trace the owners of copyright material this has not always proved possible and I would like to take the opportunity to offer apologies to any copyright holders whose rights have been unwittingly infringed.

I must acknowledge the support of my parents, who have been unflinching in their encouragement to pursue my chosen path. Since beginning this project I have found a wife and gained a young family. They have been expected to make considerable sacrifices whilst this manuscript was completed. Clemmie and Alfie have not always been able to understand why I could not come and help them ride their bikes or toss around the rugby ball, but they have helped remind me of my priorities in life. Understandably, for them a book needs to have pictures! Finally, my wife Charlotte deserves my gratitude and love for unstintingly supporting me and on occasion reminding me of the necessity of returning to my study!

N.J. Crowson
Bournville
April 2006

# Introduction

At the beginning of the twenty-first century it appears difficult to envisage that enthusiasm for European integration was ever a significant strain in Conservative thinking and policy. Yet Conservative administrations were at the vanguard of Britain's bid to become a member of the European club: from Winston Churchill's battle cry for a united Europe in 1946, through Macmillan's 1961 European Economic Community (EEC) application, to Heath's successful accession in 1973 and then with Thatcher's and Heath's support for the 'Yes' campaign in the 1975 referendum. Subsequent Conservative administrations have committed Britain yet further to the integrationalist path with the acceptance of the European Exchange Rate Mechanism (ERM) and the Maastricht Treaty. To explain how, and why, the party has undergone such a reversal in attitudes is the principal purpose behind this book. It will offer a fuller appreciation of the political world in which Conservative European policy has been framed and pursued since 1945. It will explore the shifting stances inside the party within an economic, political and international context as the Conservatives adjusted to the decline of Britain's world role and the loss of empire. The analysis blends the high politics of Westminster with the views of the party's wider activist base.

## The narrative[1]

The very concept of 'Europe' in the 1940s and 1950s was only in the process of being defined: how it would be characterised and how it would relate to other policy issues shaped whether it attracted or repelled Conservatives. The geopolitical realities of the Cold War meant that territorially the 'vision' was confined to Western Europe. The need to sustain the capitalist model of Western Europe saw this vision increasingly become articulated in terms of trade policy. In British eyes plans for 'union' were too much of a commitment, implying a tight, formal structure, whereas 'unity' was a more accommodating term that allowed for changing circumstances. In other words: with Europe but not one of Europe. The Schuman Plan for a European Coal and Steel Community in 1950 met with a lukewarm response from the British Labour government, unwilling to contemplate European limitations on its policy planning. It probably did not help matters that the parliamentary debate on Schuman took place the day after North Korea attacked its southern neighbour. Yet despite non-British participation in the Schuman Plan, during the early 1950s the means for defining Europe still remained open. The 1957 Treaties of Rome changed that. The Eden Conservative government had only sent a Board of Trade civil servant, Russell Bretherton, to 'watch' over the 1955 Messina negotiations, and Britain was not a signatory to the treaties. Two Communities were created by these agreements: the European Atomic Energy Community (Euratom), and the EEC. The EEC proved ultimately to be the main platform for integration, but at the time it was not necessarily clear that it would prove more successful than Euratom, or that either would succeed. Yet by 1961, as Macmillan's government launched a bid to secure British membership of the EEC, it was apparent that an economic model, with a strong political intention, was the driver for integration. That Britain's first two attempts to join the new European Community were rebuffed in 1963 and 1967 contributed further to the unease with which Britain viewed the continent. Much of the debate centred on whether entry served the national interest. Unlike the continent, there were only limited appeals to the ideals of furthering the peace and overcoming nationalism. When at last Edward Heath successfully negotiated entry in 1970, the bitter parliamentary ratification process saw each side seeking to demonstrate that the costs/losses outweighed the benefits. It was a largely negative debate. Political expediency meant few were prepared to comment that perhaps the costs were acceptable in order to serve a higher purpose.

Domestic considerations have nearly always informed the stance of the British government's European policy.[2] Although Britain joined the Community in 1973, within two years, at the behest of Wilson's Labour government, the British electorate was asked to confirm British membership in a referendum. Two-thirds said 'yes' to continued membership.[3] The challenge now for politicians was to make British membership work. The opening decade of membership was largely one of conflict over the scale of the British budgetary contribution to the Community. This reached a climax with the Fontainebleau settlement in 1984. Thatcher's strident nationalist tone during these negotiations was designed specifically for domestic consumption, both in the electorate and within the Conservative Party. It was important for Thatcher to demonstrate her nationalist credentials. Critics of her economic policies, such as the abolition of exchange controls and the freeing of capital movements, suggested these were contrary to the national interest.[4] 'Challenging' Europe allowed her to distract the electorate.

Alongside Britain, Ireland and Denmark had also joined the Community in 1973. In 1981 Greece became the Community's tenth member and the applications of Spain and Portugal were being considered. Concern was being expressed in some quarters that the persistence of national interests within the Community was hindering Western Europe's recovery from economic recession. This downturn had been provoked by the second oil crisis of 1979. Whilst the Japanese and US economies had been quick to recover, the European Community (EC) still remained stuck with high unemployment and low growth. What emerged were plans to negotiate a new EC treaty, which would strengthen the powers of the EC institutions at the expense of those of the member states. This eventually became the 1986 Single European Act (SEA). The Thatcher government had been supportive of the SEA because of concerns to free the internal market.[5] The reforms included removing non-tariff barriers to trade and extending the principle of free trade to service industries, such as financial services. There was less enthusiasm for French ideas that the freeing of the market should be accompanied by further economic and political union, or that a 'social' dimension guaranteeing workers rights and conditions should be introduced. This proved to be a significant turning point in the Conservative Party's response to Europe.

Once again external events influenced the subsequent development of the European Union (EU). Attempts by Mikhail Gorbachev to reform the Soviet Union's economy and the subsequent relaxation of Moscow's economic grip on its satellite states in Eastern Europe provided significant opportunities. Then in 1989 the reunification of Germany brought new challenges, and once more raised fears about a resurgent Germany dominating Europe. The outcome was the continued enlargement of the EU. Spain and Portugal joined in 1986, with Austria, Finland and Sweden gaining admission in 1995. The British government of John Major was welcoming of enlargement, sensing that this was the best way to support the fledging capitalist economies of Eastern Europe, but was less receptive to any ideas of closer political union, of a common European foreign policy, to a European Social Chapter, let alone a common European currency. In contrast, the European Commission, headed by Jacques Delors, saw the growth of democracy and capitalism in Eastern Europe as a threat: EC integration needed to be accelerated or else the project risked destruction.

A new constitutional treaty, Maastricht, which recognised the economic, social and political aspirations of the European Union, was signed in 1992. At Maastricht Major managed to remove the federalist intent from the treaty details and secure opt-outs for Britain from the single currency and the Social Chapter. The ratification process proved a difficult experience Europe-wide, and the British experience was no less so. Major had behaved in a manner consistent with past British governments in their European negotiations, including Thatcher's, but the Conservative disunity arose because the 'tone and tenor' of the debate had changed: 'The effect was that ideas mattered intensely in Conservative political debates about Europe.'[6] Matters were not helped by the currency crisis that befell Europe in the autumn of 1994. Since 1978 Europe had been trying to reduce the impact of currency fluctuations by tying the EC economies together under the European Monetary System (EMS). Callaghan's Labour government did not join EMS; nor did Thatcher's. It was not until 1989 that Thatcher agreed to allow sterling to join EMS's successor, the ERM.[7] The problem was that keeping the currencies within their permitted valuation bands on the currency markets required frequent governmental intervention in terms of both monetary policy and propping up the currency. The crisis reached a head in the aftermath of Maastricht as currency speculators on the money markets forced the British pound out of the ERM. Black Wednesday, as it was dubbed, was followed by the devaluation of sterling and other European currencies, including the French franc and Italian lira. Beset as it was with the difficulties of the ratification of Maastricht, this was the last thing the Major government needed.

Despite this setback the European Commission pushed ahead with plans to introduce a single European currency, the euro. Britain refused to join and in January 2002 the national currencies of continental Europe disappeared forever. Britain has since remained outside the euro zone, and is pledged only to join if strict economic conditions, as defined by the Treasury, are fulfilled. The European project has continued with further enlargement, two additional treaty agreements (Amsterdam 1997 and Nice 2000) and then in 2004 plans to adopt a European constitution.[8] This was scuppered following the French and Dutch referendum rejections.

This short narrative implies that 'Europe' has been defined as the European Union. In reality this represents only one aspect of a multifaceted view of European integration that has both historically and in more contemporary terms been articulated by Conservatives. For this party there is more to 'Europe' than purely the European Union. Europe has included more than a purely economic and trade angle: it includes political, technological and security components. Institutions such the Western European Union (WEU), the North Atlantic Treaty Organisation (NATO), the Council of Europe and the Organisation for European Economic Co-operation (OEEC) form as an important element of Conservative views of Europe, as does resisting the 'federalist' activities of the European Union.[9] The Conservative experience of Europe has just as likely occurred in one of these alternative European institutions as it has in the activities of the European Union. This fits with a general Conservative world-view that believes Britain's 'world power' influence can be measured by participation in breadth.

## The historiography

This study draws upon a broad range of historical and political debates. On one level this is a study of the Conservative Party, on another it is about Britain's world role and relationship with Europe. Being a work of contemporary history, it straddles conventional primary source-based history and the theoretical discourses of political science. It is necessary to explain the debates that this book engages with, taking each of the broad 'subject' subsets in turn.

For many contemporaries and academic observers Britain's relationship with Europe since 1945 has been one of missed opportunities.[10] Edmund Dell saw the failure to participate in the 1950 Schuman Plan as a significant wasted opportunity.[11] Roger Broad accuses Labour of 'arrogance' over Schuman, but believes that with Messina the Conservatives 'were even more arrogant'.[12] For Alan Milward, Britain's failure to contribute to the 1957 Treaties of Rome was 'a serious mistake'. Warming to his theme, he says:

> In refusing to join, British governments were weakening the nation more than defending its sovereignty. They were left to carry their own burdens of welfare and agricultural policy and the consequences for manufacturing industry were immediate. Economically and politically Britain's role became increasingly peripheral and the benefits from not having joined the Communities were reduced to no more than the preservation of that same illusion of independence which led to the mistake in the first place.[13]

This criticism is not the sole preserve of historians. Key actors on the European stage have joined in. Leon Brittan laments the 'mistake' of 'not being there' in 1966 when the EC agreed the Common Agricultural Policy (CAP).[14] For Francis Pym, the Thatcher era was typified by an awkwardness that alienated Britain's European partners.[15] For other grandees of the party, when it came to non-participation in the single currency this amounted to a betrayal of Britain's national interest.[16] All of this represents the phenomenon identified by Anthony Seldon as the politicisation of history by 'self-styled Europeans'.[17] Disentangling the rhetorical political myth from the historical reality is the key challenge of this work.

Diplomatic historians of European integration have demonstrated the importance of Britain's extra-European commitments in explaining why this country was reluctant to join in European co-operation. Europe was one element of a wider global strategy that the British used to sustain a world role.[18] Economic historians have shown the significance of Britain's external economic policy in highlighting attitudes to European integration. The desire to sustain sterling as an international currency via sterling–dollar convertibility meant Whitehall's economic mandarins saw little benefit in joining a project that only created a position of equality and which downgraded the importance of the British currency.[19] This work contributes to these sectorial analyses by offering an explanation of the domestic party political context of Conservative European policy.

Studies of Britain and Europe have largely concentrated upon the process of government administrations. Near contemporary accounts, such as Camps or Beloff, provided an early and necessary narrative framework for understanding events.[20] Camps proved particularly important because of her privileged access to policy-makers. Even the Conservative Party called upon her services from time to time. Broadly sympathetic to the cause of European unity, she did demonstrate how the economic, political and strategic differences between Britain and Europe explain the reluctance of British policy-makers to embrace the supranational project.[21] Little was added to Camps' account of the first EEC application until releases of material during the 1980s in the National Archives facilitated a spate of studies that sought to explain the reasons why Britain did not participate in the Messina process and why Macmillan decided to apply for membership in 1961.[22] These studies contributed to a developing literature on Britain's role in European integration since 1945. This has been followed by studies of Wilson's 1967 application.[23] What is clear is that reference to both political and economic determinants is necessary to understand British decision-making. Studies of more recent episodes have been left to either journalists or political scientists. That Britain's relationship with the European Union continues to have a contemporary relevance has normally been the spur for these enquiries.[24] Overall these have contributed to a much larger body of research concerned with Britain's relationship with continental Europe.[25]

That Conservative governments took many of these decisions is important, but understanding the rationale of these administrations from the perspective of the Whitehall bureaucracy is not the purpose of this book. These aspects have been well covered by both diplomatic and economic historians. Instead it seeks to understand the position taken by these administrations from the party political dimension. Its primary focus is upon what the Conservative *Party* thought on the issue and how its views impacted upon its leaders. Consequently this book represents a contribution to both the history of Britain and Europe relations and the development of Conservative historiography by examining how the party reacted to, and influenced, European policy from 1945 onwards, not just at the level of parliamentary elites but by including the wider party in the narrative. In doing so this offers a counterbalance to the dominance of studies that have taken the views of the political elites as the explanation of the pursuit of policy. With foreign policy it has been recognised that external policy is not made in a vacuum and that it responds to a series of different pressures, whether financial, military, strategic or domestic.[26] Sometimes the policy-making process prioritises some aspects over others, asks some questions but ignores others and blends potentially conflicting bodies of evidence to reach a policy outcome.

The past twenty-five years have a seen a growing academic understanding and appreciation of the functioning of the Conservative Party machine.[27] Despite the party being in opposition since 1997 academics continue to show interest in both the party's organisation and episodic phases, both historical and contemporary.[28] Many have been exercised by the question of whether after three successive general election defeats the party can survive at all.[29] This represents a contribution to understanding that question since it was the divisions over Europe that undermined publicly the leadership of John Major, and the humiliating withdrawal from the ERM that destroyed the Conservative's longstanding claim to be the only economically competent party. Then his successors have sought to use opposition to 'Europe' as an electoral asset and yet failed to secure electoral success. What relevance does Europe have as an electoral tool, and how historically has the party sold the issue?

Writing in 1994 in a survey of Conservative historiography, Stuart Ball observed that the Europe's 'impact on the party has received remarkably little direct examination'.[30] It was largely that observation that prompted this particular study, and surprisingly Ball's observations still remains true. The study of Europe's impact on *the* party has largely been left to political scientists, contemporary participants or political biographers.[31] There have been a number of episodic studies, but none has attempted a substantial archival-based longitudinal study. Sue Onslow's 1997 monograph[32] observed the role of Conservative backbenchers in formulating European policy, in the period 1948–57. Its particular strength was the use of oral testimony. She concluded that the Europeanists were a small force that enjoyed success in opposition from 1945 to 1951 whilst Churchill was interested; thereafter 'Europe' had served its political purpose. Ewen Green has drawn a comparison between the historic lineages in Macmillan's economic rationale for favouring EEC entry and his earlier Edwardian views on tariff reform. The means of securing the nation's economic well-being in an interdependent world relied no longer on the Empire but on other European countries.[33] A number of studies have made claims in their titles to explore Conservative European policy since 1945, but in reality they have been studies of the party in recent memory. John Turner concluded with the observation in 2000 that Hague had succeeded in making Euroscepticism 'a potential vote-winner in any future election'.[34] The results of 2001 and 2005 might suggest otherwise. In a similar manner Anthony Forster offered an analysis of Euroscepticism in both the Conservative and Labour parties. This study saw scepticism as an 'article of faith' and argued that it was weakened because of the divisions between the Labour and Conservative adherents. Conservative Euroscepticism especially is seen as a unique phenomenon borne out of the circumstances of the late 1980s and early 1990s.[35] This strain of scepticism was ideologically driven. The weakness of this study was that it failed to offer a primary source-based analysis of the historical nature of Conservative Euroscepticism. Consequently many of its assertions will be challenged in the course of this book. Jim Buller and Helen Thompson have both examined the Conservatives' adoption of the ERM.[36] Buller used a number of theoretical models to evaluate the period from the adoption of the SEA to the ERM and advance a 'Europeanisation' thesis to suggest that the Conservative leadership under Thatcher and Major saw considerable domestic advantages in linking further the British economy with Europe, but that this unleashed unintended consequences: namely even greater integration and a fresh bout of Euroscepticism.[37] A considerable body of literature has grown up around evaluating the voting behaviour of individual Conservative MPs and using this to understand the ideological composition of the Conservative Party. Largely driven by the work of Philip Norton in the 1970s and 1980s, these political scientists have provided the data which allow the historian to gain a sense of the scale and chronology with which Euroscepticism has re-emerged in the Conservative Party since the late 1980s.[38] Although Conservative parliamentarians generally accept that it is not their position to create policy, 'we are failing in our duty if we do not help *form* it'.[39] This study goes further by also seeking to explore the role of the Conservative activist, and to understand his or her relationship with the parliamentary party, the party organisation and the leadership.

## Methodology

From the late 1970s the historiographical debate was reinvigorated by the first releases of governmental records dating back to the original moves towards European integration, which sent a new generation of doctoral students scurrying to the archival coalface. The annual release of governmental documentation under the thirty-year rule does have a distorting effect on historical enquiry. Although it has been demonstrated that it is possible to reconstruct an account of a particular governmental administration without recourse to government documentation, there still remains an insatiable thirst to plunder the latest releases from the National Archives (TNA; formerly Public Record Office (PRO)).[40] The convenience of working from one archive can be understood. Yet one academic feared that the historian of the twentieth century, swamped by the volumes of archival documentation, risked being 'overwhelmed … into interpretative surrender'.[41] Others have made swipes at the 'PRO mafia'.[42] Our understanding of the administrative practises of Whitehall has been greatly enhanced as a result. Yet a larger methodological issue has also been raised, asking whether detailed scrutiny of Cabinet records and Whitehall minutes actually enables the historian to add anything fresh, other than greater detail, to the conclusions drawn by contemporary accounts.[43] This study has therefore taken a different methodological approach in the hope that it will cast fresh light on a subject about which much has been written. This approach involves blending the national and regional records of the Conservative Party with a survey of constituency association records and adding to these a sample of personal papers of Conservative politicians. It may be that the 'tyranny' of the National Archives has just been replaced by the 'tyranny' of the Conservative Party Archive.

## The sources

The sources used in this study are of vital importance in understanding the questions posed. The use of the minute books of local Conservative associations offers a key insight into the world of political activism. These activists are the party's visibility within a constituency responsible for providing the necessary organisation to help secure the election of Conservative candidates at local, national and European elections. The autonomy of the association to select its own prospective parliamentary candidates, normally drawn from an approved list provided by Central Office, gives it a powerful position within the party structure. And whilst a considerable proportion of the associations' time is spent fundraising and providing a social focus for sympathisers, they do seek to involve themselves in discussions about political policy. This certainly challenges the suggestion that associations were merely for ceremonial purposes and to provide for canvassing purposes at elections. It also needs to be recognised that from the 1950s onwards these associations began to experience a declining, and ageing, membership, emphasised by political de-alignment. This reinforced a trend toward a diminishing status and role for an association within the affairs of a local community. For the historian the difficulty rests with the increasing professionalisation of minute-taking, which by the 1970s has reduced considerably the usefulness of many of these records; merely recording a subject for discussion, with perhaps a sentence explaining the conclusion reached. This has the potential to make the study of Conservatism once more an elusive topic, because it reinvokes the party's greatest strength: silence. This means that whilst for the 1930s it was often easier to trace the nature of a discussion, and the difference in views offered, and to attribute characteristics to the stances taken, this possibility diminishes with each subsequent decade.[44] This experience is further hampered by the decline in political reporting in the local press, which might previously have carried near verbatim reports of significant public meetings such as annual general meetings. From the mid-1960s onwards such reportage is increasingly confined to the occasional short paragraph, usually making announcements of an event or meeting and playing a secondary role to reports on the latest village fete or details of trials from the local courts. Only during by-election campaigns is the level of coverage more widespread. This does not mean that it is impossible to reconstruct the attitudes of the party's activists. The correspondence files between associations and Central Office, plus especially the area agents' files held within the Conservative Party Archive, can be particularly useful. Add to these the records of the Conservative Political Centre and its regular discussion group briefs and it becomes feasible to gain an understanding of the thought processes of the more committed rank-and-file party member. Additional difficultly comes with the increasing application of the thirty-year rule on archival holdings, something that the Conservative Party at both local and national levels generally adheres to. Again, this can be circumvented by recourse to the private papers of politicians and resources such as the Thatcher Foundation, which have made available online images of the Conservative Shadow Cabinet minutes until 1979, as well as other miscellaneous items, documents that are otherwise closed in the Conservative Party Archive.[45] The final issue is the sheer volume of documentary material that exists and whether to apply rules of selectivity. For example, shortly before the draft of this book was completed many records for the Conservative delegations to the European Parliament in the 1970s were deposited with the Conservative Party Archive. The decision not to consult them was taken after considering whether further research would substantially alter the conclusions already drawn, alongside the normal issues of finance and time constraints that befall the research active historian. It will be for the reader to determine whether the analysis suffers as a consequence.

## Preamble

Structure-wise the book has adopted a thematic line, based around two chronological opening chapters. This inevitably means that some aspects or events will receive less coverage than readers might desire. The intention throughout, though, has been to provide the best sense of how the Conservative debate has evolved.

Peter Morris has argued that divisions over Europe amongst the grass roots 'are a response to elite divisions rather than their cause and that they originate within the party elite'.[46] And yet to reach this conclusion his analysis has concentrated exclusively upon the parliamentary elites. This assessment would appear to confirm the idea that the Conservative Party is an oligarchic organisation. This would appear to contradict the historical analysis of the past twenty years. These studies, particularly Ramsden's and Ball's, have shown that the influence of the rank and file can be channelled through two means: first, via the connections of leading figures in the National Union and Central Office, who always have regular and unpublicised contacts with the chairman and leadership; and, second, through the reaction of Conservative associations to policy initiatives. There is a need too to consider external policy as a tool in Conservative domestic statecraft and to pose the question about the degree to which the responses of the grass roots act as limitations on a leader's manoeuvrability, and whether they have an 'initiative' role in policy formation? It raises questions about the relationship between parliamentary elites and their grassroots followers. Are these contacts infrequent and often disagreeable, if ultimately obligatory assignations? Or are the local activists, particularly the constituency association officers, a vital conduit for the analysis of public or party opinion? Despite the various mechanisms that Central Office has in place for monitoring, and responding to, party opinion there is a sense of unwillingness to engage with the wider party on issues that are perceived to arouse activist hostility.

Jim Bulpitt has suggested that until the 1980s Britain's relations with the EC should be seen 'as just another zimmerframe' that allowed Conservative leaders to subvert foreign policy to domestic concerns.[47] This carries echoes of Maurice Cowling's conclusions about the linkage between 1930s foreign policy and domestic party politics.[48] The process of European integration has obliged the Conservative Party to confront a major strategic choice concerning Britain's future role in the world political economy. Cowling has dated the beginning of this debate to May 1940, when a parliamentary revolt obliged Neville Chamberlain to resign as prime minister.[49] Rab Butler, who at that time held a junior ministerial position in the Foreign Office, appears to concur, telling Annie Chamberlain that her husband's death saw the end of a traditional policy 'which had been responsible for so much of England's greatness'.[50] Cowling's argument is that the collapse of Neville Chamberlain's government and the formation of the Churchill wartime coalition government reversed the previous rationale for Conservative foreign and domestic policies that had sought to contain the pressures threatening Britain. The argument suggests that this political realignment forced the Conservatives to allow the regeneration of the Labour Party, to ally with the USA in order to achieve victory, but at the ultimate cost of the loss of the British Empire. This loss of empire, combined with a concern about economic subservience to the USA, obliged Conservative leaders to look for an alternative means of interdependence, namely closer economic links with Europe, in order to preserve Britain's world role. Running with the Cowling interpretation, it is evident that through skilful party management the Conservative leadership was able to conduct negotiations to join Europe while marginalising their own dissidents in Parliament and the wider party, and ultimately impose this realignment upon the party and Britain. However, over the past decade the internal Conservative bloodletting over Europe and the increased ascendancy of the Eurosceptics imply that the debate is far from settled. Yet it needs also to be recognised that European unity first became a high-profile issue in 1929 with the Briand Plan. Much of the debate about 'appeasement' in the 1930s stemmed from differing perceptions of the need for Britain to intervene in the affairs of continental Europe. Even before these events, Britain had 'been under pressure to interest itself closely in events on the continent'.[51] In 1897 Lord Salisbury observed that

> the federated action of Europe ... is our hope of escaping the constant terror and calamity of war, the constant pressure of the burdens of armed peace, which weigh down the spirits and darken he prospect of every Nation in this part of the world. The Federation of Europe is the only hope we have.[52]

Consequently questions such as 'What is Europe?', 'What is Britain's relationship with Europe?' and 'How does Europe fit within Britain's economic and external relations framework?' have troubled the Conservative Party for much of the twentieth century and back into the nineteenth. Since 1945, Europe has manifested itself through political projects and plans for organisation. Prior to that date, Europe was a series of nation-states linked by loose confederations or alliances. That said, the growing global economic dynamics and issues of interdependence meant that Europe was a British 'problem'. The difficulty has been a premise that Britain's island status somehow offered a uniqueness that distinguished it from the 'continentals' of mainland Europe. This crude 'superiority' complex has hindered the Conservative debate.

Aside from the need to realise that much of the Conservative debate has revolved around the 'nature' of European integration, it is also worth dwelling on what was considered 'Europe'. 'Europe' may be taken today to mean the European Union, but it was by no means a settled phrase until the 1960s. Is there a vision that can be described as Conservative? Ultimately this has been as much influenced by circumstances, especially political considerations, as by theoretical notions. At a basic level, a view exists that, broadly speaking, Europe is defined by an adherence to Christianity. Yet Europe's diversity means that it can only be conceived as a geographical expression. As Michael Ancram, shadow foreign secretary, explained in May 2002,

> 'Europe' is a concept. It is a collective, broad-brush description, not a nationality. It is a geographical entity, rather than a 'land' with the true sense of belonging that flows from that term. ... [The] multiplicity of descriptions of Europe also hides a massive diversity of languages, peoples, cultures, economies and histories. Some aspects are shared. Many more are different. One has but to look at the patchwork quilt of the history of Europe. It underlines the infinite diversity in our continent which cannot be straight jacketed by simplistic definition.[53]

The territorial division of Europe between capitalist and communist blocs in the years after the end of the Second World War reinforced this sense of British concern for Western Europe. From the earliest days of Winston Churchill's rally call for a united Europe this was politically portrayed as absolutely essential to reverse the threat of Communism and offer the potential of liberation to those Eastern European nations subjugated under Communist tyranny.[54] On the face of it commitment to NATO and Britain's East of Suez role made it appear as though circumstances were very different from the inter-war period. Until 1961 this Cold War actually reinforced traditional British limited liability approach to Europe and integration. After 1961 significant elements of the Conservative leadership began to articulate the view that the EC was the framework and employed a rhetoric that emphasised the western versus eastern division. However, the collapse of the Soviet Empire in 1989 and the perceived need to export western liberal economic and democratic ideas to the former states of the Warsaw bloc have meant that again Europe is seen on a much wider basis.

Technological advances have also been responsible for obliging Conservatives to revise their perception of where Europe's, and Britain's, interests rest. Austen Chamberlain pointed in February 1930 to the fact that the growth of interdependence arising from 'the development of the means of rapid communication both of ideas and persons' meant that 'the world has narrowed'.[55] In 1932 Stanley Baldwin felt it necessary to warn the British people that because of the advances in aircraft development Britain had now to look upon the Rhine as her frontier. The division of Europe after 1945, and the presence of British armed forces on the Rhine, meant that, militarily at least, many conceived this as Britain's natural border.[56] The collapse of the Warsaw bloc and the retreat of Communism encouraged many Conservatives to advocate enlargement. As Britain sought EU membership, so it emerged that the idea of Europe should not solely be conceived in terms of the Six. Rather, enlargement was a preference.[57] In more recent decades the Conservative Party has been keen to promote the inclusion of Eastern Europe in the economic integration processes, using enlargement to dilute the overly integrationist tendencies of Brussels. 'Our Europe today', declared William Hague 'should not end at the banks of the Oder and the Danube'.[58] This is harking back to an older vision of Europe as Christendom, but also represents a deliberate Conservative vision that wishes to diminish the Franco-German influence within the EU and offer Britain renewed status as the arbiter of the balance of power. At the same time the physical and political boundaries of Europe have been broken down. The emergence of budget air travel and the growth of the internet have encouraged more Eurosceptically inclined Conservatives to argue that the EU is an outmoded concept, owing to its rigidity and its being fashioned on outdated economic and political concepts.[59] It is in the rhetoric that a sense emerges of the conflicting ideas of what 'Europe' is, in Conservative eyes. As Milward has noted, it is

> two opposed constructs neither closer to reality. Either it was an entity which, if Britain led it, would restore the country's prosperity and increase its security, or it was an entity which would weaken Britain's economy, reduce its security, curb its freedom of action, and perhaps even bring to an end the very long history an independent British state.[60]

The chapters which follow will illustrate how and why Conservatives' attitudes to European integration have evolved.

# 1 Conservative moves towards Europe, 1945–75

'Like chasing a girl'[1]

British entry into the EEC and Edward Heath are indelibly linked. On 22 January 1972 in a ceremony in Brussels he signed the Treaty of Accession on behalf of Britain. At the third British attempt a Conservative prime minister had succeeded in taking Britain into Europe. It was a personal triumph for Heath, who had played a central role in negotiations for over a decade and appeared to conclude a process initiated by Winston Churchill in 1946. It represented a substantial milestone for the Conservative Party, which against its natural hesitations and core ideological values had been convinced that entry was both necessary and welcome. This conversion had taken nearly a quarter of a century, it had been uncertain, but in the event the Conservatives had become the party of Europe. How, and why, did the party decide it should join Europe? Moving chronologically through the earliest proposals for European unity to the creation of the EEC to British entry and confirmation of membership in 1975, this chapter explores the reaction of the Conservative Party, which for much of this period was the party of government. What makes this transformation all the more significant is that at face value it appeared as though involvement in Europe ran contrary to the party's heart and yet its leadership had managed to convince the head.

## The opposition years: the Council of Europe and the Schuman Plan

Pushed ignominiously into parliamentary opposition in July 1945, the Conservative Party morbidly sought to look for a suitable medicine to stabilise the slide towards political oblivion. Whilst the likes of Anthony Eden, Rab Butler and Lord Woolton attempted to resuscitate the party on the domestic front with organisational and policy reviews, the ever-restless Winston Churchill, now demoted to being a mere party leader, sulked on the international stage. His particular rallying call became a united Europe, something enthusiastically received by the continental political establishment of Western Europe and encouraged by American presidents anxious that Europe should quickly re-establish her democratic and economic credentials and play an active role in the containment of Communism. In a series of speeches, most famously at Zurich University in September 1946, he called for a 'United States of Europe'. Churchill's 'vision' was for a more united continent able to resist Soviet Russia via increased economic and political strength. Britain would act as a sponsor, enabling her to retain a world role, sustain the Anglo-American alliance and avoid risking disloyalty to the traditions of Britain's Empire and Commonwealth.[2]

Suitably enthused, his son-in-law Duncan Sandys launched the United Europe Movement (UEM), which quickly became a Europe-wide propaganda organisation propagating the Churchillian message of a united Europe.[3] Its inaugural meeting at the Royal Albert Hall on 14 May 1947 heard Churchill question whether 'the states of Europe [are] to continue for ever to squander the first-fruits of their toil upon the erection of new barriers, military fortifications, tariff-walls and passport networks against one another'. It was time for Britain and France to take a lead.[4] Sandys, and the UEM, then convened the Hague Congress, 7–10 May 1948. It was attended not only by European politicians, but also representatives of industry and literature. From the Congress emerged the desire to seek a form of European parliamentary assembly. Churchill was the 'central figure' at the Congress, acting as *President d'honneur*.[5] In his address to the Congress he spoke of the need not just for economic and political co-operation but also 'a parallel policy of political unity'.[6] But much of Churchill's European rhetoric was symbolic, lacking in specifics: the details and practicalities were for others to sort out. When challenged by his longstanding political ally Robert Boothby as to what was meant by 'a kind of United States of Europe', Churchill refused to be drawn but declared: 'We are not making a machine, we are growing a living plant'.[7] As well as Boothby, Churchill was accompanied to the Hague by other Conservative stalwarts like Anthony Eden, Peter Thorneycroft, Harold Macmillan, David Maxwell-Fyfe, Peter MacDonald, David Eccles and Walter Elliot, many of whom were also members of the UEM. Churchill had the attention of not only his party colleagues, but also many of the political establishment of Western Europe.

Inspired by these Churchillian flourishes, governmental representatives from ten countries agreed the creation of the Council of Europe in May.[8] It comprised two components: a committee of ministers and a consultative assembly, which would be made up of political delegates from the signatory nations. It was quickly evident that expectations differed between countries. The Benelux bloc and Italy tended most to favour the idea of adopting a federalist institutional model with executive powers being granted to the Parliamentary Assembly. France accepted the Assembly but looked to integration as a means of constraining Germany, whilst Britain, Ireland and the Scandinavian nations were determined to avoid any loss of national sovereignty and emphasised the intergovernmental nature of the Council. To European federalists it was a disappointment. Power rested with the Committee of Ministers, where a single national ministerial act of veto could scupper any action. It also controlled the Council's budget and secretariat, decided on new members and appointments and dictated the size of a member nation's delegation and budgetary contribution. The Assembly was purely consultative, able only to make recommendations to the Committee of Ministers and, whilst permitted to discuss matters of European unity, was precluded from any discussion relating to defence. As a consequence, 'having asked for a magic carpet' European federalists 'felt they had been forced to settle for a straight jacket'.[9] The Council Assembly may have been purely an advisory body but it introduced a whole generation of Conservatives to the concept of closer European co-operation. It became a form of adult education for a succession of young parliamentarians.[10] Many, such as Duncan Sandys and Peter Thorneycroft, who had seen service as Tory Strasbourgers, were to become involved in later British governmental attempts to join the EEC. For the first three decades of its existence it comprised purely Western European members and was concerned with Western European issues, but during the 1980s and 1990s it took on a new role in the democratisation of Central and Eastern Europe as its membership swelled to forty-five nations.

The format of the Council of Europe was very much shaped by the British as a non-federalist, intergovernmental organisation. The active participation of Churchill, Macmillan and other Conservatives at the Assembly's inaugural session in 1949 raised expectations about the likelihood of a positive British European policy as and when the party returned to government. Yet when the Tories returned to office in 1951 the Tory Strasbourgers proved surprisingly impotent at imposing a European agenda on the Churchill government, despite many holding middle-ranking to senior ministerial positions within the British Cabinet. The question that consequently baffled so many political observers and frustrated continental politicians was why did the Conservative Party after 1951 fail to deliver upon the expectations and promise offered by Churchill over the previous five years? Some European politicians, perhaps typified by Spaak's resignation as president of the Council of Europe Assembly in 1952, felt frustrated that the British, having created the vision, failed to provide the practical leadership.[11] This encouraged them to look for alternative means of securing their economic and political goals, which led to the creation of the EEC, with its European Parliament, which has overshadowed the Council of Europe ever since, ensuring it is 'no longer enormously important'.[12]

So why was the Churchill peacetime administration lukewarm to the moves towards European unity? The answer can be found at several levels. First, and most importantly, Churchill had recognised that Europe was an issue that afforded him easy opportunities to embarrass the Labour government, as exemplified by the attacks on Labour's handling of the 1950 Schuman Plan negotiations.[13] Europe was an arena where he was feted as the saviour of liberated Europe, and proved a distraction from the drudgery of domestic opposition politics. Furthermore, it enabled Churchill to present himself as a major national leader above being purely a Conservative Party leader. There is a sense in which Churchill tried to present his European vision as a 'national' policy, rather than a specifically Conservative one, and that it was for the party to consider the merits of adopting his agenda. It was also an area where the rhetoric was more important than the actions. The vocabulary of Europe used so effectively by Churchill was also part of the problem. The contemporary use of words like 'unity' and 'federation' was widespread but there was little attempt to define what these phrases meant.[14] Furthermore, confusion could be caused by translation. 'Union' is such an example. In the articles of the Council of Europe the English text uses the phrase 'closer unity', the French, '*une union plus étroite*'.[15]

With a Conservative return to office the European unity issue had served its purpose; then as now, it was not an issue that drew particular electoral support and therefore the more pressing needs of running the domestic economy, of building new houses and continuing to revive Britain's world position were paramount.[16] This is not to suggest that British involvement in European unity was not part of rebuilding Britain's world role. Rather, the role envisaged for Europe in this process was not entirely as suggested by the rhetoric, especially as understood by an audience in the late twentieth and early twenty-first century. Britain was not looking to lead a move towards political federation; nor did she see much need to unite economically with the continent. Britain was still in 1950 the pre-eminent European economy by a considerable way and based upon all economic indices.[17] Conservative rhetoric on European unity took the premise of Western Europe acting as a single entity to resist the encroachment of Communism and the Soviet military threat.[18] This could be best achieved through British participation in WEU and NATO. This was what Conservatives meant by European unity, the defence of Europe. It fitted with a particular reading of history that saw Britain unite during periods of history to resist the domination of Europe by an aggressor: whether it was Elizabeth I, Henry IV's Grand Design, the Holy Alliance, the Congress of Vienna or the congress system.

This concept of a defence of Europe fitted into the perceived model of Britain's world as articulated by Churchill at the 1948 Llandudno Conservative conference and reiterated by Anthony Eden, as foreign secretary, at the 1953 Margate conference. When they spoke of three circles – the Commonwealth, Western Europe and America – Conservatives envisaged these blocks over-lapping, with Britain as the common denominator. This left Britain in a unique leadership position, enabling her to maintain a leading world role. Because this was a formula that articulated Conservative desires for a restoration of Britain's world power it was largely unquestioned, and Churchill was afforded the opportunity to articulate his European vision unchallenged. He was not alone in this vision, and importantly it was one shared by the Foreign Office and its Labour foreign secretary, Ernest Bevin. The weakness of Churchill's model was that it assumed that Britain's leadership roles in the Commonwealth and in Western Europe and with the USA could be sustained and combined, and yet as Macmillan later conceded little thought was given to how this might be practically achieved.[19] Further, as the 1950s developed the United States was increasingly distracted by sustaining the Cold War with the Union of Soviet Socialist Republics (USSR). Decolonisation meant that increased numbers of colonies were now pursuing their own trade and economic affairs, with Britain less able to influence their general policies. The average Conservative activist was more concerned with the need to promote the imperial linkages and support the calls for imperial preference.[20] Herbert Williams, chair of the party's voluntary wing, the National Union, denounced Churchill's pro-Europeanism, likening it to a Colorado beetle undermining British trade. It was a denouncement that earned him a rebuke from the party chairman, Lord Woolton.[21] It did not occur to, or was slow to impact upon, the Conservative mindset, that the leaders of continental Europe, particularly France and Germany, were not to be content with military unity. They foresaw opportunities for economic interdependency and for Europe to challenge economically the supremacy of the USA as a single trading bloc. It is clear that too often Conservatives would dismiss European initiatives on integration, implying that the goals were too ambitious to realise and too far into the future to worry about. This is not to suggest that they should have foreseen the development of the EEC, but this short-term arrogance was, and remains, a fatal weakness in the Conservatives' European strategy. Too often Conservatives have failed to absorb the continental mentality of conducting diplomacy and the idea that often 'positions' are crucial to the future evolution of Europe over a ten- or twenty-year period. Those who gained experience attending the fledgling European assemblies could be alert to this difference. As Macmillan observed, the continental tradition reasoned '*a priori* from the top downwards, from general principles to practical application', whereas the Anglo-Saxon method was to argue '*a posteriori* from the bottom upwards, from practical experience'.[22] At the same time, too many were caught up in a mindset that, dressed up as patriotism, provided a misrepresentation of the realities of the world, such that Churchill could tell the American State Department in 1954 that 'only the English-speaking peoples count: that together they can rule the world'.[23]

The difficulty for Britain, and especially Conservatives, was the legacy of the empire. Within the political psyche of the right, the position of the empire was paramount in explaining Britain's uniqueness. The economic, familial and political ties with the empire and dominions meant that this dimension always had to be considered in relation to any other form of European association Britain was considering. In 1949 amongst Conservative activists the calls for the extension of imperial preference, whereby goods imported from the empire were subject to preferable rates of tariff, were vocal.[24] The issue of European unity must be considered in relation to the party's internal debates about imperial preference and the role of the Common-wealth. If few Conservatives were concerned with Europe, the same was not true of empire. It was to be a difficult heritage to shake off. Even as late as September 1995 John Major, in his Leiden speech, would talk of the importance of the Commonwealth in Britain's world role.[25] This association with the empire in part explains some of Britain's reluctance to participate in the early stages of the European unification process. At the time arguments about the viability of helping create a European economic market seemed hollow given that in the period 1950–4 the empire/Commonwealth supplied 49 per cent of British imports and took 54 per cent of its exports.[26] This compared to British exports to Western Europe amounting in the late 1940s to only 25 per cent of total exports, admittedly a larger figure than in the 1930s, but a form of trade that did not at the time greatly help close the dollar gap.[27] That the party's 1947 industrial policy statement had virtually ignored Europe, declaring instead that 'the principle of granting preferences, which has been the lifeline of our Commonwealth and in particular, of our Colonies, must be preserved', confirms the dominant economic train of thought at that time.[28]

For continental Europe the priority was to promote its recovery from the wartime destruction it had suffered. If the Council of Europe had been a move towards political unity, then the economic dimension would be given momentum by the suggestion of Robert Schuman, the French foreign minister, that Europe should create a European Coal and Steel Community (ECSC).[29] The invitation to the British Labour government to participate was extended in early May 1950 but declined. The Conservatives might have been in opposition but the subject matter was not necessarily new, at least among those few representing the party in organisations like the British Committee of the European League for Economic Cooperation (ELEC). There had been no wider party debate.[30] The leadership took the stance that it favoured joining the negotiations and sought to gain political capital by criticising Labour's non-participation. At one level the Schuman Plan forced the Conservatives to wrestle with their future economic vision. Memories of the parliamentary battles over the nationalisation of Britain's staple industries were still at the fore of the Conservative consciousness. But this was not as contentious as the possible political implications of Schuman's plan. Not all in the party were willing to sanction British participation, amongst them Enoch Powell. He, along with five other Conservative MPs, defied the whip and supported the Labour government's stance of not participating in the discussions when the issue was put to the vote in the House of Commons.[31] As explained Henry Legge-Bourke, MP for Isle of Ely, his rebellion was based upon the belief that Schuman was a 'move towards European political federation'.[32]

Although during the war years Conservatives had been prepared to tolerate supranational organisations on the understanding that these were temporary, this was no longer acceptable and many felt that the ECSC was merely giving legitimacy to a cartel. It would be far better for these industries to compete under private enterprise. The leadership recognised that for the most part it was an opportunity to embarrass Labour. Tory Strasbourger David Eccles was highly critical of Labour's 'feeble' efforts at co-operation with Europe, whilst Irene Ward, who represented an industrial North East constituency, feared the consequence of not sending a British delegation to the talks would be French and German collusion on coal prices, which would squeeze British coal exports.[33] What the internal Conservative debate about Schuman revealed was that those Conservatives who had been to Strasbourg were more inclined to favour British participation than those who had not and who were prone to considering the issue strictly in national terms.[34] This was demonstrated by the enthusiasm Harold Macmillan and David Eccles showed for the issue by publishing in July 1950 alternative plans for a non-supranational coal and steel institution. This preference for intergovernmental organisation was the main difference from the Schuman Plan. It also marked a turning point, when a new breed of Conservatives first elected to Westminster in 1950 nailed their colours to the European standard. Airey Neave spoke of the need 'to put our case and demand our conditions. As it is, we are going to be left looking very silly'.[35] In light of later events it was notable that Edward Heath chose Schuman as the subject for his maiden Commons speech, a speech in which he emphasised the claim of the Tories to be the pro-European party.[36] What is evident is that these speeches saw the pro-European Conservatives rehearsing what would become the stock themes of their argument over the coming decades. Britain should go into Europe and take the lead; to remain aloof would be fatal; with this opportunity missed, the terms of entry would only become more awkward. This contemporary view was nowhere better encapsulated than in the party's own briefing prepared by the Conservative Research Department:

> If we want to dictate terms – better still if we want to be in a position where we do not need to dictate terms on which European integration can move towards [sic] gradually – we have to lead, not follow.[37]

For the pro-Europeans the Schuman Plan and the arising ECSC would now enter the political mythology as the 'missed opportunity'.[38] The reality, though, was that within the Conservative ranks enthusiasm for Europe was confined essentially to a few middle-ranking figures: there was no widespread missionary zeal. The majority of the party viewed the issue with ambivalence. During one party meeting the overwhelming majority of speakers backed Schuman, but the silence of the audience suggested that a majority of the parliamentary party were adopting a position of indifference, if not hostility.[39] They were prepared to accept that European unity was a bulwark against Communism largely because of Churchill's involvement. Lord Woolton, party chairman, warned that members of the executive of the party's voluntary wing, the National Union, were 'disturbed' about the risks a customs union posed to British industry and agriculture but were also 'attracted by the idealism on the one hand, and the military necessity of Western Union on the other'.[40] Activist motions on Europe only started reaching the National Union from 1948. Whilst these took positive views, they largely reflected the Churchillian vision. Thus Yorkshire area activists expressed hope in March 1948 that 'the

United States of Europe [would] readily materialise' if a European conference was called.[41] Europe did not become an agenda item at the party
conference until October 1949, and then Duncan Sandys was ordered by the
chairman of the 1922 Committee to tone down the positive European tone of
the conference motion.[42] Consequently it called for all measures of European
unity to be 'consistent with the full maintenance of the unity of the British
empire and continuing collaboration with the U.S.'[43] More broadly, Conservatives could argue that the creation of the ECSC in May 1951, with Belgium,
France, (West) Germany, Italy, Luxembourg and the Netherlands as members,
represented only one industrial sector and did not harm British core economic
interests. It is easy to dismiss the ECSC as inconsequential, but it wrested the
leadership of Europe away from Britain. Within a matter of months the
Conservatives were elected back into office, with expectations that Churchill's
positive European stance would lead to a radical repositioning of Britain on
the continental stage.

## European defence and free trade areas

In fact its return to political office in October 1951 obliged the Conservative
Party to face up to the realities of European integration. Aside from the
need to be considered alongside the pressing demands of the domestic situation, the moves towards European integration were being conducted within
the context of the Cold War, with Europe divided between Communist East
and Capitalist West. Debates amongst activists, at a constituency and regional
level, showed a preoccupation with the Soviet threat, but scant concern for
the matter of European unity in any economic or political sense. Activists
were rather patronising towards Europe, suggesting that the continent was
incapable of organising its own defence against Soviet aggression. The
Conservative Political Centre sought the views of activists on Europe in
1949 as part of its 'Two-Way' discussion, using a pamphlet by Robert
Boothby, *About Western Union*, as a discussion starting point.[44] What the
485 constituency responses showed was that the Churchillian ideal of
European unity was accepted, within the parameters of an anti-Communist
defence mechanism that was essential to peace and prosperity.[45] Since June
1950 a hot war had been fought in Korea against a Communist enemy, with
British regular and conscript forces participating. Not surprisingly, then,
issues of defence were placed high on the integration agenda, not least with
regard to how best to reintegrate West Germany into the international arena.
Since the end of European hostilities, Britain had kept four army divisions
and the Tactical Air Force in Europe. The 1948 Berlin Airlift and the formal
partition of Germany emphasised the fragility of the European peace.

The creation of NATO in 1949, to provide Western Europe with its military security, was largely welcomed by Conservatives, who felt a degree of
military federation was a necessary compromise to link the USA and Europe
together in their opposition to Communism. Despite a definite strain of

anti-Americanism in Conservative thinking, especially at the activist level, Conservatives largely displayed a preference for the maintenance of the Atlanticist alliance. Even leading Europeanists like Robert Boothby believed this the better option than a solely European military deterrent.[46] With the USA committed to the defence of Europe, those Conservatives sympathetic to closer European co-operation argued that NATO provided the military reassurance which would allow the Council of Europe to concentrate on promoting political unity. This was, of course, a peculiarly Conservative reading of how European unity should develop: along intergovernmental lines, with co-operation through association rather than participation. In this immediate post-war decade it appears evident that Conservatives were seeking to shape Europe in the British mould. This revolved primarily around defensive matters, enabling Britain to maintain her world position. Economics was not really an issue. Unsurprisingly, activists, given the party's hostility to Labour's nationalisation, when asked about this economic planning were opposed.[47] It would only be from the 1960s that the economic argument for joining Europe became predominant. What was not appreciated in the 1950s, from the time of the Schuman Plan onwards, was that these were conscious efforts on the parts of the French and the Germans to revolt against the vision of a British Europe. Conservatives, especially the pro-Europeans, were too slow to appreciate this.

Warning signs that the French were not content to play second fiddle to the British emerged in October 1950 with the Pleven Plan, which proposed the creation of a European Defence Community (EDC).[48] The plan included proposals for a European defence minister responsible to the European Assembly, a European Defence Council of Ministers and a single European defence budget. Ironically the proposal would flounder not because of British intransigence but because French parliamentarians rejected it in August 1954. Despite Churchill and other Tory Strasbourgers having floated similar proposals for a European army and European defence minister at the Council of Europe in August 1950, the prospect of EDC filled most Conservatives with horror, not least Churchill.[49] His supporters argued that he had been advocating a 'grand alliance', that there were intergovernmental safeguards and an option for a national government to withdraw. In contrast these Pleven proposals were militarily incompetent. But it also revealed divisions within the Conservative camp, and amongst both Europeanists and opponents.

The autumn of 1951 marks something of a watershed. Strasbourg Tories had been making a major effort to impress upon their continental counterparts that the Churchill government would seek to work to strengthen the Council of Europe. David Maxwell-Fyfe, the home secretary, had been authorised by the Cabinet to make a statement in November 1951 that the Conservative government would give the European army issue 'thorough examination'. However, within hours Anthony Eden, the foreign secretary, had succeeded in creating 'an unhappy misunderstanding' by comments to a press conference in Rome in which he denied that Britain could ever join a

European army, but was willing to support EDC because it had US support and to him offered the only solution to the issue of German rearmament.[50] This deflated and demoralised the party's Europeanists. Less than a month after resuming office it appeared as though the new Conservative government was going to follow in the footsteps its Labour predecessor. Continental politicians were similarly exacerbated, too; Paul Henri Spaak withdrew from the Council of Europe and determined to work through alternative forums to achieve European unity, which the United Kingdom could not scupper.[51] In contrast, Harold Macmillan took the view that the French plans were doomed to failure and that Britain should stand aside to allow this, thus providing an opportunity for Britain to step into the breach and propose a practical alternative. As he would lament, 'I always thought EDC a folly and it would do nothing but waste precious time. So it has proved'.[52] However he had conceded to the French ambassador in early 1951 that it might be possible to have a British contingent 'included in the European army, even if the greater part of the British contribution was made direct to the Atlantic force'.[53]

Fear of American isolationism was one of the reasons why in 1950 Macmillan had seen a European army as imperative. But there was also a need to reassure Conservatives, especially amongst the activists, that German rearmament would not enable Germany to become the dominant continental power again.[54] The episode confirmed too that whilst European integration might form part of Churchill's general belief system, championing it was purely a rhetorical exercise to sustain a domestic political agenda. Others feared that it would weaken Britain's leadership role in Europe. The EDC's supranationalist intentions were abhorrent. Robert Boothby confessed he was 'opposed to this with my head and with my heart'.[55] As the negotiations during 1951 and 1952 gradually watered these elements down, and the primacy of NATO was assured, some, like Henry Crookshank, the health minister, felt reassured that EDC would be 'an integral part of the Atlantic defence system'.[56] For others, like Henry Legge-Bourke, who were anti-European, the very thought of the primacy of NATO being challenged and a European joint command created was a heresy.[57] What the EDC proposals succeeded in achieving, if temporarily, was an alliance of convenience in opposition between the pro- and anti-European wings of the party. For the British they wanted to bring about controlled German rearmament without hitching it to a European political authority. As a consequence, in March 1952 Eden put forward a plan for the various Western European communities to come together under the authority of the Council of Europe. For Eden the incorporation of Germany into the western defence system would allay French fears about a resurgent Germany. Drafted by Anthony Nutting, the junior Foreign Office minister leading the Strasbourg delegation, the Eden Plan was seen as a minor triumph by the party's Europeanists, who thought they had managed to reverse the 'Little Englander' attitude of the foreign secretary. In reality, despite their best efforts in Strasbourg, the plan was badly received by their European counterparts, who suspected that, more than dragging their feet, the British were seeking to derail the European project.[58]

When the EDC idea collapsed Eden seized the opportunity to resolve the issue of German rearmament within the NATO framework, 'a European box inside an Atlantic box'.[59] He proposed an extension of the 1948 Brussels Treaty to include the accession of West Germany and Italy. Thus the Western European Union (WEU) came into being in October 1954. It recognised West Germany as a sovereign nation and permitted limited and controlled German rearmament. In return, Britain agreed to maintain its existing army and Royal Air Force (RAF) levels in Germany. WEU's council and secretariat were based in London until 1993, before transferring to Brussels, whilst the Parliamentary Assembly was in Paris.[60] Conservative delegates to the Council of Europe explained that a German contribution to NATO was a 'strategic and military necessity' if the balance of power was to be sustained in Europe, whilst British public opinion saw Germany's entry into NATO as a 'real safeguard'.[61] Once the WEU had been agreed its institutions were created on an *ad hoc* basis. John Maclay, who became the first president of the Assembly of the WEU, saw it as 'a very instructive operation because we found ourselves trying to create a new Parliamentary Consultative Assembly ... the terms of reference ... [were] inserted at three o'clock in the morning, and we had to start the thing from scratch'.[62] In fact, the precise wording of Article IV was exactly as described: 'The Council of Western European Union shall make an Annual Report on its activities and in particular concerning the control of armaments to an Assembly composed of the Brussels Treaty Powers to the Consultative Assembly of the Council of Europe.'[63] The Council of Europe was keen to tie the WEU Assembly in to its activities. A Conservative-sponsored resolution determined that the WEU Parliamentary Assembly should coincide with the Council of Europe Assembly; that it should have a right of reply; that there should be an overlap between committee membership of the two organisations; and that it should have the right to receive and comment upon the budget.

The WEU Assembly held its first session on 5 July 1955, but it quickly became evident that it would make a minimal impact. In a sense, the Assembly of the Council of Europe already performed the functions of the Consultative Assembly. The situation was such that 'it is very important that there should be no friction between this new organisation and the Council of Europe'.[64] The membership of the Assembly was drawn from the Council of Europe delegations. Furthermore, NATO made most of its military functions redundant. It was not, and could not be, a vehicle for European integration, which suited many in the Conservative Party perfectly. It did prove awkward for the Macmillan government when the 1957 Sandys Defence White Paper proposed cutting the size of the British Army on the Rhine to 50,000. Any such cut required the WEU's approval and, as Macmillan admitted to his diary, 'the reception of our plan for cutting our forces was pretty chilly'.[65]

Originally conceived as a bridging operation after the collapse of the EDC talks, Conservatives gave its conception a warm reception. Pro-Europeanists saw it as an olive branch from Eden, and those who had opposed his support for EDC made their acclamation for the WEU well known. Julian Amery wrote to Anthony Eden:

> I always hoped for a solution on these lines rather than for EDC itself. As things have turned out, however, I feel bound to admit that your previous support of EDC has greatly strengthened our position for carrying out the new policy.[66]

Indeed there seems to have been universal Conservative approval for WEU, because it 'exemplified British, rather than Continental techniques, [and] allowed for organic growth'.[67] In a similar vein, Macmillan confided to his diary that 'it has been a real pleasure to see England leading Europe'.[68] This self-congratulation was not without apparent good reason for it 'reinforced the impression that the experiment with integration *à six* which had begun in 1950 had reached an unexpected end by 1954'.[69]

For Conservatives WEU fitted with their preferred model of European co-operation, namely intergovernmental association. Furthermore, it was not seen as detrimental to the favoured option of Atlanticism. There was the problem of the French. Almost immediately they were perceived as working to undermine the organisation. 'The rats', wrote Anthony Nutting, 'set to work to eat away the foundations of confidence on which it rested'.[70] Thus continued a familiar theme of the intransigent French that has blighted Britain's integration experience. It is clear though that despite its apparent impotence the British increasingly saw WEU as an important forum in which to reinforce their commitment to Europe. It is noticeable in the run-up to Macmillan's 1961 EEC application that ministers used the WEU to express their preference to consider further acts of integration.[71] Following de Gaulle's veto Conservatives revisited the issue of whether the WEU might be used as the forum in which to promote and develop Britain's European credentials. Heath told the party's Foreign Affairs Committee that the WEU could be used as 'a forum for discussion and negotiation' and that reforms of the organisation, such as supplementing the existing foreign minister-level meeting with a bi-annual heads of government session, might be a positive step forward.[72] Amongst Conservative Europeanists the idea of exploiting the WEU was tempting, as the debates during February and March 1963 amongst the party's Foreign Affairs Committee reveal.[73] However the party's senior leadership, particularly Home and Macmillan, were nervous about discussing defence matters with the Five and feared they might distract from NATO.[74]

## EEC and EFTA: at sixes and sevens

The French rejection of EDC and the creation of WEU created a false sunset for the Conservatives. Eden and the Foreign Office could congratulate themselves on having seen off the integrationist agenda for the foreseeable future. In reality those continental politicians keen to unite Europe were now seeking to achieve this goal through avenues that could not be vetoed by the British. The convening of a multinational meeting at Messina in 1955 began the discussions. Britain was invited but considered it worth sending only a civil servant, Russell Bretherton, who withdrew after the early phases of the discussions.[75] The consequence was the signing of the Treaties of Rome on 25 March 1957 by the Six. These treaties created the EEC and Euratom. This outcome was certainly unexpected by some Conservatives. The chairman of Rushcliffe Conservatives, having returned from visiting Italy and France, confidently reassured his activists that the negotiations were 'unlikely of fulfilment for at least a decade'.[76] Complacency was commonplace, and not for the first time would Conservatives misunderstand the nature and process of the EC integration process. Many believed that the proposed EEC could do no economic harm to the UK, and that any potential damage could be dissipated if the construction of a British-led alternative free trade area could be achieved. To an extent the change in leadership from Eden to Macmillan following the fallout of the 1956 Suez Crisis and the distraction of having to rebuild Anglo-American relations left the Macmillan government too busy to follow European events. However, signature of the Treaty of Rome did refocus minds in certain quarters. Some Conservatives foresaw a danger that the creation of a European economic and atomic bloc not only threatened economic exclusion of the UK but would lead to the unravelling of Britain's carefully constructed European vision, leading to the collapse of NATO and WEU.[77] The Treaty of Rome also offended backbench Conservatives because the Six's decision to include their overseas territories within the EEC tariff boundaries had consequences for Commonwealth trade and British agricultural products.[78] The Macmillan government's response was to try and negotiate an industrial free trade area (FTA) excluding all overseas areas. But FTA immediately met with suspicion. Lord Salisbury felt that

> we could be misled by the fact that the economies of European countries have expanded more rapidly than have those of Commonwealth countries during the past five years. If we could return to our old Conservative policy goal of United Kingdom producer first, Commonwealth producer second and foreigner last we could probably turn misgivings and opposition into something like enthusiasm.[79]

The Six perceived it as a British attempt to undermine their own initiative, whilst Conservative activists and backbenchers had their Commonwealth heartstrings tugged. Negotiations to create a European FTA of the seventeen

OEEC member nations failed in December 1958 when the French vetoed the proposals. Selwyn Lloyd, chancellor of the Exchequer, was 'not unduly disheartened by the breakdown of the free trade area negotiations. I think we have to have a period in which counties concerned can re-think their attitudes and then just start again'.[80] In fact, the 'start again' was immediate, with an attempt to establish a rival to the EEC, with a European Free Trade Area (EFTA) of the Seven. This was signed on 21 November 1959.[81] Macmillan's chief whip, holidaying in Italy, questioned, 'don't you think that in our island we have a special aptitude for *not* seeing the other country's point of view?'[82]

Although Macmillan was not faced with a backbench revolt over EFTA, backbench MPs' disquiet, and that of the activists, was widely reported. The *Economist* observed that activist opposition was considerable and that 'some Conservative MPs could now win local applause by climbing on this bandwagon'. Furthermore, the views of the 'Expanding Commonwealth Group' showed these Conservative imperialists 'are more critical of freer trade arrangements with Europe than Conservative MPs have been before'.[83] One Bristol activist, 'perturbed' at Macmillan's pro-European policy in preference to a pro-empire policy, feared it was part of the 'licking of the American boot'.[84] The original FTA proposal would have had a market of 200 million people, whilst the Seven had only 40 million. Critics were apt to suggest this was too small to provide a viable competitor to either the EEC or the USA.[85] Ministers were keen to reassure the Commonwealth lobby, arguing that EFTA gave Britain new markets whilst still retaining old imperial market links: 'a new conception ... but ... following Mr Joseph Chamberlain's lead'.[86] Activists were nevertheless concerned that EFTA would lead to increased unemployment and decreased British prosperity.[87] The agricultural lobby was warned that UK agricultural prosperity was dependent upon a high level of industrial activity and that if excluded from a European trading bloc British exports would suffer.[88] Common lines amongst EFTA advocates were that such a bloc would liberalise trade, that it was British led, and that it was both a necessity and a natural evolution which if avoided would be tantamount to suicide.[89] There were hopes that it would extend Britain's trading opportunities regardless of the development of the Six. Some even thought that its creation would oblige the Six to abandon the EEC project and join with EFTA to form one large free trade area.[90] A further strand was that EFTA was a bulwark against Russia; as Sir William Cocker told Accrington Conservatives, 'if we could have economic ties with Europe it would prevent them from looking to the East for help'.[91] This debate showed a large body of supporters, anxious to consider an alternative that excluded Britain from the common market, but who were reluctant to sanction anything that might harm economic and political links with the Commonwealth. In a sense the arguments over EFTA were to prove a mini test run of future disputes over closer European ties: the speculation about parliamentary and activist revolts, and the activists complaints that these new and complicated changes were not being adequately explained by the leadership.[92]

**The first EEC application**

EFTA has been characterised by some as a British means of securing EEC membership by virtue of negotiating entry as part of a trading bloc rather than as an individual nation.[93] Whether this was the case or not, it quickly became apparent to the Macmillan government that EFTA was not delivering as expected and that progress was constrained by its weakest member. Furthermore, it was increasingly evident that Britain no longer enjoyed the reputation of being a world superpower. Suez had only too clearly demonstrated that. But was a British application to join the Six the answer? If it was, then it would represent an apparent historic reversal of British policy. Although the publication of Macmillan's diaries has challenged the perception that Macmillan was inconsistent about his stance on European integration prior to 1957, considerable academic effort has been spent evaluating the decision to bid for EEC membership.[94] One minister attributes the decision to move from the expedient alternative of the FTA to the failed entry negotiations of 1961–3 to the influence of civil servants Frank Lee and Herbert Andrew, and Peter Thorneycroft, chancellor of the Exchequer from 1957 to 1958 and one-time Tory Strasbourger. Two significant events are also flagged up. Macmillan's visit to the USA in 1959–60, during which it was indicated that the US supported the creation of the Six, and the appointment of Edward Heath as Lord Privy Seal in July 1960, which was 'quite decisive'.[95]

On 13 July 1960 the Cabinet had decided that Britain should 'draw closer' to the EEC but refused to commit to an application. A month earlier Macmillan had sent a questionnaire on the subject to all government departments. Speculation amongst the parliamentary and national party that Macmillan would launch an application for EEC membership had been rife since spring 1961.[96] It came as little surprise when Macmillan rose in the House of Commons on 31 July to announce Britain's intention to seek accession to the Treaty of Rome. What did surprise many was the relatively lacklustre manner in which Macmillan delivered his short statement.[97] The prime minister emphasised three problems that the negotiations with the Six would have to resolve: the relationship of the other EFTA nations with the EEC, the agricultural exports of the Commonwealth to Britain and the position of domestic British agriculture.[98] Macmillan's words were intended for both domestic and European consumption. These were the issues that had exercised the Cabinet. Sovereignty appears not to have been mentioned; rather, entry was presented as a free trade exercise.[99] Significant also was the Cabinet's insistence that Britain could 'transform' the EEC into an 'outward-looking group of nations, mindful of its responsibilities to the world as a whole'.[100] For the Conservative Party the issue of agriculture was of considerable political importance, but it was of equally great economic importance to the French. The decision by Macmillan to apply illustrated a basic condition in the leadership/party relationship. It is easier if a particular political party is in government to persuade its wider party to accept new policies, whilst the longer a party is in government the less its leaders depend on ideas from the grass roots and the more they adopt the views of external opinion formers.

The speculation about an EEC entry application galvanised the Conservatives' internal dissidents, who formed a Common Market Committee on 25 July 1961, just days before Macmillan announced his new position. Quickly tabling an early day motion (EDM) that criticised a potential application and expressed the fear that it would compromise British sovereignty was intended as a parliamentary shot across the bows of the prime minister. During the two-day House of Commons debate that followed Macmillan's announcement, Robin Turton, Derek Walker-Smith and Peter Walker led the Conservative critics' assault. This was parliament's first set-piece debate on the EEC, but it would prove a rehearsal for Conservative backbenchers to lambaste the front bench about its pro-European proclivities. When the House divided on 3 August, twenty-four Conservatives abstained on the Labour amendment and twenty-nine abstained on the main government motion, with Anthony Fell actually cross-voting with the four Independent Labour Party (ILP) MPs.[101] That the government won its vote by 313 to 5 meant it was now clear to launch its application, but the level of abstention suggested the absolute necessity of negotiating satisfactory entry arrangements. Writing to thank his whips, Macmillan admitted that

> a great issue like the Common Market which involves a reorientation of much Conservative thought and tradition is a pretty big thing to undertake. Of course I realise that the crunch will come if and when negotiations are concluded successfully. Still, we have made a great impact and once more the Conservative party is seen to be adaptable and flexible ... those Conservatives who abstained fell into two very clearly defined groups. There were about half who did so out of real conviction with which I sympathise, and the other half were those who are disgruntled on things generally and seize any difficulty to exploit.[102]

This final observation is important because it suggests that Europe had the potential to become a force for party disunity.[103]

Concern about disunity was evident amongst the National Union executive reviewing the forty-two motions received for the 1961 annual conference agenda on the EEC. Several, like Worcester's, were critical, and elements of the executive were anxious not to appear to be stifling debate and urged 'that in the selection of motions ... no overriding weight would be given to the Government's views'.[104] Evidently, from the conference podium senior ministers, such as Sandys, were not beyond making it a loyalty test and warning that any negativity would be interpreted as a vote of censure on the government. Macmillan himself devoted a fifth of his closing address to the very matter, and his entire 1962 conference speech was on the EEC application.[105]

Almost immediately the pace of the negotiations caused difficulties.[106] The Six had agreed to talks on 26 September, with the first ministerial conference taking place on 10 October. At a further meeting in early November it was agreed that a number of working parties should be created to consider particular aspects; however, the detailed negotiations did not begin proper until 8 May 1962. Throughout early 1962 senior ministers sought to reassure the parliamentary party that everything was progressing according to plan.[107] Negotiations slowed down because the EEC not only had to reach agreement with the UK, but also had to agree to everything amongst themselves. In addition, the EEC was wrestling with two big issues concerning its future development: the CAP and political co-operation. The ongoing discussions and compromises that arose over CAP made Britain's negotiation position more difficult. Many Conservatives were optimistic that British agriculture would not prove a barrier, but domestically there was considerable concern amongst the farming and horticultural communities that entry would damage their livelihoods.

From the summer of 1961 Central Office had been alarmed by reports it received from Tory-held rural constituencies suggesting the degree of 'farming' support for the Anti-Common Market League (ACML).[108] Area agents went to great lengths to cover ACML meetings and provided their superiors with disturbing reports of crowded and enthusiastic meetings where government policy was lambasted, often by backbench Conservative MPs.[109] Although Central Office increasingly believed a commitment to the EEC would help the party win the next election, loyal activists were wont to complain that there was no direction from Westminster as to how they should challenge the anti-Marketeers' propaganda, and that the Macmillan government was failing to articulate the reasons why entry was necessary. It was appreciated that the need to negotiate prevented an explanation of the bargaining position, but when this was combined with a lack of apparent progress in the negotiations there was understandably a sense of unease about the advisability of the application. As Edinburgh North Association's review of 1962 concluded, the application 'was never widely understood' by the electorate.[110] It did not help either, activists complained, that the uncertainty about entry had a negative impact upon Britain's trading position, which exacerbated the unemployment figures, thereby further contributing to the government's unpopularity.

The drawn-out nature of the negotiations had a further complication, namely that there were increased calls from those who wished to see Britain seek an alternative to EEC membership. Certainly, by the autumn of 1962 the pace of negotiations was exasperating nearly all quarters of the party. But was it Britain's fault or the Six's? One conference delegate complained:

> If I issue an invitation for a meal and I get a reluctant response, that person can expect a cool reception. Why, therefore, are we surprised that we are getting a cool reception in Europe? The time for dragging our feet is past.[111]

The delays were not good for morale. Area agents were reporting disquiet from the grass roots, even 'despondency' suggested one area chairman, and alluding to a growth in support for the anti-Marketeers because of a sense that the terms could not be that good.[112] The prognosis from Iain Macleod, party chairman, was little better: without any 'hard news' of success in the negotiations 'we are going to go on suffering', he reported to the prime minister.[113]

The evidence for the lack of a wider debate about the advisability of entry is exemplified by opinion polls that showed two-thirds of voters did not know whether Britain was a member of EEC or EFTA, or else gave an incorrect answer.[114] Throughout the negotiations those who approved of the government's initiative outweighed those who disapproved, although the proportion offering no opinion remained high. Support, though, had peaked at 53 per cent in December 1961, falling to a low point of 36 per cent in June 1962. There was a partial recovery during the summer of 1962, only for support to decline steeply from October.[115] In 1962 Churchill was drawn into the argument over the application after he was forced to rebut the claim by the sceptic Lord Montgomery of El Alamain that he had agreed that Britain should not enter the EEC. His statement gave a hint of his opposition to the government's policy and this would have carried great weight with the constituency associations of the party where misgivings were the strongest.[116] Partly there was a presumption amongst senior Conservatives that once negotiations had been concluded the necessary government campaign would successfully swing opinion behind the application.[117] The party chairman was most anxious to undertake this education process. He estimated that a large majority of floating voters were slightly inclined towards opposing entry, but were open to persuasion if given a clear lead. His sense was that the country's head was convinced but its heart was not.[118]

Some sections of the party were forecasting the likelihood of failure as early as May 1962. Anthony Eden let it be known to the prime minister that he saw similarities between the pace of negotiations and his experiences with EDC. He proposed that the government should 'cast round in our minds very discreetly for what possible alternatives there might be, so as to have some idea ready if a crisis occurred'.[119] The Conservative Research Department had also been at work considering a plan B of what the options would be if the application failed.[120] Should negotiations fail, then the government saw two pathways: either play up the failure and appeal to the nation's jingoism or withdraw from WEU and bring British forces on the Rhine home.[121] The pro-Europeanists considered it necessary to continue to argue the merits of a successful application and reassure doubters that entry would not destroy the British way of life.[122] The reality was that once in the negotiations the government had little choice but to remain at the table until an outcome one way or the other was reached, not least to reinforce the impression that it was de Gaulle's sabotage. As a senior Conservative from the West Country warned the prime minister's aides:

> If there were to be a change of policy and we were to back out of the
> negotiations it would be disastrous. Not only would it be wrong, but it
> would ensure we lost the election.[123]

The application negotiations must be seen within the context of other events
that provided distractions. The year 1962 was not a successful one for the
government's public relations image. The huge defeat inflicted upon the
Conservative candidate by the electors of Orpington on 14 March 1962 and
other by-election defeats suggested a resurgence of the Liberal Party.[124]
Rising unemployment and issues about Commonwealth immigration were
matters of pressing concern, whilst the scandals over the George Blake spy
ring and the Vassall and Galbraith affairs horrified, fascinated and titillated
the electorate in equal measure. When combined with the advent of television satire, with *That Was the Week that Was*, it all helped to further dent
Macmillan's 'Supermac' reputation.[125] The series of by-elections in November
1962, which included the intervention of a number of anti-Common Market
candidates, confirmed the potential dangers.[126] Senior Conservatives advising
Macmillan, like the party chairman Macleod, wanted to explain more
clearly to the electorate why they favoured EEC entry, but Macmillan seems
to have been reluctant to directly launch an offensive. He warned ministers
that their pronouncement on Europe should be restricted to 'general support
in broad terms' but that no commitments or explanations should be given
'which will come back on them if and when we find the terms are not just
what we would like'. He drew back from issuing ministers with a directive as
that was 'a little dangerous' if the media got hold of it, but suggested that
the pro-European message could be promoted through organisations like the
Federation of British Industry and Britain in Europe (BIE).[127] That ministers
heeded this request is shown by an analysis of ministerial parliamentary
statements. Only 31 per cent spoke positively about the advantages of entry,
whilst 68 per cent succeeded in adopting a neutral position.[128] Even after de
Gaulle's infamous '*Non*' press conference on 14 January 1963 some held on
to the hope that last-minute talks could salvage the negotiations, as 'failure
is a bitter prospect'.[129] Heath spent 15–18 January making a last bid at
summitry, but the damage had been done and a further meeting on 28–29
January between Britain and the Six confirmed failure.[130]

## Surviving the veto?

The veto was a major blow to Macmillan's government. The party's potential re-election strategy had been pinned on the assumption of success. The
government's internal critics were quick to apportion blame and suggest that
failure was at least in part because the government had 'been trying to have
it both ways' by maintaining the special relationship with America whilst
trying to be a good European. But it was clear who the principal villain was:
France.[131] One noted Europeanists, Anthony Meyer, told the 1963 party

conference that de Gaulle had 'destroyed the basis of confidence on which was laid the Common Market's achievements. It may be, indeed, that he has destroyed the political dynamism of the Six'. Similarly the 1964 *Campaign Guide* saw fit to quote Hallstein's February 1963 comment that the 'results of an interruption affect the Community as a whole, not just one member state'.[132] Blaming France had the potential at least of deflecting the worst of domestic criticism.

For some it was a stratagem that carried dangers. Iain Macleod was concerned in case there was an internal party backlash, with Conservatives turning their backs on Europe. This would involve the hazard of leaving the Liberals as the only 'European' party in Britain. At the same time Labour was going to make political capital by 'blame'.[133] Given that so much emphasis in the argument for EEC entry had been placed upon the dangers of economic isolation for a Britain outside the community, now that this had occurred the pro-Europeanists realised that the issue of British industrial and economic international competitiveness was 'of supreme importance' whilst domestically concentrating on maintaining an 'effective incomes policy'.[134] Some attempt was made to put a gloss on the veto. One internal strategy document pointed to 'the upsurge on the continent of political goodwill towards Britain' as an 'undoubted gain', but how best to capitalise on this?[135] In the immediate aftermath of the veto there were suggestions that perhaps Britain should redirect her attentions to the WEU or the Council of Europe, but it is noticeable that the anti-Marketeers did not contribute to this debate.[136] Others suggested that Britain should concentrate on the Five and effectively by-pass the French.[137] This was based upon a fundamental misconception of how the EEC was structured and operated and was an option the Cabinet rejected. The veto meant that as long as France was opposed to British entry it mattered little what the remaining Five thought. If Britain wanted entry it was to the French that attention should be paid. So although Princess Margaret's March 1963 visit to France was cancelled, the government still remained committed to the Channel Tunnel and the supersonic airliner project.[138] In reality these were not viable alternatives, and as long as de Gaulle remained in charge of France 'there was', as Heath conceded, 'certainly no short-term prospect of a resumption of negotiation'.[139] The hunt was now on for a possible alternative that would help facilitate a future reapplication to the EEC.

The political repercussions within the party after the failed application were significant: political reputations were either enhanced or irreparably damaged. The relationship between Macmillan and his party chairman, Macleod, were fundamentally weakened, with each losing confidence in the other. In contrast, despite having been Britain's chief negotiator, Edward Heath saw little blame attributed to him.[140] A prostate health-scare in late 1963 panicked Macmillan into retirement, and saw his replacement with Alec Douglas-Home. The 1964 general election was narrowly lost, and, stung by criticism of the manner in which he had become leader, Home introduced a leadership ballot system and announced his intention to stand down. It was Ted Heath who emerged victorious, and who now began the process of preparing his party for a return to office and for a future in Europe.[141]

The European debate re-ignited within the party in 1965. The party conference that autumn faced twenty-four pro-European resolutions. Notable was the absence of any debate on either the Commonwealth or empire for the first time since the end of the Second World War. Furthermore, during the defence debate Enoch Powell referred to the United Kingdom as a European power.[142] It all suggested that the Conservative Party was facing up to the new realities of Britain's international position. Also, for the pro-Europeans it appeared that perhaps after all de Gaulle was realising the advantages of an intergovernmental Europe after the 1965 Luxembourg Compromise. The compromise was that national vetoes could be applied to any issues which were considered to affect a member's 'vital' interests. This suggested that France now favoured a Europe of Nations and no longer demanded federalist unity. Activist opinion also appeared to be swinging towards favouring entry. The 1965 Conservative Political Centre (CPC) discussion groups demonstrated that activists saw the advantages of access to the large EEC markets, favoured a confederal structure but opposed direct elections to the European Parliament. This pro-European trend appeared to be confirmed with the following year's conference, which received twelve pro-European resolutions and then endorsed the desire to seek British membership by 1,452 votes to 475.[143] It should be noted that the total number of resolutions received on European affairs only represented a small fraction of the total conference resolutions submitted, suggesting that in terms of its saliency the issue still ranked relatively low in Conservative activist concerns.

## Labour's 1967 application

Labour, having won a narrow majority in 1964, was able to consolidate its grip on power when it won additional seats in the 1966 general election. Wilson's administration found itself faced, from late 1966, with growing calls for a second British application to the EEC. Wilson formally announced the application in May 1967 and sought parliamentary approval.[144] Some commentators saw this application as an attempt politically to trump Heath's hand, which he had been gently nurturing. The application certainly placed the Conservative opposition in a difficult position. The ranks of the pro-Europeans within the Conservative Party had been swelled by the 1964 and 1966 general elections and it was hardly feasible, or likely, that Heath would suddenly renounce his European credentials. The stance of the Conservatives was summarised in an internal briefing document prepared by the pro-Europeanist Gordon Pears: 'Our main concern here must be to avoid being tied too closely to the actual conduct of the negotiations and so being associated with their failure if they do fail.'[145] This assumption of failure was central to the Conservatives strategy during 1967. Apart from meaning that they must not be tarred with any blame in the event, it also encouraged them to seek to try and deflect domestic elec-toral attention away from Europe, 'increasingly to the mess that has been made of the economy and [to] relate this to Europe by pointing out that whatever the outcome of the negotiations, we must first put our own house in order'.[146] In other words, if the Conservatives were in power this applica-tion would stand more chance of success because the British economy would be structured in a manner that complemented an application. This reiterated the message of Labour's economic incompetence, which had been a core Conservative theme since 1929. This call had been flagged up by one of Heath's working committees in March. It had been suggested that the Conservatives should take the attack to Wilson, stressing the need for a reduction in government expenditure to help maintain the balance of payments and looking to develop an internal monetary policy that was less dollar reliant.[147] The tactics were evident at the party's 1967 autumn confer-ence, where it was deemed wrong, both politically and technically, to concentrate on Europe.[148] That said, the conference received seventeen Europe-related resolutions: ten urging the continued search for entry; three demanding specific terms for New Zealand, agriculture and education; with four calling for alternatives to be considered. However, once the party's contacts within the diplomatic service began reporting the likelihood of a veto Heath returned to the attack.[149] He exploited the Opposition Day debate in November, arguing that Wilson's application was evidence that he was moving 'along the path we have urged him to take', but that 'the adop-tion of more clearly European attitudes in virtually every field of external policy' was required.[150] Heath adopted a dual strategy: to secure credit for the Conservatives as the pro-European party, but also seeking to strike a blow blaming any veto on Labour because they had misunderstood many of the issues, issues that the Conservatives had foreseen and with their past experi-ence of the 1961–3 negotiations would have resolved. Behind this, though, was a question of what would happen in the event of a veto: could a future Conservative government seriously contemplate another application?[151]

The Conservative leadership was clearly alert to the need to be seen to have considered alternatives to the EEC, but essentially alternatives that had a European orientation. In advance of Labour's formal announcement of its application the Conservative Research Department was preparing briefs on alternatives.[152] Through the summer and autumn of 1967 the party's Commonwealth and Europe Committee anticipated amongst the electorate 'widespread disillusion' following a second veto, but was concerned that there should be a concerted effort to bolster party opinion towards continued support for the European project. The answer, they thought, lay in seeking alternatives that would enhance a future British application by a Conservative government.[153] For the pro-Europeanists the concern with the veto was that it would open up the divisions within the party and mean that non-European alternatives 'may suddenly be resurrected'.[154] And, as predicted, the anti-Marketeers took the issue up with the parliamentary party's Foreign Affairs Committee, arguing that Britain should look after her own interests, promote a British vision of Europe through NATO and EFTA and consider strengthening Commonwealth trade whilst evaluating the viability of the North Atlantic Free Trade Agreement (NAFTA).[155] Neil Marten, the former chair of the party's Foreign Affairs Committee, was even more blunt with Heath:

> We have been rebuffed twice and we really cannot continue to live in this uncertainty in the future. It is bad for industry and business, who have been waiting for the 'advantages' of entry too long. Now, we must press on our own and look at alternatives.

Given that entry had first been proposed in 1961, '[t]here seems no reason why we should not change our views somewhat in that time and with the experience of persistent refusal by the French'.[156] Heath was unlikely ever to sanction a radical swing away from Europe, but with encouragement from leading Europeanists, like Douglas Dodds-Parker, he indicated willingness, at least for appearances' sake, to consider the alternatives.[157] This went some way to pacify the anti-Marketeers, especially as they were brought into the consultation process. The second prong of the Europeanists' defence was to ensure they did not make any further enemies in Europe. Whilst anti-Marketeers were critical of the failure of Germany to take issue with de Gaulle and of the pro-British elements within the French establishment, the pro-Europeanists sought to capitalise on the belief that 'European politicians are more angry with the French than are the British'.[158] As part of this charm offensive a number of leading Conservatives wrote to the major European newspapers deploring the veto but pledging the intention to fight on.[159] EEC membership remained the best aim and 'we must also not let down our many European friends'.[160]

Various policy committees, such as the Committee on Europe (Policy Research) and the Commonwealth and Europe Group, were authorised to make studies of the alternatives to EEC membership. The influence of these committees was restricted by the agreement:

> That it was not for it to question the party's continuing commitment to Europe. This was and would remain official party policy. ... If ever it were to be questioned, it could only be done in the full foreign affairs committee.[161]

These policy debates involved both pro and anti-Europeanists and the range of subject papers considered was varied and wide-ranging.[162] The motivation behind these committees, at least from the perspective of the party leadership, was to help facilitate British admission to the EEC at the earliest date possible. Some pro-Europeans were worried that elements 'want to re-open the whole question of whether we should join the community'.[163] At the same time other Conservatives sought to marry the conflicting interpretations of floating the 'vision' of a European community that included some African nations as 'associate members', along with the Mediterranean nations, Spain, Portugal, Greece, Turkey and Cyprus.[164] Evidently the Conservative preference for widening not deepening the Community has a historical pedigree. The Committee on Europe illustrates a significant feature, namely the relative co-operation between the pro- and anti-Europe factions of the party during the late 1960s and early 1970s.[165] This contrasts with the situation during the Major years where the debate was far more polarised.

### Third time lucky? The successful 1970 application

The arrival of a new French president at the Elysée Palace reopened the possibility of a renewed British application. Although they were still in opposition, internal Conservative briefing papers suggested that the French would be ready to consider allowing talks from spring 1970. Despite the window dressing of considering alternatives, Heath had no intention of being deflected from his real intention of EEC membership. Advisors and party officials sought the advice of diplomats and European officials to gauge the ways and means Britain could best secure entry.[166] In addition policy research was directed to areas – such as European collaborative technological projects, Western European defence and the 'Europeanisation' of sterling – where previously the party had done little more than make vague statements. This chimed with the view of the party's Europeanists, who thought that it would demonstrate the party's commitment to the European project.[167] It was recognised, though, that any fresh EEC application would have to resolve a number of issues. There was concern that under the current CAP rules, agreed in July 1966, that 20 per cent might be added to food prices in Britain.[168] The problem of Commonwealth trade, especially in areas where there was considerable EEC surplus, would have to be addressed. Whilst sterling was thought to be less of a serious obstacle since the 1968 Basle agreement, any moves towards monetary union would raise questions about sterling's international role. This led to questions about Britain's economic position, which had been used as a pretext for the 1967 veto. It was felt that the restoration of a balance of payments could run in tandem with negotiations. There would also be the matter of the other likely applicant nations, Ireland, Norway and Denmark, as well as the question of whether there should be a period of transition prior to full membership.[169]

Heath was keen to ensure that Conservative policy commitments were best suited to harmonisation with the EEC. There was certainly a consensus amongst the Europeanists that harmonisation, a continued commitment to free trade and measures to encourage British industry and the 'City' to consider Europe their natural market 'would economically identify Britain more closely with Europe'.[170] This was especially true of taxation, and a commitment to introduce value-added tax (VAT) at the same level as the EEC was adopted.[171] The problem, now clearly recognised, was that having not been there at the beginning meant that with each passing year the terms and conditions of entry potentially became more unpalatable, or at least less satisfactory from the British perspective. This was part of the thinking behind Heath's address to the British Chamber of Commerce in Paris in May 1970. He urged that the Six must be prepared to allow British entry 'on terms which are tolerable in the short term and clearly and visibly beneficial in the long term'. He argued that there were three requisites of British participation: a move towards a more satisfactory environment for competition; greater freedom of choice; and an increase in the standard of living. In order to reinforce the idea that Britain would not join at any cost he suggested: 'we are not seeking shelter in the Community from the storms of the outside world. We have lived and thrived in that world among those storms for many centuries, and we can do so with equal success in future.' This final sentence left his own internal sceptics asking whether, if this was true, Britain needed to make a further application.[172]

Heath launched Britain's third application in June 1970, just twelve days after the Conservatives had won a general election with a thirty-seat majority. The party's manifesto had promised to open negotiations with the EEC but avoided an overt commitment to entry; nevertheless Heath considered the result a sufficient mandate. Once again the negotiation process was drawn out, but the tone was more optimistic than previously. The view was not 'whether' but 'when' Britain would join; however, the pace of negotiations was again frustratingly slow.[173] The government's negotiation team, initially led by Anthony Barber, and then by Geoffrey Rippon following the Cabinet reshuffle necessitated by the sudden death of Iain Macleod, was keen not to portray any sense of pessimism. Rippon did admit that because the Treaty of Rome was 'four pages of principles and four hundred pages of exceptions' discussion would be tough.[174] When pressed by elements on the Conservative Foreign Affairs Committee in November 1970 about whether Britain intended to continue thinking of alternatives to EEC membership, Rippon's response was 'that the negotiations could be harmed were Britain to sound too pessimistic about the chances of their succeeding'. The problem at this stage was that thus far the negotiations had been fact finding and there was little to report on.[175]

With the negotiations concluded in June 1971 a White Paper was published the following month, signalling the beginnings of a drawn-out parliamentary battle as the European Economic Communities Bill worked its way through its various readings. In July Heath rejected the need for a referendum on the entry terms and told the party's National Union's Central Council that the House of Commons had the constitutional sovereignty to decide, but not with a free vote.[176] Within the government, and the party, there was a debate about the timing of the vote on the EEC. The backdrop to this debate was the perceived position of public opinion. The polls suggested that, at worst, the electorate was against entry; at best, apathetic.[177] The unpopularity of the government had been confirmed by the Bromsgrove by-election defeat in May, and the decision of Macclesfield Conservatives to select an anti-Marketeer candidate for their forthcoming by-election suggested party activists sensed the growing mood of the electorate. The chief whip, Francis Pym, favoured delaying the vote until after the summer recess so as not to give the appearance of having rushed MPs in their decision.[178] This was certainly the message Central Office was relaying to constituency officials, reassuring them that 'the Government has been careful to allow adequate time' for MP/constituency consultations.[179] Others within Number 10 were more eager. 'My own view is that the dangers of allowing Members to go away for the recess without taking a vote in principle are probably the greater', wrote Douglas Hurd in a memo to Heath on 7 June, 'and that it would be worth sitting well into August for this purpose'. Hurd was not so much motivated by a concern about the impact of the electorate on their MPs as fearful that without a parliamentary lead the party's activists had the potential for unpredictability during the autumn conference season.[180] In the event the views of the chief whip prevailed and Heath was given a fillip when the party's annual conference accepted the terms for entry with a substantial majority of 2,474 to 324. This conference vote, rather like the 1962 Llandudno conference EEC vote, was important because it reassured the leadership that it was winning over constituency opinion, which would help to influence the uncommitted centre of the parliamentary party. The conference vote was mirrored in the CPC 'Britain and Europe' discussion, which involved 4,030 activists: 3,055 favoured entry, compared to 475 objectors, with 12 per cent either abstaining or being undecided. This total for 'undecided' mirrored the party's own internal polling. There were some regional variations, with Scottish activists proving the most enthusiastic proponents for entry whilst a quarter of Welsh and Western activists were hostile.[181] A further internal battle was also fought about whether to impose a three-line whip on the vote. At the eleventh hour a decision to grant Conservative MPs a free vote ensured Commons approval was also secured by 356 to 244 on 28 October, after five days of debate. The rebellion of thirty-nine Conservative MPs was more than counteracted by the connivance of the Labour pro-Europe rebels with the Conservative whips.[182] The government ignored demands for a referendum on the issue and easily defeated a Labour amendment making such a call, by 284 to 235. Despite anti-Marketeer optimism that they could inflict a defeat on the government in the committee stages, they failed to prevent the second reading being carried by 309 to 301 in February 1972. The bill received its final approval in July 1972 despite sixteen Conservative rebellions and four abstentions after 300 hours of parliamentary debate time. Heath had won all 104 votes during the five-month passage of the bill. Assured of entry, Heath resisted the temptation to create a Ministry of

Europe, instead ordering all departments to consider the harmonisation of their methods with those of Europe in their own sphere.[183] However, if Heath thought he would reap the political benefits of securing entry he was to be sorely disappointed. His premiership was to be dogged by the persistent inflation, strike action and low growth that began to affect all Western economies, ending the boom conditions of the 1950s and 1960s.[184]

## Renegotiation and the 1975 referendum

Heath was ousted from Number 10 following the February 1974 general election. Although the election had been dominated by the question of who governs Britain, the EEC had played its part in Heath's demise when in the dying days of the campaign Enoch Powell had urged Conservative anti-Marketeers to vote Labour.[185] Labour's manifesto, with its pledge to revisit the terms of Britain's EEC entry, particularly the CAP and Britain's budget contribution, also promised a popular vote on EEC membership, which offered the potential for withdrawal.[186] In reality Labour's attempted renegotiation was little more than window dressing, but must be understood within the context of internal Labour politics and its own divisions over Europe. The October general election gave Labour a slim majority of four seats. The decision to call a referendum, which Wilson proposed to Cabinet on 21 January 1975 and publicly announced two days later, was provoked by the very real splits within the Labour leadership.[187] The date was set for June. The renegotiated terms were put before parliament on 7–8 April.[188] The Conservative leadership had been sceptical about the benefits of such a debate, since 'Parliament would in effect be committing its sovereignty to the referendum process'.[189] With Conservative and Liberal support, Wilson won the vote to stay in the EEC by 396 to 170. When the House divided only eight Conservative MPs voted against Labour's renegotiated terms, with a further eighteen abstaining.

The timing of the referendum could perhaps have not been worse for the Conservatives. On 4 February Heath was challenged, and defeated, for the leadership of the Conservative Party. Margaret Thatcher secured final victory on 11 February. Airey Neave, Thatcher's campaign manager, successfully persuaded her before the second ballot to make a statement which would reassure pro-European Conservatives. She did this by paying tribute to Heath for securing entry and promising to pick up where he left off: 'The commitment to European partnership is one which I fully share.'[190] A meeting with pro-Europeanist Conservatives on 3 March confirmed that she 'did not at that time have definite views on the future of Europe'.[191] However, flushed with success she famously declared that Europe was 'Ted's issue' and deliberately played a low-profile role in the 'Yes' referendum campaign. The party also had difficulties with the concept of a referendum. The Shadow Cabinet expressed concern during the parliamentary debate on the referendum White Paper 'that if we argued on the details we would be seen as giving tacit acceptance to the idea of a referendum'. However, there was 'also a feeling that we should not impede the Bill unduly, which would go through anyway, and thereby put ourselves in a difficult position for the actual referendum campaign'.[192] When there was a further parliamentary debate it was agreed that the necessary message was one of Conservative unity on the EEC issue.[193] That only five Conservative MPs went into the opposition lobby on 11 March 1975 suggested that this was pretty much true.

The 'Yes' campaign was directed under the umbrella of the BIE group led by Con O'Neill, the retired Foreign Office diplomat. The 'No' campaign coalesced under the National Referendum Campaign (NRC) and was headed up by Neil Marten, the Conservative MP for Banbury. Although clearly these groups were multi-party coalitions, the fault-lines within each went along traditional party lines. For example, because Wilson had decided that he would only speak on Labour platforms, the Conservatives retaliated by restricting Thatcher's campaign to Conservative-only events.[194] Thatcher was concerned that her party's role in the campaign must not be eclipsed by BIE, whilst some of her close advisers were suggesting that BIE was essentially a front to undermine her leadership.[195] Further, Conservative pro-Europeanists were told not to campaign in strong Labour areas: 'This should be left to Labour pro-Europeans.'[196] Willie Whitelaw confessed that, as a vice-president of BIE, 'he had to keep a close watch on the Liberals who seemed determined to squeeze party advantage out of the referendum'.[197] Likewise, within the NRC there was barely disguised hostility between the left-wingers of Tony Benn and Barbara Castle and the right-wingers of Enoch Powell.[198] On an individual level, opposing personalities were on civil terms; however, the press, sensing political divisions, were only too willing to accentuate them.[199] In the view of Whitelaw, it was no accident that so many of those he regarded as untrustworthy should be included in the 'No' camp.[200] What the mainstream of the party was successfully doing was implying that the anti-Marketeers were somehow suspect. This was all the easier because of the behaviour of Enoch Powell in breaking with his party and advocating that its supporters vote Labour in February 1974. He had broken the loyalty code of the party's ethic. This perhaps explains the biggest difficulty the 'No' campaign had, for although many of its key messages on sovereignty and national identity potentially appealed to Conservative voters, those articulating the message where either traitors or 'Reds'. The 'No' campaign conclusion was that the Conservative vote 'had been lost largely due to the Red Smear and the Anti-Benn campaign; also the isolation argument and the feeling that Mr Callaghan had, in fact, renegotiated better terms'.[201]

The Conservative organisational structure was brought into support the 'Yes' campaign. This was vitally important to the 'Yes' campaign, and although the ultimate result might have raised questions about the validity of organisation and traditional canvassing methods, a professional party organisation was something denied to the 'No' campaign.[202] Central Office agents were asked to report on the activities of the 'No' campaign.[203] By mid-May

Central Office had distributed 10 million leaflets on Europe, 6.5 million on behalf of Britain in Europe and 3.5 million of its own.[204] The Shadow Cabinet took the view that encouraging the Conservative vote 'on the doorstep' would probably be more 'decisive' than the media.[205] Peter Thorneycroft, the newly appointed party chairman, repeated what his predecessor Willie Whitelaw had told activists in January. He wrote to all associations urging them to maximise the 'Yes' vote whether as individual associations or as part of BIE.[206] The Shadow Cabinet was anxious that Thatcher reinforce the message and suggested circulating appropriate examples from her speeches on the EEC.[207] Between 15 March and 4 June Thatcher made over a dozen public statements on the subject.[208] Advice was offered to activists about where they could secure additional funds to fight the campaign, be it from Central Office coffers or from the European Movement or BIE. On the recommendation of the area agent, Newcastle West Association secured a grant of £30 from 'Keep Britain In' to cover meetings and leaflet production, whilst West Midlands Young Conservatives approached BIE to help offset some of the £970 it intended spending on the forthcoming campaign.[209] With just over a month before polling, the Conservatives estimated that seventy Conservative-held seats had well-organised 'Yes' campaigns, in another sixty to seventy something was happening and in the remainder nothing as yet.[210] In many ways this reflects the general division of the party. The enthusiasts and sceptics, who were small in numbers, were based on the peripheries of the party. A portion of 'loyalists' followed the leadership line, whilst the majority remained agnostic.

One of the difficulties was that in those constituencies where the sitting Conservative MP was an anti, the advice was less than clear cut. In the end the expectation was that individuals might campaign through BIE. The last time Britain had seen anything comparable was the privately organised 1935 League of Nations Union Peace Ballot. Then, as now, the organisation and personnel of the local Conservative associations were sought to help marshal the vote.[211] The difference then had been that the leadership was unwilling to sanction participation and anxious to minimise the turnout.[212] Now the reverse applied. To mobilise the vote it needed a sense of magnitude. As Dudley Smith (MP for Warwick) emphasised, it was 'essential' to keep living standards and preserve peace in Europe:

> It was not a political battle in the terms [to] which we have become accustomed. It was a battle about the future survival and prosperity of our country; a battle about the idealism of well-ordered and co-operative societies; a battle about peace and hope for our children and those who come after them.[213]

The 'No' campaign was divided between those who spoke about high food prices and those who spoke about the loss of sovereignty. In addition they argued that there was a risk of unemployment, especially in those regions furthest from the continent. The 'Yes' campaign countered that jobs would be created from membership, that Britain had no alternative, but that this would not risk British traditions. The outcome of the 5 June referendum was an emphatic rejection of the anti-Marketeers message. Of those who voted, 67 per cent were prepared to accept the renegotiated terms and remain in the EEC. Only the Western Isles of Scotland showed a majority for the No's. It was exactly as the polls had been predicting: a two-to-one majority.

The result was a major disappointment to the anti-Marketeers, but hardly surprising, as Cyril Black concluded, given the 'overwhelming forces and resources used against us'.[214] The 'Yes' campaign had been in planning for many months, had secured significant financial backing, especially from business. Lord Drogheda, John Sainsbury and Alastair McAlpine had been seeking financial backing and by May 1975 raised £1,481,583.[215] In contrast, the 'No' coalition secured only £8,000. The sceptics failed to have the referendum legislation impose an upper limit for campaign spending, but did secure a government subsidy of £125,000 for each side.[216] The 'No' campaign had been unable to match the professionalism of the BIE campaign and failed to secure vital support from the media. Only the *Morning Star* supported the 'No' campaign, and all the pro-EEC editorials in papers like *The Times* and the *Daily Telegraph* and the cartoons in the *Daily Mail* were free advertising. This last lesson was one the 'No' campaign would not forget. Senior Conservative anti-Marketeers, though crushed by the result, hoped that 'disillusion with the Market will grow and the time may well come when the whole issue will have to be considered and fought again'. Some even felt there was a historical parallel, suggesting that if Neville Chamberlain had held a referendum on Munich in 1938 he would have won, 'but the men of Munich are now dishonoured, and Winston Churchill – the outstanding leader of the minority at that time – has been abundantly vindicated'.[217] Party loyalties, especially at the grass roots, might have helped secure the referendum's success, but Europe was now an issue for parliamentary rebellion, as the 1990s would testify. Anti-Marketeers, confident that they were latter-day anti-appeasers, had their thoughts articulated by Edward du Cann, chairman of the 1922 Committee, when he declared that 'there is always a higher loyalty than party loyalty – loyalty to one's country and what one honestly believes to be her best interests'.[218]

The 1975 referendum was important because it began a process of realignment in British politics. It accelerated the feature of division within the Labour Party, which would result in the 1981 creation of the Social Democratic Party. Senior Conservatives sensed the potential opportunity during the referendum campaign. Whitelaw thought the inter-party co-operation in the 'Yes' campaign was 'bringing about a subtle change of mood. This might be opening up possibilities for the future'. He meant by this that if the Labour Party drifted too leftward elements of the party's right and pro-Europeans might consider a switch to the Conservatives. This was not such a far-fetched idea in 1975. Historically the Conservative Party had a very successful record of absorbing disaffected elements of the opposition parties. Others welcomed the resumption of party warfare on the completion of the ballot. Douglas Hurd admitted it had been pleasurable working alongside people who were usually political opponents and consequently he 'never lost the habit of discussing any subject comfortably with men like Roy Jenkins, John Harris and Bill Rodgers, who had been my fellow campaigners'.[219] It was also, though, important in redefining the Conservative agenda, in a Thatcherite mould. Thus began the gradual transformation of the Conservatives from the party of Europe into the party of scepticism that entered the twenty-first century. The argument began to be articulated that obsession with EEC entry from Macmillan's application had been to the detriment of a 'clear Conservative programme' which would 'provide a positive alternative to socialism' and allowing Labour to seize the 'initiative'.[220]

The success of the referendum brought to a close a long-running debate, which had been conducted since 1946. In hindsight it was apparent that this was only the conclusion of a battle; the war still needed to be won. The Conservative Party had been forced to confront its core ideological values by its leaders and appeared to have accepted that they were the party of Europe. By reaffirming the entry of Britain to the EEC the British people now presented the political establishment with the challenge of finding Britain's place in Europe.

# 2 From EEC to EU, 1975–2006

## 'In Europe, but not run by Europe'?

The Conservatives in opposition from 1974 to 1979 could still be seen broadly as the least divided of the main parties when it came to Europe. They were a pro-EEC party. The anti-Marketeers appeared, as a force within the party, to have dwindled, deemed irrelevant due to the scale of the 'Yes' vote in the 1975 referendum. Now the issue was deliberately kept low key. This position suited the new leader Margaret Thatcher, who was yet to form her strident views on the matter, because there was no wish to detract from the objective of questioning Labour's domestic record. The discussion that did occur on Europe after the referendum revolved around four areas. One was a general sense that Wilson and then Callaghan were taking a passive role in European affairs. This was largely because of Labour's internal divisions, but it meant that in Conservative eyes the EEC continued to be dominated by the Franco-German axis. The matter of direct elections to the European Parliament exercised minds the most. The matter of Britain's budget contribution to the EEC was an irritant, along with the issue of whether Britain would participate in the Franco-German proposed European Monetary System (EMS). With the exception of direct elections, these were not issues that really registered with the party's grass roots. One phenomenon of the post-1975 Europe debate was the extent to which it was confined to within the parliamentary party until the 1990s. It should also be seen as significant that, unlike the last opposition period, 1964–70, there was only one policy group considering European matters: direct elections to the European Parliament.[1] Yet as Thatcher led her party into the 1979 general election there appeared to be a positiveness about their attitude to the EEC. They were critical of Labour's obstructiveness, and made promises of renewed British leadership and entry into EMS if the election was won.[2]

## Direct elections

Since Britain had formally joined the EEC a non-elected delegation of British representatives had been eligible to sit in the European Parliament. This was only a temporary arrangement because direct elections to the European Parliament had been agreed in principle at the 1974 Paris Summit.

Party advisors had reacted positively to the proposals, considering them 'very much in the interests of the Conservative Party, as the Party which has spearheaded our entry into Europe'.[3] This was an aspect of Europe that appealed to the activists. They had been calling for direct elections since the 1972 party conference. In 1973, of the forty resolutions concerning Europe twelve called for direct elections. The 1975 party conference received sixteen motions welcoming the implementation of direct elections, in most cases urging the earliest implementation and suggesting they would help the electorate feel part of Europe.[4] Unsurprisingly, anti-Marketeers like Neil Marten were more worried, fearing 'further loss of sovereignty' because the European Parliament would gain new legislative powers which would overrule Westminster.[5] These views reveal that the debate about direct elections centred on two questions of principle: whether Britain should participate in an election to an assembly that threatened to usurp some of the legitimacy of the Westminster Parliament, whilst the matter of electoral system raised the possibility of proportional representation (PR) and if adopted might prove the necessary precedent to ensure its implementation for Westminster elections.

In December 1975 the European Council had agreed that the first European-wide elections should be held in mid-1978. However, the whole European process had to be delayed after Callaghan's direct elections bill gained parliamentary approval but had the proportional representation element rejected by 319 votes to 222 in December 1977.[6] The Conservative position on this issue was anything but settled, and there was considerable internal debate. Thatcher's view was that the advice she had received 'made rejection necessary'.[7] The Labour government's April 1977 White Paper had proposed consideration of four systems: first past the post (FPTP); national list system (NLS); regional list system (RLS); and single transferable vote (STV). STV was clearly the least-favoured system, whilst any idea of the party lists system was considered 'alien to British traditions'.[8] Concern was also expressed that regional lists presented problems from the point of view of party organisation.[9] Some, like Angus Maude, were less 'dogmatic' about the electoral system. They believed it likely that in time a Europe-wide system would be adopted and had 'no objection in principle' to proportional representation for Euro-elections whilst keeping first past the post for Westminster elections.[10] Indeed Ted Heath, Francis Pym, Peter Walker, James Prior, John Younger and Ian Gilmour all voted for PR.[11] Likewise, the Conservative Group for Europe supported PR 'in principle', using the additional member system.[12] Thatcher was particularly suspicious of the idea of a set of European parliamentarians who would not be constrained by the normal channels of Westminster, and for this reason she favoured the traditional electoral procedure of first past the post.[13] Amongst party managers some anxiety existed about how the party's anti-Marketeers would behave during the legislative process and whether they would consider tactical voting against Conservative interests in order to scupper the bill.[14] In the event 229 out of 280 Tories supported it, compared to only 132 out of 308 Labour MPs.[15] Yet in an ironic twist a Conservative amendment to secure voting rights for British citizens resident in Europe was defeated in February 1978 only because the Conservative MP members of the European Parliament failed to return to Westminster in sufficient time.[16]

In the event Parliament rejected the PR element. As a consequence the bill had to be reintroduced and the whole of the EEC had to put back the election date to 1979. These elections now provided the party with 'a great opportunity to use its unique organisation to ensure that the Party is represented in strength in the European Parliament'.[17] The job of explaining to the party activists what this all meant fell to shadow Europe minister Douglas Hurd, who was also still working in a part-time capacity for Britain in Europe. It was a tedious and repetitive experience. He admits in his memoirs, 'A tiny handful of Conservatives in each constituency were enthusiastic, another handful hostile, most bemused'.[18] This represented a classic affirmation of how the party has typically responded to the whole subject of European integration. Once the technicalities of the election process were ironed out, fresh concerns arose about how these elections would be funded, as well as some internal argument about the manner in which the prospective European candidates would be selected.[19]

In the first direct elections on 7 June 1979 the Conservatives won sixty out of the seventy-eight seats available and gained 51 per cent of the vote.[20] The result was tarnished by the poor turnout: only 48 per cent. Electoral interest in the European elections might be minimal, but many observers were relieved to see that the election mirrored the national outcome of the previous month – a feature of European elections thereafter. The difficulty would be that, having now won both the national and European elections, the Conservatives were once more the party of government, and with that came the responsibility for dealing with Europe at a time when the whole area was viewed with apathy.[21]

## Thatcher's budgetary battles

The last years of Callaghan's Labour government had seen Britain's net financial contribution to the EEC rise steeply, even accounting for the 1975 refund deal. In 1979 the net contribution was £780 million and this would worsen in 1980 when the transition to full membership was achieved. This made Britain the second largest contributor to the Community after Germany, despite being the third poorest member of the Community.[22] On taking office in 1979 Thatcher was advised by Treasury officials that EEC membership was costing Britain £1 billion a year, largely because so little was received from CAP.[23] In addition the import/export balance of payments had to be taken into consideration. By the end of the 1970s the value of UK exports represented 33 per cent of gross domestic product (GDP), compared to 21 per cent in the mid-1960s, whilst the value of UK imports at the end of the 1970s was 30 per cent of GDP, compared to 23 per cent for the mid-1960s.[24] Given the relative weakness of the British economy, the economic costs of EEC membership were politically significant.

Thatcher was determined that the situation could not be allowed to continue and renegotiation of the British contribution was necessary. She warned her European counterparts in June 1979 that she was unwilling to see Britain as the funder of the EEC at the expense of asking the British electorate to forgo social and economic improvements.[25] She seized upon a figure of £1,000 million rebate based upon the claim that 'for every £2 we contribute we get £1 back'.[26] This was a battle that pitched her not just against the idea of 'Europe' but also against the leaders of Europe. For four years, until 1984, the issue of the British contribution threatened to disrupt all matters European.

In her memoirs Thatcher places a nationalistic spin on the renegotiations. She was defending Britain's honour, with the Europeans acting in self-interest and with bad manners. When the matter was raised during the Dublin Summit in November to December 1979 their reaction had been 'un-English'.[27] Portraying the talks in these terms may well have served to project a retrospective Eurosceptic message, but it also suggests that Thatcher still failed to appreciate, and understand, the European way of conducting business: namely the need to seek compromises and build coalitions to achieve consensus and drive the European project forward. That said, observers such as Roy Jenkins felt that her European counterparts had treated her poorly.[28]

One of the most persistent themes running through Conservative thought on Europe was a perception that Britain could shape and direct European matters. Once a member of the Community, Conservatives sensed that Britain should be playing a leading, and distinctive, role. The problem was, and this could never be admitted to for electoral purposes, that Britain's late entry, combined with economic weakness, meant playing a secondary role to the Franco-German axis.[29] This Thatcher was unwilling to acquiesce to and in retaliation she adopted a more adversarial approach to dealing with her European partners. This was demonstrated in March 1980 when she threatened to withhold Britain's VAT contributions. A former private secretary is doubtful that the 'handbagging' method was the only option open, but concedes that it probably provided a quicker resolution than 'conventional' diplomacy might have done.[30]

The budget negotiations were conducted within the context of economic recession, where instead of a European response individual nation-states sought to resolve their own economic woes without recourse to broader more integrated policies. Thatcher's attempts to renegotiate Britain's budget contribution also challenged many of the national interests of leading Community members. In accepting EEC membership in 1971 Heath had been forced to adopt economic and industrial policy models that were ill suited to Britain's industrial and agricultural base. Thatcher had pledged in

1979 that she did not intend to be a 'soft touch': 'we shall judge what Britain's interests are, and we shall be resolute in defending them.'[31] These became the matters of Community budget, balancing the inequities of CAP whilst imposing monetary constraint on the EEC's spending and subsidies regime.[32] This view had formed early into her leadership after a visit to the European Commission in December 1977.[33] By the 1980s Thatcher spoke of 'our money' and contrasted the austerity of Britain with the fat-cat image of Brussels bureaucrats and CAP-generated food mountains.[34] This was a period when opinion polls showed that Thatcher was the most unpopular prime minister since polling began, and the nationalistic tone of Thatcher's European rhetoric was as much an electoral device as evidence of intent.[35] In negotiations it was stressed that the EU budget was the first part of a broader twofold approach to Europe. The budget negotiations might be negative but future British policy priorities were not possible until the European Union reformed its finances.[36]

Not every Conservative desired such a combative approach. The so-called 'wets' within cabinet, individuals like Francis Pym, the defence secretary, were concerned that Thatcher was whipping up anti-European sentiment amongst the British electorate and similarly alienating Britain's European partners.[37] In May 1980 a temporary compromise on the budget was reached which gave Britain two-thirds of the rebate Thatcher was demanding. Thatcher later claimed to have regretted accepting this, but attributes the agreement to the persistence of Peter Carrington, the foreign secretary.[38] The negotiations had been delegated to Carrington and Ian Gilmour. Thatcher was none too pleased with the terms they presented to her in May 1980, not because they had succeeded at her expense, but rather because the grievance was more valuable than its removal. She could 'win some kudos and popularity as the defender of the British people against the foreigner', noted Gilmour; 'a running row with our European partners was the next best thing to a war; it would divert public attention from the disasters at home'.[39] But this was only a temporary solution to cover 1980–1; it 'remained a most provocative piece of unfinished business' that would require further compromise in June 1982, before final solution in 1984.[40] The appointment of Geoffrey Howe, as foreign secretary, was a turning point in these negotiations depending upon whose version of events you encounter. It has been suggested that a patient Howe complimented Thatcher's aggressive and direct manner of negotia-tion.[41] In contrast Howe is blamed for going 'native' whilst at the Foreign Office. Thatcher has subsequently suggested Howe had an 'almost romantic longing for Britain to become part of some grandiose European consensus ... it was to bring us no end of trouble'. Her critique is that he conceded too easily at Fontainebleau and that the 66 per cent rebate was gained despite and not because of Howe's strategy.[42] The reality was more, as the political scientist and seasoned political observer Dennis Kavanagh has concluded, that Thatcher's policy on Europe up until 1988, whilst one of resistance, ulti-mately displayed willingness to compromise.[43] This aptly points to the

inherent contradictions in Thatcher's European position. Despite challenging many of her natural instincts she was prepared to work both to
enhance the project and against it. This the journalist Hugo Young has
likened to a religious faith, where the individual thinks they ought to be
atheist but cannot take themselves beyond fluctuating between attending
church and taking an agnostic position.[44] Thatcher's stance was not without
critics, most notably Heath and Pym, who felt that Britain should concentrate on leadership.[45] This potential for leadership appeared possible in the
moves towards developing a European monetary system.

## Towards a single market

The European Monetary System came into being without Britain after
Callaghan's Labour government had ruled out participation. Its purpose was
to tie together the exchange rates of the EEC member states, thereby formal-
ising economic co-operation, with the long-term objective of achieving
economic convergence. In the relative luxury of opposition the Thatcher
Shadow Cabinet had, after fairly detailed discussion, reached a 'tolerably
clear consensus' that committed them to supporting the system, believing
that it was the correct both politically and economically.[46] The party's June
1979 Euro-election manifesto reiterated the party's support for EMS and the
objectives of currency stability and closer co-ordination of national economic
policies: 'we shall look for ways in which Britain can take her rightful place
within it.'[47] Furthermore, EMS appeared to be working, although this owed
much to the weakness of the Deutschmark, which enabled the other countries to maintain their parity.[48] Yet it is clear the party's position was
motivated largely by opportunism, in a manner similar to the Churchill
opposition years before 1951. On assuming power in 1979 the Cabinet's
public enthusiasm suddenly cooled, as with Treasury support it was argued
that the conditions were not yet suited to British entry into the EMS. As
Lawson had warned, it was 'a hideously complex and awkward issue, both
economically and (more importantly) politically'.[49] What is more, other
senior Conservatives were concerned that because it was a Franco-German
initiative it did not offer Britain the opportunities she needed for leadership.
But underlining all these discussions was a political tension between remem-
bering that 'our own party had European obligations' and that the wider
party was potentially vulnerable to the anti-Marketeers' arguments.[50]

Although EMS succeeded in its early years it did little to help instigate a
recovery from the economic malaise Europe experienced in the early 1980s.
This encouraged the Germans and Italians to consider means by which the
institutions of Europe could be enhanced at the expense of national governments to invigorate the decision-making process. This gained momentum at
Stuttgart in June 1983 with the Solemn Declaration on European Union,
which included plans to relaunch the integration process. This process was
given further impetus by the European Parliament adopting the Draft

Treaty on European Union in February 1984. Elements of the Conservative leadership saw this as an opportunity to develop 'Thatcherism on a European scale'.[51] Yet with the passing of time Thatcher has come to the view that EMS was a mistake into which others bounced her.[52] Commentators such as Hugo Young sense the irony that after her hand-bagging Europe over budgetary contributions Thatcher failed to appreciate that the single market was an acceleration of the unification process and a challenge to the nation-state.[53] And yet Thatcher was a willing participant in the move towards a single market. She saw in the Treaty of Rome a commitment to the free market and believed that the Community's structure helped restrict the impact of Communist parties in other member states. Hence the ambition of the European Commission to create a proper internal market met with her approval.[54] EMS guaranteed majority voting in the Council of Ministers and increased the powers of the European Parliament to amend legislation. In addition it covered measures to liberalise the EEC's internal market. It was this latter development that encouraged the Conservatives: the 'external product of a domestic strategy aimed at entrenching the perceived governing benefits of neo-liberal economics.'[55] Furthermore, in her view the persistent use of national veto had made a mockery of the Common Market ideal. The single market would remove the anomalies these vetos had created and relaunch the European Union in a British vision. The new direction of Thatcher's thinking had been suggested in the White Paper *Europe: The Future*, which had first been introduced at the Fontainebleau Summit in June 1984. There appeared to be little that was new or radical in this paper, but it reveals the re-emergence of the link between supply-side problems and the significance of exporters needing international markets. This has been interpreted as evidence of Thatcher's intention to seek the 'Europeanisation' of British political economy in order to bring external pressure to bear on supply-side issues, secure domestic autonomy and have free market ideas accepted,[56] the high point of which was to be the SEA.

The architect of SEA, Lord Cockfield, was a former member of her Cabinet, and she used her full political power to ensure the parliamentary ratification of the Act, which included provision for majority voting in the Council of Ministers.[57] Importantly, too, unlike EMS, the SEA was a British-led initiative, which meant that it was advantageous to the British. When the SEA was ratified in February 1986 it cleared the way by 1992 for the free movement of goods, capital services and labour. It expanded the areas of EU interest to include foreign policy co-operation, the environment and social policy, and increased the powers of the European Parliament, giving it a veto over any single market legislation.

At the time the Single European Act appeared to meet with broad acceptance from the Conservative Party.[58] During the parliamentary debates there was widespread absenteeism (particularly from the Labour Party) and only forty-three MPs opposed the third reading.[59] Other events were gripping the attention of politicians and the media. All this unfolded against the back-drop of the Westland affair and the Heseltine and Brittan resignations. The wets had long championed the idea, whilst the neo-liberals saw it as a consolidation of the free market and the entrenchment of their own economic views at the European level. The expressions of concern were only belated and initially muted. However, there was concern that the SEA would impact upon the role and function of Parliament and that it provided increased powers for the European Parliament.[60] Edward Du Cann, the former chair of the 1922 Committee, was amongst those who voted against, arguing that it undermined national sovereignty. So why was it so easily moved through Parliament? Ministers successfully portrayed the SEA as an example of Britain's leadership role.[61] Similarly, they were able to present the SEA as being what business and the City of London wanted. Obviously the size of the Conservative majority played its part, as did Labour's own internal divisions, but also it has been observed that during the 1980s the parliamentary party placed European matters low on the political agenda. This was evidenced by the low attendance at parliamentary debates.[62] The low turnout was, according to one backbencher, 'a measure of the way in which European debates have almost become a part of our domestic scene and can be gathered from the attendance this afternoon in the House of Commons. They rate slightly below Scottish housing debates'.[63] This suggests that MPs absorbed the generalities of European policy without evaluating the details. Ian Gilmour takes the view that the constitutional implications of the Single European Act in 1986 were significant enough to warrant a referendum.[64] But this was retrospective. Indeed, what the single market did was consolidate, and give fresh momentum to, many of the disparate aims set out by the European Commission over the preceding thirty years. At the same time, it has been suggested that 1986 marks the first evidence of a split within the Conservative leadership on Europe, as Thatcher clashed with her most senior colleagues over the desirability of British membership of the ERM.[65] Whereas Thatcher had expectations that the single market would mark the final stage in the construction of the EEC, 1992 was ultimately used as an opportunity to expand the role of the European Union into previously untouched policy areas that challenged the sovereignty of the nation. This occurred because of the ambiguity of language in the SEA preamble, and the title of Article 20 enabled the EU to force the pace towards a single currency, which had never been Thatcher's intention.[66] As Howe lamented,

> in domestic politics one had at least the feeling of being able to control the speed and manner in which policies developed. But in the Community we often seemed to be on a remorselessly moving carpet.[67]

The expectation that the SEA would herald a long period of calm was misplaced. The problem was that the European Union under Commissioner

Jacques Delors saw Europe as a bicycle: you kept pedalling or else you fell off. So what did this mean for the Conservative Party? It marked the beginnings of a gradual awakening period that within seven years had raised the stakes and changed the game's rules. In its aftermath it became apparent that the SEA was anything but Thatcherism in Europe, and if Thatcher could not make membership work for Britain, some posed the question as to whether anyone could?[68]

Thatcher's awakening to the European threat was her September 1988 Bruges speech. She famously declared: 'We have not successfully rolled back the frontiers of the state in Britain, only to see them reimposed at a European level, with a European super-state exercising a new dominance from Brussels.'[69] It was in effect a rejection of her government's previous approach to Europe. It signalled her opposition to Europe's growing centralism and the creation of a European state. It was also an admission of failure: failure by her governments to find a satisfactory position for Britain within Europe.[70] But, just as importantly, this shift in stance would have profound implications for Thatcher's leadership. As Nigel Lawson observed,

> the Conservative Party could be successfully led only by someone who took their stand in the centre of the spectrum on this issue, where the silent majority dwelt. Margaret's evident determination to lead the Party from one of the two extremes of the spectrum spelt nothing but trouble.[71]

The 'conversion' was important too because it indicated that Euroscepticism was moving into the mainstream, legitimising views that previously had been dismissed as held by cranks and extremists. Some suggest that this was actually the point when the credos of the anti-Marketeers were replaced by an ideology of Euroscepticism based upon a critique of the European Union.[72] The flaw in this interpretation is that it accepts at face value the Eurosceptics' own claim to uniqueness, without questioning why they should make such a claim, and which ignores the longer-term historical linkages between the anti-Europeans of the 1940s and 1950s, the anti-Marketeers of the 1960s and 1970s and the Eurosceptics of the 1990s.

## The European Exchange Rate Mechanism

For the increasingly sceptical Thatcher the problem was that the European Union had decided exchange rate control was not enough.[73] Both Germany and France, especially after France being forced to devalue the franc in January 1987, were increasingly attracted to the need for monetary union to isolate their own economic strategies from global pressure. It was at the Madrid European Council in June 1989 that Thatcher reluctantly agreed that sterling could join the ERM provided it was within a broad band of 6 per cent and that in return the second and third stages of the Delors plans for a common currency were postponed pending further consideration. She had been bounced by the axis of Lawson and Howe, with her chancellor threatening resignation if she did not commit to the ERM. From this point onwards her relations with her two most senior ministerial colleagues would be fraught. This was significant given the key role both men had played in implementing Thatcherism: it threatened the very basis of Thatcher's leadership. In July Howe was moved from the Foreign Office and within three months Lawson had resigned, citing the persistent intervention of Thatcher's advisor, and implacable opponent of ERM, Alan Walters. Within the Cabinet debates Thatcher had found herself isolated in her scepticism towards the ERM, highlighting the divisions amongst the Thatcherite praetorian guard, being able to rely only on Biffen and Ridley. Tebbit was favourably disposed for party political reasons, whilst Parkinson, Lilley and Redwood all supported the party's 1987 manifesto group desire to endorse entry as a future policy goal. It left Thatcher looking increasingly isolated.[74] It suggested too that Europeanism had the upper hand.

When in October 1990 the Rome Summit convened, Thatcher found to her considerable annoyance that Europe had taken another step forward. The summit called for an intergovernmental conference on monetary and political union, a process that would culminate in the Maastricht Treaty.[75] Given that Thatcher thought this had been ruled out at the Madrid Council, this raised doubts in Eurosceptic minds about the balance of power in the European Union and posed the question of whether Britain had any political leverage.[76] In her battles with the European Union Thatcher had sought to avoid calls for intergovernmental conferences and any form of treaty amendment for fear that such an event would open up a Pandora's box with the potential for federalist advancement. It risked provoking domestic opposition from the party's own backbenchers. In the event it was not Thatcher but her chancellor, John Major, who would lead the British negotiating team as prime minister in December 1991. Thatcher was subjected to a leadership challenge sparked by the resignation of Geoffrey Howe.[77] Thatcher had angered Howe by briefing journalists outside the Rome Summit room on a line that contradicted the agreed Foreign Office negotiating position and which attacked the European commissioner Jacques Delors.[78] The next day in the House of Commons Thatcher made her infamous 'No, No, No' speech, which again attacked Delors and his plans to make the European Parliament the legislature for the Community and the Commission the executive. This speech confirmed in Howe's mind that there was now a 'fundamental' division between him and Thatcher over European policy and that resignation was the only option. The resolution was confirmed during his final Cabinet meeting (held before he informed Thatcher of his decision), at which he was subjected to a sustained diatribe from Thatcher, which caused considerable embarrassment around the Cabinet table. When Howe delivered his resignation speech to the House of Commons two weeks later he insisted his resignation was down to disagreement over the substance of European policy and that he felt like a cricketer being sent to the crease only to find on facing the opposition that his bat had been broken by his own captain. As Thatcher left the Chamber she confessed to her party chairman, Kenneth Baker, 'the game is over'.[79] Michael Heseltine seized the opportunity to initiate a leadership contest, and although Thatcher topped the poll her majority was not sufficient under the rules. Advised that her authority had been severely damaged, she reluctantly resigned. John Major and Douglas Hurd now entered the contest to challenge the Heseltine bid. Major drew strong support from the Eurosceptic/Thatcherite wing of the party, who perceived him as Thatcher's heir, and he subsequently won the contest. This would later backfire as it heightened the sceptics' sense of betrayal over the Maastricht Treaty.[80] But Euroscepticism itself was not a sufficient reason for voting for Major. The other candidates drew upon this support too: Biffen voted for Hurd, whilst Richard Shepherd supported Heseltine's bid.[81] However, unlike in the 1950s and 1960s, 'Europe' was now a test of a Conservative politicians' standing.

## Maastricht: 'game, set and match'?

In contrast to his predecessor, John Major appeared from the beginning to take a less antagonistic approach towards the EU. Speaking in Bonn in March 1991 he let it be known that it was his wish that Britain be at 'the heart of Europe'.[82] This sort of language did not go down well with the party's resurgent Eurosceptics. In June a leaked Bruges Group memorandum attacked the drift of the government's European policy, whilst Thatcher made a speech critical of European Union in Chicago.[83] Further controversy was provoked in October when the Selsdon Group manifesto included a call for the virtual withdrawal of Britain from the European Union, prompting several ministers to tender their resignations from the group.

These Eurosceptic concerns during the summer and autumn of 1991 were being fuelled by Dutch plans to enhance the federalist commitments of the draft Maastricht Treaty and a belief that there was a 'hidden agenda'.[84] Although the plans to extend the remit of Community institutions to foreign and defence policy found little favour with wider European governments, the matters of EMU and the Social Chapter remained on the negotiating table for the Maastricht Summit. Addressing the House of Commons in advance of the summit Major sought to mollify his Eurosceptic colleagues. He reassured them that he would not 'accept a treaty which describes the Community as having a federal vocation'. This meant no EMU for Britain, no diminution of NATO's role or Community interference in foreign, defence or domestic policy, and the Social Chapter could not be allowed to threaten Britain's economic competitiveness. His causes would be the enlargement of Europe and subsidiarity. This latter phrase was the idea that more decision-making should occur at the national level rather than regional or European levels. Reviewing this parliamentary debate, it is clear that although the numerical numbers had not yet rallied to the Eurosceptic standard, the rhetorical skirmishes based on opposition to EMU and a referendum demand were to provide the battlefield of the subsequent civil war.[85] Major not only faced difficulties over his negotiating positions from within Parliament, but also figures in the Cabinet, particularly Baker, Howard and Lilley, were unhappy about the potential risks to sovereignty, immigration and frontier controls and the Social Chapter. Major did not secure the Cabinet's mandate until 5 December.[86]

He did return from the intergovernmental conference in December 1991 having secured two opt-outs for Britain from the single currency and the Social Chapter and insisting on the removal from the treaty's text of the Union's federal intent. Although Chancellor Lamont and he would battle it out in their memoirs about who exactly secured these opt-outs at the negotiation table, the fact remains that this was hailed at the time as a victory for British negotiation and a central achievement of his premiership.[87] Major was conforming to the model of placing a marker in the discussion sandpit, but being prepared to compromise and adjust the marker's final placement. But the compromises he achieved fell within the criteria of Conservative acceptability: preserving the interdependent nature of European institutions, maintaining parliamentary sovereignty over matters of currency and taxation and resisting any further legitimisation of the trade union movement. It seems that Major might have been prepared to offer a referendum on the new treaty had it not been for Thatcher's public and personal attack on the issue before he left for Maastricht.[88] When the small print of the new treaty was considered it was clear that Major had not retained all his pledges of 20 November. Maastricht set up a 'pillared' structure whereby the role of the European Community was expanded to include two new areas of policy co-operation: Common Foreign and Security Policy (CFSP) and Justice and Home Affairs (JHA).

What the Conservative Party really thought about Maastricht at this precise moment was probably the least of Major's worries. When Parliament debated the treaty over two days (18–19 December) the numbers of projected Eurosceptic rebels dissipated. In the event, instead of a predicted rebellion of about forty, only seven Conservatives voted against the government, with a further three abstaining. Domestically his administration was faced with the need to fight a general election. With the opinion polls suggesting the likelihood of a Kinnock-led Labour government it seems that the ratification process for this treaty would fall to a different administration. Political survival was the absolute necessity. Yet against 'expert' predictions John Major won the 1992 general election, with the vast majority of Conservative candidates having endorsed the treaty during the campaign.[89] This propelled the ratification of the treaty high up the new government's agenda. There were good grounds for optimism that this would be a relatively straightforward process. Europe had played no big part in the election campaign and senior figures took the view that the 'argument within the Conservative Party was not extinct but it had died down'.[90] Some of the senior sceptics, like Thatcher and Tebbit, had since the election moved to the House of Lords. Furthermore, the party's overall reaction to the treaty's signature on 7 February 1992 had been broadly acquiescent.[91] On 21 May the bill received its second reading by 336 votes to 92 (after Labour abstained), with only twenty-two Conservatives voting against.[92] As Hurd admits in his memoirs, 'the way through to ratification seemed tedious but sure'.[93] The committee stage was scheduled to commence on 4 June. It appeared that European matters were working in Major's favour, especially as the momentum towards integration seemed to have been checked by the less than enthusiastic welcome for Maastricht from the peoples of Europe. 'Game, set and match' was in retrospect rather presumptuous, but not an unrealistic assessment at the time.[94]

It was these expressions of continental public doubt that gave the Conservatives' internal debate fresh fuel. The Danish 'No' vote of 2 June threw the whole British legislative process into question and re-energised the sceptics. Tony Newton and the whips warned Major that the second reading rebels would now gain fresh recruits and discussions took place about postponing the legislation.[95] This was confirmed by the eighty-two signatures secured for the 3 June Early Day Motion calling for a 'fresh start' on Europe. Significant was that around twenty of these signatories were newly elected MPs, and the fact that, despite suggestions by the whips that many had signed unaware of the implications of supporting an EDM, only four MPs subsequently withdrew their name suggests the implausibility of this critique.[96] The Eurosceptics appeared to be gaining support for their argument that Maastricht was a step too far, that it represented a fundamental new direction for Europe in terms of the range and power it ceded to a central authority. This was no longer the common economic market which Britain had accepted in 1973, but a radically different proposal, a European Union, with economic and monetary union, a single currency, a common foreign and defence policy and legal uniformity. It appeared that the prophecies of the 1971–3 anti-Marketeers were proving remarkably accurate. Hurd pessimistically confided to his diary: 'we are holed below the waterline.'[97] Eventually the decision was taken to reintroduce the bill in the autumn after the Irish and French referendums, but with Britain taking the presidency of the EU for six months from July it proved a difficult period.[98] The whole issue of Maastricht became entangled within a web of broader questions relating to leadership and policy. This partially explains why the negotiated opt-outs were insufficient to satiate the demands of the Eurosceptics. The matter is complicated further by the emerging divisions over economic policy amongst former Thatcherites, which can be traced back to 1986. The Thatcherites splintered between the nationalists, who supported EU membership but who increasingly opposed moves towards a single currency because of the challenge to nationhood and independence, and the neo-liberal integrationists, who see the single market/currency as an opportunity to enhance the principles of the free market and are therefore prepared to consider further integration (short of federalism) as a necessary response to the interdependence of the European economics.[99]

Circumstances conspired further to make the passage of the Maastricht legislation still more difficult. Britain had formally joined the ERM in October 1990, but was spectacularly forced to withdraw on 16 September 1992. Major's government spent £10 billion trying to defend the pound against the currency speculators. However, the momentum proved unstoppable, and after a last-ditch bid to control the money markets with a huge rise in interest rates to 15 per cent, the chancellor was obliged to withdraw from the ERM. Black Wednesday, as it was dubbed, threw the whole European monetary programme into chaos. The incriminations were immediate. In light of events the resolution from Lancashire Central Euro-constituency submitted for the coming party conference in Brighton appeared hollow. It was one of those typically congratulatory types of conference resolution that believed 'the ERM has made a significant contribution to the dramatic reduction in inflation and hopes that, in the interests of British industry and commerce, it will be possible to enter the narrow band as soon as possible'.[100] It also highlighted the expectation associated with the ERM: that it was a mechanism for controlling inflation. Thatcher sought to distance herself from responsibility, arguing that history showed that no fixed exchange rate system, whether the gold standard or Bretton Woods, had ultimately survived. Nor was she prepared to blame the Germans. After all they had merely been looking after their own interests by maintaining a strong Deutschmark, something she would have been inclined towards.[101] The Eurosceptics flexed their muscle by laying down a second 'fresh start' EDM on economic policy on 24 September and secured sixty-seven signatures.[102] Despite calls for his sacking, Norman Lamont remained as chancellor until June 1993. When he did resign he was prepared to blame both the French and the Germans for the ERM collapse. He defended his belief that ERM had 'dramatically' controlled inflation. Thatcher was accused of short-termism by agreeing to entry in 1989 because it offered the opportunity to cut interest rates. He suggested too that the vast majority of the Cabinet had no say in the decision, with entry being 'foisted on the party by a small cabal'.[103] More generally for Eurosceptics Black Wednesday was confirmation that participation in further economic integration would restrain still more British room for manoeuvre.

The party's growing division was to be publicly aired at the 1992 Brighton party conference. Normally Conservative conferences have a reputation for being stage-managed 'unity' rallies. This conference had received 1,190 resolutions from constituency associations. Of these, 196 dealt with Europe and foreign affairs and 77 with the economy (including the ERM).[104] The conference hall saw the Eurosceptics in full voice, galvanised by Norman Tebbit, who when he asked conference delegates if they wanted to be citizens of a European Union was greeted with a very audible roar of 'No!'[105] The press and media emphasis upon Tebbit's speech overplays the scepticism of the conference activists. There is also a danger in purely citing the number of resolutions received on Europe, which can further overstate this scepticism. It should be noted that the topic that drew the most resolutions was law and order, with 215.[106] It fell to Douglas Hurd to close the Europe debate. In his memoirs he makes much of the fact that he felt Tebbit had successfully cowed the pro-Europeans in the audience. There were also many undecided, who rallied to Hurd's call for unity and warnings of divisions on the lines of 1846.[107] This call for unity would become a familiar refrain over the next five years, but such public calls for harmony merely served to reinforce in the electorates' mind, and the medias', the party's schism. The divisions spilled out of the conference chamber into the foyer, where Christopher Gill (MP for Ludlow and a Fresh Starter) was confronted by party vice-chairman Tim Smith and ordered to stop selling HMSO copies of the Treaty on European Union for the reduced price of £1. For Gill it was 'now glaringly obvious that the gloves are off and that this is going to be a fight to the finish'.[108]

The government narrowly succeed in winning the two parliamentary votes (with majorities of six and three) for its 'paving motion' on 4 November 1992, although it did require some wheeler-dealing in the lobbies – a concession to delay the third reading until after the Danish referendum was offered to certain waiverers. One difficulty the government faced was that the case they presented was essentially defensive, illustrating that the treaty could do no harm to Britain: 'But these negative arguments did not amount to a battle-cry.'[109] Major was buoyed, though, by his belief in parliamentary sovereignty and that the recent 1992 election had given him a mandate to push through the Maastricht Treaty. When rumours spread around Westminster that Eurosceptics intended to support a Labour amendment critical of Major's opt-out, the party machine was galvanised into action. The Conservative Research Department produced a thirteen-page briefing document, which liberally quoted from Thatcher. As Ian Taylor, vice-chair of the Positive Europeans, explained:

> Those thinking of voting for the social chapter will have to be reminded about all the things Margaret Thatcher said on the subject. We need to embarrass Margaret Thatcher herself. Embarrassment is a reasonable tactic.[110]

What it revealed was the deep fault-lines that Europe had sent through the party. But it also showed that leadership was so preoccupied with the parliamentary battle that it was failing to 'sell' Maastricht to the wider party and the electorate. A leaked CPC report based upon the responses of 350 activist discussion groups noted that many 'claim insufficient knowledge and understanding of the treaty'. As a result of this ignorance and 'partly because of the often confusing and contradictory claims made about Maastricht, there was widespread suspicion and even bewilderment over the treaty'.[111] This has been such a common complaint amongst activists since Macmillan's 1961

EEC application that it implies an almost deliberate attempt by the party leadership's to ensure that control of the European debate is retained amongst the Westminster elites. During the bill's committee stages the Eurosceptics fought a constant guerrilla war, tabling over 600 amendments to the three-clause bill. Bill Cash alone was responsible for 240 amendments, and he voted against the government on fifty occasions.[112] They also argued that ratification should be subject to a referendum; if this was granted their parliamentary opposition would cease. In an attempt to force the issue on 21 February 1992 Richard Shepherd (Aldridge-Brownhills) had proposed his own bill for a referendum on Maastricht.[113] In July 1993 the Conservative sceptics finally extracted their revenge on Major and combined with Labour to defeat the government over the Social Chapter.[114] Major immediately announced a vote of confidence and won by thirty-nine votes.[115] However, the divisions were not healed by the revelation of Major's off-camera reference to senior right-wing Cabinet colleagues as 'bastards'.[116] Maastricht was finally ratified on 2 August 1993, despite a last-minute attempt by Lord Rees-Mogg to mount a legal challenge. If Major had hoped that Maastricht's ratification and the collapse of the ERM would push back the timetable for the implementation of the single currency he was to be disappointed. The desire to keep the European bicycle in motion saw the French and Germans push for its rapid implementation.

## The single currency

Ideas of a single currency had been moving in European circles since the 1960s.[117] Heath might have refused to participate in the 1973 EEC discussions on monetary union, but the Werner report of March 1971 explicitly set out the objectives towards currency conversion over a twenty-year timetable, something that appeared to be overlooked by many of the pro-Europeans in 1971–3 and dismissed by the sceptics as unworkable.[118] Again this suggested a failing amongst British politicians, not just Conservative, to appreciate the nature of the European integration process. Statements of positions as a device to achieve a form of consensus were the driving force of the integration movement. Now, with the acceptance of Maastricht, the EU was keen to implement the single currency.

Against the discussions over the single currency the Conservatives' European civil war continued. In January 1994 the government accepted the Ioanninan compromise on the blocking minority in the EU Council of Ministers. In March Tony Marlow called for Major's resignation after what he perceived to be the prime minister's U-turn.[119] This was the first time since 1963 that a Conservative backbencher had openly called in the House of Commons for the resignation of a prime minister. The need to address the matter of the Council of Ministers voting system had arisen because of the proposed enlargement of the EU. From January 1995 Norway, Sweden, Finland and Austria would join the EU. Under the existing arrangements

Britain had 10 out of 76 votes, whilst 23 were required for a blocking minority. The changes would mean a total of 90 votes and a veto threshold of 27. A survey of backbench Conservatives found that a three-to-one majority were opposed to any change in the present voting system. A CPC report also showed that a 'substantial majority' of activists were in favour of the larger EU nations having disproportionate voting powers over smaller nations. A small majority favoured 'additional rights of veto'.[120]

In November 1994 Major survived a confidence vote on the European Communities (Finance) Bill by 330 to 303 votes. Major's eventual response to these repeated challenges was to withdraw the whip from eight rebel MPs who had abstained in the vote on 28 November. Sir Richard Body made it nine when he resigned the whip in solidarity. Major's action backfired and the 'Whipless Nine' merely provided a focus for the Eurosceptic tendency and eventually Major was obliged humiliatingly to reinstate the whip on 24 April 1995.[121] The party's civil war was spreading. In 1995 Marcus Fox was challenged for the chairmanship of the 1922 Committee because of his pro-Major stance. Fox had angered sceptics by acting as a conduit for Major's threats of electoral disaster should he lose the November 1994 vote on the Community budget increases.[122] Fed up with the attacks on his leadership, Major took the surprise decision to offer himself up for a leadership vote. John Redwood resigned from the Cabinet and, supported by the Eurosceptics, offered a challenge. Although Major won, it showed that one-third of his parliamentary party did not support him.[123] Further embarrassment was inflicted when in December the government was defeated in the EU fisheries 'take note' motion. Three Conservatives voted against and seven abstained. Although generally the Maastricht rebels, and especially the whipless MPs of 1994–5, kept the support of their local associations, it became clear in the aftermath of Major's successful defence of his leadership in June 1995 that activists, no doubt conscious of the imminence of a general election, had come to expect greater displays of loyalty.[124]

During 1995, and particularly 1996, the increasingly dominant matter of European debate was the single currency. In adopting the euro European states would be voluntarily ceding economic policy to a Central European Bank. This was critical because it would terminate the supranational character of the European Union.[125] A straw poll of 100 backbench Tories in advance of the parliamentary debate showed 40 were against the single currency, whilst 22 were positive Britain should join. The remainder were of the view that membership should be dependent upon the correct circumstances. The majority thought 1997 was too soon to participate and a significant minority thought the party's next election manifesto should rule out membership.[126] These views reinforced an EDM which 100 Conservatives had signed supporting the view that it was not in the nation's interest to join a single currency in 1997. This was mix of hard-line sceptics like Bill Cash and Norman Lamont and middle-roaders like Tom King and David Howell.[127] Major used the 1 March parliamentary debate as an opportunity to declare that membership was 'a matter of practice not principle'. He admitted the constitutional implications

> would be the most sweeping changes in fiscal and monetary manage-
> ment which this House, with its history of control of supply, had ever
> considered and accepted in all its long and proud history.[128]

In fact Major's favoured stance became, as he tried to balance the views of his warring party, to advocate a policy of 'wait and see'. Major was in a no-win situation. He was under fire from those who felt he should definitely rule out euro-membership, whilst the pro-Europeans were dissatisfied by the lack of commitment.

Major's Eurosceptic critics accused him of 'sleep-walking into monetary union' and warned the single currency was 'irreversible and points towards a European state'.[129] Others played the sovereignty card, warning that Parliament would be reduced to 'part of our traditional pageantry rather than our government'.[130] The former MP for Pembroke, Nicholas Bennett, thought 'wait and see' was 'intellectually untenable. The single currency is a matter of political and economic principle'. The government either had to refuse to join as a matter of principle or announce a referendum.[131] Positive Europeanists did attempt to argue the single currency's merits. Ted Heath saw favour if purely to prevent currency speculators:

> There is no single market in the world with more than one currency. If
> you have more than one currency people cheat and manipulate their
> currency so that they can get a greater share of the economic activities
> of the union.[132]

Heath's interview for the weekly journal of Parliament, *House*, can be read two ways. First, it can be interpreted as an attack on those who wished to keep Britain out of the euro because they were denying its inevitability. Second, it reads as a veiled criticism of German monetary policy and carries a degree of euro-caution. However the majority of the parliamentary party appear to have been reasonably satisfied with Major's stance.[133]

As the debate about the advisability of joining the euro intensified during 1996, so too did calls for a referendum on membership. In June 1996 seventy-eight Conservative MPs supported a demand for a referendum. Belatedly pro-Europeans began a media fight back through a series of letters signed by senior grandees such as Edward Heath, Geoffrey Howe, Douglas Hurd and William Whitelaw. In their first letter the authors sought to sound a clarion call for Britain to return to the Churchillian vision of a positive, internationalist Europe. For them,

> the tragedy of Churchill's Zurich speech was that, for too long, it did
> not inform Britain's post-war policy. We have sought to distance

ourselves from Europe rather than decisively shape it ... we have been working to catch up ever since.

To rule out British membership would be 'to betray our national interest'.[134] Julian Critchley thought ruling out the single currency would cost the Conservatives the next election and suggested that in doing so Major

> would also be acting in the past tradition of British statesmen of both parties; namely to miss every bus but the last, and then spend time complaining that we were not in Europe at the formative stage of any policy.[135]

For some pro-Europe sections of the party the perceived anti-European position of the leadership was intolerable, and in Emma Nicholson's (MP for Devon West and Torridge and former deputy party chairman) case it led to her defection, on 29 December 1995, to the Liberal Democrats. As an issue Europe was proving particularly taxing on intra-party unity. Many of the senior ministerial resignations of the past decade had been over matters European: Michael Heseltine (1986), Nigel Lawson (1989), Nicholas Ridley (1990), Geoffrey Howe (1990) and Derek Heathcote-Amory (1996). Over the next six years the party under Major and Hague was to suffer a series of defections to other political parties specifically because of the European issue: Lord McAlpine (former party treasurer) and George Gardiner (MP for Reigate until deselected) both joined Goldsmith's Referendum Party, whilst another right-winger, Adrian Rogers (previously candidate for Exeter in 1997 election), defected to the UK Independence Party (UKIP). A number of pro-Europeans, Hugh Dykes (MP for Harrow East until 1997) and MEP Bill Newton Dunn, followed Nicholson into the Liberal Democrats, whilst Peter Temple Morris (MP for Kidderminster) and Anthony Nelson (MP for Chichester until 1997) joined Labour. The divisions can be observed by noting that since the anti-Common Market League (ACML) was formed in 1961 Conservative MPs have been involved in at least eight ginger groups on Europe.[136] Names such as the Bruges Group, No Turning Back, European Foundation, European Research Group, Positive Europeans, 92 Group, Fresh Starters, the Conservative Group for Europe and the European Movement are familiar in the corridors and smoking rooms of Westminster.

At the same time the apparent scepticism of many of the party's grass roots appeared to continue. The 1996 Bournemouth conference had received 23 motions urging *no* participation in a single currency, whilst 16 had backed Major's 'wait and see', but with the proviso that a referendum would be called if entry was recommended.[137] A poll by *The Sunday Times* of 100 constituency chairmen in advance of the 1997 general election found that when asked to name one action Major could take to help win the election, 12 suggested he 'say no' to a single currency and a further 8 felt more clarity or a referendum on Europe would improve matters.[138] In fact the Cabinet had been edging towards this position by publicly agreeing that EMU entry in 1999 was 'unlikely'.

In the 1997 manifesto official EMU policy was to negotiate and decide.[139] Only 34 MPs seeking re-election endorsed this position, whilst 75 MPs, including 3 ministers, clearly stated their opposition to EMU. The 1997 general election was little short of a massacre for the Conservatives. A record number of frontbenchers lost their seats and one-third of successful Conservative MPs had majorities of less than 5,000 votes. Major immediately resigned. William Hague emerged as the 'compromise' victor from the electoral ballot and immediately set about confirming his Eurosceptic credentials. Of the five candidates who contested the 1997 leadership battle, Hague probably had the least-defined position on Europe. Michael Howard, Peter Lilley and John Redwood were on the Eurosceptic right. Kenneth Clarke represented the pro-European left. During the campaign Hague had hardened his stance towards EMU, implying his opposition in principle in an attempt to pick up votes from Lilley and Howard supporters, and eventually he won by ninety-two votes over Clarke in the third ballot.[140] He appointed prominent Eurosceptics to the Shadow Cabinet, having declared that only those prepared to oppose EMU entry for the 'foreseeable future' could be considered. In October the Shadow Cabinet agreed to reject EMU membership for ten years, but not for all time. This was certainly a more Eurosceptic position than Major's 'wait and see' policy, but it was still a moderated form of Euroscepticism that suggested flexibility. It was also an attempt to establish 'clear blue water' between the Conservatives and a pro-European Labour government. The announcement by Gordon Brown, Labour's chancellor of the Exchequer, in October 1997 that Britain would not enter the EMU during the current Parliament, but would look to join in the future if the single currency proved successful and fulfilled his five economic tests, allowed the Conservative leadership to emphasis their differences from Labour. The electorate's choice was between a Labour Party committed to entry and a Conservative Party who had legitimate economic and political reasons for opposing entry.

Hague was under pressure from both wings of the party. Peter Temple Morris threatened to leave the party unless its Euroscepticism was moderated, whilst Paul Sykes, a Eurosceptic party donor, was warning he would not commit further funds unless EMU membership was ruled out for ten years.[141] Hague took the view that the single currency was too much of a gamble: 'why bet the whole of the EU's success of the past 40 years on a single horse called EMU?'[142] Senior figures were warning of the potential dangers of the party's rightward drift. Norman Fowler urged caution: 'It is a debate, not a war. We want neither threats of separate parties nor mutterings about expulsions.'[143] Pro-Europeans were attempting to argue their case but found themselves being verbally roughed up by the Eurosceptics, who sensed they were now in the ascendancy.[144] It is noticeable that within a year Hague had lost three pro-European shadow ministers: Ian Taylor and David Curry (both in October 1997) and Stephen Dorrell (June 1998). The clarion call of senior pro-Europeans in the *Independent* that EMU was 'the right policy for our country, and it is one we shall continue to commend with conviction' sounded rather hollow and it is clear that many Europeanists feared they were being labelled 'disloyal heretics'.[145] At the same time it is evident that the Eurosceptics were not getting it all their own way. When former MPs Nicholas Budgen and Tony Marlow threatened to stand on an anti-federalist ticket against official Conservative candidates in the 1999 Euro-election, both men were threatened with expulsion from the party if this course of action was undertaken. Then Adrian Rogers, the right-winger and the party's 1997 candidate for Exeter, wrote to the *Daily Telegraph* urging Conservative supporters to vote for UKIP in the European Elections. When threatened with expulsion he defected to UKIP.[146]

In an attempt to consolidate his position Hague announced in September 1998 that he would ballot the party's membership over the single currency. Not everyone responded positively. Nicholas Budgen argued that it ran contrary to the ethos of parliamentary sovereignty and saw the ballot as 'a test of loyalty, not of opinion'. He sought to compare the position of the Eurosceptics with that of Churchill when he opposed Chamberlain's appeasement policy: 'he was not bound by guidance from focus groups or even from his constituency association.'[147] A pro-European Conservative sought a different analogy: 'The referendums in some of the jollier third world dictatorships have after all shown us that voting does not always equate with democracy.'[148] Others wondered whether Hague had hit upon a formula that would allow the party to feel it had debated the issue and then unite behind the leadership. Certainly that was the view amongst the 1997 intake of Tory MPs.[149] The ballot also bears a similarity to Ted Heath's tactics in 1971 when he personally insisted that the party conference take the highly unusual step of voting on the pro-European conference motion. Here were party leaders using the 'will' of the party activists to enforce their chosen policy and reiterate to the parliamentary party their position of authority and legitimacy. The process of the ballot was not without controversy. There was a failure by the Post Office to deliver 8,000 ballot papers and when the results were announced only 202,674 of the 344,157 dispatched ballot papers had been returned. However, Hague's policy of ruling out joining the single currency until at least the end of the next Parliament was endorsed by 84.4 per cent of the vote.[150] Critics, like Heath and Heseltine, argued that the non-return of 41.1 per cent of the ballot papers was an indication of opposition to Hague's policy and therefore the majority of the party's membership was in fact favourable to the single currency.[151] Further complaints were made that the ballot offered no opportunity to express alternative views. Others were more emphatic: 'Until we see how the euro works', wrote MEP Tom Spencer, 'I regard a policy of opposing British membership … as being as intellectually indefensible and politically unwise as one that argues for our immediate membership'.[152]

Europe was increasingly brought to the fore during Hague's leadership. Based upon an assumption that the Conservatives needed to win back core voters who had defected to the Referendum Party in 1997, Hague officially positioned his party as the Eurosceptics' choice. He made a series of speeches both in Britain and abroad on this theme. In establishing a Conservative critique of EMU Hague sought to emphasise the 'uniqueness' of the British position, which stressed that the British economy lacked convergence with the European economies: Britain had a larger financial services sector, home ownership and pension provision than European counterparts, which when combined with Britain's flexible labour market, low taxation and trade with non-EU nations meant Britain could be more influential outside the euro zone.[153] His most controversial speech was in Fontainebleau in May 1998. He criticised the EU's lack of democratic accountability and warned that 'the original danger which confronted the founding fathers [of the EEC] has gone. If anything the threat comes from the opposite, the artificial repression of nationality'.[154] Such speeches provoked angry responses from former senior Tories. Heseltine branded the speech more extreme than anything Thatcher had said, whilst Major thought Hague's policy was 'absurd and crazy'.[155] Hague's theme throughout was 'In Europe, not run by Europe', a phrase coined in 1997, which became the title of the party's 1999 European election manifesto. The message was that Europe had to choose between integration leading to a European 'superstate' and a more flexible Europe. This idea of a flexible Europe echoed Conservative policy from the mid-1990s, but Hague and Maude took it a stage further. It was argued that all EU member states should accept the core elements of a free market Europe, but that the opt-out for non-core activities where member nations wished to pursue policy at a national level should be enshrined in a new treaty provision.[156] In February 2000 Hague launched the 'Keep the Pound' campaign with a nationwide tour speaking from the back of a truck. This became the central theme of Hague's message for the 2001 election campaign as he counted down the number of days left to save the pound.[157] Although the official party line was to rule out the euro for the duration of the next Parliament, declarations like Thatcher's of 22 May that Britain should 'never' surrender to the single currency reinforced the message of implacable hostility.[158] The doomsday scenario portrayed the general election as being the last chance to save sterling. This carried particular risks, which were all too familiar in the long anti-Europe campaign: namely a poor turnout in support of the Conservatives would imply a weak electoral adhesion to the Eurosceptic message and potentially could be more damaging. It left the Conservatives looking like a single-issue party, obsessed with Europe.

The problem was that it was still evident that the divisions within the party were far from healed. In July 1999 Kenneth Clarke wrote in *The Times* that he was in 'broad agreement on the big issues of Europe' with Blair's Labour government.[159] The internal disciplining of party members, which culminated in the expulsions of Julian Critchley and Tim Rathbone for backing Pro-European Conservative candidates in the June 1999 European elections, further highlighted the internal feuding. The fragility of the situation was clearly illustrated by the row in November 2000 over the Blair government's plans to commit British troops to Europe's Rapid Reaction Force: plans which were condemned roundly by the Conservative leadership but which provoked counter-attacks from pro-Europeans like Howe and Hurd. The Hague leadership team, though, appeared confident that a sceptical European stance would prove the Conservatives' electoral trump card at the next election.[160] This was a risky strategy. The 1999 European elections may have provided encouragement that a Eurosceptic campaign appealed, but to have secured a 35 per cent share of the vote in a low turnout election was hardly conclusive.[161] The reality was that the electorate, true to form, was less concerned about the European debate than the level of taxation, the position of education and the state of the National Health Service (NHS) and the parties' abilities to deliver in these areas.[162] The Conservatives were still perceived as a divided party. As Sir Anthony Grant urged, Hague needed to 'state what they are *for*'. The anti-Euro position was clear, but the Conservatives needed to address domestic issues 'that concern the eighty per cent of the electorate apparently uninterested in the EU'.[163] The electorate concurred in 2001 when it gave Blair his second term in office and once more humiliated the Conservatives. It was evident that the Conservatives' core campaign issues of Europe, tax and asylum were perceived as irrelevant to the 'Missing Conservatives'. It sent out a message of extremism and implied that the party was out of touch with the electorate's key concerns.[164] Matters European were perhaps not helped by outbursts like Peter Tapsell's likening Blair's European policy to that of Josef Goebbels, which reinforced the message of extremism.[165]

With Hague's resignation, a protracted leadership contest took place under new rules which provided the grass roots with the opportunity to vote for the first time.[166] Of the five candidates, Michael Portillo, Iain Duncan Smith and David Davies were noted Eurosceptics, Michael Ancram was perceived as a moderate Eurosceptic and Kenneth Clarke as the token Europhile. Portillo campaigned for a return to core values and a reduced emphasis on the euro until a referendum. Clarke was urging a more moderate European position, ceasing opposition to Nice, the euro, and the Rapid Reaction Force. But an unwillingness to defend his own European stance had the consequence of reopening the European wound. Both Duncan Smith and Davies needed to widen their appeal, hence both men made pledges about including pro-euro colleagues in any Shadow Cabinet they formed. Ultimately it was a battle between Duncan Smith and Clarke. In the final run-off Europe came centre-stage. Clarke backtracked on Nice, indicating that he would continue the party's opposition to the treaty, whilst Eurosceptics would be given key Shadow Cabinet briefs. Duncan Smith attacked Clarke's extreme views on Europe and argued that these would destroy the party. That 57 per cent of ballot papers were returned by

1 September, well before official hustings were completed, implied that Duncan Smith was trading off his anti-Maastricht reputation.[167] His election meant that he was now party leader only nine years after entering Parliament.

Almost immediately he sought to take a decisive stance by emphatically ruling that a Conservative government would never join the euro. Whilst this can be perceived as the action of a hard-line Eurosceptic, it should also be seen in terms of an act of domestic statecraft. The categorical nature of the position meant that it was no longer deemed a 'live' issue, thereby depriving the media of an issue around which to highlight Conservative divisions and to detract from attempts to reposition the party, and instead offering the potential of presenting an air of unity to the electorate. It could also be seen as a mild rebuke to Hague's overt emphasis on the issue, which created the impression that the party might be a single-issue group.

It is noticeable that Europe as an issue was quickly pushed to one side to the extent that Iain Duncan Smith (IDS) instructed his MPs to talk about issues other than Europe. The internal divisions over Europe remained, and within the party a power struggle between the modernisers and the traditionalists ensued, with Europe representing one fragment of that battle. A leaked Central Office memo written by Dominic Cummings suggested that IDS would be well advised to refrain from agreeing to front any 'No' referendum campaign about the single currency.[168] Duncan Smith was anxious to distinguish his leadership from Hague's; hence the very deliberate downplaying of the key themes of the 2001 general election: Europe, tax and asylum. This was particularly apparent during 2002 as Duncan Smith sought to define the party's policy options. The few public pronouncements on Europe made it clear that the leader's Eurosceptic tone had hardened. Duncan Smith warned the party could never accept the euro under his leadership, whilst the shadow foreign secretary, Michael Ancram, denied that Britain would take the 'damaging course' and leave the EU under the Conservatives because it would be 'forfeiting authority and benefit', but warned that treaty renegotiations were a necessity.[169] Through all of this the possibility of a referendum on the euro had been consistently in the background. A euro referendum may well prove a decisive moment for the Conservatives, but the reluctance of the chancellor, Gordon Brown, to accept the euro has kept the Conservatives from the brink. At the same time it was evident that now the euro had been launched the federalists within the EU were keen to drive the agenda forward once more through the adoption of a European Constitution. Under the December 2001 Laeken Declaration a Convention on the Future of Europe, chaired by former French president Giscard d'Estaing, was charged with drafting a European constitution that would then go before an intergovernmental conference of the EU member states, on which Conservatives served as representatives of the House of Commons.[170] The expectation was that this constitution would found a new European Union, separate from the member states, endowed with new powers and its own legal personality. In anticipation of this, eighteen

Conservative grandees, including Major, Hurd, Howe, Clarke and Heseltine, supported a proposal by Lord Brittan, then chairman of the Conservative Group for Europe, for a wholesale revision of the key European treaties. In a document entitled *The Future of the EU: A Positive Conservative Approach*, they put forward the case for reforming the institutions of the EU to make them both more accountable and more understandable to the citizens of the EU, and they proposed that the whole body of EU treaties should be simplified and divided into two. The most important articles should be set out in a new list of Treaty Commitments, whilst the less important provisions should be contained in a set of Treaty Rules. They concluded with a warning:

> Reform must be put in the context of a broader political vision. A vision of an EU whose whole purpose is to enable its Member States and their citizens to deal more effectively with the increasingly complex economic, political, social and security problems affecting all our lives.[171]

This exemplifies the commonality that can exist between the two factions of the party, at least in the agreement about simplifying the European Union treaties. Derek Heathcote-Amory offered the Eurosceptic response to the European convention's proposals for a constitution. Concerned that the proposals failed to resolve the democratic deficiencies of the EU, Heathcote-Amory was a signatory to a minority report to the European convention that argued against the need for a constitution, instead favouring a slimmed-down treaty which reformed the EU's institutions, retained the national veto and created a Europe 'organised on an interparliamentary basis by means of a Treaty of European Cooperation'.[172] The problem for the Conservatives was that domestically they were failing to make political headway. With them still trailing in the opinion polls, dissatisfaction rapidly grew with IDS's leadership. Subjected to defeat in a vote of confidence, he resigned.

With Duncan Smith's ousting and the coronation of Michael Howard there was little change in the party's European policy emphasis. Europe was kept in the background whilst Howard attempted to redefine his image and policy ideals.[173] Howard did, though, seek to explain his vision of Europe in a speech to the Konrad-Adenauer-Stiftung in Berlin in February 2004. He reminded his audience that it was always Conservative governments who had made positive contributions to Britain's involvement in the EU, from the 1961 application to the 1986 Single European Act, and that he had no intention of withdrawing. However Europe required a 'new deal', which would allow flexibility, be based on co-operation and not on coercion and respect national sovereignties. Therefore he opposed the euro and the European Constitution and had 'grave reservations' about an independent European defence initiative, which would undermine NATO.[174] It appeared that the collapse of the European Constitution negotiations had removed that spectre for the moment; however, the March Brussels conference led the EU to declare their intent to resolve the issue by June 2004. Whilst Blair and the

Labour government claimed that the constitution was merely a tidying-up exercise, the whole proceedings alarmed the Conservative Eurosceptics. They became particularly vocal about demanding a referendum, based upon the argument that in fact this constitution, apart from being alien to the British political system, represented a significant revision of the EU treaty clauses. Although the EU as an organisation in 2004 was unrecognisable from the organisation the British people voted for in 1975, it could still be argued that it remained a treaty organisation between nation-states which had formed an association for common purpose; a European constitution would change all that and should therefore be subject to a referendum.[175] The referendum demand became a key policy requirement of the party's 2004 European election stratagem. Seeking to disarm this, Blair's government conceded in April that there should be a referendum on the European Constitution, and immediately neutralised the issue. The timing and question would be the government's decision, and many observers thought it unlikely that Blair would acquiesce to an autumn 2004 poll, and presumed that the 'pledge' would be held over to a third Labour term of office. In the event the French 'No' vote and the Dutch rejection of the constitution nullified the need for a British referendum and for the time being ended the prospects of a EU-wide constitution. Electoral defeat, yet again, in the 2005 general election saw Michael Howard's replacement by David Cameron. It is unclear whether Cameron intends to try and moderate his party's Euroscepticism. His pledge to move the party's MEPs out of the European People's Party grouping suggests a continuation of the recent trend. Yet warnings have also been given to those Conservatives who advocated withdrawal from the EU that such a stance will not enhance the prospects of promotion to shadow ministerial posts.[176]

# 3   The issues and debates

## 'Head versus heart'

Since its conception, the idea of European integration has forced Conservatives to confront many of their core ideological values. The overarching issue has been the kind of Europe they wish to be involved with. Despite attempts by the leadership before 1988 to portray Europe within the narrow parameters of being a purely economic matter that was necessary to reverse Britain's decline, the continuing and protracted debate has opened a Pandora's box of issues which question Britain's world role, peace and prosperity, national sovereignty and patriotism, the nation's economic foundations, as well as its political and legal integrity. The saliency of these issues has ebbed and flowed over the decades. Each camp within the party has sought to undermine their internal opponents' values whilst promoting their own positions and seeking to win the support of the party's silent agnostic majority. The pro-Europeans succeeded best at this until the late 1980s. Thereafter a succession of events, the Single European Act, Maastricht, Black Wednesday and more recently the euro and the European Constitution, enabled the Eurosceptics to proclaim their values as once more legitimate concerns. Taken at face value the party's core values would suggest an instinctive hostility towards Europe, yet party managers for much of the post-war era managed to convince the party otherwise, making it believe that a pro-European policy was not only advisable but necessary: the only option. Addressing each of the issues in turn will enable a greater appreciation of how, and why, the debates have evolved and help the reader understand why the current Conservative Party leadership largely supports a Eurosceptic position.

## Atlantic or European world power?

Whilst in recent decades the European debate has had a distinctly economic edge, in the longer term the issue has as much revolved around discussion of Britain's world role as it has concerned political and economic issues. It has been of central importance since the debate first emerged in the immediate post-Second World War years, as Britain was seeking to hold on to her world power position. Although clearly eclipsed by the new superpowers of

Soviet Russia and America, Britain still retained her empire and economically was much better placed than continental Europe. This meant that there were, as one senior Foreign Office official put it, two and a half world powers.[1] But this faith was a declining value. Surveys of British elite opinion found that, whereas in 1959 72 per cent saw Britain as the third power in the world, by 1965 this had declined to 39 per cent, with only 8 per cent expecting Britain to occupy such a position by 2000.[2] Today's Conservative Eurosceptics would claim not to recognise this negativity. This enables them to dismiss the rationale that British involvement in the EU was necessary to give Britain international status. They would argue that Britain, economically and diplomatically, outperforms continental rivals, meaning that Britain's renewed status on the world stage renders 'the concept of a pan-continental state as a hangover from an earlier era'.[3]

After 1940 the new alliance with America and the need for both US military and economic assistance to sustain a divided Europe brought a new dimension to British thinking. This was most famously articulated through Winston Churchill's 'three circles'; the perceived wisdom being that Britain uniquely straddled the European, American and imperial world dimensions. Yet this Churchillian vision was as much a compromise designed to hold his party together as it was a sham in *Realpolitik* terms. Within the party elements prepared to champion one or other of the dimensions could be found. What Churchill was seeking to demonstrate was that each was a legitimate theatre, but that rather than one gaining primacy at the expense of the others, the overlapping of concerns meant Britain was well placed to play an important world role as a form of honest broker. It was a vision accepted, and put into practice, by a Foreign Office under a Labour foreign secretary.

Fuelling the debate about whether Britain should position herself as a European or Atlantic power were latent suspicions towards the French, Germans and Americans. Elements of those sceptical about closer European involvement were not willing to trust the Americans. They remembered that American isolationism (which translated into self-interest) in the inter-war years had left Britain to act alongside France as 'policemen' of the world, yet operating in an international order of Wilsonian construction. Imperialists suspected that American enthusiasm for British involvement in Europe stemmed from a desire to see the end of the Commonwealth and destroy imperial preference.[4] There existed widespread activist suspicion well into the mid-1960s that the USA, motivated entirely by self-interest, was placing undue pressure on the British government.[5] Anti-Americanism as a force ebbed and flowed, peaking after Bretton Woods, Suez and following Macmillan's 1961 EEC application. At the same time it must be remembered that the European debate for nearly forty years was conducted within the context of the Cold War. The division of Europe and the potential threat of the Soviet Union's Red Army led many Conservatives to argue that Europe alone could not hold the breech. The emergence of the USA as a world superpower, both economically and militarily, meant there was an equally forceful wing of the party which favoured the Atlanticist approach. The American alliance meant that some Conservatives could legitimately argue that Britain should look more closely to its natural Atlantic cousins than the continent. Consequently the Atlanticists were willing supporters of the 'three circles' vision, as Eden's 1953 Margate conference speech on the subject demonstrated.[6] It was a view rearticulated by Thatcher at the conclusion of her Bruges speech:

> Let us have a Europe which plays its full part in the wider world, and which looks outward not inward, and which preserves that Atlantic Community – that Europe on both sides of the Atlantic – which is our noblest inheritance and our greatest strength.[7]

Certainly until the 1960s there was a strain of anti-foreignerism amongst activist thought. Agents reported a 'deep-seated insularity' and observed a feeling that 'Wogs start at the channel'.[8] This translated more specifically into hostility towards France and Germany. The explanations for this are a mix of crude nationalist values and stereotyping as well as fear. A sense existed that political or economic tie-up with former enemies was a betrayal of fallen comrades and the Commonwealth who had fought at our side.[9] Allied to this was a concern that Germany would use European unity to once again dominate Europe.[10] The 1969 party conference received thirty-five resolutions on Europe, most of which expressed concern about future German influence in the EC. What the pro-Europeans succeeded in doing from the 1960s was to argue that Britain's active participation and leadership could best dilute this.[11] Two successive twentieth-century wars against Germany have helped cement a strong strain of anti-Germanism in Conservative thinking. This paranoia has been utilised by the Europeanists to justify British participation in the affairs of the continent. Macmillan, with both the EDC and ECSC, expressed fears about the consequences if these went ahead without British participation. 'Was there not a danger that if it went through', he told Cabinet in December 1951,

> the position in ten years would be still worse. There would be a European Community which would dominate Europe and would be roughly equal to Hitler's Europe of 1940. If we stay out, we risk that German domination of Europe which we have fought two world wars to prevent.[12]

This was theme the Macmillan Cabinet returned to in January 1958 when examining FTA, believing that the European nations risked 'passing gradually under the domination, both political and economic, of the Federal German Republic' if they failed to reach agreement with the UK.[13] With the successive French vetoes much of the hostility was diverted towards France; however, the suspicion towards Germany has never entirely evaporated, as

Thatcher's reaction to German reunification illustrated.[14] From the 1980s the concern was not about the danger from Germany militarily but rather economically. Nick Ridley's ill-judged 1990 comments about Germany in an interview for the *Spectator* were intended to highlight that the ERM was essentially flawed because of the strength of the German Deutschmark, its interest rates and the monetary policy of the Bundesbank.[15]

Aside from anxieties that the Franco-German axis sought to dominate Europe, there was a feeling that France, especially, was using European unity for self-aggrandisement. Even amongst the party's pro-Europeans there was a distinct strain of Francophobia. As Maurice Macmillan observed in late 1962, many of the problems with the Treaty of Rome were due to French intransigence and because they 'had insisted on trying to feather-bed French agriculture'. His Father in 1959 had similarly caricatured France, whose 'idea of Europe has been that Europe should build a wall around itself: in other words a protectionist attitude'.[16] Some even doubted after the second veto whether French self-interest would ever allow her to accede to British entry.[17] Blaming the French for failures on the diplomatic stage was an ideal means of deflecting domestic opinion. Hence when discussions about reforming the Council of Europe failed in the early 1970s it was due to French self-interest: 'so many of whose nationals are employed at the Council of Europe HQ.'[18] Many have taken the stance that the French have tried to use the EU as a protectionist tool, which is detrimental to Britain's reliance on imports. The vetoes confirmed suspicions that France was hostile to British EU entry and subsequently opposed reforms of EU institutions because of her own self-interest and a fear that Britain would seek to diminish France's leadership and influence. Although many Conservatives have thought that France's own actions and intransigence have left her at times isolated, this weakness has not been exploited fully by successive British governments. The French self-interest is nowhere more self-evident that in the CAP, which has been engineered to her benefit, and this, when combined with other EU economic initiatives, covered up French economic inefficiencies and fragilities.[19]

What the Europeanists succeeded in doing was restraining this anti-foreigner attitude and converting the world power argument into a positive attribute of the European cause. Thus David Eccles could argue in 1950 to his Wiltshire activists that without British participation in Europe 'we should lose our place as a Great Power and make more probable another war'.[20] Therefore European unity not only secured Britain's position, but provided peace and stability. There was no alternative. Similarly, Winchester Conservatives heard in 1960 how 'essential' EEC membership was to enable Britain to 'remain a world power of consequence'. During the 1940s and 1950s pro-Europeans acquiesced to Churchill's three circles model and argued successfully that a 'united Europe' was necessary for the defence of Western Europe, although they were anxious not to do anything to under-mine NATO and therefore America's commitment to Europe. Addressing the Council of Europe in 1954, Peter Smithers warned Europe never to isolate itself from America: 'our liberty depended upon the alliance between Europe and the United States – "Let us never forget that in our calculations".'[21] Proponents of this argument were at pains to emphasis that British involvement in Europe did not require Britain to choose between America and Europe. Rather, because America wanted Britain to be involved, it provided Britain with the all-important linkage role and as a consequence a position of leadership. It was argued that British entry into the European Union would enhance Atlantic security and shore up the East/West balance. British, French and German quarrels would be terminated and provide the conditions for foreign policy co-ordination, giving Western Europe a greater cohesion and consequently enhancing NATO. Heath took the view that entry would secure international power status for Britain and France at the head of the EEC: due to our global responsibilities, nuclear capabilities and United Nations Security Council membership.[22] However, for the Euro-enthusiasts, as the Conservatives returned to office in 1951, so the 'three circles' model appeared increasingly unsustainable. It was felt that the US was distracted by its own standoff with the USSR, whilst the growing independence of the Commonwealth, both economically and politically, further reduced British influence. The rapid economic recovery of Europe after wartime devastation was the cue for 'mooring' Britain to the continent. The time was now ripe for a third European force. Yet they failed to convince Churchill of the legitimacy of their arguments and Britain remained aloof from continental developments.

Atlanticists were concerned that greater European independence threatened to provoke the Americans back into isolation and unilateralism. Others were concerned for the division of Western Europe between the Sixes and Sevens. With the creation of EFTA, Martin Redmayne speculated with Macmillan about the need to reach an agreement with the Six. 'Time is not on our side,' he warned the prime minister.

> I am sure therefore we have to produce a new idea, a new turn in events, and that must be to bring the Americans once again onto the European stage. A second Marshall plan. ... If the USA saw Europe falling apart they would have to find ways of bringing us together again. The President would agree that a divided Europe must seriously weaken the West in the struggle against Khrushchev's economic offensive.[23]

In other words, the economic unity of Western Europe was an American interest not least because it strengthened the capitalist alliance against Communism.

The difficulty was that in economic terms the Atlantic alliance was one-sided and therefore pro-Europeans could successfully argue that it was in Britain's trading interests to look to Europe. Heath thought it odd, given British trade with the United States in the early 1960s amounted to only 8 per cent, that it was necessary to maintain a Washington embassy with 750 staff. In 1963 British trade with the EEC was 20 percent and increasing, yet in Brussels there were only four officers and clerical support.[24] The whole contested nature of the Atlantic alliance was evidenced by those Conservatives who argued that EEC entry would weaken the strength of the British–American special relationship, whilst other elements argued that entry, far from weakening these bonds, would actually strengthen them.[25] Following the 1963 veto and Douglas-Home's accession to the leadership, his front bench team had rejected turning to the USA for fear it would turn Britain into a backwater. Douglas-Home was never outspokenly pro-European and was widely perceived as an 'Atlanticist'. As Heath's foreign secretary he took the view that Britain had no alternative to seeking entry, but chose to concentrate on foreign policy issues other than European ones. He did chair the Cabinet's European Policy Committee, perhaps a tactic reminiscent of Macmillan appointing a doubting Rab Butler to chair a similar committee in 1961–3. Heath subscribed to the view that the economic and political gains of entry were mutually reinforcing, for a stronger economy would help Britain to secure her world role and strengthen the Atlantic alliance as a consequence.

Rhetorically many Conservatives have persisted with Churchill's 'three circles' model, arguing Britain's uniqueness in straddling these differing alliances. As Malcolm Rifkind, the foreign secretary, told the October 1995 party conference, he saw Britain as an Atlantic nation as well as a European one and believed that Conservative ministers would fight to create an Atlantic Free Trade Area.[26] Speaking in the aftermath of the 2001 terrorist attacks on the World Trade Center, Michael Ancram, shadow foreign secretary, warned those in Britain and Europe against indulging in anti-American rhetoric because 'America is a sovereign superpower with vast resources. Europe is not. We need America far more than America needs us. We must stick to the partnership of Europe and America'.[27] Emotionally, Conservatives have tried to hang on to an illusion of Britain's former imperial importance, but in real terms this circle has adopted the persona of a mirage.

## End of empire

Yet linked to Britain's world power claim after 1945 was the presence of her empire. Although Britain emerged from the Second World War with much of her empire reclaimed, a process of decolonisation was quickly implemented by the 1945–51 Labour government, and accelerated under Harold Macmillan's 1957–63 administration. Many Conservatives suspected the hand of America in pressing the cause of decolonisation.[28] The imperial wing of the party was able to accept a Europe of intergovernmental cooperation to resist Communism, but unwilling to concede that it offered a new economic relationship that would provide greater prosperity. From 1949 the debate about imperial preference was high on the Conservative agenda. To counter this, the party's more progressive, pro-European wing sought to argue the benefits of Europe as a mix of the two arguments. Leo Amery's contribution to the 1949 conference combined this approach when he argued that if Britain co-operated with Europe it would not relegate Britain to the role of a province within a European super-state; nor would it exclude the Dominions. For someone of Amery's imperial reputation this may have appeared a startling statement, but he was firmly convinced of the European project. Charles Waterhouse, MP for South East Leicester and a staunch imperialist, admitted after Suez that it was necessary for Britain to re-evaluate her international position. He recognised that America was 'anxious' for Britain to look to Europe, but suspected they hoped to see Britain further disassociate herself from the Commonwealth as a consequence. He thought there should be a dual policy of promoting the Commonwealth and looking to Europe, but accepted it was 'not an easy policy to work out'.[29]

Activists saw the empire as an explanation for Britain's uniqueness. This view was encouraged by organisations like Henry Page-Croft's Empire Industries Association and parliamentary groupings likes the Expanding Commonwealth Group chaired by Patrick Maitland.[30] Yet from the 1950s onwards through into the 1970s there were diminishing emotional ties as empire became Commonwealth. Partly this was helped by support for Europe of pro-empire men like Leo Amery and Duncan Sandys. Also there was the transfer of emotional support from the colonies to the white Dominions. This was due in part to the failure of many Commonwealth nations to retain democracy, the assertive dictatorial personalities who took over these nations and because of Conservative fears about Commonwealth immigration. Also importantly, by the late 1960s some of those previously advocating a pro-Commonwealth message, like Peter Walker, were now promoting Europe.[31] It is noticeable that activists in 1962 still ranked Commonwealth ties high as a reason for hostility to EEC entry, but also felt that Britain had nursed these ailing economies long enough, and that it was time to free them and allow Britain to benefit economically.[32] If in the 1960s the anti-Marketeers had been able to point to the concern of Commonwealth leaders about the implications of entry, by the 1970s it was widely appreciated that the Commonwealth took entry for granted. Although Commonwealth prime ministers gave a cautious endorsement to entry negotiations in 1961, the wider Commonwealth was open to provocation, as Peter Walker's 1962 tour of Australia revealed.[33] Members of the Commonwealth Affairs Committee repeatedly criticised the Macmillan government for not adequately consulting the Commonwealth in 1961–2, whereas when the subject was revisited in the 1970s the Commonwealth attachment had all but disappeared. By the late 1960s successive EEC negotiations had resolved many of the Commonwealth trade issues. The principle outstanding problem was New Zealand butter and meat. Nearly 90 per cent of New Zealand butter was exported to Britain, and along with cheese and lamb it was an area with EEC surpluses.[34] Yet there was confidence that New Zealand would be able to secure an association agreement under Article 238 of the Treaty of Rome. At the same time the decline of the Commonwealth as a market for British goods was being emphasised. It was down from 35 per cent in 1958 to 22 per cent by 1969.[35] Prominence was also being given to the argument that entry would give Britain extra economic clout, which would enable Britain to help underdeveloped members of the Commonwealth.[36] The argument's successful penetration of the party was confirmed by internal polling, which showed in August 1970 that only 3 per cent thought EEC entry would be bad for the Commonwealth.[37] The decline of the Commonwealth link has been important in explaining the broader support for Europe. This was particularly true by the 1980s. 'The next generation can't remember a time when we weren't in Europe', observed Edwina Curry, 'just as I regard hankering after an Empire as slightly dotty'.[38]

## Defence of Europe

Linked to arguments about Britain's world role was the discussion of how best Britain could contribute to the defence of Western Europe. Since the collapse of Communism and the rapid absorption of Eastern European nations into NATO and the EU this has been an issue of declining significance. As the decades have receded since the cessation of the Second World War, those active politicians with direct experience of that war have dwindled. So it is not surprising that the military dimension of the integration process should have reduced. The economic and political rationales for continued European unity might dominate the European debate today, but this should not distract from the reality that for at least two decades after 1945 the military unity option was the preferable avenue for many Conservatives. The defence of Western Europe is one sphere in which many Conservatives would claim Britain had shown particular leadership.[39] In the context of the Cold War climate the idea that Conservative politicians had moulded the post-war security environment claimed many adherents. Both NATO and the WEU have been forums in which Britain has been prepared to pursue this. The death of Stalin in March 1953 would diminish, but not quell, Cold War anxieties. When Churchill launched his concept of a European army at Strasbourg in August 1950 the rationale was both to help contain the Russian threat and to provide a safe context for German rearmament. The outbreak of the Korean War two months earlier also added to the pertinence of the proposal. The particular conditions of the Cold War made the military dimension an imperative for many Conservatives. As Cuthbert Headlam, MP for Newcastle Central, admitted in February 1949

> the necessity for some kind of union among the western nations if any halt is to be made on Russian and Communist progress westward – of course the main thing is to achieve a system of defence.[40]

Some Conservatives were convinced that if Britain joined the EEC it would increase the imminence of Soviet tanks rolling across the plains of West Germany towards the channel ports.[41] Other Conservatives seemed willing to accept some form of military federation as a defence against the USSR.[42] British participation in the defence of Europe was seen as part of a tradition of seeking unity and allies to resist aggressors.

The debates and arguments that surrounded the formation of NATO and WEU have continued and rebounded over the decades since. The end of the Cold War has led to new debates about the strategic mission of NATO, but its primacy as *the* defence organisation for Britain is not in question. Core has been the Conservative preference for intergovernmental organisations that required association rather than membership. As Macmillan told the French ambassador in 1951, 'The British w[oul]d never accept a Parliamentary control by a sort of sub-committee of the European Assembly'.[43] Accession to NATO might have required the British to pool its sovereignty. Under her membership Britain is committed to intervene in the common defence if another member is attacked, and to accept a foreign commander for such an operation. But this was a necessary price to pay for a continued Atlanticist presence in Europe. 'This pact', observed Cuthbert Headlam, 'is a step in the right direction and one welcomes it'.[44] Furthermore, NATO was perceived as a limited step towards decreasing nationalistic jealousy. The primacy of NATO has remained sacrosanct ever since. Whenever proposals for a European army or a purely European deterrent have been floated, whether in the 1950s or 1990s, Conservatives have been unable to accept a European structure (whether for armaments, logistics or command) which is linked but not integral to NATO. Thus during 1995–6 Major's government was keen to promote reforms of the WEU, not least given its intergovernmental nature, and to establish for it a specific, and limited, military role which did not impinge on NATO and at the same time distracted from the French and German ambitions for a Euro-corps.[45] In March 1995 Major proposed that a WEU military force might be given specific operational tasks such as rescue missions, peacekeeping and embargo and sanctions enforcement. The key was that the WEU was intergovernmental.[46] This represented the Conservative governments attempts to water down EU plans for a common European foreign policy and army that were on the agenda for the intergovernmental conferences of 1996–7. As Michael Portillo explained in 1996, the attraction lay in it not being an EU-based defence pact, which meant that it did not have to take account of the views of the EU institutions and nor was it subject to majority voting decisions.[47]

Throughout there has been a suspicion of French motives. Continental Europe has criticised the British for playing the awkward role; however, this is considered unjustifiable in the military sphere. The defence of Europe, leaving aside intervention in two world wars, is a sphere in which Conservatives would consider that Britain has more than fully demonstrated participation. Of course, French politicians have sought to undermine these

Anglo-Saxon initiatives, not least because of their own nationalistic agenda. Thus de Gaulle's nuclear aspirations and bloody-mindedness encouraged him to pursue 'independence' from NATO, thus undermining an organisation 'not designed for exercises in reconciliation of political differences'.[48] Fortunately the forum of WEU was able during the late 1960s and early 1970s to provide the point of liaison between the French and NATO. Likewise, when the French proposed the 'reactivation' of WEU in 1984 leading Conservatives like Thatcher, Howe and Heseltine were wary, fearing that it was a deliberate plot to undermine NATO.

## Common European foreign policy

In the past decade, closely associated with the discussions about European defence has been the matter of a common European foreign policy. Brought to the fore at Maastricht, it has proved a provocative concept. Britain may have been able to claim in 1945 that it remained a world power, but by the 1970s this was evidently not the position. The advocates of closer European co-operation have long argued that Europe needed to become a 'third' force in foreign affairs, 'expressing the united views of countries allied closely to the United States yet remaining distinct from it'.[49] Such a vision required the closest of Anglo-Franco-German co-operation. In many respects what was envisaged here was little more than a continuation of traditional European diplomacy, with Britain seeking to sustain the balance of European power. The plans for a common foreign policy implied that a nation-state would lose its sovereign right to determine its own foreign policy. Sceptics like Walter Sweeney, MP for Glamorgan 1992–7, attacked Maastricht because, although it appeared that the government had retained a veto on a Common Foreign and Security Policy (CFSP) as outlined in Title III of the treaty, concessions on policy-making in the arena had been given up. With the proven ability of the European federalists to push forward the integrationist agenda using the most innocuous of treaty language, this was concern enough.[50] This proved to be the case with the Amsterdam (1997) and Nice (2000) treaties. Michael Portillo articulated an increasingly common view in April 1998 that EU development should confine itself to economics rather than seek the attributes of a super-state. In a thinly veiled attack on the previous Conservative administration, he warned that Britain should stop criticising EU policies only to then acquiesce. Ministers should stick to promoting calls for liberal markets and sovereign nation-states.[51] Recent events have done little to reassure Conservatives. They argue that CFSP has proved itself 'a trail of failures', evidenced by Europe's failures over the Israeli–Palestinian issue, Zimbabwe, the undermining of NATO and the divisions over Iraq.[52] This goes to the core of recent Conservative concerns about the European project, namely that the objective is a federal European super-state that reduces the nation-state to the role of regional administrator and which absorbs the traditional functions of the nation-state into a political and economic union.

## Political union and federalism

It is the extent to which European unity expects political union, and what is means by political union, that has become of central importance to the Conservative discussions about Britain's relationship with Europe. The matter of political union revolves at two levels. First, it is whether the European Union is, or should be, an 'economic' and/or a 'political' organisation; second, there has been a debate about the level of integration between the federalists and the functionalists. The functionalists favour the use of intergovernmental structures to tackle specific problems that could be best resolved by co-operation. Given the rhetoric of Euroscepticism since the 1990s it might perhaps seem surprising that many of the early conservative protagonists for European unity could be classed as 'functionalists'. As Maxwell-Fyfe explained to the House of Commons in 1948, he favoured those 'who believe that the way to greater union is the common attack on varied problems and the function and co-operation inherent in their solution'.[53] Similarly, Leo Amery made clear his opposition to federalism, arguing that the 'real solution' lay in 'securing effective co-operation between governments as governments'.[54] During the application phase the debate revolved around whether the objective of the EEC was a federal state of Europe, and then whether the EEC's aspirations of economic and monetary union inevitably led to political union. Considerable efforts were made by pro-Europeans to reassure, faced with a repeated barrage of questions on the issue in party committees and correspondence, particularly between 1967 and 1973. It was accepted that both public and party opinion were 'disturbed' by the idea of a United States of Europe.[55]

Federalism was not mentioned in the Treaty of Rome and, once a signatory, it would not 'project us automatically and defencelessly into a federal or supranational structure'.[56] Senior ministerial figures were adamant that political union was not on the agenda, but accepted that 'European union', 'a concept which has yet to be precisely defined by the Community', was an intended goal.[57] Hindsight suggests that many of the protagonists misunderstood the nature of European decision-making. When controversy arose about the foreign secretary, Douglas-Home, sitting on the Werner Committee in 1970 to discuss monetary union, ministers denied it was a commitment to federalism.[58] Whilst the members of the Six on the committee thought they were moving towards a commitment to proceed to monetary union, the British were trying to restrict it to the specifics of identifying what was required and then establishing the machinery to implement it.[59] There was a worrying vagueness about definition that concerned many anti-Marketeers, especially when 'anxieties are increased by the out-and-out federalist case being made by the European Movement, with which the Conservative Party is so closely identified in the eyes of the public'.[60] The defence of the Europeanists was that even if the EC wished to advance a federalist agenda the national veto would always ensure that at every stage successive governments would be able to safeguard British interests.[61] Eurosceptics since 1992 would argue that this defence has no validity because the extension of qualified majority voting and the legal judgements of the European Courts of Justice have undermined the role of government as the ultimate arbiter of policy, and the European constitution idea just reinforces this trend.

Some Europeanists have been willing to openly advocate federalism, individuals like Anthony Meyer and Bill Newton-Dunn. That over sixty Conservative MPs were willing to sign an all-party Early Day Motion in 1948 calling for long-term federal Europe implied there was support in the earliest days. West Midlands Young Conservatives in 1976 accepted federalism was a 'taboo' subject but they foresaw that federalism was 'the best answer' for the 'future development of a democratic Community'.[62] The reality is that it is less than clear exactly what is meant by 'federalism'; it is another of those words in the European debate that is freely used but is imprecise in meaning. The ambiguity behind Churchill's European message suggests that he was probably not opposed to federalism in principle, but felt that it was a long-term consideration which might be possible if it took a non-institutional route: 'To imagine that Europe today is ripe for either a political federation or a customs union would be wholly unrealistic. But who can say what may not be possible in the future.'[63] Realistically Churchill was a functionalist rather than a federalist, which meant supporting the creation of intergovernmental organisations with the responsibility for specific and limited functions, as typified by his European army proposal.

For the Europeanist Anthony Meyer, federalism was defined thus:

> Those things which are best done at a European level should be done at that level; that those things which are best done at a national level are best done at that level; but also that those things which are best done at local level should be done at that level.

'When this concept is express in an institutional structure', Meyer explained, 'it is called federalism, and I support it'.[64] Edward Heath has sought to argue that the issue of federalism is a smokescreen that portrays a fundamental misunderstanding of what the European Union is. Writing in *International Affairs* in 1988 he argued that he did

> not believe that it is very productive to talk about federalism and non-federalism. The European Community was created *sui generis*. There has never been anything like it before in the world ... and the final form of its organisation will be *sui generis*.[65]

It is a debate that has not gone away, and the 2004–5 debates about a European Constitution bought the spectre of a federal Europe back into the political consciousness. Implicit, though, in the developments towards a common foreign policy and political and monetary union is the consequential loss of sovereignty by the nation-state.

## Sovereignty

Sovereignty is a 'major feature of British heritage', declared Welsh Conservative activists, not in 2005, but in 1962. This is indicative of a long-running concern that has exercised Conservatives. The parliamentary debate of August 1961 that approved Harold Macmillan's intention to bid for EC membership saw anti-Marketeers like Derek Walker-Smith rehearsing the arguments about the potential loss of sovereignty, both parliamentary and economic, that have continued through into the twenty-first century. Smith questioned why sovereignty needed to be sacrificed and was unable to accept that economic realism required Britain to join a supranational organisation rather than continue to favour intergovernmental operations. Furthermore, he warned that the EC intended to become more than a purely economic union, and that political union was the goal, which risked Britain surrendering the power of political decision-making.[66]

During Macmillan's application sovereignty was high among Conservative activist concerns, not least because sections of the media (particularly Beaverbrook's *Daily Express*) and the Anti-Common Market League were playing the issue 'to the full: exploiting an emotional; and deep seated feeling which is harboured by our good and solid citizens'. The concerns were largely related to the political and constitutional implications of membership, rather than fears about a decline in economic sovereignty. Conservative area agents reported anxieties that entry would mean the end of the monarchy or the destruction of the British electoral system. Only from the North of England was a sense of pragmatism sounded when the area agent reported 'strong opinion' that sovereignty would be effected no worse by EU entry than it had been by British membership of NATO and the United Nations.[67] Similarly, the party's own internal polling in 1970–1 showed that loss of sovereignty ranked second as a concern after rising food prices.[68] It is important to note that often the activists' 'concerns' were related to appeals for further explanation from the leadership, rather than statements of hostility.

Activists had highlighted these potential anxieties regarding sovereignty in the early 1950s when as visitors to the Council of Europe they reported that 'our people would not be willing within any foreseeable period to surrender our national sovereignty constitutionally to a brand-new European Federation'.[69] The point is that the sovereignty debate has a long pedigree and the party has not, as Norman Lamont claims, just sleepwalked into the issue.[70] With the creation of the EC, others, at a more senior level, too began articulating such views. Anthony Eden, now Lord Avon since resigning the premiership after Suez, feared the EU's intention to be a 'federation in the sense of one Parliament, one foreign policy, one currency etc. ... I do not want to become part of such a federation'.[71] He annoyed former Cabinet colleagues when he expressed his concerns to a rally of Young Conservatives in Leamington Spa.[72] He followed this with a similar warning to the House of Lords in November 1962.[73] In doing so Avon was beginning the phenomenon of a former party leader, and ex-prime minister, providing discomfort for their successor on Europe. Ted Heath and Margaret Thatcher would perfect this during the 1980s and 1990s.

Pro-Europeans like Douglas Hurd have tried to counter the current sceptics by arguing that developments in the EU since 1975, like the single market, a common European foreign policy and common currency, 'were not current in 1975' because 'these ideas came later'.[74] This in itself is really a half-truth. Many of these ideas were current in Brussels in the early 1970s and indeed had been since the late 1960s. Tax harmonisation had been on the European Commission's agenda since the mid-1960s, and Heath committed the Conservatives to introducing VAT to assist the cause of entry.[75] Macmillan in his 1957 conversation with Guy Mollet had admitted, 'it is difficult to create a common market without a common currency and common institutions'.[76] At the December 1969 Hague Summit EC leaders had agreed the objective of achieving European Monetary Union (EMU) by 1980, although there were divisions between the Six as to whether monetary co-operation should be given first priority, with economic co-operation inevitably following in its wake, or vice versa.[77] The Monnet (1969) and Werner (1970–1) Committees were discussing a twenty-year timetable for monetary union just as Britain joined the EU, and foreign secretary Alec Douglas-Home was present at the Werner Committee discussions. One senior policy advisor expressed concern at the lack of discussion within the party about these important and topical 'hot potatoes'.[78] In part this can be explained by the verdict of Alec Douglas-Home that the argument would run for years and years whilst the European powers 'decided how far economic integration can be taken without a degree of loss of sovereignty to which one or other national unit would object'.[79] At this point, Europe's discussions were based upon an assumption that monetary union would be underpinned by the dollar and the Bretton Woods international monetary system. The latter's collapse would oblige European decision-makers to consider EMU in relation to wider structural changes in the world economy and by the 1980s a realisation that the traditional relationship between unemployment and inflation was breaking down. Elements within the party were not complacent about the impact of entry. Internal Conservative briefings during the 1970s were warning that the EU was 'dynamic', which meant that decisions were frequently taken which not only related to areas where EU authority was well established but had the effect of extending in some way the authority of Community institutions.[80] Of course, these potential future developments were downplayed, but as Teddy Taylor, who resigned as a junior minister in opposition to EU entry in 1971, admitted in 1997, Heath 'didn't hide the consequences. The tragedy is that few listened'.[81]

There were moments of frankness from Heath's ministers during the accession debates. Geoffrey Howe, the solicitor-general and the person responsible for drafting the twelve-clause European Economic Communities Bill, told the House of Commons that 'the Communities were a dynamic organisation that would evolve and continue to evolve'. In the same debate Heath admitted that additional treaties would probably occur and that these might include the introduction of majority voting within ten years.[82] Entry, though, was presented in terms which argued that as a nation-state Britain faced diminishing choices. Entry was a trade-off between the loss of 'virtual' autonomy against the influence gained as EU entry increased these choices, but with the safeguard of the national veto as enshrined by the Luxembourg compromise.[83] To Heath's administration sovereignty meant autonomy. This was typical of a changed definition of sovereignty that had occurred in certain foreign policy circles since Suez. Sovereignty was no longer an absolute concept of independence from external forces, but a relative concept of securing the greatest possible international influence. Furthermore, it was perceived that future integration would be policy orientated rather than institutional, and that this would ally any concerns about the threat to parliamentary sovereignty. As the Conservative Research Department advised, there would be some limitations on a government's freedom of action but these would be compensated by the scope for action, especially in the economic sphere.[84]

Defining sovereignty is problematic, not least because of its applicability to different spheres. Academics would appear unable to reach unanimity about what it is.[85] In the British case this is complicated by the absence of a formal written constitution. Some have suggested dispensing with the term 'sovereignty' altogether.[86] Whilst it may be convenient to dismiss the term as meaningless, any parliamentary debate on European matters will see the phrase uttered frequently.[87] Some historians of the 1961–3 British EU application have dismissed the matter as an 'irrelevance',[88] but this is a largely subjective assessment that fails to understand that the issue means something to practicing politicians. It is necessary to understand what that meaning is. After all, politicians are not just policy-makers, tacticians and administrators; they have public personas designed to win electoral support for themselves, their parties and their causes. Politicians are what they speak and publish.[89]

Since the 1990s Conservative Euroseptics have pointed to the apparent erosion of British sovereignty, an alert sounded by Thatcher's 1988 Bruges speech as it dawned upon elements of the party that the 1986 Single European Act, far from implementing 'Thatcherism in Europe', was potentially eroding British autonomy, a process then accelerated by the Maastricht Treaty, the introduction of the euro and now the European Constitution.[90] Certainly this was a view that struck a cord with party activists: one 1992 survey finding that 68 per cent concurred.[91] Likewise, recent opinion polls suggest a similar verdict amongst the electorate.[92] The argument deployed was that since the Single European Act the nature of the European Union had changed from that which they thought had been accepted by the 1975 referendum. It is argued that during the accession and referendum debates of the 1970–5 the governments of the day deliberately downplayed the constitutional impact of membership, portraying the European Union as purely a trading arrangement, for jobs and prosperity, and that the British people were deprived the opportunity to consider the sovereignty implications.[93] As Winston Churchill, grandson of the former Conservative leader and MP for Davyhulme, bemoaned in 2000, the EU as it now stood was 'a far cry' from the Common Market he had campaigned for in the early 1970s.[94] This appears as a frequent complaint. It is evident that few Conservative MPs in the early 1970s appeared aware, or even cared, about the primacy of European Union law under Section 2 of the 1972 Communities Act. This appears to be corroborated by the exchange Heath had with Brian Rathbone, the former candidate for Smethwick, at the Central Council meeting of July 1971. Heath dismissed Rathbone's concerns and used the 'pooling' argument, citing the example of the UN and the role of the veto. He continued that in the EU 'there is agreement that on a country's vital national interest this can't be overridden, so in that regard we can also safeguard our position'. This was a safeguard that was reaffirmed by the role of the Council of Ministers and the national appointment of commissioners.[95] But it is wrong to argue that there was no discussion during this period. Sovereignty was the key argument in the anti-Marketeers' opposition to accession in 1971, as it had been during the first two application attempts, and became the central plank of the 1975 'No' vote campaign. Edward Heath admitted himself in 1972 that 'sovereignty ... and the power of the House of Commons has been one of the major themes of the discussion on European policy from the beginning'.[96] Yet some academic observers of the Conservatives in the 1990s have appeared willing to swallow the Eurosceptic argument.[97] This is perhaps an understandable assessment if the Conservatives internal debate about Europe is considered from the prism of the 1990s. If historical perspective is added it is untrue, a position that even some long-term irreconcilable Eurosceptics acknowledge, although they would maintain that the erosion of sovereignty is accelerating.[98]

So what does sovereignty mean for Conservatives? William Whitelaw, a former minister and party grandee, was dismissive of the concept. He felt unable to understand constituency concerns about 'sovereignty: whatever that meant'.[99] Given his background, Whitelaw was more than aware of the legal and academic disagreements about definitions. The distinct Conservative distrust of ideological concerns, and their willingness to celebrate the J.S. Mill 'stupid party' label, means they are keen to appear as the party of pragmatism. The views of activists showed that sovereignty was essentially an abstract concern about EC entry equated with the 'signing away of rights'. In other words, sovereignty was the means and mechanism for governing. This was certainly the core definition for anti-Marketeers from the early 1960s. As one anti-Marketeer referendum pamphlet declared in 1975, sovereignty 'is not national identity, it is not economic power, nor is it the power to throw our weight about in the world. It is purely the right for self-government'.[100] The very idea of European integration challenges traditional Conservative assumptions about sovereignty. The party has consistently presented itself as the party of the Union, the constitution and the empire. Julian Critchley, who first entered Parliament in 1959, observed in the late 1990s that the imperialists of the 1950s and 1960s were 'every bit as keen to defend concepts such as "identity" and "sovereignty", as Mr James Cran *et al.* are today'.[101]

The definition of sovereignty requires further breaking down. What is evident from those Conservative politicians who wished Britain to join the Community from 1961 onwards was a belief that membership would give Britain a renewed sense of autonomy and that it would increase the range of feasible options for Britain. Margaret Thatcher herself declared in 1961 that Britain was engaged in numerous treaties and alliances which appeared to restrict Britain's freedom of action. Yet entering into 'commercial obligations and treaties was an exercise in sovereignty, not a derogation from it'.[102] The 1956 Suez debacle may well have also played its part, at least in terms of a foreign policy take on sovereignty. Now it was imperative that Britain found a means of operating as a world power that could exercise autonomy of action without excessive outside interference. EC entry would allow Britain to act alongside France as a quasi world power with a nuclear deterrent and world colonial influence.[103] Heath and his supporters would have enhanced these claims in the early 1970s by suggesting that EU membership liberated Britain from its reliance on the American 'special relationship' and enabled this country to act upon its own best interests. This Heath demonstrated through his talks with Nixon by taking the decision from December 1970 onwards that Britain should cease bilateral negotiations with the US and not take decisions without first assessing the EU's stance.[104] For those opposed to entry, or further integration, the concern has centred around three aspects of sovereignty: the ability of Britain to sustain the legal right of final decision; the ability of Britain to make decisions without excessive outside interference; and the 'politics of nationhood'.

Pro-European Conservatives are contemptuous of the 'indelible right of Westminster argument'. They accept that sovereignty is about the means of governance but would argue that in the modern world sovereignty is exercised at different levels, from the local to the regional, from the European to the world.[105] Where they part company is over the insistence that it is a static concept that requires defending. Instead it is an ever-evolving concept, and in relation to the EU the sovereignty of each member nation has come together, something Geoffrey Howe likens to a rope with different strands intertwining to strengthen the bond and to which additional rope can be spliced.[106] Sceptics not surprisingly scorn expressions such as 'pooling' sovereignty or 'taking our decisions in common': 'they are honeyed words to express the loss of sovereignty.'[107]

It is clear that Howe's analogy about sovereignty being like a rope has a long pedigree. In 1950, when the party's Advisory Committee on Policy was discussing further defence co-ordination with the USA and NATO in Europe and the Far East, Lord Swinton argued that he foresaw no diminution of national sovereignty, 'as each nation concerned would be responsible for the efficiency of their national contribution to the overall plan'.[108] In fact this line of thinking became an integral part of the case for Europe, with proponents frequently making the point that Britain had already pooled her sovereignty through membership of NATO, the United Nations Organisation (UNO), the General Agreement on Tariffs and Trade (GATT) and WEU, and that EC membership would be no different. As Gordon Pears told Winchester activists in November 1960, 'our sovereignty has gone and it does us no good to hang on to the trappings of sovereignty. But this does not mean that we have to give up our way of life'.[109] Furthermore, as Irene Ward advanced in January 1962, once Britain became an EC member 'We shall have first class representatives on any controlling body in Europe – we run no greater risk than that we do at present'.[110] A Scottish Central Office pamphlet in 1971 warned that 'if we stay out we will be contenting ourselves with the illusion of national sovereignty, when the reality has long departed'.[111] Likewise, Geoffrey Rippon in December 1974: 'Our parliamentary sovereignty is marginal in world affairs.'[112] If Britain was outside the EU, then only the impression of having sovereignty would exist, but in reality it would be dependent on decisions taken elsewhere, such as by NATO or the EU. This was not acceptable to Eurosceptics. They countered with the argument that British membership of the United Nations, NATO and WEU could not affect British parliamentary sovereignty because none of these organisations could make law that took legal precedence over UK law. This view has received academic support.[113]

The debate about sovereignty has been a central strand of the Conservative debate since 1947. It is a debate that ranges across the economic and political spheres but is largely constrained within a concept of who governs Britain. Pro-Europeans have categorised it as an 'illusion' and argued that any actual diminution in powers has been offset by the increased position of influence and the opportunities membership of the EC has presented. For nearly thirty years this argument convinced the majority of the party, who appeared willing to accept these trade-offs. Heath from 1968 undertook to articulate more clearly the implications of membership, and as a consequence the party broadly fell in line. However, in 1986, as it appeared that Britain was increasingly unable to restrain the moves toward closer union, the doubts began to re-emerge. The problem was that Thatcher's success at renegotiating the UK's EC budgetary contribution in 1983 had reinforced an illusion of increased British sovereignty at when time when in fact the UK was losing power to the EC. The SEA provided the reality check. If closer European integration was once more perceived as a threat to British parliamentary sovereignty, it has also been accompanied by fears that decisions are being taken at a level which disenfranchised the British electorate. As a result, a demand for a referendum has been a frequent feature of the debate. Where the Europeanists of the party have failed since 1986 is in convincing the wider party that active British leadership in Europe will mitigate these risks. The perception that sovereignty is tangible, and under threat, makes it difficult for many current Conservatives to accept Geoffrey Howe's advice that 'it is not like political virginity, now you have it now you don't'.[114]

### 'Let the people decide!' Referendum demands

Defending parliamentary sovereignty is one matter, but championing referenda would appear to weaken this concept. Yet increasingly Eurosceptics have been suggesting that matters of significance on Europe should be put to a referendum. In 1911, 1930 and 1945 Conservative leaders had pledged support for a referendum.[115] Yet since 1945 referenda have never been terribly popular with the Conservative leadership, who sense them to be an 'alien' concept.[116] Largely, this opposition has centred on a concern that populist referenda undermine the very nature of a representative parliamentary democracy. Further, a widely held view is that, having conceded the principle of a referendum, where does one draw the line? This view is given credence by Labour having granted thirty-six referenda since 1997 on issues as varied as establishing a Welsh Assembly and deciding whether Hartlepool should have a mayor. As far back as the mid-1930s, as the League of Nations tried to enlist the assistance of Conservative activists in its peace ballot, it has been clear that the willingness of the activists to advocate, or participate in, referenda is not shared by their Central Office superiors.[117] Part of the concern has rested with the fear that political opponents can use referenda as rallying calls: internal as well as external. It has certainly been the case that those Conservatives championing referenda on Europe have largely, although not exclusively, come from the sceptic camp. Partly this could be interpreted as a failure to win the policy argument within the party structure, and therefore as a deliberate attempt to appeal to the people over the party's head. At the same time there is scope to accept the argument that for matters as profound as EEC entry or a European Constitution referenda represent an opportunity to educate the people about the subject.

With the Heath government's decision to apply for EEC membership arose renewed calls that any entry terms should be submitted to the British electorate in a referendum. This was rejected in no uncertain terms by Heath, who argued that Members of Parliament were representatives of the people and in a representative democracy the will of the House of Commons was sovereign. These calls for a referendum on entry terms were not new amongst Conservatives. With the 1961–3 negotiations activists had sought reassurances that a successful application would be the subject of either a general election or a referendum.[118] These reassurances were not forthcoming then, nor were they a decade later.[119] Indeed, by the 1970s senior figures like

Francis Pym, the chief whip, were warning that 'it will be impossible to sweep the referendum argument under the carpet'.[120] The leadership recognised that there would be these demands but were determined to resist.[121] Anti-Marketeers had tabled an EDM in July 1969 and Labour had moved an amendment during the EEC Bill, which was rejected by 284 votes to 235. The party's own polling in 1970 showed that six out of ten Conservative voters supported the referendum calls, whilst anti-Marketeers tried to suggest that floating Conservative voters would return to the fold if there was a commitment to a referendum.[122] Others had hoped Heath might have been persuaded to include a commitment to a referendum in the 1970 manifesto. It was a means of outflanking Labour. The argument ran that since the Labour Party were reluctant Europeans they could always convey the impression to the electorate that they would have negotiated better terms than the Conservatives. However, the people's consent was a vital element of the pro-referendum argument: 'unless public opinion favoured entry, any government would have difficulty in taking the country into Europe and keeping it there.'[123] Heath had himself spoken in May 1970 of EEC enlargement requiring 'the full-hearted consent of the Parliaments *and peoples* of the new member countries'.[124] By this Heath meant the British Parliament through MPs as the democratic representative of the British people.[125] As one of his closest aides admits, 'Ted never had in mind a referendum', but was seeking to warn the French that in negotiations he would be no pushover.[126] But those favourable to a referendum were drawn to the 'and peoples' phrase and pointed out that a precedent had been created with the pledge of a referendum on the border issue for Northern Ireland before Stormont was prorogued in March 1972. As argued Neil Marten, MP for Banbury and leading anti-Marketeer:

> The analogy of no transfer of sovereignty 'without the consent of the people' of Northern Ireland is very close and the yardstick by which their consent was tested was the referendum, which would have been held even if their Parliament had continued in existence.[127]

The Northern Irish example would again be used in the late 1990s when those advocating a referendum on British membership of the single currency would point to the precedent of the referendum on the Good Friday agreement.[128] Although it was thought in the early 1970s that a pledge of a referendum might convince some of the parliamentary doubters to support the negotiated entry terms there was greater concern that the issue was 'being used by some anti's as a weapon in the struggle'.[129] Party activists might be calling for a referendum but the likelihood that government would accept a referendum, even if its rhetorical objections were overcome, was minimal when opinion polls showed the scepticism of the electorate towards EEC membership.[130]

The debates about the Maastricht Treaty and the moves towards a single currency reinvigorated the Eurosceptic demands for a referendum. The memories of defeat in 1975 had diminished and there was a growing sense that popular opinion was increasingly questioning the value of the European project. In 1996 Bill Cash introduced a private member's bill calling for a referendum before any change to the relationship between Britain and the EU which secured the support of seventy-four fellow Conservatives.[131] The Major government was wary of the issue, but increasingly found itself backing into a cul-de-sac. The messages were increasingly confused. A leaked CPC report in 1993 showed the majority of activists did not favour a referendum, prompting Douglas Hurd, the foreign secretary, to declare: 'those calling for a referendum are undermining – albeit unwittingly – the parliamentary democracy which they say they want to defend.'[132] Yet as the party increasingly fractured over the European issue and the question of Major's leadership was subject to challenge, the carrot of a referendum became the bait to secure party unity, despite the opposition of pro-Europeans like Ken Clarke. During the 1995 leadership contest Major's former parliamentary private secretary (PPS), Tony Favell, urged Major to agree to a referendum 'before further European integration' as a means to 'save his administration'.[133] Just days earlier Hurd had told the House of Commons Foreign Affairs Select Committee of his willingness to accept the arguments for a referendum.[134] Thereafter for the remainder of Major's premiership the Eurosceptics sought to gain definitive proof of the expressions of intent by urging Major to introduce legislation for a referendum and thereby demonstrate the party's acceptance of 'the basic principle that the nation belongs to the people and to nobody else'.[135] Under Hague the commitment to a referendum became enshrined in party policy, but with a very important distinction. Whereas under a Major government a referendum would have seen the majority of the Conservative leadership campaigning for a 'Yes' vote, under Hague and his subsequent successors the leadership would have been urging a 'No' vote. The illusion of the Conservatives as the party of Europe was now firmly shattered. This was also a reflection of the party's electoral fortunes. The hammering at the 1997 and 2001 polls encouraged a belief in the need to shore up the core Conservative vote, and, encouraged by an increasingly Eurosceptic press, the belief within Central Office was that this would prove a popular message. Some Conservatives were less than convinced, warning that to demand referenda on each and every treaty amendment left the party 'without even a fig leaf to cover their intellectual nakedness'.[136]

There is a danger in the use of the referendum call tactic. Since entering opposition in 1997 virtually each EU initiative has been greeted with a Conservative demand for a referendum. This risks devaluing the referendum, and does run counter to the British democratic tradition. It is an element of popularism, proposing that the people should be the arbiters of decision-making, yet it was one of principle. Rhodes Boyson supported calls for a referendum and opposed Maastricht because he saw it as a constitutional issue:

> I firmly believe that the passage of power from the Commons to Europe should have been a people's decision and not a government or whipped party decision. The vote, to my mind, thus has no credibility and the British people can revoke it at any time.[137]

The issues of the single currency and the European Constitution do appear as serious enough issues to warrant a referendum.[138]

## Free trade versus preference

If the dangers of integration divide the party over the implications for sovereignty, then at least in recent decades there has been an expectation that at an economic level there is hope for trade liberalisation. Yet this consensus is only a recent phenomenon and masks a key argument at the heart of the Conservatives' ideological identity that can be traced back to the split in 1847 over the Corn Laws. During the 1950s and 1960s the European debate was conducted in tandem with the party's internal debate about imperial preference. The debate about preference revolved around a fundamental argument about protection versus free trade which had engaged the Conservatives, often with near-fatal consequences, since the Corn Laws. Protection had finally been enshrined at the 1932 Ottawa agreement, but by the 1950s conditions had changed. At one level the party's protectionists should have found joining the EEC acceptable as it operated a form of protectionism. The difficulty was that the Six were unwilling to grant preferences to the Commonwealth. Part of the problem was that continental politicians found it difficult to grasp how the Commonwealth functioned, but there were those who sensed a British tendency to 'fall back' on the Commonwealth as an 'alibi'.[139] The rationale for joining EFTA and the EEC was that these were free trade areas that would facilitate greater trade liberalisation. By the 1980s, as Thatcherism sought to roll back the state at home the belief that these free market neo-liberal economic strategies could be implemented on a Europe-wide level motivated the party's participation in Europe.

Britain's initial proposal for a Free Trade Area, in 1958–9, fitted into the preferred conception of British associate involvement in Europe and the avoidance of supranational bodies. As Fergus Graham MP explained, 'we were not joining it in the full sense but as "country members of a club"'.[140] The potential attraction of a European market of 200 million people was obvious, which with a growing consumer market suggested the potential for British business to win 'a good slice'.[141] The problem was that the Free Trade Area that Britain eventually joined in 1959 had a market of only 40 million, which for those Conservative who looked to joining the EEC felt was 'no substitute'.[142] It was a common criticism that EFTA was too small a trading bloc to compete effectively, and that historically and geographically it was not as favourable to Britain as EEC membership would be.[143] However, following de Gaulle's first veto elements of the party increasingly advanced the idea that EFTA had the potential to be developed into a wider customs union, with a common external tariff, and expanded to include the Commonwealth, America and Canada. These advocates were anxious to deflect Britain from its flirtation with Europe. An expanded EFTA would encourage trade in invisible exports (which was a UK strength) whilst complimenting and harmonising the existing defence and trade arrangements Britain was already committed to.[144] To the defenders of protection,

> [the] recent moves towards customs unions, common markets, supra-national organisations, and federations are the result of overlooking the economic truth that non-discrimination is a policy tending always to place the borrowing and debtor nations at the mercy of the creditor, and to necessitate centralisation of control over individual debtors' economies.[145]

The empire was 'one of the most successful experiments in international relations the world has ever seen'. The nation's standard of living and employment was largely dependent upon the resources and markets of the empire.[146] The activist attachment to preference was also clear, and something that they perceived as a 'cardinal point' of party policy.[147] There was a sense amongst the imperialist wing of the party that preference was under dual attack: from a jealous USA and the free trade principles of European unity.[148] The critics of preference were warning that its significance was diminishing and extolling activists to 'keep a sense of proportion about this'.[149] It was suggested that with many Commonwealth nations in their own right manufacturers there was an ever-decreasing empire market for British goods. In the Commonwealth's mind preferential tariffs were less important than the power to borrow UK money for investment. If Britain was to have the reserves to support this investment it needed to ally itself with the markets of Europe to rebuild resources.[150]

As the 1970s progressed the economic significance of the Commonwealth to Britain declined still further. The world economic stagnation meant that the first decade of EEC membership appeared to be rather inconsequential. However, after 1979, with a new Conservative administration passively pro-European and a new Labour opposition lurching leftward and more hostile than ever to Europe, it meant this became a key political battleground. During the early 1980s, with the Conservatives still projecting themselves as the party of Europe, they faced left-wing attacks on their European policy. Their critique essentially ran along the lines that membership of the EEC had been economically harmful to Britain, with the large deficit that now existed on Britain's trade balance with Europe contributing to the high levels of unemployment. As a consequence withdrawal was necessary. The Conservative counter was that it was extremely difficult to calculate the costs and benefits of membership given the breadth of variables that needed to be

accounted for. They were prepared to overlook the decline in British manu-
facturing performance and pointed instead to the fact that 40 per cent of
British exports went to the EEC. The withdrawal argument was economic
suicide since it put at risk inward investment and employment. This did not
mean that the Thatcher administration would gladly accept the status quo in
the early 1980s, and it would be the economic costs of agricultural support
that would prove the engagement point.

## Agriculture: from an economic to a patriotic issue

The historical association between the Conservative Party and agriculture
has been a long and key one. The championing of the farmer's corner since
ideas for closer European unity began has often been a sign of adherence to
the sceptic cause. The centrality of agriculture to the British economy has
declined rapidly since the 1960s, enabling pro-Europeans to neutralise it as
an issue. Since the 1980s the issue of agriculture has been revitalised by the
Eurosceptics and turned back to their advantage through the battles over
CAP, the French ban on British beef and Spanish fishermen, incidents that
have allowed the sceptics to support agriculture with the patriotic card.
Europe has placed the relationship between the Conservatives and the
farming lobby under considerable strain.[151] The historical precedents for the
potential breakdown of this relationship are enormous and profound for
the party: the Corn Laws and tariff reform. The perceived significance of
the rural vote for Conservatives in the Shires goes some considerable way to
explaining the nervousness with which the issue was tackled. *The Times'*
parliamentary correspondent reported in 1962 that although party managers
were privately prepared to concede that the farming lobby could no longer
break a Conservative administration, 'the theory lives on. Nor does it merely
live; sometimes it has the ring of established doctrine'.[152] Even in opposition
in 1966 the Conservatives represented thirty-one of the forty constituencies
in which more than 15 per cent of the work force was employed in farming.
Amongst the 1970 cohort of Conservative MPs seventy-nine had either an
occupational or personal link to farming.[153] Though psephological studies
have discounted the importance of the 'farming vote', it is much more significant to understand how important contemporary politicians thought the
farm vote was.

    The debates over imperial preference which so dominated Conservative
thinking of the late 1940s and 1950s meant there was a general acceptance
that if Britain ever became involved in the European process of economic
integration the needs of British agriculture would deserve protecting. As
Rab Butler warned Macmillan after the 1961 decision to apply for EEC
membership, with agriculture the 'safeguards must be such as will hold the
country or county seats'.[154] Electoral considerations aside, there was a
broader consensus within the policy-making machine that any British
involvement first in a free trade area and then later as a member of the EEC

would not necessarily be adverse to British agriculture *per se*, but would have implications for Britain's balance of payments and the cost of living. The relatively healthy position of British agriculture, which enjoyed a relative degree of efficiency and economies of scale, was considered to be a benefit to Britain. The necessity of safeguards was to protect the specialist sectors of the industry (hill farmers and horticulturalists especially) and the need to negotiate a transitional period was to lessen the impact upon food prices and Britain's trade balance.

Through the party's agricultural committee, during the late 1950s and 1960s the leadership sought to evaluate the likely impact on agriculture of Britain's involvement in Europe. Butler, who represented the conscience of agriculture within the Cabinet in the early 1960s, thought this committee played an important role in keeping the government in touch with farming and party opinion. It was largely on this committee's recommendation that agricultural production was excluded from the EFTA arrangements. The problem the Cabinet faced was that the agricultural community did not necessarily speak with one voice, but the ability of the industry to give expression to its concerns was not in doubt. The hostile reaction to a speech by David Eccles in Rome in June 1957 that appeared to contradict assurances that agricultural products would be excluded from EFTA agreements was not untypical.[155] When the party's Advisory Committee on Policy met to debate one of the agricultural committee's reports the division of opinion was clearly apparent. Henry Legge-Bourke, who represented the constituency of Isle of Ely, with its considerable horticultural interests, suggested EFTA would have a 'profound effect' on agriculture, whereas Lady Davidson was more sceptical and suggested a 'considerable division of opinion in the industry' over the likely impact.[156]

When ministers began to consider whether to apply for EEC membership in 1960 the committee was again asked to report. The committee secretary, Peter Minoprio, prepared a 'draft' interim report for ministers that indicated that the committee had 'little doubt that arrangements could be made to accommodate British agriculture within the Common Market framework'. However, this position was later modified to conclude that agriculture should not present an impossible barrier to entry provided safeguards were achieved. Through the winter of 1960–1 the committee tried to decide what these safeguards should be, but could only conclude with a majority verdict in July 1961 that they should be 'stiff terms'.[157]

Throughout the first application period Central Office, through its network of area agents, paid close attention to the mood of the agricultural community. It was estimated that as many as seventy to eighty Conservative seats were at risk if the farming vote was alienated.[158] Reports that meetings of the Anti-Common Market League were attracting large rural audiences and being addressed by disaffected Conservative MPs caused a certain degree of alarm about the potential electoral threat to safe Conservative seats. Several by-elections during 1962, such as West Derbyshire and

Norfolk South, provided opportunities to test the mood of the agricultural community. The intervention of anti-Common Market candidates added to the potential danger. The conclusion of one party committee after the loss of South Dorset in November 1962 was that the government needed to show 'its determination to defend the special interests which we have always said must be adequately safeguarded'.[159] Party officials were also concerned that in addition to the ACML, the National Farmers' Union (NFU) was stoking the farmers' hostility.[160] Considerable efforts were made throughout the 1960s to try and convince the NFU of the need to join Europe, but with little success.[161] In fact what agents were reporting back was that opposition to EEC entry appeared to be confined mainly to the small-scale farmer, the hill farmer and the horticulturalist. There was also a sense that many farmers were open to persuasion and there were frequent calls for the production of pamphlets that explained the situation for agriculture.[162]

However, if the farming community was not as hostile as expected there was considerable concern that the reported increase in food prices and the cost of living that would ensue with EEC entry were worrying the wider electorate. The cost of food was to be a key battleground throughout the 1960s and 1970s. The clarion call of cheap food carried considerable resonance with the electorate, and harked back to the protection versus free trade debates of the previous hundred years. Consequently both the pro- and anti- groups spent considerable time trying to establish how much extra EEC entry would mean for the household food bill. Supporters of entry were willing to concede that entry would lead to higher food costs, but argued that this would be offset by price falls for particular commodities, increased agricultural efficiency and a reduction in indirect taxation.[163] By 1969 Shadow Cabinet estimates were that food prices would rise over five years by no more than 14 per cent upon entry.[164] This was certainly one of the more moderate estimates, with figures ranging from 4 per cent to 33 percent, and these from pro-entry elements of the party! What is evident is that numerous factors could be brought into play which affected the calculation of the figure: devaluation of the pound had a big impact, as did the agreement in 1966 on the Common Agricultural Policy, whilst the terms of any entry, such as the length of transition period, were all features that needed to be accounted for. What was beyond dispute was that the party's own opinion polls showed that increased food prices were widely expected by the electorate and these price hikes were the main reason for opposing entry.[165] As a leading Europeanist warned in late 1970, the anti-Marketeers were winning the argument and successfully associating the EEC with higher living costs.[166] A minister was reported to have suggested that meat prices would increase upon entry, but that this would be offset by a fall in wine costs. One angry Bristol constituency official tartly admonished Central Office: 'It is not our habit to dine on table wines exclusively, a good piece of meat at a reasonable price is more to our taste.'[167] It was clearly evident amongst party activists that hostility to food price rises was one of the key complaints.[168] As the party chairman observed to the minister responsible for the negotiations:

> There is no doubt that we face a major and difficult task in convincing the party in the country of the merits of the case for entering Europe and if we can go some way towards meeting this very difficult objection, our task will be that much easier.[169]

When added to the bogey of the Common Agricultural Policy this made it potentially difficult to reverse the opposition to entry.

When Conservative policy-makers first considered the mechanisms of the newly agreed CAP in 1966 they concluded that compared to the UK system of guaranteed prices by deficiency payments CAP was 'no less effective in ensuring a fair return to the farmer. In fact *it has much in common with the system which the Conservative Party has put forward for British agriculture*'.[170] Many had expected that the EEC member nations would have found it impossible to find a system of agricultural support that they could agree upon and which worked.[171] Once they had, it became quickly apparent both that it was not working, with the French and Germans both wanting contradictory outcomes, and that it was not such a beneficial system for the British. For those anxious to secure Britain's final entry, the 1969 CAP crisis was seen as of potential benefit, raising expectations that it would provide the incentive to the French to agree to renewed negotiations about British membership. But it was also warned that the CAP system was 'impossible' for Britain.[172] The problem for Britain was that CAP would mean giving up the scheme of deficiency payments to farmers subsidised through indirect taxation in exchange for a system of guaranteed prices which only encouraged overproduction and higher prices. It has been estimated, though, that in the last year of operation this scheme cost £1.5 billion.[173] Furthermore, the EEC generated revenue from levies on imported foodstuffs from outside the Community that hit Britain hard because of her reliance on food imports. It was these conditions that Heath was obliged to accept in 1970 with the concession of a six-year transition period. It was, as one leading anti-Marketeer proclaimed, only 'some marginal tinkering', and because of French intransigence Britain had been obliged to accept as the price of entry the 'major villain of the piece', CAP.[174]

From this moment CAP was elevated in the consciousness of Conservatives to a position as the 'root of all the troubles in Europe today'.[175] But for pro-Europeans it is a 'convenient target' that obscures the fact that Britain's predecessor deficit system was just as costly.[176] Images of grain and butter mountains and wine lakes entered the political mindset, encouraged by Thatcher's determination to 'handbag' Europe. CAP took up almost 70 per cent of the entire EEC budget in 1979. The Eurosceptics have succeeded in making the issue one of 'them' and 'us', the inefficiency of European, especially French, agriculture being protected from genuine free trade by their national governments' self-interest. The hostility of activists has remained. Between 1992 and 1995 party conference received forty motions critical of CAP.[177] In February 1988 Thatcher succeeded in securing minor reforms to CAP which went towards decreasing agricultural surpluses and granting a fresh rebate to Britain. However, the influence of farming groups in both France and Germany would ensure the system's survival. Some in Britain, such as Ben Gill, a president of the NFU, have held CAP up as an example of successful European Union policy, but most Conservatives see it as a distortion of free trade principles, 'an extreme form of protectionism'.[178] It implies that the majority of the EU is half-hearted in its commitment to free trade, and this legitimises Britain's reluctance to embrace the European project. Even amongst the pro-European lobby there has been a willingness to admit to the problems of CAP. For them the remedy lies in reform, particularly in removing the risk of surpluses by reducing quotas.[179] Reform is the watchword because CAP is 'indefensible socially, economically, ecologically, environmentally and morally'.[180] The implications of agricultural reform may ultimately be confined to a small section of the economy, but as the European project has gained momentum its impact has broadened.

### The single market, monetary union and the euro

British leadership within Europe has been one of the 'key' defences of the Europeanists. John Major was able to define the outcome of Maastricht negotiations as 'game, set and match' because having a British presence at the negotiating table meant securing significant concessions. Where the Eurosceptics have successfully advanced their cause since the mid-1980s has been through concentration upon the argument that the vision of British leadership in Europe is a myth. They suggest the EU, through a combination of the Franco-German axis in league with the European Commission, has consistently found the means to undermine Britain's negotiated position and hasten the pace of integration. In the sceptic version of events the single market in 1992 was intended as 'a liberating measure, eliminating barriers to trade and allowing free markets to flourish. In practice, it has been used to open up a vast new regulatory chapter of harmonised standards and controls'.[181] One of the strategies of the Eurosceptics has been to imply that the opt-outs (single currency and Social Chapter) are not nearly as watertight as portrayed by the government. They pointed to the ability of the European Court of Justice (ECJ) to erode the opt-out and said that because other member states were implementing the changes by implication Britain would have to join in the future and accept legislation it had no role in shaping. Sceptics would argue that government had not learned the lessons of SEA and complacency meant subsequent governments were prepared to accept treaty statements which appeared innocuous but which offered incentives to European federalists to push the integration agenda still further. This was one reason why under Hague the Conservatives proposed that the

ECJ should be reformed so that if it interpreted EU legislation in a manner different from that intended by the draft legislators it would then be subject to immediate amendment.

Since the Single European Act the right of the EU to interfere in the economic sovereignty of a nation-state by determining monetary and taxation policy has become a central debate. It has been an issue on which the Eurosceptics have made considerable play. In July 1992 the chancellor Norman Lamont accepted the EU Commission's right to set VAT at 15 per cent in exchange for an opt-out for children's clothes, fuel and whisky. This was an important psychological hurdle because, as Norman Tebbit complained, it was 'contrary to 1,000 years of British sovereignty' and meant the British people had lost control over taxation.[182] A 1994 survey of the parliamentary party showed that privately it had considerable concerns about the EU's plans to harmonise VAT.[183] VAT is for the electorate a constant source of irritation. Its adoption is entirely due to EEC entry. During the 1966 general election Conservative candidates had been briefed that the harmonisation of taxation was a 'more distant' aim of the EEC.[184] Yet in less than twelve months the Conservative Research Department was urging the Shadow Cabinet to make it a 'definite item' on the party's programme because the adoption of VAT 'would be powerful evidence of "meaning business" as far as the Community was concerned' and would score domestic political points because Labour were 'napping' on the issue.[185] The huge volume of work done in opposition for the adoption of VAT is difficult to understand without appreciating the European context. The Conservatives adopted the implementation of VAT as party policy on the understanding that the European Commission was prepared to accept different rates between countries and specific national opt-outs.[186] Thus the taxation debate has evolved from being presented as a necessary harmonisation measure to an issue of sovereignty, with the national ability to determine taxation levels under threat. If national rights of taxation are a sacred cow, then the proposed abandonment of sterling for a common European currency has obliged Conservatives to radically question their values.

National currency has been an important part of national identity since coinage first began being exchanged. It has the ability to evoke strong emotions. For the Conservative Party the pound (or sterling) has been a vital element of testing the economic virility of the nation. Its role as a reserve currency on the world money markets has been perceived as vital to economic well-being. So it was unsurprising that moves towards a European single currency, the euro, were greeted with such suspicion by many Conservatives. The debate since the mid-1980s has become more than an economic one, given that monetary union is as much a part of the European Union's political agenda. This whole debate has split the Conservative Party wide open, destroying the carefully constructed premise that the European project was an economic experiment that was necessary to reverse Britain's economic decline.

For some the very survival of the EEC as a customs union required the development of common fiscal and monetary policies.[187] Others expressed anxiety that a common currency was the EEC's aim.[188] However, these speculations were conducted within the framework of the future well-being of sterling as a reserve currency. The 1969 Hague Summit agreed the objective of monetary union by 1980. This was confirmed in the Werner report, which advocated the abolition of exchange rates and the adoption of a single currency, but within an international monetary system underpinned by the dollar. This was something that would be undone by the collapse of the Bretton Woods system. Party policy wonks felt able to dismiss the likelihood of a common currency, especially as 'there is no timetable laid down'.[189] However, with a successful British application likely after 1970 the presence of the Monnet and Werner Committees caused unease in certain circles. Geoffrey Rippon could only seek to assuage doubters with the assurance that the EEC had agreed not to undertake any further commitments in this field 'which might prejudice our negotiations'.[190] However, for those charged with anticipating the likely impact of entry upon British policy-making the limitations imposed upon economic policy (particularly because of budgetary contributions) would 'be further restricted by the development of economic and monetary union'. Warning was given that decreased control over economic policy would reduce the scope for engineering favourable economic conditions around the electoral timetable and that Britain had to appreciate that the EEC was 'dynamic'. This meant that decisions were frequently taken which not only related to areas where Community interest was well established but also had the effect of extending in some way the authority of Community institutions.[191] This would be a lesson painfully learned by the Conservatives, as the implementation of the Single European Act would reveal a decade later.

As the first steps towards economic union progressed, the Conservatives had the luxury of being the party of opposition. The Callaghan government rejected the opportunity of British participation in the EMS, but the Conservatives' 1979 manifesto pledged that consideration would be given to membership if the economic situation was correct. As Thatcher fought her budgetary battles with Europe, others, especially Howe and Lawson, were looking at the relative success of EMS. Their conclusion was that the system of semi-fixed exchange rates had generally been successful in fulfilling the objectives of monetary stability and policy convergence. The 1986 Sterling Crisis encouraged those who thought British membership of the ERM would insulate the domestic economy from the current unpredictability of policy in a global world where the outcomes increasingly failed to reflect the underlying economic conditions. Those favouring entry into the ERM directed their argument at different levels. In economic terms they argued that it would minimise the impact of exchange rate fluctuations but also act as a restraint on domestic inflationary pressures. Even as the pound came under sustained pressure in 1992, proponents of the ERM, like Howe, were arguing membership was 'absolutely right' because it helped 'to reinforce our discipline against inflation'.[192] The British leadership question was also reintroduced. Warnings from the likes of Howe and Heseltine that Britain must not repeat the mistakes of the 1950s were linked to the line that if it was part of the ERM Britain could use it as vehicle to slow down and divert the pressures for greater integration.[193] In other words, this was an opportunity for Britain to shape the Community's future development in its own vision. In October 1990 sterling joined the ERM at a rate of DM2.95. Rhodes Boyson likened it to 'a twelve-legged race in which twelve runners had their legs tied together and were then made to run. Of course they all fell down'.[194] In less than two years John Major's government was forced humiliatingly to withdraw. Divisions had emerged amongst the Thatcherites even before Britain joined and now became very evident.[195] And despite the problems of Black Wednesday, the European Union was not going to be deterred in its ambitions to create a single European currency.

In retrospect it is clear that the agreement of the Single European Act in February 1986 marked the fracture point of the Thatcherite monetarist alliance. The SEA had been imposed upon the party with the argument that it offered the opportunity to entrench neo-liberal economic values at the core of the European Union and constrain the moves towards further economic and political integration. The reality proved that the Euro-ratchet effect – the ability of EU organisations to continually and explicitly penetrate the British political process – was taking hold.[196] Belatedly, those like Thatcher who were sceptical of the EU's benefits realised that the SEA was now a tool for further integration. Her former allies, such as Howe and Lawson, argued that further integration (short of federalism) was necessary to protect neo-liberal values. What emerged after 1986 was the growing cohesion of the Eurosceptic arguments, which gained mainstream coverage with Thatcher's 1988 Bruges speech.

The principal line was that Britain had tried and failed to make the European Union work. Specifically this broke down into four areas of critique. First, the inequity of application of the legislation by member nations quickly became evident. This was particularly so in the area of air transportation and in the banking and insurance sector. What this suggested to the sceptics was that it would require further sovereignty concessions to achieve a true single market. Second, there was the commissioners' use of harmonisation to push the federalist agenda. Sceptics pointed to the use of the qualified majority vote in areas of health and safety which ran counter to the desires of the British government and also to a series of legal decisions handed down by the ECJ and the British Law Courts which emphasised the primacy of European law over British. Between January 1973 and January 2003 102,567 EU directives had been imposed on Britain.[197] Third, there was a sense that, having failed to transplant Thatcherite values into the European system, it was now more than likely that the EU would become Christian or Social Democrat in purpose and therefore be an alien creed to the British system. Finally, the SEA had been portrayed as a means of halting further integration, when in fact it had given the process fresh momentum and the Commission was now a rival to the British government's sovereignty.[198]

Although in the 1960s the idea of a common European currency could be dismissed as far away, by the 1990s it was an impending reality, with Britain 'on the conveyor belt'.[199] Whilst the average British voter showed little interest in the matter, the political elites descended into division and rancour. One 1995 survey of the parliamentary party found that privately 68 per cent were opposed, with 33 per cent prepared to sign an EDM in February.[200] Sceptics portrayed the potential loss of the pound as a crisis for British national identity. Hague's nationwide 'Keep the Pound' campaign, launched from the back of a truck in February 2000, was intended to try and tap into the electorate's supposed patriotism, but it is evident that Europe as an issue carries little saliency when compared to matters such as tax, law and order and education. In the view of some, Hague was playing a dangerous game by attempting to make 'Europe' a people's issue after the Establishment had spent so long trying to keep it the preserve of the political elites.[201] He repeatedly emphasised that the agenda of the single currency was political rather than economic. In doing so, the bogey of a federal Europe was caricatured, with all that this entailed for the consequential loss of sovereignty, the constitutional implications of a centrally set interest rate, and the absence of democratic accountability.

Once the euro came into being its first tests were economic, rather than political. Sceptics pointed to its initial weakness on the currency markets, and argued that this both damaged the pound and threatened British jobs because of the knock-on effect for British exports.[202] Furthermore, they made play of the 'one glove fits all' nature of the euro and argued this denied individual national governments the chance to tailor economic policy to suit their national needs.[203] This had potentially dangerous consequences, warned Portillo in a speech to the Institute of Economic Affairs in January 1998: 'If we shoe-horn the nations of Europe into an artificial union, we will not abolish nationalism, indeed we risk stirring it up.'[204] After 1997 leading Conservatives abandoned the 'wait and see' policy of John Major and began to articulate the economic case against EMU. It was pointed out that the British economy possessed unique features (such as a flexible labour market, with a large financial services sector and a history of low taxation) that made convergence with the European economies difficult. This economic 'uniqueness' meant Britain could be more influential outside the euro zone.

How the euro has been received by British industry and the City has been keenly contested.[205] Under Hague, John Nott was commissioned to chair a panel of economists and businessmen to consider the case for preserving sterling. The Nott report concluded that there were not only powerful economic reasons to avoid joining the euro but also political arguments against, namely the loss of national control over key economic decisions and diminution of self-government. The media empires of Murdoch and Black in propagating their message have ably supported the sceptics. But what are the alternatives? Can Britain remain outside the euro zone? Hard-core sceptics like Norman Lamont and John Redwood have argued for Britain's permanent exclusion from monetary union, but appear unable to propose alternatives.[206] William Waldegrave speculated whether Britain could leave the EU and survive in its shadow, free from the dangers of its central economic control but benefiting from the proximity of its market.[207] In making this bold declaration Waldegrave was in effect committing a heresy by admitting that it did not matter if Britain no longer counted, and therefore challenging a central tenet of Conservative post-war thinking that Britain required and could offer a leadership role.[208] The weakness of the Waldegrave thesis was that by withdrawing from the EU Britain would become subject to its tariffs, with the implications this carried for the British export market. If Britain adopted an 'associate' status in the manner of Norway, then that experience suggested Britain would still be forced to accept the bureaucratic controls that Waldegrave was seeking to avoid.

In contrast, the limited numbers of Conservatives prepared to argue the case for the single currency have made much of the economic imperatives. The single currency offers an environment for more reliable Europe-wide economic growth through low interest rates and price transparency. The stability offered to the currency markets, especially in light of the ERM fiasco, offers further inducement.[209] They deny that the loss of control over interest rates would signal the end of the nation-state and point to the arguments offered by Alan Milward that closer European Union has seen the consolidation of the nation-state rather than its demise.[210] The historical case has also been made, with Ken Clarke reminding the European movement that there was a de facto union between Britain and Ireland and others pointing out that previously Britain has been involved in other international monetary 'unions' such as the gold standard and Bretton Woods.[211] What is clear is that this issue fails to secure unanimity. Yet one area of European policy that gains a better degree of Conservative consensus is enlargement.

## Enlargement

The matter of Conservatives championing the cause of 'enlargement' within the EU has a historical pedigree. During the 1971 debates about entry James Spicer floated the idea that the European community should include some African nations as 'associate members' along with the Mediterranean nations Spain, Portugal, Greece, Turkey and Cyprus.[212] Although some Europeanists were concerned in the 1970s in case it led 'to a slacking of the pace of integration', the issue gained additional pertinence with the collapse of the Soviet Union and the return of Eastern European nations to democracy.[213] Whilst pro-Europeans argued that the EU should concentrate on ensuring that its existing institutions and member nations were operating effectively, some sceptics began pointing to enlargement as a means of diluting the integrationists' agenda. The pro-Europeanists were divided. Chris Patten saw no contradiction between an enlarged Europe and greater sovereignty sharing in the future.[214] In contrast, Ted Heath was emphatic in his belief that it was 'quite wrong' to admit ex-Soviet bloc countries. They were economically too weak and lacked democratic stability. Here Heath was echoing the fears of EU Commissioner Delors, who feared Eastern Europe threatened the integration project. Heath was also adamant that British support for enlargement was counterproductive: 'the plain fact is that the other members interpret it as being the British way of blocking any further development within the Union'.[215] Here there was certainly a strong grain of truth. Nicholas Ridley had called for the admission of the EFTA nations and middle Europe as a means of widening, rather than deepening, the impact of Maastricht. The EU has sensed this danger. They have used the enlargement agenda as an opportunity to consolidate the integration process by ensuring the conditions of entry avoided opportunities for opt-outs. Furthermore, the concern that larger numbers at the Council table might hinder the decision-making process led directly to the moves towards the European Constitution. This has 'concerned' Eurosceptics, who again see a British-led development being hijacked by the federalists.[216] Following the failure of the Treaty of Nice (2000) to agree reforms to CAP, Hague warned that this must not be allowed to stand in the way of enlargement:

> For us, Europe could never end at the Iron Curtain that once divided East and West. We have always believed that a European Union worthy of the name had to include our fellow Europeans who were suffering under the tyrannical shackles of communism.[217]

This was put more succinctly by shadow foreign secretary Francis Maude: 'Enlargement is our moral imperative.'[218] Generally, although differing on motives, support for enlargement is a theme most Conservatives can agree upon, and this insistence on enlargement 'is a historic legacy of which we should rightly be proud'.[219]

What becomes clear through the various debates the Conservatives have had on European issues is that the pursuit of power can make people stomach policies they dislike. In the case of Europe many within the Conservatives were willing to take this course for the sake of pragmatism. Once it appeared that Europe both threatened the fabric of the power base they sought to protect and appeared to be an electoral liability, with the growth of explicitly Eurosceptic parties, then matters changed and the party witnessed a growing ideologically driven debate. Only time will show whether a return to government obliges the path of pragmatism.

# 4    The Conservative Europeanist

It has been noticeable that since 1945 there has always been a body of pro-European Conservatives willing to promote the cause of closer European integration. To define them as a group would attribute to them an artificial cohesion and consistency that has not been the case. Importantly these pro-Europeans have promoted the cause not because of direction from the party's leadership, but inspite of it. Since 1997 these Europeanists have been in rapid retreat, with few Conservative politicians prepared to admit to being 'Europhiles'.[1] This chapter will seek to examine the motivations, forums and personalities associated with promoting the Conservative Europeanists' cause. Furthermore, it will offer an assessment of why these Conservatives have lost the initiative and failed to convince the party's rump of the benefits of their cause.

## Definition

Who have been the party's Europeanists? Both in the media and amongst academics there has been a tendency to label elements, or individuals, of the Conservative parliamentary party as Europhiles. The rationale for this may be one of simplicity and clarity, but the reality is anything but simple and clear. Political scientists have recognised this problem and have sought to define further the typological characteristics of the pro-European elements of the party.[2] This still implies a degree of cohesion that does not exist, but it does offer the opportunity to make more realistic assessments of the relative numerical strengths of these sections within the party. Because of this lack of cohesion it would be best to consider Conservative Europeanism as a 'tendency'. It is important to understand that there are degrees of enthusiasm for Europe. To label a Conservative either a Europhile or a pro-Europeanist is just too vague, and does not allow for those who might subscribe to the cause because it is perceived as politically expedient at a given moment in time. When considering the views of those who might have been considered Europeanists in the period 1948–50 it is evident that a broad range of views existed, from those who expressed a preference for Britain sponsoring the continental process of integration to those who wanted to see British participation in a European confederal structure. Therefore some attempt to specify the necessary characteristics is required.

At the extremity are those who have championed either the cause of integration or its furthering (military, economic and political), who have been dismissive of the concerns about sovereignty, arguing that by 'pooling' sovereignty Britain has enhanced her world influence, and who in more recent times have advocated British membership of the single currency. It has been this element that has often taken a position in advance of the leadership. Sometimes this has been with the tacit approval of the leadership, as during the 1947–50 era or again during the late 1960s, when there has been political advantage in having a non-leadership voice for Europe. At other times, as in Major's position with the single currency, their advocacy has been awkward.

There is a more centrist position that takes a positive attitude towards Europe, sensing that the process of integration is inevitable, but which believes that British involvement and leadership can seek to revise unpopular elements, such as the Common Agricultural Policy, the Commission or the European Courts of Justice. At times these centrists have felt frustrated by the perception that the party leadership is not seeking to provide a lead to Europe from within this process. But typically this Europhile Conservative has been more willing to toe the line with the official leadership position, although since 1997 this loyalty has been strained and it is clear that the number of those who might be labelled as such has declined.[3] The difficulties associated with definitions and labels is perhaps apparent from two studies that have sought to evaluate the European typological layout of the Conservative Party. One suggests that 23 per cent of the 1997–2001 parliamentary party could be considered Europhile, whilst another suggests that 29 per cent could be seen as pro-Europeanists.[4] The difference in margins can be explained by examining the figures both offer for the 'undecided' or 'agnostics': figures that range from 17 per cent to 12 per cent. What is perhaps surprising is that between one-fifth and one-third of the parliamentary party could be deemed Europeanists after 1997. But what is also clear is that in percentage terms this is a relatively constant figure throughout the entire post-war Conservative Party.[5] Particular electoral intakes have helped bolster the Europhile numbers, as in 1950 and 1966.

## The historical Europhile

Although the emphasis of this study is on the Conservative European debate after 1945, it needs noting that a few individuals within the Conservative Party did champion the cause of a United Europe during the inter-war years. Their numbers were small, and it would be too easy to apply hindsight and to overstate their significance because of the names involved. Individuals like Winston Churchill and Leo Amery at one time or another during the 1920s and 1930s were attracted to the ideas of Briand and Count

Coudenhove-Kalergi.[6] The increased economic challenges presented by America, Russia and Japan had persuaded some to consider the possibilities of a European Customs Union. More generally this was an issue that drew the attention of Liberals and elements of the left, rather than Conservatives.[7] However, the attraction for some Conservatives in the late 1920s was the prospect that a United Europe would assist the balance of power by neutralising the German threat and would provide France with the assurance of security.[8] The difficulty was that much about the European idea was framed as philosophical abstractions, which only promoted distrust amongst many British politicians. When the Briand government actually put something into concrete form in a plan for a federal Europe in 1930 the British Labour government rejected the plan, arguing that it would damage empire ties as well as the prestige and authority of the League of Nations.[9] Furthermore, the question arises as to exactly how these 'adherents' saw Britain fitting into the model for European unity. In the Edwardian era, Churchill had been attracted to the federal ideas of Lionel Curtis. Austen Chamberlain saw merit in these ideas too and wondered whether they were means to deal with the Irish problem in 1918. Both these men in the 1930s wrote articles on Britain's relations with Europe, which with hindsight would offer a potential lineage with post-1945 thinking.[10] This also suggests that both men saw Britain as a sponsor of European unity rather than a direct participant.[11]

## The Strasbourg years

Whilst Churchill provided the figurehead for European unity in the immediate post-war years, behind the scenes a small number of individuals were responsible for trying to put substance to the Churchillian rhetoric. Many of them served as delegates to the Council of Europe and earned the subrogate 'Tory Strasbourgers'. Potentially they held a position of influence, having the ear of Churchill, but at this point they were the 'emerging generation'. The problem was that they proved incapable of convincing their colleagues of the merit of their ideas, and once the Conservatives returned to office most were given portfolios with only a domestic dimension. The difficulty to some observers was that they had created an expectation which was not delivered by the Churchill government.[12] The impotency of the Tory Strasbourgers must in part be explained by the struggle between Churchill and Eden over who had supremacy in foreign policy-making. The Strasbourgers were most successful whilst enjoying Churchill's tacit support, but once near to power caution set in, and it is evident that their influence waned whenever Churchill was persuaded to adopt an Eden line. This was clearly illustrated in November 1951 by the debate about Britain's involvement in the European army. It also exposed the divisions amongst the Europeanists and as a force left them in disarray. It was left to a small core around Amery, Smithers and Boothby to continue to try and promote alternative military and economic arrangements. There was a larger moderate grouping who hoped to see

Britain join the European Coal and Steel Community, but who were disheartened by the apparent indifference of Eden and the Foreign Office. This tendency included the likes of Beamish, Boyle, Hope, Maclay, Nicolson, Longden, Kerr, Roberts, Hay, Foster, Harris, Hallett, Pitman, Black, Fraser and Tilney.[13] But the majority of the party accepted Eden's view, preferring 'association' to 'participation' and the wish for Britain to continue to play a world role based on the Atlantic alliance.

Even amongst those closely involved in the early days of the European movement it is worth noting the differences of emphasis and interpretation. Churchill, with his 'three circles' (Europe, empire, English-speaking peoples), precluded placing the greatest emphasis upon Western Europe. Also, as a free trader at heart he was inclined to underestimate the degree to which old tariff reformers in the party resented US influence over Britain and the significance of this. Duncan Sandys considered the days of empire numbered and feared that if too closely allied with US Britain would become too subordinate to count on the world stage. His vision of union with Europe was based on an economic integration modelled along lines of the Marshall Plan that would eventually lead to military integration. In contrast Julian Amery was anxious to avoid a 'Balkanised' Europe. He saw a European Commonwealth as a counter to Russia and thought the issue might revive the party's electoral fortunes. What these differing interpretations illustrate is that the European idea was still fluid: the exact form and purpose of European unity remained very much a matter for debate. Even for those who could agree upon the objectives there was often less unanimity upon the means.[14]

## Edward Heath

With the death of Edward Heath in 2005 it was clear that his obituarists saw Europe as his legacy.[15] It was also apparent that during the last twenty-five years of his life his European views had almost become a caricature. Yet those who observed him at close quarters during the 1960s and early 1970s felt he 'had never taken an emotional attitude towards the Common Market'.[16] Such a claim does overly stretch credibility, but its uttering was intended to emphasise that Heath's enthusiasm was based upon incontrovertible evidence, and thereby to seek to dismiss the alarmist claims of his critics. Yet Heath and his biographers have made considerable claim to the importance of his pre-war and wartime experiences in helping shape his views, and it does seem likely that his early interest was kindled here.[17] Whilst his critics might lament his 'single-mindedness', his supporters agreed that Heath's mastery and detailed knowledge of the subject created a favourable impression.[18] Much has been made of Heath's maiden speech to the House of Commons on the Schuman Plan as having been indicative of his position. More crucial to Britain's relationship with Europe was Heath's appointment as Commons' spokesman for the Foreign Office, which in the view of one senior minister was 'quite decisive' in pushing an EU application to the top of Macmillan's priorities.[19] Once leader, his role in advocating European affairs was undeniable. A party official noted that Heath had 'a direct involvement going rather beyond his involvement as leader in other sectors'. Whilst this could be explained by his 'expertise' and background, political expediency and the prominence of the issue in the House of Commons, particularly during 1967, must be accounted for.[20] Heath's natural enthusiasm did not blind him to the political realities of championing the issue. It is clear his political antennae told him when to downplay the issue, as with the instruction that the 1967 conference foreign policy resolution should avoid any mention of Europe, and in 1973 when he appeared reluctant to champion the cause of MEPs, sensing that the issue only made a negative impression upon the electorate.[21] Likewise, he was often careful with his public utterances, wary of providing the anti-Marketeers with ammunition. Typical was his dislike for the word 'terms', 'which has a connotation of supplocation [sic] or even surrender', and his preference for using 'arrangements' instead.[22]

## The converts

The heyday of the Europeanists was the 1960s and early 1970s, during which time their key tactic was to win over doubters to their cause.[23] But just occasionally they succeeded in converting apparently implacable opponents. Understanding this conversion helps explain the potency of the Europeanists' arguments during this period. It suggests much about the changing perceptions and confidence within the party regarding Britain's place in the world order. The examples of Peter Walker and Henry Legge-Bourke are revealing for these very reasons. Peter Walker had entered parliament as MP for Worcester after a by-election in March 1961 and immediately sought to promote a Commonwealth alternative to EEC entry. He was part of the initial discussions that led to the formation of the ACML. His Worcester Association forwarded a motion to the 1962 annual conference stressing the likely damage entry would inflict on Britain.[24] Yet by 1970 he was a member of Heath's Cabinet and an enthusiastic supporter of entry. Why this change of attitude? Much has been attributed to the role of Heath. Walker had acted as his campaign manager in 1965 and as a result become exposed to Heath's way of thinking. The key reason was that by the late 1960s it had become evident that the pattern of imperial trade had been transformed, meaning Walker's original vision for a combination of the EFTA nations and the more important Commonwealth nations was now impossible. Australia and New Zealand had begun to look towards the Japanese market, whilst Canada's economy was increasingly an extension of the United States'. Britain now traded much more with Europe and in the 1970 negotiations the problems centred on West Indian sugar and New Zealand dairy produce. EFTA was by 1970 on the verge of collapse, with Britain and Denmark seeking EC membership. Walker now accepted that there was no alternative other than entry, and that as an EEC member Britain could help secure it as an outward-looking organisation.[25]

The diminishing position of the Commonwealth goes some way to explaining the conversion of Henry Legge-Bourke. He had been wounded during the Second World War and seen his brother captured in 1940. He had also lost his father and uncle in the Great War. Although he hailed from a different generation to Walker, Bourke was also firmly wedded to the party's imperialist tradition. He was an active member of the Suez Group. The long-term representative of Isle of Ely, Bourke had defied the party whip over the Schuman Plan, accusing it of supranational ambitions, and had been critical of the 1961 application.[26] His opposition was based upon a mixture of concern about the lack of support for the empire and concern that European entry would have an adverse affect on many of his horticultural and farming constituents. A former Regular solider in the Royal Horse Artillery, he was considered by many of his contemporaries to be a man of great integrity and honour.[27] By 1971 he had advanced to a position of seniority on the backbenches and served on the 1922 Committee. He appears to have taken the decision that his constituents should have the opportunity to explain their views on entry; hence his decision to hold a postal referendum. That so few bothered to return ballot forms convinced Bourke that Europe as an issue carried little pertinence and that therefore the arguments being advocated by the anti-Marketeers were clearly deemed to be irrelevant.[28] He appears to have satisfied his concerns that EU membership threatened British nationhood, and reached a conclusion that entry would restore its declining influence.[29]

Given the diversity of positions that can be taken within the spectrum of Europeanism, it comes as little surprise that there is an equally broad rationale that can explain a particular Europeanist's adherence to the cause.

## The legacy of the war

When considering the issue of Europe over a long chronological period it is inevitable that the significance of different factors will vary between political generations. One such case is the experience of the Second World War. Not surprisingly it was a much-cited factor in the 1950s and 1960s and still carried a resonance into the 1970s. Heath specifically referred to it in a television broadcast to the nation on 8 July 1971:

> Many of you have fought in Europe, as I did, or have lost fathers, or brothers, or husbands who fell fighting in Europe. I say to you now, with that experience in my memory, that joining the Community, working together with them for our joint security and prosperity, is the best guarantee we can give ourselves of a lasting peace in Europe.[30]

This appeal was based upon the direct experience of war: either the actual experience of battle and its aftermath scarred the individual or, as a result of the strategic complexities of fighting as a coalition, international friendships were formed that proved influential. In the late 1990s Heath accepted that his support for European unity had 'always been coloured' by his wartime experience.[31] For Willie Whitelaw, his visit to the liberated Belsen camp along with the trauma of a tank engagement at Caumont Ridge that left twenty-two of his tank battalion dead in July 1944 'almost certainly contributed', his biographers' believe, 'to his instinctive support for the idea of European cooperation, which he consistently regarded as crucial to the establishment of peace and reconciliation between Germany and her former enemies and victims'.[32] Others, like Percy Grieve, MP for Solihull 1964–83, who had spent time in France before 1939 and served with de Gaulle and the Free French during the war, saw support for the EEC as a logical progression of their experiences.[33] Grieve would serve on the Council of Europe and Western European Union from 1969 to 1983. Meetings with continental figures who would come to play leading roles in the politics of Europe after liberation were also profoundly important. John Maclay credited Jean Monnet, whom he got to know in Washington in 1944, with getting him 'very interested in the whole European thing', whilst Douglas Dodds-Parker became 'a convinced "European"' after dining with Spaak in 1941 following the Special Operations Executive (SOE) dropping his first saboteur into Belgium.[34] Of course, the 'war experience' has not been the sole preserve of the pro-Europeanists, and many Eurosceptics used the Allied sacrifices as justification for their hostility.[35] Although one academic analysis from the late 1990s offered the view that the Conservative Party has 'no hope of reconciling herself with the future until the generation that fought or grew up in the Second World War has passed', what has become more apparent in recent decades is that the memory of war continues to be used to promote the differing positions.[36]

Linked to this has been a persistent theme that had Britain pursued alternative diplomatic options before 1939, then war would have been avoided altogether. The 'failure' of appeasement should not be underestimated as a motivation for promoting European integration. An example of this would be Henry Legge-Bourke, who 'converted' to the cause in 1971. Feeling obliged to explain his new position to a constituent he referred to his belief 'that if there had been a Common Market in the 1930s and before the First World War, neither of the wars might have taken place because Britain's influence in Europe could have been far greater than it was then'. Similarly, Douglas Dodds-Parker took the view that he had 'always been convinced that had we such a meeting place [as the Council of Europe or WEU] in the 1930s, we might well have avoided the Second World War'.[37] Implicit in both these last statements was the belief that somehow Britain was in decline and that EU membership would help reverse this. It was also an explicit affirmation that Neville Chamberlain's appeasement of the dictators contributed to war in 1939. This is a legacy that the post-1945 Conservative Party has felt terribly uncomfortable about and consistently sought to disassociate itself from.[38] The anti-appeasement rhetoric can be extended to many of the leading proponents of closer European co-operation: Churchill, Heath, Macmillan, Boothby, Leo Amery, all of whom made considerable play of their credentials as internal opponents of Chamberlain's foreign policy, and each of whom has acted as cheerleader and manager for Britain's moves towards Europe.[39] This is a consistent tradition within patriotic Conservatism. Nor is it a theme that has diminished with time: thus, the Tory Reform Group's *Reformer* magazine was urging loyal Conservatives in 1999 to support the Britain in Europe campaign by reminding its readership thus:

> In 1940 over 80 Conservative MPs failed to support Chamberlain in a confidence motion. In doing so they not only helped save this country, they also helped the Conservative party from being associated irrevocably with appeasement.[40]

In other words, with the dawn of the twenty-first century Euroscepticism might be in the ascendancy but the pro-Europeans needed to draw upon the experience of the anti-appeasers and take courage to put country before party. Key to this Europeanist argument was the claim that European unity offered the means to contain Germany. But over time it was extended to claim that it offered a wider European peace. However, as the European Commission sought to establish its right to present a European foreign policy after Maastricht, some moderate Europeanists felt that it failed at its first challenge and questioned whether this diplomatic ambition was a step too far. As one notable Europeanists warned in the mid-1990s as Yugoslavia descended into civil war:

> What price now the claim that we have built a Europe free from war, when a part of our continent is convulsed in war, when European powers struggle again to bind the bleeding wounds in the Balkans?[41]

That the opening moves of the European integration process were conducted under the conditions of the Cold War also adds to the 'appeasement' analogy. It is notable that those who championed Britain's involvement in the late 1940s and the 1950s frequently pointed to the need to provide a bulwark against the Soviet Union and Communism, the idea of a 'third force'. In this sense the Fascist dictators of the 1930s had been transposed with Stalin. The Conservative leadership of the 1930s might have been unwilling to actively co-operate with the other nations of Europe to encircle Germany diplomatically and militarily, but post-war European co-operation offered an opportunity to learn from past mistakes and by acting as a collective bloc resist further Communist advances and safeguard Western democracy and capitalism. Yet until 1961 many in the Conservative leadership used the Cold War to reinforce the tradition of British limited liability.

## Political expediency and missed chances

Political memory is concerned more with perceptions than historical authenticity, and so just as the rubbishing of appeasement offered opportunities for political realignments the fallout from the 1956 Suez debacle offered fresh chances for reinvention. It was after Suez that a 'missed opportunity' thesis began to take hold amongst pro-Europeanists. The 1957 Treaty of Rome left these Conservatives questioning why Britain had not been one of the signatories only a decade after playing a key role in the creation of the Council of Europe.[42] For them it was clear that the Churchill Government of 1951–5 had welched on its opposition promises and as a result of a failure to actively engage in the integration process surrendered the leadership of Europe to the Franco-German axis.[43] An early example was Robert Boothby, who tendered his resignation from the United European Movement because he was disgruntled with 'successive British governments, which have so often led us up the garden path and left us there'.[44] The resignation was more a response to Boothby's belief that his former colleagues had snubbed him than a principled attack on the European leadership of Churchill. It was shortly withdrawn. Ultimately it was less Churchill than the negating role of Anthony Eden at the Foreign Office that was perceived as the real reason for Britain's reluctance to become involved.[45] Although historians have seen this as unfair, amongst contemporaries it was a difficult perception to erase.[46] Eden was horrified by the criticisms from former colleagues, like Maxwell-Fyfe and Macmillan, to the point that he considered threats of legal action.[47] The Foreign Office has often been perceived as a negative influence, driven by a distrust of the French. When attending the November 1968 Congress of the European Movement in the Hague, Ted Heath made a speech in which he said there could be no Europe without France. It was a speech poorly received by some Foreign Office officials and provoked one of Heath's advisors to lament that '[i]t had just become an article of faith that the French were impossible'.[48] The attacks upon the failed leadership of Eden and Churchill were conducted both in private and in public. The publication in 1960 of former junior Foreign Office minister Anthony Nutting's *Europe Will Not Wait* continued the theme, arguing that Britain had lost a unique opportunity by failing to assume the leadership of Western Europe since the war.[49] Kent activists heard Peter Kirk in February 1961 criticise both the Conservative administration of 1951–5 for having 'missed a priceless opportunity of gaining leadership in Europe' and his party's contemporary leadership, which 'he doubted even now … knew what the Government's policy was towards closer ties with Europe'.[50] Heath used the 1967 Godkin lectures to develop this thesis further, explaining that British non-participation in the 1950s was due to a leadership 'thinking in terms appropriate to the nation-state' and that they had failed to appreciate that newer forms of international co-operation such as OECD and WEU, though an improvement on the past, were not enough.[51] The question with this approach is that, given that so many of these critics had served under Churchill and Eden, why had they proved so moribund at converting government policy? Or is the more convenient expression that opposition offers the luxury of criticism?

Since entry was secured, the 'missed opportunity' argument has been used to admonish those reluctant to support the further development of the EU. 'Too often, Europe has been seen not as an opportunity, but as a threat', chided a group of senior Conservative former ministers upon the twenty-fifth anniversary of Britain joining the EEC.[52] Similarly, Douglas Hurd argued that Britain could not ignore the Maastricht process: 'we made that mistake in 1957, and later had to join something that others had designed.'[53] Once more there was the suggestion that somehow Britain's negativism about developments within the EU was going to prove costly as it would leave others to shape the developments that Britain would mostly likely in time actually participate in.[54] Julian Critchley warned John Major in 1996 against ruling out British membership of the single currency:

> He would be acting in the past tradition of British statesmen of both parties; namely to miss every bus but the last, and then spend time complaining that we were not in Europe at the formative stage of any policy.[55]

The choice of phrase here is interesting. 'Missed every bus' could be seen as a deliberate echo of Chamberlain's infamous press briefing that Hitler had 'missed the bus', and it was seeking to tar and shame Major with the 'appeasement' brush. Some Eurosceptics have been equally critical of the tendency to complain about European developments, only for a British government to eventually accept the arrangements.[56] Consistently being a tail-end Charlie appears a poor way in which to establish British influence. The idea that somehow Britain has missed the boat has established itself in the pro-European arguments, but linked into this was the argument that if Britain joined the EEC it would provide a forum for increasing the world-wide prestige both of Britain and of Europe itself. Thus Richard Luce felt able to reassure his Shoreham constituents in 1971 that 'Europe with the United Kingdom in her community would be stronger and more influential than Europe without us'.[57] Lord Dalkeith took this argument further, suggesting that British membership would help reverse 'a fundamental flaw' in the EEC, namely its inward nature, because Britain's Commonwealth ties made it outward looking and global, which would 'be of such immense significance in helping to weld the Western minded nations together'.[58] All of these themes were moulded into the party's policy statement on Europe in 1967:

Among the leaders of this new united Europe we can regain an influence in the affairs of the world and a control over our own destiny which changing circumstances have been taking from us. We have already missed too many chances to take this position which belongs to us; we must not wait any longer.[59]

From this also stems the argument about whether being part of Europe diminishes Britain's national identity. As one MP explained in 2000, Britain faced a choice of whether to remain isolated or seek to influence from within: 'That was true in 1975 and is true today: are the French any less French or the Germans any less German for being part of the EU?'[60] This has probably proved the most difficult element of the pro-European argument to articulate. The general ambivalence towards the EU since entry, and the frequent portrayal of European debates as being 'them' versus 'us', has meant that there is no sense of thinking that national interests are fundamental to the EU process. As one of Heath's European advisors explained in 1972:

To 'think European' is not to turn one's back on national interest and enter some realm of vapid theorising, but to consider how national interest can be furthered within the framework of the enlarged Community in a way which assures the interests of the Community as whole.[61]

## Reverse decline

Suez had shown the limitations of Britain's imperial position and demonstrated that Britain could no longer sustain a world role: militarily, diplomatically or economically. It had revealed the fragilities of the relationship with America and undermined one of the key post-war visions of Conservative foreign policy.[62] It resulted in Macmillan securing the party leadership.[63] Recognising that Suez had revealed Britain's economic fragilities and destroyed the pretence of world power status, Britain had now to find a means of improving her economic performance and creating a new global role. The challenge was to convince the party, and the electorate, that this was the only course of action.

Central, though, to the pro-Europeanists' motives was the belief that participation in European unity would reverse Britain's decline, both politically and economically. Churchill argued in 1948 that European unity presented 'an opportunity for Britain to resume on a new plane her moral leadership in world affairs'.[64] It is evident that by the 1960s many senior Conservatives subscribed to this verdict, and this was filtering down to the 'thinking sections' of the party.[65] Philip de Zulueta believes that Macmillan sought 'to join the European game in order to stay in the world power game'.[66] James Prior ascribes Heath's desire for EEC entry to being motivated by 'a very definite attempt to break out of the vicious circle'. Similarly, Robert Carr sensed that 'Heath was determined to lead Britain out of inertia and the EEC was to be the spring board'.[67] The 1970 application was certainly presented in terms that stressed the benefits of economic integration and political multilateralism. This represented a dilution of Britain's 'traditional' preoccupation with strength, security and uniqueness. This is perhaps typified by those who began to argue after the 1963 veto that Britain could further her position by viewing Europe as an opportunity for scientific and technological co-operation, with the obvious knock-on affects this would have economically.[68] The Anglo-French co-operation over Concorde and the Channel Tunnel were practical examples of this.[69] It was a theme Airey Neave, MP for Abingdon, was prone to articulate, although he did have business and constituency reasons for making this a hobbyhorse.[70] Heath's advisors in 1970 were warning that it would difficult to measure the longer-term benefits of membership, so consequently favoured articulating a futuristic computer-driven vision. If Britain combined with Europe, 'together we have the ingredients for our technological revolution'.[71] Similarly, it has been often argued that, economically, Britain and Europe combined could offer a new trading bloc. Within weeks of his becoming leader in 1965 the Carrington Study Group had presented Heath with a report on foreign policy. This report was pro-European and argued that membership of the EEC would secure Britain a political and economic role in a grouping that could rival the USSR and USA. It suggested entry was in 'the highest interests of Britain and Europe alike' and demanded that 'we should not be left out' of either economic or political union.[72] Similar arguments were heard within Macmillan's Cabinet and again in the late 1990s as the EU enlarged into Eastern Europe.

## Economics and markets

The economic arguments for closer British association with Europe have only really come to the fore since 1957. The primary argument has been the size of market that the EEC offered Britain. One of the oft-cited reasons against EFTA was that its potential size of market was too limited.[73] As Alresford Conservatives heard in July 1961, the economic argument was one of scale. The world saw four trading blocs, the Soviet, American, Chinese and a growing Europe. 'Amongst all these people what were 50 million British to do?' The UK needed to go into partnership and the EEC was the best option: 'it made commonsense to make common cause with the like-minded Christian nations in Europe.'[74] Similarly, Shoreham activists heard in 1971 that the UK risked being 'dwarfed' by rival economic blocs if she remained outside the EEC.[75] This argument became all the more pronounced with concerns about Britain's 'decline', and individual pro-European MPs were liable to point to the specific economic advantages entry might bring to their region.[76] Advocates suggested that throughout the 1960s the EEC economically outperformed Britain and had caught up and overtaken Britain in terms of standard of living.[77] When Central Office produced a pamphlet making these exact claims in 1971 this provoked furious rebuttals from the anti-Marketeers.[78] Statistics by their very nature are open to interpretation, but both sides of the argument never shied away from making their claims. The difficulty with using economic statistics in arguments is their intangibility to the non-specialist. This has meant that both sides of the argument have had to seek means of explaining to the wider party and electorate what this would translate into.[79] Pro-Europeanists were particularly worried in 1970 that the anti-Marketeers were making considerable headway with arguing their case because they had succeeded in making the higher cost of living attached to entry stick at the forefront of the public mind.[80] This led to stunts such as press conferences to highlight the cost of similar goods in a shopping basket bought in London and Brussels.[81]

Pro-Europeanists could also point to Britain's growing trading relationship with Europe. They argued that entry has increased Britain's export prospects, which in turn has increased the investment incentive. When defending the Maastricht agreement foreign secretary Douglas Hurd reminded his critics that 57 per cent of British exports went to Europe and that foreign inward investment was based upon the assumption that Britain was part of the EU.[82] Michael Heseltine suggested that this represented as much as 40 per cent of all American and Japanese investment into the EU being directed towards Britain. Further EU investment into Britain had increased from £5 billion in 1975 to £35 billion in 1995.[83] Similarly, Chris Patten chose a CPC Jubilee lecture to remind his audience that Britain had attracted the 'lion's share' of Asian inward investment because it was inside the European Union, arguing for it to be as open and free trading as possible, and for Britain to practise what she preached. He then linked this argument to a familiar refrain about leadership: 'we have been winning the arguments. Now is the time to lead the field, not to leave it.'[84]

## British leadership

If EU entry would reverse Britain's economic decline, then equally important was the argument that entry would provide a forum for Britain to exert her international prestige and leadership. Linked to this was a desire to contain Germany both militarily and economically. When the French Assembly rejected the European Defence Community (EDC) in August 1954 Macmillan revisited his Cabinet paper of February 1952 on the subject to satisfy himself that his prediction of failure had been correct: '"Federation" of Europe means "Germanisation" of Europe. "Confederation" (if we play our cards properly), should be British leadership of Europe.'[85] When the party considered proposals for Euratom in 1956 Thorneycroft warned that 'if we were not associated with them in some form, the leadership would pass to others'.[86] Again in 1959 Macmillan's Cabinet ministers were concerned that non-UK participation in the Treaty of Rome meant that West Germany was once more the economically dominant power in Europe.

One study group in 1965 was arguing that once Britain was a member of the EEC this would allow her to push policies that were in her own national interest, secure a large slice for Britain and aid the Commonwealth.[87] The leadership argument was used successfully during the 1960s and 1970s to undermine the sovereignty thesis of the anti-Marketeers. The myth of diminished sovereignty because of entry was countered by the argument that Britain was already dependent upon decisions taken in places other than Westminster and that if Britain was part of the EEC her leadership could mould some of these exterior factors.[88]

Since entry, the leadership argument has been sustained and developed. Conservative participation within the European Parliament and the European Commission has been pointed to, although these are hardly areas that strike any resonance with the British electorate. During the 1980s Thatcher's successes in reforming the EU budget and targeting CAP were heralded as examples of Britain reforming the EU for the wider European good.[89] Similarly, the SEA was heralded as transplanting British economic values to the wider Europe. In a sense Thatcher's infamous Bruges speech was intended to remind both Europe and, perhaps more importantly, a domestic audience that Britain expected to have a commanding voice in Europe's future development and that France and Germany would ignore this at their peril.

## Forums

If the differing motives for promoting a European position can be understood, it is also important to gain a sense of the environments in which European policy is discussed and formulated. Over the decades the Conservative Europeanists have sought to promote their message through a number of different forums, both in and outside the party. It is also necessary to distinguish between those which were policy orientated and those which were intended as opinion shapers, whether parliamentary groups, think tanks or pressure groups. Within the Westminster Parliament the subject-specific party committees provided a discussion forum within a hierarchical structure.[90] In policy terms the Foreign Affairs Committee (FAC) represented the apex of the pyramid, but it only discussed Europe 'from time to time' and 'usually only in general terms'. This was a committee the anti-Marketeers used both to press their cause and as an opportunity to quiz ministers in private. With European matters the committee's main value was 'providing an opportunity for sounding the opinion of Member who are not specialists on the subject'.[91] The presence of a whip at its meetings, and during Macmillan's premiership his PPS Knox-Cunningham, ensured that the leadership was closely kept in touch with backbench views.[92] The FAC would also on occasion request that a specific frontbencher appear before them or call external specialists to address them, such as Miriam Camps, who in February 1965 spoke to the committee on the current state of

European affairs.[93] Whilst the committee's main duty was to gauge and monitor opinion rather than be a conduit for the evolution of ideas, technically the committee represented the forum at which official party policy could be questioned.[94] The FAC was willing to sanction policy discussion on Europe, but usually only with explicit leadership encouragement.

In May 1966 the FAC created, at Heath's request, the Committee on Europe (Policy Research), chaired by Lord Balneil. Its main function was 'studying various aspects of British entry to the Common Market and producing papers on them'. No meetings were held between May and November 1967 until the outcome of the second application was known.[95] In December 1967 the FAC decided to reconvene the committee under the chairmanship of Richard Wood, third son of former foreign secretary Lord Halifax. It held its first meeting in January 1968 with the aim of studying 'the various possible relationships open to Britain while full membership of the EEC remains denied to us'.[96] Membership of this sub-committee included both pro- and anti-Europeans, but it is evident that Richard Wood restricted the opportunity for the anti-Marketeers to use this forum to challenge policy by both limiting the number of meetings held and securing a 'majority view' in support of his position.[97] In December 1968 this sub-committee was split into two: a NAFTA group and a Europe Committee that would merge with representatives from the defence and finance committees.[98]

The Committee on Europe was not the only policy committee considering European matters during 1967. The Commonwealth and Europe group, under the chairmanship of William Gorell Barnes, had been formed in May 1966. Its membership was not exclusively parliamentarian.[99] Given the party's imperial heritage this group had the potential to be a hotbed for anti-Marketeer sentiment, but in fact it proved the opposite. Its activities were considered 'extremely valuable' by pro-Europeanists within the Conservative Research Department.[100] Under its terms of reference the group was directed towards producing short papers 'of constructive use for the guidance of the party leadership'. It could decide to publish them; however, such reports were viewed as a contribution towards discussion, and could not be presented as official policy.[101] Its first three meetings heard from 'authorities' speaking on different aspects of European policy. At Heath's direction the group decided to direct their research efforts to the issue of sterling and the future of the sterling area. This led to the creation of joint working party with the Parliamentary Group on Monetary Problems in July 1966.[102] In May 1967 anxiety about duplication led Gorell Barnes and Balneil to agree that their respective groups should split the workload.[103] As a consequence the Barnes group began to consider the issue of 'association'. A sub-committee was formed in August 1967, chaired by David Bagnell, to study this issue. Its 'draft' report was ready in December, but to the annoyance of Barnes the 'draft' was forwarded to the leadership before the main committee had the opportunity to consider it.[104] This bore similarities to an earlier incident in 1960–1 when an interim report from the Agriculture

Policy Committee that had been drafted by its pro-European secretary Peter Minoprio was forwarded to the Cabinet before the committee had had an opportunity to discuss and amend it.[105] At the time this was interpreted as a deliberate attempt to circumvent the anti-Marketeer committee chairman, Anthony Hurd.

Outside Parliament a succession of organisations, both party specific and pressure groups, have drawn upon the views of Conservative Europeanists, assisted with publications and propaganda and provided a source for political journalists. Some have had very limited durations; others have, chameleon-like, adjusted with the political landscape. The earliest was the United European Movement (UEM). Duncan Sandys established it in 1946 on the instruction of his father-in-law, Winston Churchill. It was an inter-party group to promote the ideal of European integration in Britain and in Western Europe. From this emerged the British United Europe Committee on 16 January 1947. Labour refused to participate, fearing that it was purely a tool for Churchill to attack Attlee. When it was formally launched on 14 May 1947, with a rally addressed by Churchill at the Albert Hall, it became clear that Conservative and Liberal members dominated the organisation. Leo Amery was a vice-chairman, something it was hoped would convince the imperialists that the movement was not anti-empire. Robert Boothby also served on the committee. In 1948 it relaunched itself as the UK Council of the European Movement, co-ordinating with other groups in Western Europe. In March 1956 Julian Amery followed in his father's footsteps by taking the chair. The usefulness of organisations such as UEM and later Britain in Europe has not gone unnoticed by senior pro-European Conservatives. These groups have often been used as a means of softening public opinion to the European issue. As Macmillan suggested to Julian Amery in 1955 when he proposed Amery co-operate with his foreign office officials: 'There is of course no reason for the European Movement not to go a little ahead of the Government but it will be very helpful if both are travelling on parallel lines.'[106] It is clear, though, that elements within the UEM were less than enthused by the lack of support the Conservative government had been giving since 1951.[107] Indeed, after the UEM hosted an economic conference at Westminster in April 1949 Central Office received a stinging rebuke from a UEM delegate who complained about the 'almost disastrous lack of Conservative-thinking support' and warned that the Conservatives had taken the non-party ethos of UEM too far: 'It would, therefore, be disastrous if the British representation continued to be deprived of responsible industrial and right-wing representation.'[108] Marjorse Maxse, after reading the report, was moved to observe that the party 'had apparently learnt nothing from the lessons of The Hague and Brussels'.[109]

There have been times when the European Movement has been too advanced in its views even for leading pro-Europeans within the Conservative Party. This was particularly the case under Gladwyn and then Wistrich. In 1966 twenty-two Conservative MPs sat on the executive of the European

Movement, with Chataway, Hynd, Matthew, Rippon, Sandys, Julian Amery, Maurice Macmillan, Beamish and Howell being especially active. However, with echoes of the Conservative complaints about the League of Nations Union during the inter-war years, pro-Europeans were wont to bemoan the limited Conservative participation and express concern that businessmen and federalist intellectuals dominated the European Movement.[110]

Britain in Europe has been a haphazard organisation. Formed in 1957, during the 1960s it had a reputation for being a 'more active, intellectually more committed and politically tougher body' than many of its sister groups.[111] In the summer of 1969 it merged with the British Council of the European Movement to form the European Movement.[112] It was re-branded Britain in Europe in March 1975, and intended as the umbrella organisation that would co-ordinate the 'Yes' campaign in the referendum. Willie Whitelaw and Reginald Maudling appeared on the launch press conference platform alongside two senior Labour figures. Ted Heath had been invited, but was 'pulled', not at Thatcher's insistence, as was reported, but because of Labour's inability to find more than two ministers to attend.[113] It had in fact been organising its activities from December 1974 but was intent on not launching itself until the Labour Cabinet had declared its position. This was largely motivated by a concern to make life easier for the pro-Marketeers within the Labour Party and prevent the loss of the 'Yes' vote by alienating Labour voters.[114] Michael Heseltine and Kenneth Clarke shared a platform with Blair and Brown at the relaunch of the Britain in Europe group on 14 October 1999. Both men had during the previous summer made their intentions to support Britain in Europe clear. In July Clarke had written of the long pro-European tradition within the party and 'as a patriotic Tory I have consistently believed that on that big, broad issue, what he [Blair] says is right, which is why I will be fighting alongside him'.[115] Similarly, Heseltine told the *Express* that because the single currency was the 'over-riding national interest' he would be 'shoulder-to-shoulder with Tony Blair in the Britain in Europe campaign'.[116]

What is clear is that over the decades Conservative Europeanists have been active in a whole range of groups and committees with overlapping functions and memberships. Consequently the names of organisations like Positive Europeans, the European League for Economic Cooperation (ELEC), Conservative Mainstream, the European Union of Women and the Tory Reform Group have been associated with promoting the European cause behind the scenes to the party's wider activist base.[117] Since the Conservatives were voted out of office in 1997 it has fallen to the party's ex-ministerial grandees like Hurd, Whitelaw, Brittan, Clarke and Heseltine to provide the 'public' face of the Conservative pro-Europeanists. Either touring the newsrooms or writing for the media these people have been newsworthy because of their former position and because they are challenging the official line of party policy.[118]

When Macmillan launched Britain's 1961 application, party officials were anxious to gauge how the party was responding to the negotiations. Agents consistently reported that the young were supportive of entry.[119] This youth support has often been utilised during party conference season to ensure that critics are given a hard time. In both 1961 and 1971 the Young Conservatives sought to mobilise the Europeanist support. Many wore large 'Yes' badges at the 1961 Brighton conference and were responsible for taunting Derek Walker-Smith during his speech from the platform, having draped banners from the auditorium balcony.[120] Similarly, in 1971 Walker-Smith was barracked and every pro-European utterance from the platform greeted gleeful by a block of Young Conservatives in the audience. One reason for this support was offered by John Gummer, a Young Student Tory in 1962, who observed: 'young people want to take part in something that is above the level of ordinary politics. The ideal of the Common Market could fill this need.'[121] Another explanation for the youth wing's pro-Europeanism is young people have 'no emotional link with the Commonwealth'.[122] This might be truer for the 1970s, but the fact that a number of the Young Conservative national leadership came together in 1961 because of their desire to promote the Commonwealth and ultimately formed the Anti-Common Market League suggests that the youth movement merely reflected the broader divisions within the party; that is, there were two small wings either for or against EEC entry, with the majority taking an agnostic position, but one ultimately loyal to the leadership. Also, Young Conservative membership was in rapid decline. Figures suggested that a membership of about 80,000 during the early 1960s had declined by half by the 1970s.[123] With this decline in number came a fall in the average age of the membership, with many below twenty years of age, but it appeared that by the 1970s the leadership was more radical and trenchant in its views. The cynic must also wonder whether career advancement explains the position in the 1960s and 1970s, with many of the Young Conservative leadership wishing to appear loyal to the leadership to help their own chances of securing seats in Westminster.

Another forum that was attracting the younger generation of Conservatives was the Bow Group. Founded in 1950 by a group of university friends, by 1960 it had a membership of about 800. Many members subsequently moved into ministerial posts, such as ex-chairmen Geoffrey Howe and Enoch Powell. The Bow Group offered a platform for these emerging politicians to express their views through a range of publications, including the journal *Crossbow*. They weighed into the European debate shortly after the Treaty of Rome was signed. The reputation of the Bow Group had been forged by its research-driven pamphlets. Having championed the cause of decolonisation it was perhaps inevitable that Europe should become an issue for the group, especially as the post-imperial age required Britain to consider its trading role and relationship with the continent. In 1957 Russell Lewis wrote *The Challenge from Europe*, which argued the benefits of joining the Six because it would free up capital and labour. With Macmillan's application the group again returned to the subject, publishing in June 1962 *Britain and Europe*.[124] Published under the pseudonym William Russell, it was in fact a collaborative effort between five different authors. As a result the publications committee decided the 'draft had been patchy in quality' and therefore asked Russell Lewis, now working as a press officer for the EEC's Community Information Office, and John MacGregor to rework it.[125] The following month a supplement to the group's magazine *Crossbow* looked at the constitutional implications of entry.[126] There was a tendency for the group's pro-Europeanists to downplay the political implications of entry and enhance the economic benefits. As Patrick Jenkin argued for *Crossbow* in June 1960:

> We must recognise that unless were are prepared to gradually sink to the status of Europe's off-shore island, we must identify our interests with those of our nearest neighbours and form a single coherent unity which can stand on its own and compete with the other major powers. If this involves a surrender of sovereignty, then so be it. For that way, and that way alone, lies our future as a power capable of influencing world events.[127]

To imply that all within the Bow Group were pro-European in the early 1960s would be an exaggeration. The Bow Group was a mix of progressive pro-European economic liberals (the likes of Russell Lewis and Jock Bruce-Gardyne) and pro-Commonwealth progressives like Robin Williams. It was significant because it represented the young, educated middle class – the party's target electoral audience. It reinforced the impression that 'youth' was pro-entry and emphasised the role of the group in the intra-party debate.[128] Yet, it appears that the same divisions which afflicted the Young Conservatives and the party more generally applied to the Bow Group. The publications committee had only narrowly approved publication, by 20 votes to 18, of the 1962 *Britain and Europe* pamphlet; likewise, in 1963 a similarly narrow vote (21 to 17, with eight abstentions) approved *No Tame or Minor Role* by Sir Robin Williams and Len Beaton, which argued the case for remaining outside the EEC.[129]

What was clear was that whilst only small numbers of Conservatives during the 1960s were involved in the specific European pressure groups, many more were broadly sympathetic to the cause as a result of their association with groups like the Young Conservatives and the Bow Group. As a consequence this was the spur for the launch of an explicitly Conservative organisation, the European Forum, on 20 May 1969. Heath, Home and Harold Macmillan agreed to serve as honorary officers. With an initially restricted membership of 150 it was confined to opinion leaders, MPs and prospective candidates.[130] It quickly established an agricultural study group under Nick Ridley, Eldon Griffith and Peter Kirk.[131] At its 1970 AGM the European Forum resolved to re-brand itself the Conservative Group for Europe (CGE) and elected Tufton Beamish as chairman. An executive committee of twenty-six, including ten MPs, was established and individuals like George Gardiner (chief political correspondent for Thomson Regional Newspapers) and Geoffrey Tucker (public relations officer) were brought into the organisation.[132] Beamish worked closely with Central Office, requesting both money and the names of industrialists and City types who might be approached to join CGE.[133] The group was intended as 'an association ... for those enthusiastic for British entry' into the EEC.[134] During 1971 the bulk of the parliamentary party joined, so that by the mid-1970s it had nearly 200 MPs as members, plus a further 1,200 external individuals associated.[135] Its purpose was not to win over the anti-Marketeers but to concentrate on the 'doubters' and to consolidate the pro-European case. CGE provided the framework within which the pro-entry campaign in Parliament was able to operate. This campaign was largely co-ordinated by Norman St John Stevas, who acted as an unofficial whip. He was able to provide party managers with assessments and intelligence on the strength of the European parliamentary camp. There was the potential for some margin of error in these lists. For example, Stevas listed William Clark (MP for Surrey East) as a pro-European because of his membership of CGE. Yet the MP in question wrote to the party chairman indicating he had yet to make his mind up, as the final terms of entry were still not known.[136] Williams caused the CGE's Jim Spicer considerable discomfort during cross-examination in a 1976 select committee hearing. He challenged Spicer's assertion that the organisation was 'not part of the Conservative Party' and reminded him that many backbenchers were members not because of conviction, but from perceived necessity.[137]

The CGE was crucial to helping Heath win the parliamentary vote in October 1971. The group had held a series of seminars in the House of Commons on European matters; 'doubters' had been flown to Paris at CGE expense, whilst another party of MPs was sent to Brussels to see the European Commission in operation. In addition they arranged a series of dinners and conferences and ensured that all MPs, except for the antis, received frequent mail shots of pro-entry literature.[138] The advantage of CGE for the leadership was that as a 'front' organisation it allowed the European message to be pushed hard without necessary causing alienation from the government, and it allowed Heath to keep the whips in reserve as the 'ultimate deterrent' to rebellion. Beamish was considered to be doing 'an excellent job revitalising the old European Forum'.[139] He had personally campaigned for Ted Heath in the 1965 leadership campaign, had been a vice-chairman of the 1922 Committee, and as Knight of the Shires was seen as a crucial link for this constituency of the party.[140] As with the anti-Marketeers, CGE ensured its membership covered the relevant party committees and planted questions to ministers to ensure their case appeared in a more favourable light.[141] The group provided pro-European speakers for meetings around the country, published speakers' notes and reprinted applicable speeches for Conservative activists to absorb, as well as publishing the

*Tory European* magazine, which George Gardiner edited. In early 1971 CGE decided to establish three advisory committees to promote liaisons with the Young Conservatives, to co-ordinate activities with the women's section of the European movement and to keep the group in touch with developments in the agricultural sector.[142] The co-operation with the party's youth wing led to a fringe meeting on EEC enlargement at the 1971 Brighton conference addressed by Erik Blumenfeld (CDU), Bernard Bestremau (French Independent Republicans) and Hans Nord (Secretary-General to the European Parliament).[143] The responsibility of providing links with like-minded continental partners was not popular with Beamish. He admonished Anthony Royle in December 1971:

> I am a little unhappy to have continuing responsibility for keeping in touch with like-minded parties in an enlarged Community, as I simply do not have the facilities or the resources (we are stony broke at present) to do the work properly, and in any case I lack the necessary guidance.

Beamish was evidently resentful that he was doing the party's dirty work but not receiving what he perceived to be the necessary support, emotionally and financially.[144] Money was always an issue. CGE drew largely upon the support of the European Movement. In 1971–2 this totalled £4,524, rising to £18,000 in 1973, but was cut by half the following year. Beamish succeeded in raising £2,000 in donations in 1971–2. However, once entry had been achieved revenue generation became difficult, 'partly because the appeal had lacked a figurehead'. Even the appointment of a fundraiser made little impact.[145] Gilbert Longden, a long-term supporter of European unity who had been a Council of Europe delegate in 1953–4, replaced Beamish as chairman in 1973, whilst Miles Hudson, previously of the Conservative Research Department and an ex-advisor to Alec Douglas-Home, was appointed as director in December 1974.

When the issue of a referendum became a real possibility party managers were once more alert to the potential benefits of the CGE 'alongside and in total concert with the Conservative party, and, wherever possible, the European Movement. Only after a successful outcome of such consultation can the Conservative Group for Europe afford to return to a forceful independence'.[146] In fact this highlights one of the problems that the Conservative Group for Europe has experienced, namely that it lacks a perception of independence and is merely an extension of Central Office. This sense of frustration has become particularly true as the Eurosceptics have gained ascendancy in the party. For Anthony Meyer, still smarting at his expulsion from the party for supporting the Pro-European Conservative Party in 1999, the CGE 'has, alas, long been a toothless poodle of Central Office'.[147] In anticipation of the 1975 referendum, the CGE proposed a six-month expenditure plan that totalled over £34,000; the problem was that 'everyone ... wanted money for the European campaign, particularly the Young

Conservatives'. As a consequence it was agreed that 'European enthusiasts should be encouraged to make their activities self-financing so far as possible, merely applying for funds to meet the shortfall through the Party but not from the Party'.[148]

The fortunes of the CGE since the 1975 referendum have reflected the growth of Euroscepticism. By the 1990s it was estimated that membership had reduced to forty MPs. Heseltine was president from 2001 to 2004 and David Curry its chairman. It sees its role in the twenty-first century as being to 'promote Britain's vigorous and purposeful membership of the European Union and a Europe built on Conservative principles'.[149] Nevertheless its perceived value remains: John Major considered the group important enough to address it specially during the 1995 leadership contest.[150]

The concern for party managers has always been to prevent the divisions over Europe descending into schism, in the manner of the Corn Laws in the mid-nineteenth century. In recent times the defections of individual pro-Europeans to other parties suggested this wing of the party was the most vulnerable element. This potential danger was confirmed in May 1999 when former MEPs John Stevens and Brendan Donnelly launched the breakaway Pro-European Conservative Party and contested the Euro-elections. The 1999 European elections were the first to be contested under a regional list variant of proportional representation and both men were disgruntled that they had gained low positions on the official Conservative South-East list. They considered this to be a deliberate attempt by the party to exclude pro-Europeans. Their decision to break with the party was strongly criticised by Kenneth Clarke. Yet ten former Conservative MPs and MEPs, including Lord Gilmour and Julian Critchley, gave them support and were expelled from the official Conservative Party. That the Pro-European Conservative Party only secured 1.4 per cent of the vote in the elections suggested that they had failed to attract disillusioned Conservatives, and appeared as additional evidence for Central Office that Euroscepticism had electoral appeal. In December 2001 the breakaway party was wound up and its remaining members joined the Liberal Democrats.[151]

# 5 Selling Europe

'A pretty big thing to undertake'[1]

Only since its return to opposition in 1997 has hostility to further European integration become enshrined in official Conservative policy. Before that date the party's leadership had consistently portrayed it as the pragmatic party of Europe. Yet amongst its broader ranks the party has contained a significant portion who are at best indifferent to the European project and at worst openly hostile. Internal party assessments suggested that even those who toed the leadership line 'are unable to put over convincing arguments for joining'.[2] This poses the question of how, and why, the party leadership successfully pursued a European agenda against the wishes of many of its membership.[3] This would appear to confirm the perception that the Conservative Party is an oligarchy handing policy down from on high. The suspicion exists that the leadership has deliberately sought to keep the European debate at an 'elite' level, and has been fearful of allowing the issue to become a populist discussion point. However, it will be suggested that the leadership has often lacked courage over Europe, feeling inhibited by the perceived hostility of its own supporters. The leadership has not so much led the party as reacted. This has resulted in a position whereby, in the considered view of Lord Cockfield, 'public relations about Europe has a very long way to go, and perhaps more in the UK than most other countries'.[4] In order to assess this state of affairs, it will be necessary to explore both the rhetorical message and the practical 'selling' of that vision.

One of the challenges that the leadership has faced is that it has three distinct audiences to satisfy when explaining Europe: the Westminster parliamentary party, the wider Conservative activist base and the electorate, particularly Conservative and floating voters. Each audience has a slightly different agenda and their expectations and perceived usefulness to the party vary over the electoral cycle. A key complaint throughout, whenever there is a Conservative government, is that they are not doing enough to actively explain their European policies. What will be shown is that to an extent this criticism is true, but it fails to appreciate the complexity of the situations and the subtlety of the means by which 'Europe' is sold. There is also an additional very important point: the 'uninformed' complaint does not necessarily mean 'hostile'; something that the leadership have on occasion been slow to appreciate. However, since 1997 the issue has been further complicated by the electoral presence of the Referendum Party and UKIP, which has convinced some within the Conservative leadership of the validity of the Eurosceptic message as a vote winner.[5]

Before moving to consider the actual mechanics of selling the European message, the changing nature of that message will first be explored. Through the late 1940s and 1950s the Conservative leadership largely saw the issue of Europe as an external concern of foreign affairs. Churchill intended, despite the apparent rhetoric of his Zurich speech, that the French and Germans should develop European unity. Britain as a superpower would remain aloof from, but supportive of, the integration experiment.[6] This stemmed from a British uniqueness in having avoided invasion and retained an empire. Some contemporaries recognised Churchill's model for what it was: a compromise which appeased all factions of the party but that was flawed because of the assumption that no real decisions needed to be made between these different spheres of influence.[7] Churchill went to great lengths to promote the European message as non-partisan, but a policy that the Conservatives ought to consider. The consequence was the perception that Churchill was 'sponsoring' the unity process for both Britain and the continent.[8] This meant that the Conservatives could 'show that we as a party have our own conception of foreign policy', which was 'an improvement on that of the [Attlee] Government'.[9] It also raised the expectation, particularly on the continent, that a Churchill-led government would be proactive, promoting, and participating in, European integration.

When the Conservatives did return to government in 1951, both Churchill's and Eden's administrations were characterised by a general apathy towards integration, with Europe's purpose presented as providing economic stability and a defensive barrier for Western Europe against the encroachment of Communism.[10] There was a desire to see Europe continue along its integrationist path, tinged with an unwillingness to appreciate the continental objective of political union and integration. This would mean that once the debate began about EEC membership it would be defined in narrow economic terms rather than broader political parameters. To remain aloof fitted Britain's superpower role. It enabled Britain to downplay the loss of empire by the counterweight of the Anglo-American alliance. At least until 1956, as Alan Milward has observed, the consensus was that moves towards integration seemed 'at best irrelevant to Britain's economic self-interest and at worst a political nuisance which had to be tolerated'.[11]

The signing of the Treaty of Rome appears to have provoked little party comment. The persistence of a belief that Britain could best exert leadership over Western Europe by strength outside Europe remained. The leadership line was to suggest that it would do little harm to Britain, and if it did this could be dissipated by the creation of a British-sponsored free trade area.[12] In part this was because the Conservatives were still caught up in the fallout from Suez. One consequence of Suez was that it severely dented Anglo-

American relations. This brought into sharp relief a realisation that to reverse Britain's apparent economic decline she required new markets. The emphasis was still upon the need for means of association, rather than supranational organisations.[13] The creation of the Seven, EFTA, was presented as an opportunity: opening new markets whilst preserving Britain's imperial tradition.[14] Under Macmillan's leadership, particularly after the 1959 general election, elements of the party began to explore the possibilities of an application to join the EEC and to prepare to re-educate the party, presenting Europe as an alternative to empire.[15] It has been a familiar tactic to use the issue of Europe as a means of asking both party and country to reconsider Britain's world role. The Europeanists presented the fledgling EEC as a purely economic organisation that lacked a wider political agenda.[16] But they warned that non-British participation also possessed dangers for Britain.[17] It would enable Germany to dominate Europe economically. Yet these views were very much in the minority amongst the wider party.

Once the decision had been taken to seek EU membership the 'there is no alternative' (TINA) argument came to the fore: it not necessarily desirable, then inevitable.[18] The ability of the EEC to generate economic growth was vastly favourable to attempting to sustain the old model of imperial preference.[19] Membership might entail some institutional restructuring, but with the necessary safeguards negotiated the economic benefits would substantially outweigh the few domestic economic costs. The long-term federal and political union implications could be overlooked by defining the European ideal as an economic panacea for Britain's declining economy.[20]

The 1963 de Gaulle veto left the Macmillan government seeking to fill the vacuum. Macmillan was warned of the need 'to steady party and public opinion and to maintain business and international confidence'. It was agreed that the line should be taken that the policy had been the correct one and that the veto was only a temporary setback that was the fault of the French. Britain was committed to seeking entry and would continue to co-operate with Europe.[21] However, as the party's 1964 *Campaign Guide* made clear, with entry denied, Britain would seek to reduce tariffs in GATT and loosen trade restrictions, pledges that were at variance with the position of the Six.[22]

Back in opposition from 1964, the position remained that entry was the preferred option but that they expected Labour to make a mess of any application. The change in the party leadership from, first, Macmillan to Home and then Heath in 1965 was important in terms of the internal debate. The party was cautious over Europe during the 1964 election, sensing that the failure of the first application weighed against them. Interest re-emerged from 1965 with the selection of Heath as leader. As the chief negotiator during the first application he had established his credentials as a leading Europeanist. Wilson's 1967 application placed Heath in a difficult position. If the negotiations succeeded Wilson would have trumped him, but whilst they were being conducted it was hard for Heath to criticise without appearing to do so purely for his own party political gain. The tactic was to appear to be offering constructive criticism, to observe that given the Conservative's experience with the 1961–3 negotiations Heath had the superior knowledge and expertise, and to attack the economic competence of Labour, which was undermining the strength of the British application.[23] The purpose of the Conservative message during this phase was to state that Wilson's government needed to negotiate special terms that protected British agriculture, enhanced the nation's status and thereby were of benefit to the Commonwealth. Once it became clear that de Gaulle would again veto Britain the emphasis of the Conservative message switched to reiterating the need to continue seeking membership, especially so as not to let down the Five.

The party's 1970 election manifesto had only committed the party to open negotiations, but the message was that entry was inevitable and desirable. Heath had been warned in late 1970 that 'enthusiasm for the European idea has to be rekindled at the grassroots of the party', and there is plenty of evidence to confirm this verdict.[24] Recent party conferences had suggested the activists, after two successive vetoes, might prefer the consideration of alternative options. To this end Heath had been seeking to show public opinion that Britain would not join the EEC at any cost whilst trying to demonstrate to Europe, and especially France, that Britain was prepared to play a 'good European' role.

Once entry had been secured the leadership believed there was no great enthusiasm for Europe and was willing to sit back and take stock. There was an anxiety not to draw too great attention to the domestic consequences of entry for fear of an electoral backlash over a sense of Britain being penalised for late entry. Instead, after entry in 1973, the Conservative leadership presented Europe and its institutions as being ripe and ready for modification under British direction. In reality this was an illusion but the strategy suited both Heath and then Thatcher for electoral purposes. At the same time a sense existed that despite all the promises the European project was not yielding the anticipated benefits and there was a clear sense of introspection.[25] During the February 1974 election the party avoided making Europe a central feature of Heath's re-election campaign, despite advisors urging the need 'for re-stating the case on which we entered Europe'.[26] This was largely because Labour had moved away from a bi-partisan position to one that advocated renegotiation and a referendum. Pro-Europeanists within the Conservative hierarchy had become concerned that the achievement of entry was being downplayed. They 'feared people would blame Europe for everything that went wrong'.[27]

In the aftermath of the 1975 referendum, it suited the new Thatcher leadership to downplay European issues. When Europe did arise as an issue the themes were consistently that Wilson's government was failing to offer an alternative to the Franco-German axis, and was failing to address the economic consequences of membership, whether budgetary or the EMS.

The key issue was direct elections to the European Parliament, and despite internal debate about the method of election, here the message was simple: 'our aim is to be ready for direct elections, and then to win them.'[28]

The period 1979 to 1984 was witness to a continued awkwardness over British EEC membership. Europe was used as a domestic tool to distract from social and economic difficulties, high unemployment and the 1984–5 coal strike. Thatcher was unwilling to accept Britain playing a secondary role to the Franco-German axis. She argued that Britain should judge what its interests were and then defend them: in reality this meant restraining the Community budget and reforming CAP. The fragility of the British economy made these issues all the more politically sensitive. The thrust behind the British argument was that unless the EU reformed its finances Britain could not consider sanctioning future developments in the Community. EEC support for the Falklands mollified some Conservatives, but the reality was largely indifference amongst the majority.[29]

Having resolved the issue of the Community budget from 1984 there was a Conservative desire to impose free market ideals on Europe and rein in the bureaucracy of the EEC. This was presented in the manner of Britain being able to offer leadership to Europe. The ambitions to create an internal market were welcomed and interpreted as a willingness to place the European market in a competitive global market. The SEA was portrayed as a commitment to the free market and enshrinement of neo-liberalism, with the constitutional impact being downplayed. However, as the 1980s progressed there was a growing sense that Brussels was using the SEA and other EU legislation to expand rather than consolidate its remit. The pace of development towards monetary union was a sign of Europe's growing centralism and a desire to create a European state. Divisions now emerged within the leadership message, as some elements began to fear the political consequences of economic unity whilst others saw it as a necessary evil due to globalisation and the interdependence of the European economies.

When Major emerged as leader in November 1990 his immediate challenge was to seek to balance the factions in his party whilst taking his country to war to liberate Kuwait. The rhetoric towards Europe was less strident than Thatcher's, but a similar message of concern remained about the overly rapid development of economic union. The idea was that Europe needed a period of consolidation to adjust to the new economic conditions and to seek to seize the opportunity to widen the EU to embrace the countries of Eastern Europe so recently freed from Soviet repression. Widening rather than deepening was the preference. John Major had a difficult (near-impossible) task to try to balance the two wings of his party, whilst mollifying the Eurosceptics by sounding more Eurosceptic than he would have wished because of the threat they posed to his parliamentary majority. The confusion within the leadership message was evident in a series of media interviews given on 19 February 1997. Macolm Rifkind told BBC Radio 4's *Today* that on balance the party was 'hostile to a single currency', only to be contradicted by Kenneth Clarke, all of which provoked an *Evening Standard* headline of 'Rifkind v. Ken: Now It's War'.[30]

After 1997, the post-mortem suggested that the party had lost is core voters, some to the Referendum Party. Only if an explicit Eurosceptic stance was adopted would these voters return to the party. In a sense Hague's position was a compromise that stopped short of ultra-Euroscepticism. The message was one of opposition to the euro for at least the next parliament, whilst promising a referendum on the matter. Europe became one of the core messages of Hague's leadership with his pledge to save the pound and the countdown to the number of days left to rescue the currency from oblivion. The defeat of 2001 suggested to some Conservatives that this was too much and portrayed the party as right-wing extremists out of touch. Under first Duncan Smith, then Michael Howard and since December 2005 David Cameron, the Eurosceptic tone has not been diminished; if anything it has been consolidated, but it has not been given the same prominence. When it has been, the message is of the Conservative desire to see a more flexible, free market Europe, which would necessitate Britain renegotiating her treaty obligations.

## The mechanics of selling

Of the three constituent groupings that the party leadership must react to, the parliamentary party has always remained the most significant, and a disproportionate amount of resources, both in terms of time and money, has been devoted to it. Why? The nature of the democratic process is the simple answer. Members of Parliament as representatives of their constituents have the responsibility for determining the outcome of legislation. For issues of a more contentious nature, like Europe, the risk always exists for a backbench rebellion to inflict serious damage on the legislative programme. This John Major found from the Maastricht Bill onwards. To this end successive Conservative leaderships have considered it necessary to seek to 'persuade' the parliamentary party of the sense of its European policy before seeking to explain its position to the wider activist and electoral components. As Anthony Royle declared in September 1970 about the timetable for legislating for British accession to the EEC, the main objective 'is to achieve the maximum vote in favour of our policy in the House of Commons'.[31] The leadership has not overlooked the party's activists but usually this motive has a secondary aim of bringing pressure to bear on the parliamentary party from below.

Set-piece parliamentary debates and parliamentary divisions are the public expression of the party's views on a given issue. It is also noticeable that Conservative governments experienced the greatest difficulties over their European policies in 1971–2 and 1992–3 when their majorities were small and the dissenters believed that they held the potential balance of power. The size of a government's majority in the lobbies is taken as a measure of the administration's virility, and the lengths to which party managers will go in order to deliver the necessary majority are well documented.[32] They range from political persuasion and bullying and bribery from the whips to connivance with opposition rebels who might be prepared to abstain if a motion for debate is phrased in a particular manner.[33] Personal ministerial interventions to strike bargains with potential dissidents, such as Michael Heseltine's pledge to Michael Carttiss not to hold the final reading of the Maastricht Bill until after the Danish referendum, are an example. This particular act is credited with ensuring that Major's government secured the narrowest of majorities for the bill's second reading.[34] The threat of a political implosion can also be sounded, an appeal for party self-preservation often overriding the 'country' considerations of dissenters. Harold Macmillan took it upon himself on the eve of the two-day debate on the 1961 application to let a leading anti-Marketeer believe he would resign if more than thirty Conservatives rebelled against the government.[35] In the event Macmillan's 'whips produced a wonderful result'.[36] The risk that the Maastricht rebels ran was that if they removed Major from office it would have probably resulted in a Labour government pledged to even more support for Europe. On losing a key Maastricht vote in July 1993 Major called a vote of confidence and comfortably survived, if only to have to endure further political sniping. However, these events represent the public climax of what can often be a long drawn-out process of political persuasion.

The mechanisms and avenues open to party mangers for selling Europe to the parliamentary party were varied. The use of patronage has been a common feature. The promise of a promotion or position on a key party committee was a carrot often dangled by the whips to entice compliant backbenchers to ask appropriately worded supplementary or oral parliamentary questions or to table an early day motion. James Cran found himself offered a PPS position in December 1991 in a bid to deflect him from criticising the Maastricht Treaty.[37] Patronage could also be used as a means of education. Heath, when chief whip, took the view that membership of the delegations to the Council of Europe could only help persuade backbenchers of the value of Europe.[38] At the same time efforts were frequently made not to enflame the internal opposition by instructing senior frontbenchers not to make potentially provocative statements about Europe. Macmillan imposed such a gag on ministers in 1962, instructing them to keep their pronouncements on Europe vague and without policy commitments. This would ensure that the momentum was sustained without risking the loss of 'the general sense of confidence and advance'.[39] This avoidance of provocation was potentially doubled edged. The opponents and proponents of European integration have been equally willing to use parliamentary questions to further their cause, through either eliciting or imparting information. A blatant example was the question from Tom Boardman to the prime minister in July 1971. He asked Ted Heath for his views on the latest opinion poll that showed 45 per cent of the electorate favoured entry and were responding to responsible leadership. Heath's reply merely thanked his questioner for the information.[40] Equally the ministerial non-answer has often been to the fury of the sceptics. Foreign Office ministers were accused in late 1970 of showing a 'contemptuous attitude' to the House of Commons by providing answers to Europe-related questions that fell 'well below the standard of average common sense, sometimes totally failing to answer the question, sometimes being so off-centre that they are virtually meaningless'.[41]

One of the constant dilemmas has been about whether to freeze the critics of European policy out of the system. The inherent danger to this is that it risks creating a disgruntled element whose loyalty to the leadership may not be relied upon. It chances turning a split into a schism. Since 1997 this has been most likely to come from the pro-European wing. A breakaway Pro-European Conservative Party, formed by ex-MEP John Stevens, unsuccessfully contested the 1999 European elections and resulted in the expulsions from the party of former MPs Julian Critchley and Tim Rathbone. Pro-Europeans appeared on the same platform as Labour ministers for the relaunch of the 'Britain in Europe' campaign in autumn 1999.[42] Ex-ministers have not shied away from criticising policy pledges. More generally party managers have been more pragmatic. This must, in part, be because absolute enthusiasm for the European project has been limited and in reality the debate is polarised, with the majority agnostic. Edward Boyle, who denied that he could be labelled a 'Eurofanatic', recognised nevertheless that 'this issue couldn't be just put under the carpet' and ignored.[43]

Whilst the polarisation of the debate is a typical feature, it is not the rule. Amongst the parliamentarians this is usually most accentuated during times of significant legislation, such as the Accession Bill or the Maastricht Treaty. Leading anti-Marketeer Neil Marten bemoaned in 1971 'the sad feature' of the lack of serious contact between the party machine and the antis, which he suspected was 'all part of the strategy'.[44] Yet during the preceding period of opposition there had been quite deliberate attempts to include leading critics of Heath's pro-Europeanism in the policy-making machine. It was a window-dressing exercise, since the remit of these policy discussions was tightly controlled. Nevertheless there was willingness during this period towards a relative degree of co-operation in publicising the issues between pro- and anti-factions. Similarly, at Cabinet level the tactic of collegiality has been employed to good effect. Rab Butler, who was widely perceived as being one of the Cabinet members least enthusiastic about Macmillan's 1961 application, was given responsibility for chairing the Cabinet committee which overlooked the Brussels negotiations. The intention was to ensure that Butler, as the leading representative of the agricultural lobby, was committed to loyally supporting the government's policy. But also the expectation was that it would give Butler the opportunity to reassure himself that Britain's agricultural interests were being protected. His initial opposition was based upon his concerns that entry was not compatible with the needs of Britain's farmers. The experience initially did little to change his attitude, with him still believing that 'the simpler, down-to-earth farmers are all against it', with the implication that his agricultural Saffron Waldron 'seat is fundamentally at stake'.[45] His deliberate inclusion in a national speaking tour during 1962 convinced him that the farming fraternity was not as hostile as he had been led to believe. Consequently he was able to assure Macmillan during a private dinner in August 1962 of his full support for the application.[46] Analysis also of parliamentary statements on Europe by the Conservative parliamentary party during the period 1961–3 reveals that over four-fifths of the debate came from the backbenches.[47] This suggests that the whips were keen not to appear to be restricting debate and thereby used the Chamber of the House of Commons as a pressure safety valve.

Having the party machine at your full disposal is a significant advantage in promoting the leadership's policies. For Europe this has meant that at key moments the party's MPs have received briefs explaining the cause. *Common Market Topics* was distributed weekly to MPs from November 1962 until de Gaulle's veto.[48] During Labour's 1967 application the Conservative Research Department provided MPs with reading lists and fact sheets concerning the pertinent issues.[49] Although dressed up as 'offering facts fairly and accurately', these briefs sang from the leadership's hymn-sheet.[50] Similar publications were produced in 1971, and again during Maastricht.[51] In at least one instance the leadership has been prepared to intervene to hinder the publication of party literature it thought detrimental to its position.[52] An innovation in 1971, which was to be copied by the anti-Marketeers, was the creation of an advisory service run by Central Office for MPs, and adopted candidates, to help them answer Common Market questions.[53] The Research Department also had the responsibility of preparing newspaper articles and letters which could be attributed to senior leadership figures,[54] and of preparing articles for pooling that might be utilised by the opinion-forming newspapers and weeklies: local and national.[55]

Stage-managing the debate at other levels has also been important. The party's national and regional conferences offer an opportunity to showcase the party and policy.[56] During the 1970s Central Office deliberately restricted the access of anti-Marketeer groups to the fringes of these gatherings, even to the extent of suppressing the distribution of pro-European literature, so that the anti-Marketeers would have no grounds for complaint.[57] Similarly, the motion before conference for debate is chosen to reflect most positively upon the leadership. During the first application one activist complained that Europe resolutions were 'so ambiguous that both pro- and anti-Marketeers could believe they were meant to support their particular point of view'.[58] European debates have been the rare occasions when a motion has actually been subjected to a vote from the conference floor. This was a deliberate device by the leadership to demonstrate to the malcontents within the parliamentary party that the grass roots supported the official policy, and was a tactic that would be repeated in 1971. Equally, avoiding entirely debates on the subject has been another response. In March 1994 when the National Union's Central Council met in Plymouth, party managers refused to accept for debate any motions on Europe – nevertheless five constituency associations submitted resolutions in defiance.[59] Similarly, with the leadership anticipating de Gaulle's second veto in 1967 it was decided that the autumn conference resolution should be 'a general one about protecting British interests' as it was 'politically and technically wrong to concentrate exclusively on Europe at this conference'.[60] Publicity stunts were another matter. During the 1962 Llandudno Conference campaign buttons pinned on Central Office workers simply said 'Yes'; these appeared rather amateurish and did not meet with the approval of all.[61]

There has been a consistency to the strategies adopted. There has been a distinct preference towards educating 'informed' opinion ahead of public opinion. This was equally apparent as the party leadership took the decision to reposition the party's stance towards the fledgling EEC, for which it was recognised that the party would require a programme of re-education. The 1959 election manifesto had made no mention of European talks, but at Butler's instigation, as chairman of the Advisory Committee on Policy, the party began preparing party opinion for a possible EEC application as early as July 1960. It was decided to circulate a statement on the EEC and EFTA 'aimed at constituency chairmen, known industrial supporters, candidates and people of that sort' in advance of the party conference. The message was to be that Britain had to adapt, whether a member of the EEC or not, and that the success of the EEC was in the interests of both Britain and her Commonwealth and EFTA.[62] This was an example of an initiative to lead 'informed' opinion (as opposed to popular opinion) whilst the implications of entry were being considered. It is evident that the Conservative leadership was constantly alert to the issue of whether it could get its European policy through. What this meant in practice was that the mood was more important than the opinions themselves.

When the 1961 application was formally announced and the necessary parliamentary approval secured there began a limited explanation programme for the wider party, but again the emphasis was upon educating the opinion formers. During the summer of 1961 ministers had half a dozen private meetings with key party workers up and down the country. This included one at Church House, Westminster, where 800 constituency representatives heard Heath extol the virtues of entry. The intention was 'to build up an informed body of Party opinion throughout the country in support of the Government's policy'.[63] However, conscious that opinion did not universally approve, there was a deliberate downplaying of the European message, allowing non-governmental organisations to take the lead in selling Europe.[64] As the negotiations neared their climax, and in anticipation of a parliamentary battle to pass any treaty of accession, lists of names were complied of MPs 'who knew the Common Market case thoroughly and could put it over' and were willing to address public meetings and/or give television or radio interviews. Also, attempts were undertaken to try and present the 'British' view to European public opinion via articles for the European press so they could understand the British attitude and reservations.[65] All this was important because behind the scenes at Central Office Iain Macleod had begun preparing the party machine to re-brand the Conservatives as the party of Europe,[66] a necessary tonic after twelve years of continuous Conservative government.

In order to stage-manage these 'educational' appeals, the party has normally undertaken detailed preparation and planning. From the time of Macmillan launching his first application bid in 1961 there was a succession of committees whose responsibility it was to promote the case for Europe amongst the parliamentary party. The first of these was the Parliamentary Group on the Common Market, chaired by Bill Deedes, who had recently been brought into Macmillan's government as minister without portfolio because of his contacts within the media. The group was created in anticipation of the successful conclusion of the negotiations and the need to prepare the ground for the passage of any accession treaty through the House of Commons. It first met on 22 October 1962, meeting thereafter on a weekly basis until de Gaulle's veto, when it moved to alternate weekly meetings before deciding to dissolve itself in May 1963. The role of this committee had been to seek the best ways to diffuse information on the EEC to the wider party. One means was the *Common Market Topics* leaflet, the content of which was the responsibility of the group and which was distributed to all Conservative MPs on a weekly basis from November 1962. Deedes also took it upon himself to provide ministers with a short twelve-line summary of the Common Market climate and the line to take in public utterances.[67] Although the decision was taken to wind up the activities of the Deedes' group following the veto, plans were activated for further publicity 'on the nature of Britain's links with Europe, as this was so closely related to our insistence on maintaining these links; and on the real nature of the modern Commonwealth, as this was so frequently misunderstood by public opinion'.[68]

Following the 1966 general election Duncan Sandys and Nicholas Ridley formed the European 'Tactical' Group. This group of parliamentarians quickly fell into abeyance but reformed in June 1967 to meet weekly whilst the House sat, with the object of discussing 'parliamentary questions, debates, tactics, and other initiatives related to Europe'.[69] In early 1967 Lord Balneil proposed to Heath the establishment of the Co-ordinating Committee on Europe as 'a means of co-ordinating Party Parliamentary Activity on Europe'. Balneil envisaged that the committee could co-ordinate the tabling of parliamentary questions and the parliamentary party's general tactics. Balneil believed:

> We should try to subject the maximum of domestic legislation and government activity to this Common Market spotlight and so build up

an awareness both in the country and in Europe that we want to discover in detail all the practical implications of our joining the Community and push forward the Country's preparations for entry as quickly as possible.

Heath concurred and a small team assembled, with each member assigned responsibility for a specific area relevant to Europe: thus James Prior covered agriculture, whilst Antony Buck's portfolio was legal and constitutional matters. Other committee members included MPs Paul Dean, Patrick Jenkin, Russell Lewis from the CPC and Gordon Pears as secretary, and it met for the first time in June 1967. The committee did identify three areas where it thought further policy consideration was necessary: tax harmonisation; procedures for the implementation of EEC regulations; and the impact of EEC standardisation on UK common standards, particularly for foodstuffs and the pharmaceutical industry. Because of the anticipation that the second application would fail, this committee had 'not had a very active life since its inception'.[70] Further, one must speculate whether the duplication of 'effort' between these various committees detracted from their effectiveness.

Again in 1970–1, it is evident that, as Rippon conducted negotiations with the Six, detailed strategic planning back at Central Office was preparing for a successful conclusion and the need to sell the terms of entry. Once negotiations were concluded in June 1971 matters moved swiftly. Douglas Hurd, working in Heath's private office in Number 10, noted on 6 July 1971, 'This is [the] eve of European battle. It has a satisfactory feel, as of an army well prepared with its charge and cannonades, now impatient for action against the odds'.[71] The campaign to sell Europe began the following day when the White Paper on Europe was published and Ted Heath made his statement to the House of the Commons, which he followed on 8 July with an evening national ministerial broadcast on the BBC. On 9 July a Conservative Research Department (CRD) pamphlet, which was an anthology of quotes on the Common Market, was distributed to MPs and peers. On 12 July there was a press conference at Lancaster House. The message emphasised the key ideas that the British people were now recognising the validity of the arguments for entry, 'in particular, that this is the best way to maintain peace and increase prosperity'. There was no alternative: free trade, NAFTA and Commonwealth preference were unworkable in the modern economic climate. A final element was the idea that Britain would be part of a European single market that offered a challenge to the economic dominance of America, China and the USSR.[72] Hurd sensed that things were going well: 'The European offensive has captured more positions than we thought possible at this stage, and there is a danger of slip from now on.'[73] Next followed a Special Central Council meeting that Heath addressed in the presence of 1,500 activists and nine TV cameras.[74] The speech was recorded and distributed to the constituencies. The debating forum then became the House of Commons, as from 19 July the White Paper was considered.[75]

The issue of Europe can rarely be separated from other matters and during August the campaign experienced external problems in the form of the Upper Clyde shipbuilders and Northern Irish situation.[76] Prior to launching the campaign, the party's own internal ORC polling had shown that the cost of living was the major issue concerning the electorate about entry: 'if reassurance could be given on price rises, cost of food etc, the main hostility to joining the Common Market would disappear.'[77] During the summer and autumn of 1971 individual associations were encouraged to hold public meetings on the EEC.[78] The Conservative Group for Europe and the European Movement were asked to target 'those constituencies with anti-Europe Members and associations, and where it is therefore difficult for MPs to make pro-European speeches'.[79] The European Movement was active in those constituencies where mini-referenda on Europe were being held. In Beckenham this helped deliver a 'Pro' vote, but only narrowly and largely because they had 'whipped up some proxy votes'.[80] The final tactic was to make the House of Commons vote a free one. The leadership was not left in any doubt that many activists felt this was the preferred course of action.[81] But Heath appeared insistent, despite the objections of the chief whip, on the requirement of a three-line whip, even during the party conference. Senior figures, like Whitelaw, were establishing contacts with Labour pro-Marketeers and Heath was even presented with an analysis of how the voting would come out in the event of a free vote.[82] In the event the decision was announced just three days before the vote. This can be portrayed as a reluctant decision on Heath's part; however, it was more than likely tactical. As early as August Heath was being lobbied to support a free vote because the margins are 'desperately narrow. A game of bluff is going on'. As a consequence the free vote decision 'should not be made known until the last possible moment'.[83]

Once it became clear that Wilson planned to put his renegotiated terms to a referendum Conservative planning for a 'Yes' vote began in earnest. The party machine was placed at the disposal of the Britain in Europe campaign. It was a campaign co-ordinated in three stages: to educate opinion formers on Europe, to conduct post-renegotiation public meetings and then to conduct the official referendum campaign.[84] Between 19 May and 2 June six editions of *Yes to Europe: Conservative Campaign Notes* were issued.[85] Conservative activists were exhorted to participate in the campaign whether with Britain in Europe or as Conservative associations to maximise the Conservative 'Yes' vote.

One important element of 'selling' the European project has been the manner in which the media has reported the issue. Particular attention has been paid to this aspect, although even the best planning cannot anticipate the unexpected: as John Major discovered when his off-camera comment about the Eurosceptic 'bastards' in the Cabinet was picked up by the live feed.[86] Attention has always been paid to the press, but with mixed outcomes. During the first application phase the press stable of Beaverbrook's was a particular irritant responsible for stirring up considerable hostility to the EEC. Given the nature of Beaverbrook, with his direct editorial input, it was appreciated that 'no very useful purpose is likely to be served by operating on anyone but Lord Beaverbrook'. It was also thought that the *Guardian* under Alastair Hetherington would be unresponsive to cultivation because of its Gaitskellite tendencies; however, a range of individual journalists and editors such as William Rees-Mogg (*Sunday Times*), H.B. Boyne (*Daily Telegraph*), David Wood (*The Times*) and Arnold Foster (*Observer*) were thought sympathetic to the government's message and were invited for individual chats with the prime minister.[87] Similarly, from the autumn of 1970 there was liaisons between Central Office Press Office, the lobby and other journalists to ensure that the entry negotiations were favourably portrayed. Heath was also advised to keep in the 'closest touch' with the editors of *The Times* and *The Daily Telegraph*, 'who are known to be favourable to British entry'.[88] This attention was not devoted solely towards the national papers; considerable effort was applied to the regional press, either through providing suitable articles or by encouraging local activists to write to the local press extolling the Conservative message. Attempts to manipulate the television coverage of Europe also occurred. During the 1962 South Dorset by-election Central Office had sought to minimise the coverage of the anti-Common Market candidate Piers Debenham, placing pressure on the BBC's current affairs programme *Panorama* and a Southern TV 'debate' with the candidates.[89] On 13 July 1971 Reginald Maudling and anti-Marketeer Neil Marten were due to appear on the BBC's *It's Your Line*. The Conservative Research Department prepared a list of twenty-five questions, which were sent out to activists with the instruction to 'ring in and put them'.[90] During the 1975 referendum the Conservatives, on behalf of the Britain in Europe campaign, undertook to monitor TV and radio programmes on Europe. This covered three aspects: ensuring advance knowledge of relevant programmes; providing quick monitoring reports; and producing transcripts.[91] At the same time Conservative representatives in the Britain in Europe team were at the fore in the negotiations with the BBC about the broadcasting ground rules for the referendum, reminding them that 'the media had also a general responsibility to inform people as fully and objectively as possible'. They accepted that the nature of news reporting should be exempt from the need to provide alternative viewpoints, but again reminded the broadcasting organisation that fair balance was expected and warned that they would be monitoring this output 'carefully'.[92] When it came to party/media relations it was certainly a case of the Conservatives wanting their cake and eating it. They were prepared to legislate to enforce broadcasting impartiality, but were not afraid to place private pressure on the media companies, whilst fostering a partisan press. The attempts to spin the media have merely continued, with ever-greater resources devoted to the matter as each decade passes.[93]

There were moments when it was deemed insensitive for Central Office to be the source of propaganda. Activists did express anxiety that they were not being presented with a balanced picture and that the advantages were being overstressed and any possible disadvantages suppressed.[94] As one MP pointed out, Central Office materials were 'obviously designed to present the most favourable picture', therefore it benefited the party if non-partisan materials were distributed.[95] Consequently there was a close connivance between Central Office and European organisations such as the Information Service for the European Community and pressure groups like the European Movement.[96] The European Movement provided Central Office with one million free summaries of the 1971 White Paper that were distributed to constituency associations.[97]

Given that until 1997 the Conservatives have been the party of government at times when significant European legislation is going through the parliamentary process it is important to distinguish between governmental and party activities. Of course, the boundaries between the two are often blurred, but it is evident that there is usually a clear division of labour, although a commonality of purpose.[98] In the autumn of 1970 the Foreign Office had devised a two-phase campaign for 'selling Europe', which would be financed by the British Council of the European Movement (BCEM). Apart from finance it was expected that the BCEM would supply speakers for non-political gatherings such as the Women's Institute, the Young Farmers or Rotary clubs. These speakers 'must concentrate on the areas of the country where the Members of Parliament are undecided regarding entry into EEC. This latter geographical reason must be kept highly confidential and not disclosed to the BCEM'. Further, it was hoped that public figures and trade unionists sympathetic to Europe would be found for major public meetings. The Conservative Party was to be responsible for its grass roots and the parliamentary party as well as establishing contacts with Labour pro-Europeans. This could not be at ministerial level as it could open them to the allegation of collusion. 'It is important', warned Anthony Royle,

> that the Foreign and Commonwealth Office is not known to be inspiring, encouraging and helping to educate public opinion, but that the operation appears to be instigated by back-benchers on both sides of the House and by independent outside bodies.[99]

The same stance had been adopted in 1962 when Macmillan's government had been happy for non-governmental organisations, such as Lord Gladwyn's European Movement and Edward Beddington Behrens' BCEM, to promote the European message. This carried one important benefit, namely that their 'statements do not commit us'.[100]

The educational process was a difficult one to call. Successive Conservative leaders from Churchill onwards have been accused of failing to provide the necessary lead to educate public opinion about the benefits of closer integration. This was a charge laid invariably by those who were committed to the idea of Europe, but also by party activists.[101] Chelmsford Association's chairman in June 1961 expressed 'general concern' and observed 'that the facts were wanted and that so far none has been published'.[102] The National Union general purposes committee observed in May 1962 the general bafflement over EEC entry in the constituencies.[103] Likewise, a CPC report in 1992 noted that many activists make 'claim to insufficient knowledge and understanding of the [Maastricht] treaty'. Consequently 'there was widespread suspicion and even bewilderment over the treaty'.[104] This also rested upon the assumption that public opinion was fluid and open to a lead. The common complaint was that the pro-European camp at the electoral level lacked confidence in its case. As the agent for the Yorkshire Area concluded in September 1962: 'Even those who are in favour of entry are, in many cases, ill-informed and would make better propagandists if they had a deeper understanding of the issues involved.'[105] In fact the consensus amongst area agents in 1962 was that if given the facts the British electorate would be less dogmatic about the hazards of entry.[106] These evaluations certainly served to strengthen the hand of then party chairman, Iain Macleod, who was keen to push Macmillan towards using Europe as a means of relaunching the party's electoral fortunes. Anxiety that such behaviour would weaken Britain's negotiating position was the rebuttal, both in 1962 and 1970–1.

During all these negotiations, first for entry and thereafter for either renegotiation or further integration, successive British governments have shown considerable reluctance to sound the clarion call. Instead an appearance of hesitancy has been adopted, with the drawing of non-negotiable lines in the sand, whether over Commonwealth preference, British agricultural interests, budgetary contributions, the Social Chapter or the single currency.[107] The preference of successive Conservative leaders has been to seek to educate specific groups of the electorate, rather than the wider electorate, as to the benefits of its European policy.[108] This in part stems from a realisation that positive Europeanism is not necessarily an electoral vote winner, but also because of the nature of the British parliamentary system, with only a small percentage of Westminster seats marginal.[109] It is the opinion formers, especially business leaders and senior local activists, who have traditionally been courted. In 1961 a series of Common Market briefings were undertaken across the country with the intention of helping 'build up an informed body of Party opinion'.[110] In turn this body would bring pressure to bear on any recalcitrant Westminster Member who might think of opposing the leadership. Similarly, between April and June 1971 a series of regional Common Market seminars were held, typically seeking to draw an audience of between fifty and seventy-five specialist press, industrialists and academics.[111] These were funded out of Central Office's special projects budget centre, but it is evident that the party treasurers were anxious to keep expenditure on 'European' matters on a tight rein, presumably not wishing to see valuable funds be diverted to matters that might legitimately secure governmental funding.[112] Another tactic during the 1971–2 period was to identify the doubters within the parliamentary party and concentrate upon converting them to the cause. This the party did via the Conservative Group for Europe, which provided seminars, fact sheets and speeches and even took specific MPs for visits to Paris and Brussels so that they could see first hand the benefits of the European project.[113]

The period 1967–8 offers a useful snapshot of the extent to which Europe was 'sold', but also reveals the limitations of the selling strategy. Within the party 1967 was clearly the 'Year of Europe'. Aside from the internal policy reviews that were instigated, the CPC chose the summer of 1967 to concentrate its activities on Europe, with a Contact Programme Briefing. The Young Conservatives also decided to make the theme of their activities 'Britain and Europe' and kick-started this with a discussion brief issued in March.[114] The CRD also fulfilled its usual role of providing specialist briefings for the parliamentary party which intended to explain the aims, intentions and features of the EEC as well as addressing the key questions of how membership would affect Britain and the impact upon the Commonwealth. The thrust of these briefings was that Britain (i.e. the Labour government) could choose to negotiate special terms that protected British agriculture, enhanced our position and thereby benefited the Commonwealth.[115] There was a growing sense that Britain's future lay with advanced technology – this required large investments and markets, which only the EEC could provide. Therefore whilst publicly downplaying Europe the pro-Europeanists 'should continue with education about Europe within the Party and so ensure that the Party was well prepared to deal with whatever situations arise next year'.[116] The conference received twelve pro-NAFTA resolutions in 1968, suggesting that now was not the time to reactivate the positive European message. Following de Gaulle's second veto Gordon Pears and Eldon Griffith suggested it would be politically sensible for Conservative officials to 'mute' their support for the EEC. However, it was necessary to defend the party's European position from attack by the anti-Marketeers. Pears felt that 'there is a need for a new group, operating perhaps *sotto voce* within the Conservative Party, to act as a continuing nucleus for the Party's commitment to Europe' and to act as a point of liaison with outside pro-Europe groups and continental contacts. The matter was cleared with the chief whip, Willie Whitelaw, and a group of private individuals met on the evening of 14 December 1967 at the House of Commons. However, this group of 'Europeans' decided to move cautiously to avoid antagonising the leadership when Heath objected, fearing that now was not the moment to aggressively relaunch the European message.[117] This suggests that Heath was allowing himself to be led by perceived party opinion, rather than seeking to shift it. This assumption gains credence when in late 1967 the CPC considered whether to revisit the European issue. The conclusion was that the activists were 'fed up with the issue now', whilst distributing any literature to agents was deemed pointless because the CRD did not 'think any of them would read it and ... for most of them the Common Market is a dead duck'.[118]

The services of the CPC have been frequently utilised to facilitate discussion with party activists on European policy.[119] An early example was the three CPC discussion pamphlets circulated in 1948. These discussions took the form of briefing documents, with attached questions being sent to CPC discussion groups in the constituencies. They would debate the topic and produce a response for the director of the CPC to evaluate. The numbers taking part in these discussions were only a very small percentage of the actual party membership; however, the programme enabled leaders to appear to be in a dialogue with probably their most active, or at least most committed, party members. In 1971 Heath was deliberately using the programme to reinforce his stance *vis-à-vis* the parliamentary party. That the overwhelming majority of CPC discussion groups endorsed Heath's position sent an important message to any 'doubting' backbenchers.[120] Over 350 CPC groups, involving a higher than average number of activists, participated in this exercise. Analysis suggested a worrying issue for the anti-Marketeers since some groups were 'reluctantly in favour' because they were unable to see any alternative. Although it is unclear to what extent these discussion groups could actually influence party policy, activists were anxious 'that it does not appear that the Conservative Government are trying to bulldoze anything through Parliament'.[121] In March 1976 a pamphlet on direct elections to the European Parliament was distributed which aimed to remind activists of the party's *raison d'être*: winning elections.[122] Further, it is likely that the reports contributed to a sense of what the party activists were prepared to tolerate, and perhaps created a climate of opinion. This is evident in the 1971 survey, where a significant number of the groups called for the House of Commons to have a free vote on entry. The importance of tone-setting was particularly high during the 1990s. Leaks of CPC reports to the press consistently suggested to John Major that the party's activist base was moving towards an increasingly sceptical position on Europe, especially as regards the single currency.[123] Add to this the difficulties he was experiencing amongst the parliamentary party and it amounted to a near-intolerable pressure to steer a more Eurosceptic line. The CPC has been sensitive to its requirement to serve the needs of the leadership. This was evident in the early 1970s when the leadership was anxious to avoid giving any prominence to the arguments of the anti-Marketeers. This clearly upset some activists.[124] It reached a climax when the CPC's director Russell Lewis refused to publish a pamphlet co-authored by Philip Goodhart and Norman St John Stevas on the case for and against a referendum. The ensuing row drew in some of the party's most senior organisational and political figures, and resulted in Goodhart determining to hold his own referendum in his Beckenham constituency.[125]

Over the decades considerable expense has been devoted to preparing and distributing literature extolling the virtues of the European project. A distinction needs to be drawn between literature provided and funded by Conservative governments and that which came from a Conservative Party source. For example, during Major's administration several such pamphlets were published. In November 1992 a guide to the Maastricht Treaty, *Britain in Europe: The European Community and Your Future*, with a foreword by Major, hit the bookshelves and was immediately dismissed by one critic as a 'distillation of the truth', whilst in June 1995 Douglas Hurd oversaw the release of *Facts and Fairy Tales Revisited*, which aimed to dispel the myths associated with the EU.[126] Both of these were examples of governmental literature. Likewise in March 1971 the Heath government began a weekly distribution, via Post Office counters, mailing lists and requests from organisations and individuals, of a series of twelve free 'Factsheets'. This echoed the Treasury 'broadsheets' issued in 1961–3.[127] The 'free' pocket-sized glossy sixteen-page brochure, at the taxpayer's expense, which distilled the contents of the White Paper and presented the material in a visually appealing manner, raised opposition hackles.[128] The Foreign and Commonwealth Office in 1971 circulated the text of eighty verbatim speeches on Europe.[129] Between August 1961 and January 1963 Central Office published twenty-three pamphlets or leaflets on the Common Market. This amounted to a total distribution of 1,948,000.[130] The extent to which such publications are actually read by the wider electorate must be questioned, and many did end up being pulped. Yet their very presence enabled the Conservative leadership to claim that they were at least trying to 'educate' opinion. Uptake could be a problem. The Executive Committee of the National Union heard in April 1962 that only 79 out of 630 constituency associations had ordered the party's leaflet on the Common Market.[131] In July 1971, as well as making copies of the White Paper available, a series of 'simple' two-page leaflets entitled 'Europe and You' were prepared for purchase by the constituency associations.[132] Ironically Conservative Central Office (CCO) fielded requests for even more simplified explanations of European policy.[133]

At the same time, such publications invariably incurred the displeasure of the sceptics, who would rail against what they saw as 'costly and biased propaganda'.[134] Not that the ability of the sceptics to distribute their own literature should be underestimated. Between 1961 and 1963 the Anti-Common Market League virtually matched the volume of literature distributed by Central Office, ensuring that 1,910,000 copies of their publications were handed out.[135] Over the decades the sceptics have repeatedly tried to persuade Central Office to include their arguments in such publications, but the likelihood that the official machine would sanction such open debate is nonsensical. After all, the function of Central Office and its various appendages remained 'to present and argue in support of the Party's official policies'.[136] The reasons for these requests have been as much financially driven as they have been ideological. The expense of publishing pamphlets and taking press advertising space has been considerable. The British Council of the European Movement spent £16,000 in 1960 running conferences and publishing a glossy magazine.[137] The ACML spent nearly £40,000 on press advertisements in 1962, which ranged from full-page advertisements in the provincial press to coincide with the September 1962 Commonwealth Prime Ministers' Conference, to membership recruitment adverts in the national press and notices in *The Times'* personal column announcing meetings and advising on speaker availability. Much of this budget came from a single individual's donation and, given that this year represents the high point of the ACML, it suggests the difficulty of financing a campaign over the long term.[138]

One noticeable difference between the 1961–3 application and 1971–3 and then the 1975 referendum was the participation of the grassroots party in 'selling' the European message. Whereas during the first application there were widespread complaints about the lack of information filtering down from the leadership to the grass roots, from 1971, although these complaints had not entirely disappeared, it is evident that associations were taking the initiative in arranging public and private meetings on the issue of Europe. During the Macmillan application these sorts of activities had largely been confined to constituencies that were represented by MPs who took a particular, usually negative, interest in EEC entry.[139] In some rare cases, as in Liverpool, local activists improvised existing resources to produce a 'propaganda medium'.[140] In part the selling of Europe from 1971 was a result of exhortations from Central Office; it was also a consequence of the volume of literature that both government, Central Office and the pro-European movements have been distributing since 1970, which left activists feeling more confident about discussing the issue. Central Office ensured that agents and CPC groups could secure specimen programmes and lists of speakers should they wish to hold one-day or half-day conferences.[141] The agent for North Dorset offers an explanation. In July 1971 the constituency MP, David James, had addressed a special meeting of the association's executive committee. This was to be then followed by a series of fifty branch meetings on the subject. The agent felt that the activists' 'chief task will be to influence public opinion in their town and village'. He was confident that 'this is the right way to go about this task rather than plunging straight into a public meeting programme without first fully briefing and winning the support of our key party workers'.[142] It is apparent also that Central Office was willing to assist those associations that were represented by anti-Marketeers, as the fact that the list of pro-European speakers provided for a series of five public meetings around the Banbury constituency of Neil Marten in the autumn of 1971 testifies.[143]

## The electoral message

The election manifestos of a political party are the most visible public expressions of a party's policy position. Consequently the importance the party attaches to 'Europe' as a vote winner can be partly determined from the prominence, or lack of prominence, the issue receives in the electoral manifestos. This reflects both how the party perceives the saliency of the issue with the electorate and the leadership's enthusiasm for the matter. An example would be the 1950 manifesto, which was a disappointment to the party's Europeanists as it made no reference to Schuman or any other European supranational authority.[144] Of course, key developments in European unity, or the anticipation of such, have rarely coincided neatly with the British electoral cycle, the exceptions being 1970 and 1992. It is apparent, though, that the wider party has tended to take a position of agnosticism, and for this reason alone the matter has been downplayed.

This can perhaps be best demonstrated by the 1970 general election. Whereas Heath considered the success of the election as a mandate for EEC entry, the party's manifesto avoided any overt commitment and merely acknowledged a wish to open negotiations. This was unlike 1966, when the manifesto had promised to 'seize the first favourable opportunity of becoming a member of the Community'.[145] Additionally, in 1970 nearly two-thirds of Conservative candidates had made no mention of the issue in their election addresses, whilst one-tenth had expressed outright opposition, a similar percentage were favourable to entry with reservations, and only 2 per cent were wholeheartedly in favour. Likewise, only 3 per cent of utterances during the campaign were concerned with the Conservative case for Europe.[146] 'This was convenient but dangerous', felt one leading Europeanist; 'the positive case for entry went by default and the field was left open to the anti-Marketeers'.[147]

This rather begs the question of whether 'Europe' is a vote winner, either championing or opposing the issue. Macmillan himself was doubtful, sensing that the state of the economy determined election outcomes since this 'is what people worry about most'.[148] It is noticeable that, in advance of the 1964 general election, constituency association chairmen, when discussing the issues the campaign should concentrate upon, made no mention of Europe.[149] Of course, at this point the party was seeking to downplay the failure of their 1961–3 application. Some within the CRD urged this was not the time for 'the party, both individually and collectively, to present a European "image"'.[150] This advice was heeded, with only 11 per cent of Conservative candidates mentioning the issue in their personal election statements. For Heath the European project was a vital element of his electoral strategy. It suggested the party's commitment to modernisation. It was increasingly felt that this was essential to winning the new target voters, including the salariat and new meritocracy. The party could show itself to be discarding its old chauvinistic image linked to empire. The 1966 manifesto indicated a Conservative government would 'seize the first favourable opportunity of becoming a member' of the EEC.[151] Still only 50 per cent of candidates mentioned Europe.[152] However, Heath found in 1966 that a commitment to entry did not command popular support. Since opinion polls were conducted on the European question from the early 1960s it appeared evident that although a significant element of the electorate were opposed to Britain joining the EEC, the matter was, and to this day remains, low on the reasons for voting Conservative.[153]

So why did the party persist with portraying itself as the 'party of Europe'? When Heath welcomed rumours that France would accept British entry, Wilson scored political points by accusing him of 'rolling on his back like a spaniel'.[154] It is evident that some activists were critical of this European emphasis, particularly as it was felt to be an incomprehensible issue for many.[155] In advance of the 1970 election, party activists warned against overplaying the Europe card, which did not go down well with the electorate, particularly floating voters, and carried the danger of making Europe too central, which, if it failed, 'leaves a vacuum'.[156] Nevertheless the electoral importance of selling Europe has been significant for the Conservatives because until the 1990s it enabled them to show their relative unity in policy and personality terms at the expense of their Labour opponents. As Rab Butler famously told the 1962 Llandudno party conference: 'For the Labour Party 1000 years of history books. For us the future.'[157] The electoral tool of advocating a pro-European stance was evident in 1962 following Hugh Gaitskell's declared opposition to the EEC and again in the early 1980s, as the Conservatives were able to look on gleefully as the Labour Party fractured over its stance on continued EEC membership. The emphasis of the message might have changed, but the underlying theme has remained consistent. This tactic proved successful, whilst the chances of electoral success were either evident or possible, but as with the debates over tariff reform in the Edwardian era and the Corn Laws of the 1840s and 1850s, once in opposition after significant electoral humiliations the debate can become bitter and factionalised.

Heath's success at securing entry could not be heralded as such in 1974 because Labour was committed to renegotiation and a referendum and therefore was suggesting that entry was still not final. Less than a quarter of Conservative candidates made any mention of the government's success in this arena. As the historian John Ramsden has concluded, 'Europe was not seen as a vote-winner even in the hour of its achievement'.[158] This has been borne out by opinion polls conducted since entry in 1973, which show that in no single month does Europe have higher saliency than other issues like tax, law and order and education.[159] This suggests a paradox; on the one hand this lack of voter saliency encourages politicians in their belief that Europe is not important, whilst it would appear that British opinion is willing to be led by politicians on Europe. The success of the 1975 referendum suggests that a more positive appeal will encourage the electorate. Macmillan was unwilling to make EEC entry the matter specifically for a general election. 'Politically this is understandable', commented the MP for Wycombe, 'but morally it may not be so'.[160] Hugo Young, the journalist, has suggested that politicians' fears about the 'people' explains the reluctance of Macmillan, Heath and other Conservative leaders to promote an overtly positive European message.[161] Yet Europe has been presented by the media as a party political battle and a metaphor for internal political strife. The poor turnout in European elections suggests the lack of electoral affinity with Strasbourg. 'To most people', the MEP Peter Price complained, 'they are invisible'.[162] But if the electorate is not shown the importance of an issue, then the matter will continue to register low in their expectations. In continental Europe the issue of 'Europe' has since the 1990s become an everyday reality of life. The activities of the European Parliament and the Strasbourg secretariat are hardly worth reporting – Europe was something its parties accepted, it was not controversial and as a result the wider population was blasé.[163] One MP from the Major era speculated that in fact many of his constituents were 'comfortable with the idea of being part of Europe, at the heart of Europe even. But that's about it', whereas continental Europe 'believe in the European dream, they believe in a united Europe, they believe in what they're doing!'[164] Rhodes Boyson, an opponent of the Maastricht Treaty, sensed the public were 'bored' by Europe, citing the low turnout for anti-Maastricht candidates in by-elections, but drew heart: 'Maybe the British public, with their instinctive sense of history, have made up their minds that Europe is going to break up in any case, so the Maastricht Treaty is not worth bothering about.'[165]

This lack of electoral affinity can be clearly seen in British European elections. Electoral turnout has been consistently low; furthermore, recent research has suggested that European elections are considered of even less consequence than local elections.[166] Conservative European manifestos have had a tendency to concentrate on the national successes or policies of the party. The party committed itself in 1979 to joining EMS, demanded 'radical changes' to CAP and promised to take the 'necessary measures' to resolve fishing policy.[167] The 1979 and 1984 manifestos were drafted almost entirely by the Westminster machine, with only the briefest of lip-service towards senior MEPs. Whilst in 1979 this had not been problematic, in 1984 there was considerable private disquiet amongst the excluded MEPs. Geoffrey Howe, who chaired the committee that drafted the 1984 manifesto, can only remember that the process had been 'warmly commended by all possible factions'.[168] *The Strong Voice in Europe* 1984 manifesto, whilst structured around European themes, was mainly concerned with the government's domestic record. It claimed credit for restoring Britain's and Europe's economic well-being and spoke of Thatcher's success against the EEC over the budget rebate and the CAP. It warned: 'we do not support attempts to force the pace of institutional reform, especially in ways which might jeopardise the defence of genuinely vital national interests.' It lacked specific policy pledges, but talked up the themes of extending free trade, implementing EEC budgetary reform and defending the national veto. Pro-Europeanists were critical, feeling that the whole Conservative campaign was being fought on too nationalistic lines.[169] Similarly pro-Europeans were critical of the party's approach to the 1989 elections. Campaigning with poster slogans of

'Stay at home and you'll have a diet of Brussels' and 'Don't let Labour in the back door', it was seen by some as 'an appalling propaganda disaster' and the blame was laid at the door of Central Office.[170] Political expediency required the party's 1994 European Manifesto *A Strong Britain in a Strong Europe* to downplay their position on Europe post-Maastricht as this was likely to draw attention to the party's internal divisions. Consequently much of the emphasis was again on the national economic recovery they had overseen. This was not really the positive campaign party activists and MEPs had been urging, but party strategists deliberately sought to keep the campaign to a minimum and to exploit any sense of national pride derived from the fiftieth anniversary D-Day celebrations.[171] Furthermore, the unexpected death of Labour leader John Smith overshadowed the whole campaign.

The election of 1999 presented the party with a new challenge. Previously it had always fought the European elections as the party of national government, which made it all the easier to trumpet the triumphs of government, but now it was consigned to opposition. Euroscepticism was also in the ascendancy. The manifesto *In Europe, Not Run by Europe* reflected this mood. However, 'a notable characteristic … was that it was exclusively devoted to European themes – unlike almost all other Euro-manifestos past and present'.[172] The position of being in opposition meant that there was little choice but to dwell on matters European. Behind the Eurosceptic rhetoric there were rather more pragmatic suggestions for reform of the European Union alongside the explicit rejection of the single currency and the federalist agenda. There were a number of themes consistent with previous Conservative views on Europe such as the primacy of NATO; opposition to an erosion of Britain's veto; a desire to cut the EU budget and reduce Britain's contribution. There was support for enlargement and free trade and a desire to increase the European Parliament's powers over the Commission. These messages were emphasised in the 2001 and 2005 general election manifestos and again in the 2004 *Putting Britain First* European election manifesto.[173] The 2004 Euro-elections were the first test of Michael Howard's leadership and although the party succeeded in becoming the largest party for the first time since 1984, the victory was hollow as it only secured 27 per cent of the vote, its lowest ever share in a European election. The result also witnessed a surge in the UKIP vote from 7 per cent in 1999 to over 16 per cent.

## Electoral tactics 1997–2005

The 1997 election defeat was so comprehensive that it decimated the parliamentary party. The casualties were high profile, such as Michael Portillo and Malcolm Rifkind, as well as numerically common. The rump of the parliamentary party appeared disproportionately biased towards the Eurosceptics, although analysis suggests that one-fifth could be classified as Europeanists.

The impression of scepticism arose because many of the post-1992 rebels held seats that were to a greater degree the safest of the safe, a feature absolutely necessary to survive in 1997. In addition a significant proportion of those Conservative candidates who entered parliament for the first time in 1997 proclaimed Eurosceptic tendencies. A disproportionate number of pro-European or loyalist MPs had stood down in 1997, to be replaced by Eurosceptics. Over 200 candidates had declared their opposition to EMU during the campaign. Surveys showed a considerable proportion of the party subscribed to sceptic views.[174] The Conservative message of opposition to EU development plus the flexible renegotiation agenda espoused by Hague was a significant departure from previous image of the Conservatives as the party of Europe, which had been cultivated since at least 1961. Within this official position it is evident that Conservative positions on Euroscepticism ranged from greater EU flexibility, through renegotiation to outright withdrawal. The profile of the parliamentary party after 1997 explains in part the adoption of an avowedly Eurosceptic line. Equally important, though, was the party's own post-mortem of the election. It was accepted that 'Europe' has contributed to the defeat. The party's Eurosceptics blamed Major, seeing his acquiescence in the European process as a betrayal of the free market and the nation-state. The disaster of Black Wednesday, brought on by Major's support for ERM, had undermined the party's reputation for economic competence. In addition the conclusion was reached that the party had failed to appeal to its core voters and now it needed to tempt back the million voters who had voted for the Referendum Party. This analysis flew in the face of academic assessment that although the Referendum Party had fielded 550 candidates there was little noticeable impact on Conservative electoral fortunes.[175] Add to this the conditions that a small number of financial backers were imposing upon party policy, and that some sceptics wished to see an even more hard-line approach from party policy. Former MPs Roger Knapman and John Browne stood as UKIP candidates in 2005. In the 2001 campaign Hague was able to limit dissent from candidates by allowing them to issue personal manifestos stating that they would vote to keep the pound without having to limit this pledge to a single parliament.[176] The difficulty was that championing opposition to a single currency and a commitment to oppose further integration failed to chime with the electorate. Hence the continued poor electoral result in 2001. If there were those Conservatives who felt that a return to the political centre ground was the answer, then this would be disavowed by the election of Iain Duncan Smith, the Maastricht rebel. Now the party was headed by a politician openly and consistently opposed to Europe. The irony that the Conservatives now more closely resembled the Labour Party under Michael Foot in 1981–3, bitterly divided and in policy terms opposed to Europe, was not lost on some observers.[177]

# 6 The Conservative sceptic

'A confederacy of zealots and lurchers'?[1]

Hostility towards British association with Europe has a long historic pedigree in the Conservative Party. Sometimes associated with the 'Little Englander' mentality, since 1945 it has manifested itself under different labels, anti-European, anti-Marketeer and Eurosceptic. The personnel involved in Conservative Euroscepticism have changed over the past sixty years. Their arguments have evolved to take account of Britain's changed international position. Although there is no single Eurosceptic position the core themes of scepticism have remained constant. The debate has a natural division point, 1975. This was the year of the referendum on Britain's continued membership of the EC. Until this event the Eurosceptics were fighting to prevent either British membership or some alternative form of closer political and economic association with continental Europe. Thereafter, they were obliged to accept membership of the EC and work from within the system to seek to reduce the EC's encroachment. The apparent abdication of Thatcher to Europe with the Single European Act appeared to suggest that adherence to scepticism was a wasted venture. In 1986 John Biffen, an implacable opponent of EC membership in the 1970s, guided the Single European Act through its guillotine stage in the House of Commons. It suggested there was no future in scepticism. But just as it appeared that the SEA was to be the death knell of scepticism it proved to be its phoenix.

Who were these sceptics, what forums and tactics have they used to promote their arguments and why were they only able to capture the leadership of the party after 1997? As with Europeanism there are grades of scepticism: moderates, who have doubts but express these within the party structure; confirmed sceptics willing to occasionally rebel; and the irreconcilables, for whom nothing can be done to convince them of the good of the European process. Euroscepticism is largely perceived as a right-wing phenomenon, which is populist, chauvinistic and reactionary. This is due to the association of individuals like Gerald Nabarro, Anthony Fell, Ronald Bell, Enoch Powell and Edward Leigh with the cause. It has also attracted those from the party's maverick fringe like Lord Hinchingbrooke and Teresa Gorman. Yet on closer inspection it becomes clear that Euroscepticism is more amorphous and that there are no neat ideological left/right divisions.

## Leadership

A noticeable feature of Euroscepticism is that it has singularly failed to produce 'national' political figures who have come to dominate the political scene. The great upheavals of the Corn Laws, Irish Home Rule and tariff reform produced their political giants, Benjamin Disraeli and Joseph Chamberlain. The post-1960 Euro-rebels have had no such figures – although the 1970s produced Enoch Powell – whilst Thatcher in the twilight of her political career has provided an elder statesman focus. Instead the 'leaders' have largely been backbenchers with reputations as experienced parliamentarians yet who have had only limited junior ministerial experience. This confirms the impression that the 'battle' has been largely restricted to the Westminster arena. It suggests that scepticism has failed to convert itself into a movement of mass appeal.

With Macmillan's 1961 application the scepticism leadership centred around a quartet of Derek Walker-Smith, Robin Turton, Peter Walker and Lord Hinchingbrooke. By the late 1960s Peter Walker had converted to Europe and had been replaced by Neil Marten. Enoch Powell, following his Shadow Cabinet sacking in 1968, took a figurehead position from March 1969, aided by his lieutenant John Biffen. With Powell's defection to the Ulster Unionists Neil Marten assumed the mantle through the 1975 referendum and its aftermath. With the revival of scepticism in the mid-1980s Biffen acted the elder statesman, advising the likes of Bill Cash and Michael Spicer. Through looking at the views of the sceptic leaders it is possible to see the continuities in their arguments. This suggests that the intellectual integrity of the leaders views goes some way to compensating for their lack political gravitas. They are not necessarily rabid anti-Europeans, and as a consequence the party's leadership, whilst dismissive of their supporters, is often prepared to engage with them directly. Major distinguished between the likes of Cash and Spicer, whom he respected intellectually, and the extreme sceptics like Gill, Gorman and Marlow. Likewise, Macmillan and Heath drew a distinction between the intellectual force of Walker-Smith and Marten and individual mavericks like Hinchingbrooke and Fell.

Derek Walker-Smith had been health minister until sacked by Macmillan in July 1960. A barrister-in-law, Walker-Smith was from the beginning profoundly concerned about the implications for British sovereignty of any EEC entry. He was called second in the August 1961 Commons 'entry' debate, probably as recognition from the Speaker that he had tabled an EDM critical of entry on 26 July. His arguments articulated in that speech proved to be the rehearsal for future Eurosceptic debates. He questioned why sovereignty needed to be sacrificed. He was unable to accept that economic realism required Britain to join a supranational organisation rather than continue to favour intergovernmental operations. He forewarned that the EEC intended to become more than a purely economic union, and that political union was the goal, which risked Britain surrendering the power of political decision-making. His alternative was for the EEC to continue to exist, but with

Britain having no more than an association.[2] It was a speech that even Harold Macmillan appreciated as a very effective critique of the government's rationale for entry and its downplaying of the sovereignty implications.[3] In conjunction with Peter Walker, Walker-Smith published a pamphlet, *A Call to the Commonwealth*, that set out to present the alternative to the EEC. It argued that Conservative foreign policy should be seeking to strengthen the Commonwealth by using it as a link between first and third worlds, thereby risking neither Commonwealth nor national sovereignty.[4] He established the 1970 Group, a dining group for anti-Marketeers that used parliamentary tactics to harass the government during the accession debates. When he addressed the 1971 Brighton party conference to jeers of 'Cheer up' from Young Conservatives, Walker-Smith argued that the costs of entry were fact but the benefits were unproven, but evidently failed to carry conference as it voted 2,474 to 325 for Europe. He went on to vote against the 1972 Communities Bill sixty-four times.

Robin Turton had entered Parliament in 1929, was a former junior minister, and also minister of health from 1955 to 1957, and from 1965 was Father of the House. He moved the amendment in 1967 that condemned Wilson's application and secured twenty-six Conservative votes. He was chairman of the parliamentary wing of the All-Party Safeguards Campaign, launched in 1970. He rebelled sixty-eight times over the accession legislation. The strengths Turton and Walker-Smith brought to the cause came by virtue of their parliamentary experience. One contemporary observed: 'what made the campaign formidable was the leadership of older men who commanded much respect in Parliament and in the constituencies.'[5] Acting as their lieutenants were Lord Hinchingbrooke and Peter Walker.

Hinchingbrooke, since taking his South Dorset seat in February 1941, had been involved in disputes over the rearmament of West Germany, the role of the Soviet Union, Churchill's suitability as leader, Cyprus and Suez. He had resigned the party whip in 1957–8, and faced considerable internal opposition from elements within his constituency Conservative association. Many of his political contemporaries felt he was a habitual maverick, but amongst colleagues he was an individual held in considerable affection. When Macmillan announced his 1961 application Hinchingbrooke became secretary for the Conservative Common Market Group. He was dismissive of the economic rationale for joining, suggesting that EEC membership would discriminate against Britain's Commonwealth. He maintained that the Commonwealth was a 'great power of influence' and that such trade was important for Britain in helping preserve the peace during the Cold War. His public stance on Europe irritated Macmillan, who dismissed him as 'mad'. His accession to the Earl of Sandwich in 1962 necessitated a by-election. Hinchingbrooke transferred his support from the official Conservative candidate, Angus Maude, to the independent anti-Common Market candidate, Sir Piers Debenham. This successfully split the Conservative vote and allowed Labour to sneak the seat in November 1962.[6] Hinchingbrooke saw this betrayal of the Conservative Party as a matter of principle. Since he was so fervently opposed to the Common Market, it would be a dereliction of his duty not to campaign: 'The effect of that would have been to claim that this [the Common Market] was a matter only for the experts.' Membership of the EEC was the people's choice and he was confident that there were 'many Conservatives' who considered that his 'views on this great problem are the proper ones for a Tory to hold'.[7] Eventually a beneficiary of legislation, Hinchingbrooke renounced his peerage and reverted to the name Victor Montagu. He managed to fight the 1966 election as Conservative candidate for Accrington, but failed to secure a return to the House of Commons before he was removed from the party's official candidates' list in May 1971.[8] This was part of a purge instigated by Heath to reduce the numbers of anti-Marketeers on the candidates' list. Following the South Dorset by-election Hinchingbrooke agreed to become president of the ACML, a position he retained for more than twenty years. In finally standing down in 1983, although motivated by personal reasons he also admitted that he 'felt that campaigning against British membership of the EEC, after the wholehearted EEC endorsement of British action in the Falklands campaign was – or would have been – inopportune and counterproductive'.[9]

The reality in 1961–2 was that the anti-Marketeers lacked a leader with the sort of public standing capable of converting the parliamentary irritation into a major embarrassment. As Macmillan observed disparagingly, 'I see no Disraeli among them; not even a Lord George Bentwick'.[10] If the early Eurosceptics of the 1960s could have hoped to secure a 'national' figure, then it would have been Anthony Eden, now resident in the House of Lords as Lord Avon. As a former party leader, prime minister and foreign secretary his views would have carried considerable weight. Yet despite his sceptical tendencies they failed to ensnare Avon, probably due to his inability ever to quite cut his loyalties ties and commit to open rebellion, whatever the issue: appeasement or Europe. In common with most Eurosceptics, Avon was emphatic that he was in no sense anti-European. He was in regular correspondence with Robin Turton during the early 1960s, confiding that 'my feeling about the Common Market is that the whole subject should be treated as a business negotiation and not as a religion'.[11] Federalism was a major concern to Avon. He feared that if Britain joined the EEC 'it must be federation in the sense of one Parliament, one foreign policy, one currency etc. So far as I can judge events on the Continent of Europe, I do not want to become part of such a federation'.[12] Eden, however, limited his public intervention to the occasional speech. He caused considerable annoyance amongst the Cabinet when in July 1962 he addressed a Young Conservatives rally in Leamington shortly after the Night of the Long Knives. 'Absolutely disgusted', vented Reggie Dilhorne, especially

> when I remember how a great many of us kept silent during Suez out of loyalty, it really shocks me that he should, after absence from politics for

so long, and I imagine only knowing one side of the case, make that kind of speech.[13]

This was followed in the House of Lords on 8 November 1962 when, having warned of the likely implications for the Commonwealth, he counselled against embarking on additional negotiations that might provide the framework for federalism.[14] Avon was conforming to the phenomenon of a former party leader, and prime minister, providing discomfort for their successor on Europe that Ted Heath and Margaret Thatcher would perfect during the 1980s and 1990s. During the 1971–2 accession debate Hinchingbrooke tried to persuade Avon to intervene in the Europe debate, but was rebuffed on grounds of ill health.[15]

Neil Marten, MP for Banbury from 1959 to 1983, was not a right-winger but came from the moderate centre-right of the party. He had served as parliamentary secretary in the Ministry of Aviation from 1962 to 1964, where ministerial convention prevented him from speaking against entry. This led him to decline the offer of junior office under Heath. Concerns about the loss of sovereignty were core to Marten's values. He was unable to accept that once an EEC member Britain would be able to shape the Community in her own interests: 'the pressure for Britain to become a state in the United States of Europe will be on. The Common Market of the Six only really makes sense if it be federal with a directly elected parliament.'[16] He defined sovereignty as 'the exclusive power of the UK parliament to legislate and tax'. This was 'surrendered' by Section 2 of the European Communities Act, and he was dismissive of the argument that the ministerial veto in the Council of Ministers was sufficient protection since this was being 'whittled away'.[17] By 1971, with Walker-Smith increasingly occupied by his duties at the Bar, it fell to Marten to co-ordinate the activities of the anti-Marketeers through the 1970 Group and links with extra-parliamentary groups like the Anti-Common Market League. The group ensured that they covered each of the party committees, tabled hostile parliamentary questions and used supplementary questions as a platform for airing their arguments. Marten likened his role during this period to that of a 'lightning conductor' for opponents of the EC.[18] During the 1971–2 legislation, Marten opposed his government on sixty-nine occasions.[19] Anti-Marketeering was a family affair: both his wife and daughter participated in the 1975 'No' referendum campaign, and Marten was chair of the National Referendum Campaign.[20] There are contradictory views as to whether he got on with Powell. Simon Heffer portrays him as one of Powell's inner circle of advisors. During 1978 when Parliament was sitting Marten would meet each morning with Powell, Douglas Jay and Labour MP Brian Gould to plot how to prevent the EEC further impacting on Britain.[21] Marten's strength and weakness was his reputation for being a parliamentary 'gentleman', but this did not prevent him from experiencing considerable difficulties with his Banbury Conservative Association, elements of which sought his deselection.[22]

After 1975 Marten's concerns were direct elections to the European parliament, plans for a Euro-passport and EMS.[23]

Powell was the most high-profile critic and *de facto* leader of the parliamentary anti-Marketeers during the 1970s.[24] Powell, though, was less than consistent in his European views. He had voted against the party whip over the Schuman Plan, but as a member of Macmillan's Cabinet he had agreed to the 1961 application and he had voted to accept negotiations in 1967, something pointed out by Tufton Beamish during 1972 debates, to Powell's considerable irritation. Powell publicly made his opposition known in March 1969. Political expediency played its part, since he had been sack by Heath from the Shadow Cabinet eleven months previously. The cause then was his anti-immigrant stance, and to adopt an anti-EEC position was a logical progression for sustaining his right-wing credentials. He now saw EEC entry as a constitutional calamity, although at the party conference of 1969 he chose to concentrate on the economic costs of entry, arguing that it would push up food prices and adversely affect Britain's balance of payments. Whilst Powell could rely upon a core of loyalists his personality and air of intellectual superiority clearly did not endear him to all. It was a dilemma:

> A difficult chap to deal with, if he insists on keeping his cards so close to his chest ... his refusal to get his own team together may prove his undoing. You can't run a country on your own. ... [N]ot to have Enoch would be rather like 'Hamlet' without the Prince, since he has become the undisputed leader of the Parliamentary anti-Marketeers.[25]

Others were more affirmative: 'Powell certainly has not got now, nor do I think will he ever obtain' the necessary parliamentary support.[26] It was not so much Powell's arguments but Powell himself that prevented his assessment from gaining broader Conservative Party support, and it would not be until the late 1980s that his analysis secured the large-scale support of the party's neo-liberals.[27] During the October 1971 debate he spoke 'forceful[ly] in a set-piece way'.[28] Part of the difficulty that the sceptic camp experienced during the 1960s and 1970s was that they lacked a sufficiently charismatic, national politician who could appeal to the wider Conservative activist and voter. Enoch Powell was the closest that the sceptic movement ever had to a 'national' figure, but he was essentially a *persona non grata* after 1974 and it is clear that from the time of his dismissal from the Shadow Cabinet in 1968 he was too divisive a figure.

John Biffen, as a former leader of the House of Commons, became the grandfather figure of the Eurosceptics after 1992. Portraying himself as the 'Fagin of Euroscepticism', Biffen was considered to be 'one of the intellectual godfathers' of the anti-European movement.[29] His physical voting record matched his intellectual hostility to the EC. During the 1972 accession legislation he voted more times against the act than any other Conservative, even Enoch Powell.[30] He acted as the informal whip for the

1970 Group. His opposition revolved around a fear that the intention of the Treaty of Rome was political: 'it seeks to bind all who sign it into a common political sovereignty.' He was deeply critical of the sleight of hand that presented EEC membership purely as 'a calculation of trading advantage' and feared that the party's history, particularly the tariff reform debate, revealed the dangers of seeking to restrict free trade. Membership would mean that 'freedom and sovereignties are surrendered beyond recall and national economic advantages are traded away for intangible benefits which belong to some misty future'.[31] Perceived during this period as one of 'Enoch's men', he acted as a conduit for Powell.[32] During the mid-1980s Biffen appeared to reconcile himself to the need for Britain to work within in the European Union and provide the necessary leadership and thereby dilute the federalist and prote ctionist agenda. To this end, as Leader of the House of Commons he was prepared to guide the SEA through its guillotine stage. In fact, Biffen was returning to his pre-1970 position on Europe. In 1967 he had dismissed the alternatives to EEC entry as 'blind alleys' and argued that Britain needed to 'economically identify' with Europe. To achieve this Britain need to harmonise much of its industrial legislation with the Six, to encourage industry to view Europe as the 'natural domestic market' and to remain avowed free traders: 'Such a policy is undramatic in its initial ambitions, but is more likely to provide a sense of direction.'[33] By 1986 he expected that enlargement of the EU would further weaken the federalist agenda, therefore when this, and the SEA, failed to halt the integrationist momentum his concern for national sovereignty was re-invoked. He had led the Conservative rebellion against ERM entry in October 1990, dismayed that the return to the managed exchange rate signalled the further Europeanisation of British economy policy and an associated loss of parliamentary sovereignty.[34] Biffen became part of the hard core that opposed John Major's line over the Maastricht Conference. He voted against the government in November 1991 after John Major sought endorsement for his proposed negotiating position, and then joined the small-scale rebellion in December 1991 following the two-day debate to discuss the outcome of the Maastricht negotiations.[35] Overall during the passage of the European Communities (Amendment) Bill 1992–3 Biffen opposed the government in 48 per cent of the votes.[36] As a consequence Biffen's name was often one of those bandied about in the press as a possible stalking horse who might challenge Major for the leadership.[37]

A significant difference between the 1960s and 1990s is that the Eurosceptic leadership could no longer be dismissed as peripheral backbencher figures that rarely moved above junior minister rank. Throughout 1990s the 'doubters' were also at the highest levels within the Cabinet, fighting their corner in the debates and earning the label 'bastards'. These sceptics, individuals like Portillo and Redwood, had gained their first junior ministerial breaks in the last days of Thatcher and were seen as carriers of her vanguard. They had accepted the Single European Act as the opportunity to implement Thatcherism in Europe and were consequently appalled at the way in which the Act was used as a means of promoting further integration, but the final nail in the coffin was the humiliation of Black Wednesday. This single event shattered the economic rationale about the equability of European economic policy and suggested that the EU was merely a conduit for German economic domination. Whereas in 1961 Macmillan had, through a combination of skill and good fortune, been able either to isolate potential doubters or convert them to the European cause, from 1992 onwards the momentum had swung in the opposite direction and the tide of Euroscepticism was creeping towards the top of the sea wall.

## Parliamentary support

Although there is a tendency to generalise Euroscepticism as a right-wing phenomenon, it would be wrong to assume that the European debate within the party is divided on an axis of left versus right,[38] just as it would be wrong to assume that because Euroscepticism did not enter the political lexicon until the 1990s there was not a historical pedigree for Euro-hostility. Throughout there always been a hardcore 'old guard' of sceptical parliamentarians. Throughout the 1960s and 1970s they numbered into the thirties, tailed off after the 1975 referendum as old age and electoral fortunes took their toll, but began to regroup during Thatcher's battles over the European budget and the implementation of the Single European Act. At the height of the 1992–3 Maastricht debate they numbered between sixty and seventy, with about forty-five willing to disobey the government on nearly all aspects of its European legislation. Variously labelled anti-Europeans during the 1940s and 1950s, anti-Marketeers during the 1960s and 1970s and Eurosceptics from the 1990s, this grouping prefer to consider themselves 'Euro-realists'.[39]

So what was the motivation for opposing EEC membership? Unsurprisingly it was varied. What would be wrong would be to consider the anti-Marketeers as a single-unified element. Academic evaluations of the Eurosceptics of the 1990s have identified different ideological strands of scepticism and yet have spoken of the pre-1975 anti-Marketeers as if they were a single unit.[40] This has partly arisen because of how the Eurosceptics of the 1990s sought to portray themselves. It has been particularly important to their argument to suggest that in 1971–2 and 1975 the governments of the day were less than honest about the implications of EEC membership and that consequently the British people were denied the opportunity to discuss the loss of political sovereignty. Michael Spicer, when explaining the motives of the Maastricht rebels, describes the original anti-Common Marketeers, who have consistently held the view that Britain should never be part of the EU, as 'hav[ing] been joined by several other groups' who have specific concerns.[41] Many of the motivations ran concurrently through both the 'application' and 'membership' phases. There is a danger in attempting to pigeonhole individuals, especially as labels can be too restrictive, but what follows describes the broad categories that explain the motivations for hostility to European integration. Particular politicians may well subscribe to more than one of the reasons.

It is clear that since the 'application phase' constitutional concerns have engaged MPs: during the 1960s and 1970s parliamentarians such as Derek Walker-Smith, Ronald Russell, Neil Marten and Enoch Powell; and in the 1990s Bill Cash, Christopher Gill and Richard Shepherd. They placed the preservation of national sovereignty at the centre of their concerns. This may well be because many have a legal background. They saw the EEC as being more than a mere customs union, and feared that the hidden agenda was closer political co-operation between member states with a consequential loss in Britain's ability to govern itself. Richard Shepherd explained the highest form of democracy as 'self-government' based in parliament at Westminster.[42] Sovereignty has been widely debated amongst Conservatives since the first moves towards closer European co-operation. This was certainly an issue the ACML heavily promoted during the first application.[43] There was an additional strand to the sovereignty argument that stressed the 'uniqueness' of the British system, both politically and economically. This fundamental incompatibility meant that Britain had nothing to gain from joining an 'alien' system that was geared to achieving the aims of the continental Europeans. This line of argument could, and often did, mutate into anti-Europeanism. This was a sort of patriotic nationalism that belittled Europeans and appealed to prejudices of the electorate.

One ideological component of the anti-Marketeers' values has disappeared. This was the empire/Commonwealth lobby. Significantly this cut across left/right political boundaries, drawing together the likes of Peter Walker, Lord Hinchingbrooke and Henry Legge-Bourke. They placed Britain's economic and political relationship with her Commonwealth, especially New Zealand and Australia, at the centre of their concerns and feared that the protectionist nature of the EEC customs union would damage Britain's special relationship with her formal empire. An example of this stance was demonstrated as early as 1948 when Herbert Williams, MP for Exeter, denounced the pro-European stance of the leadership.[44] As empire transformed into Commonwealth the ideas for preference did not disappear. Ideas were floated for a form of North Atlantic Free-Trade Area which would involve some or all of the EFTA nations, the former Dominions and the USA. Certainly one of the tactics in 1961 was to try and outmanoeuvre the leadership by getting the party to place firmer conditions on Britain's entry, including commitments to EFTA and the Commonwealth which they knew were unacceptable to Brussels. The amendment put forward to the 1961 party conference during the EEC debate was typical of this strategy.

In some cases there were individual miscellaneous reasons for opposing EEC entry. Concern at the impact of EEC membership on British agriculture was commonplace, and in time this mutated into hostility towards the

CAP. It is suggested that as many as 100 Conservative MPs would have opposed EEC entry in 1961–3 if it had included terms harmful to British farmers. In the case of a number of the Ulster Unionists who were in receipt of the Conservative whip their opposition was based upon three fears: a concern that the economic situation in Northern Ireland would be exacerbated; a fear that entry into the EEC would lead to the unification of the North and South; anxiety that the Common Market was some form of popish plot. This idea of a 'papal' plot was occasionally detected elsewhere in the UK. One constituency agent was horrified to hear such observations, but found little by way of reassurance from his area agent, who confessed to having heard similar views.[45] In this context, lamented one senior Conservative figure, the appellation 'Treaty of *Rome*' was particularly unfortunate.[46] In other instances the opposition came from Members with specialist positions perhaps having connections with horticulture (for example Henry Legge-Bourke, who represented Isle of Ely), fishing (W.H.K. Baker, MP for Banaffshire) or those having particular specialist industries, such as shoe and boot, within their constituencies and fearing the adverse effect on these industries if the EEC were joined.[47]

It is evident that by the early 1970s the anti-Marketeers could be categorised as right-wingers supported by a number of Powellites and Ulster MPs, with two or three other individuals who opposed EEC membership on specialist grounds. Analysis of the 1971 EEC rebels confirms this interpretation; what is more, the anti-Marketeers were more likely than Pro-Europeans to dissent from the party line on other issues and there was a strong positive correlation between opposing EEC entry and opposing sanctions against Rhodesia and an even stronger one between opposing EEC entry and opposing the 1972 immigration rules.[48]

These policy positions become more significant if it is realised that there was no great dissimilarity between Conservative pro- and anti-Marketeers in terms of age and university education, or in terms of constituency majority, previous ministerial experience and occupational background.[49] However, because the Europe issue revolves around debates about sovereignty and matters relating to economic and monetary policies these cut across traditional left/right divisions in the party. The ongoing debate about the single currency has split the previously united Thatcherite free market grouping. Thus those who reject the single currency because it challenges nationhood and independence find themselves opposed by former Thatcherite allies who see EMU as an opportunity to enhance the free market. When comparing the rebels of 1961–3 and 1992–3 it is noticeable that they are a coalition between senior and junior parliamentarians. Just as Derek Walker-Smith and Robin Turton in the 1960s and 1970s carried 'respect' by virtue of their seniority, so too did John Biffen and Teddy Taylor by the 1990s. The problem was that these 'elder' statesmen were less susceptible to the patronage pressures of the whips. Similarly the attraction of 'raw' recruits such as Peter Walker in 1961 and Iain Duncan Smith and others who were part of the 1992 intake to the sceptic battle ensured that they attracted disproportionate attention *vis-à-vis* the reality of their political experience.

The party's changed composition during the 1990s and the legacy of Thatcher must largely explain the growing sense of Euroscepticism. In particular the intake of new MPs in 1992 was important, individuals like Iain Duncan Smith, Alan Duncan, Bernard Jenkin and John Whittingdale, who saw themselves as Thatcher's heirs and resented the betrayal of her legacy by a Europhile Cabinet. This new group was surprisingly 'independent', as the number who signed the 'Fresh Start' motion in June 1992 and who then resisted the pressure from the whips office to withdraw their signatures testifies. Their arrival at Westminster bolstered the established Eurosceptics. Now this grouping was a blend of the 'old guard', the 'Thatcher converts' and the 'disillusioned Thatcherites'. The 'old guard' were implacable opponents of European integration, having established their credentials in 1972 and 1975. The 'converts' had established their credentials criticising the Single European Act, individuals like Bill Cash, Nick Budgen, Edward Du Cann, Ivan Lawrence and Bill Walker. The final component, 'the disillusioned' included many of the 1992 intake, but also longer-term MPs, like George Gardiner and John Wilkinson (both of whom had ironically staunchly supported entry into Europe in 1972), who resented the manner of Thatcher's departure and feared that the Cabinet Europhiles were targeting sceptics in government. They used their anti-Europeanism as a whip to beat her detractors, and contributed considerably to the sense of rancour and ill will within the parliamentary party.

It is ironic that amongst these 'rebels' of the mid-1990s were a significant number who had early in their political careers been active supporters of British entry into the EEC. The ability to about-turn appears to be an important characteristic, but one not confined solely to the Eurosceptics. John Wilkinson had as a young MP staunchly defended Ted Heath during the 1971–2 accession debates. Norman Lamont had entered Parliament in a by-election in November 1972. His maiden speech was on Europe, likening the EEC to the Act of Union: 'mortifying to the pride at first, irksome occasionally, in the long run harmonious because it is founded on interest.'[50] Some appeared to purely point with the prevailing wind. Nicholas Winterton won selection for Macclesfield in June 1971 as an anti-Marketeer, only to win the September by-election as a pro-entry Conservative before becoming one of the Maastricht rebels of the 1990s.[51] Nick Ridley, as a result of his experiences at the Council of Europe during the 1960s, admits that he was favourable to federalism; whilst George Gardiner, who considered himself a life-long supporter of British EEC membership, as editor of the party's *Monthly News* was refusing to publish any articles by the anti-Marketeers and authored a pro-European pamphlet *A Europe for the Regions* (1971).[52] In April 1986 Gardiner told Parliament that he supported the Single European Act because he believed that only by European scales of economy could the EEC hope to complete with the USA and that the SEA would overcome national protectionism and required majority voting to ensure its functioning.[53] Even Richard Body voted 'with great enthusiasm' for Heath to make his 1970 application.

The question that needs addressing is why did these Conservatives reverse their positions and become stalwarts of the Eurosceptic cause? In Body's case the conversion was fairly immediate: he had initially accepted the government's case that EEC membership offered definite economic advantages, but as the 1971 debate progressed he failed to find 'any reasoned case to support our entry on economic grounds'.[54] The particular trigger appears to have been a series of Central Office pamphlets, which he felt carried inaccurate or misleading information. He thought it was unfair to give the impression that the British economy lagged behind the Six because they were in the EEC rather than due to the economic policy of the previous Labour government.[55] Body has subsequently become one of the irreconcilables to European union, publishing a number of books on the subject.[56] He even went as far as resigning the whip in solidarity with his fellow Maastricht rebels who had been disciplined. In the case of Lamont, Ridley and Gardiner the Thatcher experiment explains their reversed positions. It seems that the reflection of Quoddle in *The Spectator* in 1964 holds true: 'the Conservative Party always in time forgives those who were wrong. Indeed often, in time, they forgive those who were right.'[57] Ridley in his memoirs suggests that he increasingly saw Europe as a Socialist incarnation, which clashed with his increased support for non-intervention and liberty. The threat of Brussels corporatism, with the dangers of inflation and state intervention, challenged the very assumptions of the Thatcher revolution.[58] Gardiner fought his conversion battle behind the scenes in the corridors and smoking rooms of Westminster, helping engineer the ousting of the pro-European Hugh Dykes as chair of the Conservative European Affairs Committee and during the 1990s using his chairmanship of the 92 Group as a means of channelling hostility towards Maastricht and subsequently John Major.[59] For elements of the party this was comparable to treason and when Gardiner, in a *Sunday Express* article in December 1996, called Major a 'ventriloquist's dummy' operated by his pro-European chancellor Kenneth Clarke, Gardiner was faced with a successful deselection attempt by his Reigate Conservative Association. This was not the first time that a sceptic had publicly overstepped the boundaries of political convention. Anthony Fell, MP for Harborough and a regular speaker for the Anti-Common Market League, was forced to apologise to his leader, Harold Macmillan, after calling him 'a national disaster' after he launched his 1961 application.[60] The public acts of disloyalty have nevertheless adversely affected the cause of Euroscepticism: disloyal by association.

A healthy distrust of Europe did not prevent some of the leading Eurosceptics from seeking to 'experience Europe'. Both Derek Walker-Smith and Harmar Nicholls offered themselves as candidates for the European Parliament. Nicholls' motivation was 'to understand the ramifications' and the experience confirmed his belief that the European Parliament was 'not likely to pass the test of time' because it carried no natural affinity with the member states.[61] In contrast Walker-Smith took the view that now that the European Parliament was a reality it must be made to work, hence his willingness to serve as a delegate to the parliament from 1973 to 1979 and his unsuccessful attempts to secure a nomination in 1979.[62] Another example was John Blackburn (MP for Dudley West, 1979–94), who despite being an 'extreme sceptic' briefly served as a member of the Council of Europe from 1983 to 1984.[63] More recently Daniel Hannan, who acted a researcher for the Eurosceptics in the run-up to the 1996 Inter-Governmental Conference and also served the European Research Group, become an MEP in 1999 for South East England.

It is in the nature of the British political system, and its adherence to party, that there can be considerable difficulty distinguishing between the public and private attitudes of politicians on a given topic. Studies have shown that there is often an imbalance between those members of the Conservative Party prepared to publicly challenge a given policy of their leadership and the views of dissent that a larger proportion are prepared to think in private. Elected Conservative MPs are naturally reluctant to give public notice of opposition to central planks of their own government's policy and to appear to be taking a leading role in mounting a militant campaign against it. The explanations for this are numerous, but what it suggests is that there is a larger body of doubters over European policy than is implied by the numbers prepared to cross-vote, or abstain in the lobbies or put their name to critical EDMs. This is true of whatever period is considered. In 1971 the whips, the pro-Europeans and the anti-Marketeers all carried out assessments of the views of the parliamentary party. It appears that in addition to those opposed to entry there were a further seventy to seventy-five MPs who had doubts about the wisdom of entry. About half of these were thought to be 'in doubt with a bias against' entry. The reasons for these doubts were varied, ranging from concerns about public opinion through to personal animosity. What was not in doubt was that both sides of the argument considered this group to be 'of vital importance', and the government particularly went to considerable efforts to convince them otherwise, to the extent that by August they estimated that all bar eleven had been converted to the government's position.[64] A similar picture of wider private doubt emerges from an analysis of the attitude of Conservative parliamentarians (both Westminster and European) as to their views on Europe in the summer of 1994. The authors of this study observed that in key parliamentary divisions over Maastricht between 10 and 20 per cent of the parliamentary party were prepared to defy the whips (either cross-voting or abstaining). However, privately the hostility was much stronger: 32 per cent of respondents thought that the disadvantages of EU membership outweighed the advantages. On EMU and a European Central Bank, whilst only 9 per cent were prepared to defy in the lobbies, 61 and 64 per cent, respectively, were privately against such developments.[65]

It is evident that the levels of concern about European integration have always been more widespread than figures for dissent registered in parliamentary rebellions suggest. Throughout the period 1961–5 there was a group of 30–40 Conservative anti-Marketeer backbenchers, with a core of 12–15 'last ditchers': 'a substantial but containable minority' was the conclusion of one 'secret' party evaluation.[66] From the Maastricht debates it became apparent that there were around 50 Eurosceptics willing to publicly rebel, of whom 20–35 could be considered 'last ditchers', and 9 even prepared to put the issue before loyalty to the party. In addition there were probably a further 80 undeclared fellow travellers.[67] Opposed to them were around 90 committed integrationists, with the balance of 130 MPs prepared 'to go whichever the wind is blowing'.[68] Whereas during the 1971–2 parliamentary session 38 MPs rebelled on one occasion, this compared to 53 MPs rebelling during the 1992–3 session over Maastricht; whilst 36 MPs rebelled between two and nine times for the accession debates, compared to 117 MPs rebelling between two and ten times over Maastricht Bill. It is also evident that the parliamentary party of 1992/3 was more rebellious in general than its counterpart in 1971–2.[69] Despite this, Major's government did not witness a growth in more widespread factionalism over non-European issues by a disgruntled right. The rebellions over VAT on fuel and the pit closure programme appealed more to the left and the involvement of the Euro-rebels was only marginal. It was clear that as soon as the debate returned to domestic issues the usual left/right or wet/dry divisions emerged. After 1997 at least three-quarters of the parliamentary party embraced a form of Euroscepticism, and the party's choice of leaders, along with its 1997, 2001 and 2005 election manifestos, reinforced this message.

## Activist base

The European debate has signally failed to capture the interest of the wider British electorate. This is evidenced by the poor turnout in European elections and the weak showing at general elections of single-issue 'European' candidates. The Eurosceptics have perhaps best succeeded at mobilising some form of activist support, but they have been unable to translate this support into a mass movement. Not that the British public are necessarily politically apathetic, as London witnessed in May 2003 with the protests at Blair's plans to go to war over Iraq or the thousands who sought to rebel against Thatcher's Community Tax. This suggests that the Eurosceptics have still not managed to 'spin' their message in a manner that has mass appeal, but also that Europe as an issue ranks low in the electorate's interest. They did succeed in stimulating elements of the activist base in 1961–3 and again after 1992, but more generally when the party's leadership has offered more dynamic direction on the European issue, as in 1965–75, the party faithful have tended to fall into line. There has been a division of opinion amongst the Eurosceptic leadership about whether the issue of Europe is an issue that can be trusted to the people. Although calls for a referendum have featured strongly in the Eurosceptic argument, there has been a significant minority who have felt that the debate should not be conducted just in sound bites in front of the television camera, but in reasoned discussion in Parliament.[70] Additionally, the decline in party political activism must be taken into account. When the Anti-Common Market League was at the height of its popularity in the early 1960s Conservative Party membership was in the region of two million; by 1992 this had declined to 750,000 and continues to drop. The profile of a grassroots Conservative Eurosceptic has not changed too much. In the 1960s it would have been a middle-aged, middle-class activist attached to the Commonwealth, who perceived themselves as patriots and who were concerned about French domination of the Europe. By the 1990s the basic profile was little different, although the average age of a party activist was now sixty-three. They are concerned about the diminution of sovereignty, anxious not to see an extension of the EU's powers and opposed to a single currency and the federalist agenda.[71] A warning was signalled to the leadership when over 1,000 party activists attending the 1992 party conference signed a 'Fresh Start' petition urging the objective 'of an enlarged, outward looking, free trading Community of European nation states and urged the rejection of any moves towards a monolithic, bureaucratic, European superstate'.[72] The endorsement that Hague received from his referendum of party members on ruling out membership of the single currency confirms the persistence of a significant Eurosceptic element amongst the grass roots. It could also be used to confirm that at least one-third of the membership are at best indifferent, or, worse, opposed, to this degree of Euroscepticism, yet saw 'non-participation' as the best action. The success of Iain Duncan Smith in the 2001 grassroots ballot for the leadership would testify to the Euroscepticism of the grass roots, but again suggests a division of opinion, with a sizeable proportion willing to support Kenneth Clarke. Yet this is not sufficient reason to explain IDS's ballot victory.

The sceptical tendency of the activist has been prominent in terms of resolutions forwarded to conference. For example, of the forty-three motions received on the EEC in 1961 for the Brighton Conference, only five voiced outright support for entry, the remainder expressing a variety of anxieties and concerns. In 1962 there were fewer resolutions on the EEC for the Llandudno Conference: thirty-one in all, of which three were explicitly against entry, nineteen supportive of entry and the remainder displaying varying shades of anxiety. Evidently by 1962 activists already had half a mind on a general election and the need to concentrate on domestic issues, which would explain the fifty-nine resolutions on taxes and rates.[73] The success of the leadership in convincing the grass roots of the advisability of entry was apparent at the 1971 Brighton Conference when sixty-nine motions of unqualified support were received, compared to twenty-five which gave qualified support and four expressing outright opposition.[74] Between 1992 and 1995 there was a resurgence of Eurosceptic motions to conference.[75] As if to validate this analysis, it is evident that the Maastricht rebels, and especially the whipless nine of 1994–5, kept the support of their local associations and retained the support of the wider Conservative electorate. Whilst this loyalty may be explained on grounds of incumbency it is clear that those constituencies that have been represented by an anti-Marketeer MP at one time or another, such as Isle of Ely (Sir Henry Legge-Bourke), Banbury (Neil Marten), West Dorset (Simon Digby) or South Buckinghamshire (Ronald Bell), have clearly discussed the matter with greater frequency, become aware of the issues and in some instances been indoctrinated with the sceptical argument: 'There is a two-way interaction between Members and their constituency associations. Members who are strongly minded one way or the other can undoubtedly influence their Association decisively.'[76] For the parliamentary party a correlation has been observed that suggests that if an MP was opposed to EC entry they were also likely to support immigration controls. This model does not appear to transfer neatly to the activist base. Norwood Conservative Association frequently passed resolutions urging immigration entry restrictions and sent a motion of support to Powell when he was sacked from the Shadow Cabinet. But the activists involved also showed a willingness to consider EEC membership, such that in July 1960 they urged a entry bid 'before it was too late', a call repeated in July 1961 before a special general meeting in July 1963 urged the reopening of negotiations, 'convinced' that entry was 'desirable'.[77] In contrast Accrington Association conformed to the model, rejecting EEC entry in favour of a 'progressively increasing association with the British Commonwealth of Nations'. There was also 'disquiet' about immigration and the association wanted compulsory medical checks.[78] This appears to support the assertion that Euroscepticism does not neatly fall between left- and right-wing ideological visions.

From 1961 the principal public extra-parliamentary expression of Conservative opposition to EEC membership was the Anti-Common Market League, a name chosen because of its parallel to the Anti-Corn Law League. The genesis of the ACML was a meeting on 26 June 1961 that included John Paul (the chairman of Kensington Conservative Association), Peter Walker (a former Young Conservative national chairman and newly elected MP for Worcester), Nicholas Scott (a local councillor and 1959 candidate for South West Islington), David Clarke (a district councillor in Hayes and Harlington and an active Young Conservative in the Home Counties Northern Area), Anthony Grant (the 1959 candidate for Hayes and Harlington), Gordon Cooper, Roger Moate (active with Greater London Young Conservatives), Michael Shay (chairman of Feltham Young Conservatives) and Jeremy Francis. Paul was a Mobil oil executive, who has unsuccessfully contested parliamentary elections in Walthamstow (1951) and Southampton Test (1955).[79] Walker, who came from the left of the party, based his opposition on trade issues and his preference for the multiracialism of the Commonwealth.[80] Both men were meeting with a group of like-minded Conservatives who had links with the Young Conservatives and/or were favourable to the idea of an expanded Commonwealth. A further meeting took place on 3 August at the House of Commons under Walker's chairmanship on the second day of the House of Commons debate on Macmillan's application. Those present were divided as to what their objectives should be: research and the dissemination of that information or a more militant form of activist agitation. When the group reconvened at Paul's Kensington home on 15 August it was evident that a definite difference of approach existed. Walker favoured the research option, urging that all efforts should be directed towards backing the Commonwealth and that this should be conducted within the party framework.[81] Others, led by Paul, felt that the government's plans for EEC entry should be attacked on all fronts, arguing that it was detrimental to Britain's vital interests. They favoured a vigorous publicity campaign to promote their message with the general public. Two further meetings at Paul's house on 21 and 28 August led to the creation of the ACML, with Paul as chairman, David Clarke as honorary treasurer and Michael Shay as honorary secretary.[82] 'Informers' alerted Central Office to the ACML's formation when it was in its embryonic stages, and then passed on very precise details about its launch and tactics.[83] The ACML was formally launched on 4 October with a meeting at Kensington Town Hall addressed by Derek Walker-Smith. However, by September 1962 it was claiming that it was open to all those opposed to EEC entry. In December 1974 the decision was taken that the ACML would merge with other anti-Marketeer groupings to form the National Referendum Campaign for the duration of the referendum campaign.[84] This was chaired by Neil Marten, and sought to co-ordinate the 'No' campaign during the 1975 referendum. After the referendum the ACML continued its activities, operating into the twenty-first century with Richard Body as its president, but very much on the periphery, lacking any regional network of substance and overshadowed by better funded, and publicity hungry, organisations such as Bill Cash's European Foundation.[85]

Initially an exclusively 'Conservative' organisation with members having to show their Conservative membership, the ACML's strongholds were in the Conservative rural heartlands. From September 1962 it sought to become a non-partisan movement, although it was never able to dispel the assumption that it was a Conservative grouping and that its leading figures were Conservative. Victor Montagu (formerly Viscount Hinchingbrooke) became its president in December 1962 and parliamentarian anti-Marketeers like Derek Walker-Smith, Neil Marten, Anthony Fell, John Biggs-Davison and Robin Turton frequently addressed the organisation's meetings, aided and abetted by former MPs like Somerset de Chair and Maurice Petherick. With the death of co-founder John Paul, and under the chairmanship of Sir Robin Williams, an attempt was made at keeping the ACML non-partisan. However, it is clear that this was not the preferred policy of significant elements on the organisation's executive, who were anxious that 'there will still have to be a distinctive Conservative view'. In 1973 the financial woes of the ACML obliged them to share offices, and personnel, with the cross-party Common Market Safeguards Committee. Again elements were concerned that this would diminish the 'Conservative' nature of their message.[86]

Its activists were to agitate internally. For example, between 1961 and 1963 they put forward forty-two motions on the EEC to the Conservatives' National Union Executive Committee.[87] In the first twelve months of its existence League speakers addressed 237 meetings, ninety-six of them by John Paul. He also addressed the 1962 Llandudno party conference as an accredited member of the Primrose League. During the Commonwealth Prime Ministers' Conference Walker-Smith, Turton and Walker addressed an audience of nearly 2000 in Central Hall, Westminster.[88] After the public meeting, publicity flyers and press advertisements were its next favoured modus operandi. By January 1963 it had distributed nearly two million leaflets or pamphlets and claimed a membership of 30,000.[89] One of its most widely distributed leaflets was a quiz asking readers to answer 'yes' or 'no' to five 'loaded' questions, and if they answered three of more as 'no' to register their opposition to EEC entry with their MP. In some parts of the country this was 'extensively' distributed door to door and it estimated that over a million had been handed out by September 1962.[90] Although some academics, such as Leiber, are dismissive of the 'threat' posed by the ACML, it is clear that party managers and the government took a different view.[91] From their perspective the threat was twofold. First, ACML supporters on the government backbenches were thought to be numerous enough to threaten the government's majority and, given that Labour opposed EEC entry, the government's control of parliament was at risk. Second, the ACML outside parliament drew on support not merely from rural areas but also from those on the right who were unhappy with government policy for a number of reasons. It had close associations with the right-wing ginger group, the Monday Club, and there was a considerable overlap of membership.[92] The Kensington Town Hall launch rally in October 1961 drew official support from groups such as the Forward Britain Movement, League of Empire Loyalists and the Commonwealth Industries Association. Whilst party managers accepted that these groups were on the fringes of the political spectrum, in sum they collectively spoke for a wider constituency of Conservative opinion. The efforts exerted by party managers to keep tabs on the activities of ACML meetings thereafter are also telling. Area agents went to great lengths to cover meetings and provided their superiors with disturbing reports of crowded and enthusiastic meetings, where government policy was lambasted, often by backbench Conservative MPs.[93] One such report from Bath observed that the audience of 120 was 'mostly Conservative of the ex-Colonial or extreme Right Wing groups in the city'.[94] This caused considerable ill will since loyalty and silence were prized virtues for Conservative activists. Central Office repeatedly found itself asked whether there was any sanction that could be taken against the offenders.[95]

It was more difficult to evaluate what electoral threat the ACML posed. Speakers might harangue their audience to reject pro-European Conservative candidates at the next election, but whether this translated into an electoral abstention of any significance is less clear. In one instance, though, the 1962 South Dorset by-election, the impact of the anti-Common Market vote could be evaluated. Lord Hinchingbrooke's elevation to the peerage as Lord Sandwich meant the vacation of the seat and the selection of Angus Maude as the Conservative candidate. However, Hinchingbrooke switched sides and supported the candidature of Piers Debenham on an anti-Common Market ticket. He secured enough votes to deprive the Conservatives of the seat. Although party managers were prepared to write this off as an exceptional result, the implication of losing a rural seat was worrying and frustrating. As party chairman, Iain Macleod complained that the intervention of anti-Common Market candidates 'is working entirely one way and against us', especially whilst pro-Common Market Labour MPs were not challenging official Labour candidates.[96]

The intervention of anti-Common Market candidates in electoral contests divided the Eurosceptic movement. Individuals like Peter Walker thought they should be arguing their position from within the party, rather than seeking to split the party.[97] Hinchingbrooke concluded immediately after South Dorset that the exercise had been worthless. He was critical of John Paul and Michael Hart for challenging official Conservative candidates at the 1964 general election, arguing that EEC entry was now 'a recessed issue'.[98] Yet by 1970 he was trying to persuade the ACML executive that they should put up candidates in as many seats as possible. It was agreed that there were risks attached with such a policy, since experience suggested that they would fare badly and this would give an impression of 'a poor Tory adherence to the anti Common Market point of view'. Some senior ACML figures were of the opinion that to challenge sitting pro-European Conservative MPs in marginal seats would let Labour into office; others formed the view that provided a constituency was represented by an anti-Marketeer it did not matter what the party label was.[99] During the 1971–2 legislative period the ACML helped co-ordinate the anti-Marketeers campaign, compiling data on the voting intentions of MPs and peers, making private approaches to the 'doubtful' and providing anti-Marketeers with parliamentary questions and information. This was a repeat of early 1962, when it had established that forty-eight Conservative MPs were opposed to the government's policy. These were classified in four groups – A1, A2, A3, A4 – and promoted or relegated as their resolution weakened or strengthened. In both instances this was testimony of the ACML's good parliamentary contacts. Further, by 1971 in constituencies where anti-Marketeer MPs were coming under local activist pressure to conform to the government's line they sought to encourage Eurosceptic constituents to rally to their MP. In some cases this took the form of adverts in local newspapers; in others ACML members were dispatched to the constituency itself.[100] One suggestion forwarded, but ultimately rejected, was that rebel MPs might force the resignation of their association officers by forcing a vote of no confidence in them, and then install new more sympathetic activists. Robin Turton thought that for those MPs who had already fallen back into supporting the government they

> had passed the stage when they would accept advice such as this, and I still think the better way is to give them fresh heart and encouragement by persuading those of their constituents who think like us to write to them on the matter.[101]

In the case of Kingston-upon-Thames, which faced a by-election with the twenty-nine-year-old Bow Group pro-European Norman Lamont as the Conservative candidate, disaffected Conservative activists formed the Kingston Conservatives Against the Common Market Organisation and put forward their own independent candidate, Edgar Scruby, who had been expelled from both the Monday Club and the Conservative Party for his attack on Nigel Fisher in the late 1960s.[102] The problem was that this, and the broader issue of campaigning, cost money. So although in the summer of 1971 the ACML could lay claim to an ever-growing network of branches, by the climax of the campaign in the autumn revenue was down 25 per cent on the previous three months, which was probably indicative of the momentum of the pro-Europe campaign.[103]

When ACML was conceived it was assumed it would be a short-term campaign lasting a few months. It sought to avoid the constraints of conventional political organisation. Its headquarters were the basement of the Pauls' Kensington House. However, the longevity of the campaign against EEC entry did oblige it to adopt greater organisational procedures, and to seek to create a grassroots network. Additionally, there were divisions within the Eurosceptic movement about the message, those like ACML willing to oppose entry on any grounds, others like Walker wishing to articulate an alterative Commonwealth vision (a message that diminished by late 1960s). The ACML, despite suggestions of amateurship, was quite clever regarding where it sought to sell its message to the wider electorate. During August 1962 a series of public meetings were held in seaside resorts and in September John Paul and Anthony Fell toured Lancashire. In addition there was an emphasis towards rural constituencies, particularly to secure invitations to address National Farmers' Union branches. In targeting these three constituents the ACML was addressing audiences that were sceptical to the benefits of Europe. Many coastal resorts were retirement areas for old-age pensioners and ex-service officers. Conservative agents had already identified that the 'old' were more likely to be opposed particularly because of fears about the cost of living and the risk of devaluation in their pension.[104] Lancashire had a reputation for 'independent' Conservatism and reports suggested opinion was 'hardening' against entry because of concerns about sovereignty and Commonwealth ties, whilst the apparent opposition of farmers was widely reported, and thought to concern up to 100 Conservative MPs with rural seats.

## Tactics

The tactics of the Eurosceptics have been tailored to operate within the environs of Westminster, the wider political electorate and the regional and national media. Until 1997 these had to be conducted in contradiction with the party organisational machine. The hindrance of the party machine plus the frequently deployed argument that the Eurosceptics were deliberately seeking to undermine official party policy, and therefore failed the loyalty litmus test, made the position of the Eurosceptics all the more difficult. The pro-European party leadership has been sufficiently alarmed at moments about the potency of the Eurosceptics' message to deploy the full resources of the party machine and, as one leading Eurosceptic observed, 'play it dirty'.[105] Sources forewarned Central Office about the impending launch of the ACML in the summer of 1961 and constituency agents and local activist officials were despatched to infiltrate ACML meetings and report on their message and deliberations.[106] Similarly, during the 1975 referendum campaign Central Office determined to 'see what intelligence can be gleaned on the activities of the anti-marketeers' and proposed using Central Office agents for this task.[107] There has also been a tradition of calling upon association officials in constituencies represented by rebels to provide reports on their activities and voting intentions.[108] In addition, Central Office has ensured that there should be no opportunity to appear to give official endorsement to the anti-Marketeer message. During the 1971 debate Neil Marten sought Central Office's help to distribute anti-Marketeer literature. Marten speculatively claimed that the literature should be jointly distributed 'because, in all fairness, our supporters who subscribe to our funds will expect to see both sides of this "great and historic debate"'. Unsurprisingly he received a direct rebuff from Peter Thomas, the party chairman.[109] Similarly, in 1975 they were denied column space in the party magazine *Monthly News*.[110] Another spoiling tactic has been to deny the Eurosceptics the opportunity to distribute literature at area and national party conferences, and thereby to seek to isolate them from the activist base.[111] At Westminster, the patronage and disciplinary system of the whips' office has been used. Although this spectacularly backfired when Major withdrew the whip from the Eight in 1994, the whips have been deployed to good effect. During the November 1992 Paving motion debate the whips succeeded in convincing many of the doubters that in effect the debate was one of confidence in John Major and if he lost resignation would be the only option. The rumours of David Lightbown's 'persuading' tactics during the Maastricht votes became the stuff of Westminster legend, with him being likened to 'the whips' office equivalent of the terminator'.[112] Similarly, during the 1971 accession debates reports about the whips' 'arm twisting' methods led Derek Walker-Smith, on behalf of the 1970 Group of anti-Marketeers, to seek an interview with the chairman and chief whip 'since this is a matter affecting Members'.[113] Another tactic of the Maastricht debate was the deliberate appointment of the Eurosceptics David Davies and David Heathcote-Amory to the whips' office to help the cause of chief whip Richard Ryder. Patronage is a key weapon in the whips' arsenal. James Cran was reportedly offered a PPS position in December 1991, which he declined. Those subjected to the pressure of the whips, though, complain too of blackmail and intimidation, and even repeat allegations of mail and telephone conversations being intercepted.[114]

The party leadership has also been happy to allow local constituency officials to place pressure on their own MP. As one internal party report observed, 'those who are in a state of doubt are much more likely to be influenced by their Association and Executive'.[115] This scenario could be typified by the experience in Weston-super-Mare in 1971, where '[t]he Common Market has certainly given us some headaches', reported the association chairman:

> Not least has been the task of persuading our member to follow the Party line! Our Area Agent has also worked on him with some success and I think you can now be assured of his (Mr Wiggins') support.[116]

Although associations jealously guard their independence to choose their own parliamentary candidates, local officials are not averse to seeking advice from Central Office and senior party figures. The agent for Walker-Smith's East Hertfordshire Association sought help to find a 'big gun' to counter Walker-Smith at their association's CPC conference on Europe in 1961.[117] Similarly, Banbury Association, represented by Neil Marten, engaged the services of party chairman Peter Thomas to pen a pro-European article for their association magazine in 1971.[118] Compromise was often the name of the game, but not before severe pressure had been brought to bear. David Mudd complained in 1971 that his Falmouth and Camborne executive was 'playing it very rough and dirty' and that they were 'basing their inquisition on the Gospel according to Central Office'.[119] In Harborough and Blaby Association, branches were sent a questionnaire on the Common Market in July 1971 to help activists raise concerns and receive answers to their queries about entry. Although the constituency agent claimed that this would leave John Farr 'in a better position to judge the issue and to give an informed opinion', the real motive was to pressure their MP by showing activist support for entry.[120] The experience of Burton-on-Trent Association perhaps typified the changed atmosphere. Whereas in 1962 the association had expressed its willingness to accept its MPs decision about entry, in 1971 association members expected their MP (who was sceptical) to support the government.[121] Similarly Alan Clark admitted during the 1975 referendum campaign that, whilst he was minded to support the 'No' campaign, pressure from his pro-European Plymouth Sutton Association was enough to prevent him doing so.[122]

When Major's government sought to move the 'paving motion' to resume progress on the Maastricht legislation on 4 November 1992 similar pressure was applied. Sir Basil Feldman, chairman of the National Union, communicated the message to constituency officers that the fate of the government was in the balance. He also wrote to *The Times* warning wavers that the party's grass roots had worked hard in April to elect them. One potential rebel, the newly elected Walter Sweeney (Glamorgan), received a fax from his association executive urging him to support the government after a Central Office official had visited the association.[123] Suspicion of Central Office intervention also occurred in Christoper Gill's Ludlow Association.[124] The compromise usually was for the association to express its satisfaction with official party policy and note the views and behaviour of the MP. However, on occasion the situation deteriorated to the extent that attempts were made to deselect the MP. This was a relatively rare occurrence, and could, as Neil Marten discovered in 1971–3, be a very bitter experience. Yet until George Gardiner was deselected by Reigate in 1997 no Eurosceptic had suffered this humiliation because of their European views. Deselection is normally an option of last resort, and usually arises because of personality problems that are exacerbated by political disputes. The latter usually provides the rationale, and cover, for the deselection.[125] These MP/association spats also raise questions about MPs' accountability and their freedom of action. These issues have been rumbling on behind the scenes for most of the century. Since the local associations retain the right of selection, many activists expect their candidate to be answerable to their views, at times in preference to the wider collective view of the party.[126] In turn the MPs turned to Burke to defend their position: 'an MP betrays his constituents instead of serving them if he sacrifices his own judgement on political matters to those of his supporters.'[127] Since 1997 the boot has been on the other foot and it is now Eurosceptic activists who have been seeking to censure pro-European MPs, as the deselection experience of Ian Taylor in Esher in December 2000 revealed. What is noticeable, though (with the exception of Gardiner), is that the national leadership has been reluctant to see opponents from the opposite side of the argument deselected and has therefore counselled caution and toleration. Although the view of Central Office is never to 'give any encouragement to any attempt to embarrass or undermine a Conservative Member of Parliament', it is evident that association officials are sometimes looking for central direction. This particularly proved the case during the 1975 referendum, when consecutive party chairmen William Whitelaw and Peter Thorneycroft wrote to association chairmen urging them to support the 'Yes' vote but failed to address 'the delicate question' of what pro-European activists should do if their seat was held by an anti-Marketeer.[128] In this, Central Office purely fudged the issue and suggested it was for individual Conservatives to act as they saw fit.

Since the time of Macmillan's first application Conservative Eurosceptics have organised themselves into a series of ginger and pressure groups, some of which are Westminster orientated and others of which have a national activist slant. The difficultly with many of these groups is disentangling the myth from the reality. This applies to the 92 Group, a right-wing dining group. Drawing its name from the address (92 Cheyne Walk) of one of its founder members, Sir Patrick Wall, legend credits the group with engineering the election of suitable members to the internal parliamentary party's subject committees and the 1922 Committee. The day before the paving resolution was to be voted on on 4 November 1992 five members of the 92 Group (Rhodes Boyson, James Pawsey, George Gardiner, Bob Dunn and John Townend) had a half-hour meeting with the prime minister to 'frankly and clearly' explain their dislike of the Maastricht Treaty, but agreeing to support the government.[129] This was deemed a coup for the whips' office and annoyed the hardcore sceptics, who felt that 'not only have they already sold the pass but then, contrary to assurances ... they go to the Press to publicly announce their intention to support the Government'.[130]

One of the difficulties has been the plethora of these groupings, often determined to pursue their own agenda, and there has only been limited success at co-ordinating their activities. This was nowhere more apparent than during the 1975 referendum campaign when the NRC was formed in early January 1975 from a menagerie of the extra-parliamentarian groups: Anti-Common Market League, British Business for World Markets, Common Market Safeguards Campaign and Get Britain Out. The NRC's foundation came with the warning not to become 'a plethora of organisations with differing policies and mutual suspicion. Let us not fall into that trap'.[131] At one level the NRC did represent a moderate success, given that it did see co-ordination between the anti-Market forces of the left and the right, even if in reality this relationship was strained. The decision to join the NRC concluded a debate that had been ongoing within the ACML since the mid-1960s, about whether they should retain a 'Conservative' appeal.[132] Tactically there has been a willingness, at a parliamentary level, to seek co-operation with elements of the Labour Party when it has been politically expedient. During the passage of the Maastricht legislation there were occasions when the Conservative rebels would ensure that the Labour whips were aware of their intentions. This collusion might consist of no more than a brief exchange of words in the corridor, but it succeeded when the combined forces of the Labour Party and twenty-three Conservatives voted against the government in July 1993, dividing the House by 324 to 316.[133] The difficulty for the Eurosceptics was that, whilst the narrowness of Major's majority made it easier to inflict a parliamentary defeat, the spectre was always present that such a division would force Major from office and would probably result in a Labour government pledged to even more support for Europe.

Behind the scenes at Westminster those parliamentarians involved in the public pressure groups were also active in the committee and smoking rooms. The first grouping to emerge in light of Macmillan's announcement was the Common Market Committee (not to be confused with Bill Deedes' Parliamentary Common Market Committee), chaired by Robin Turton. During its lifetime, membership of the Committee was about forty, although average attendance at meetings was in the low twenties. The committee first met on 25 July 1961, at which meeting the wording of a critical EDM was agreed. This motion subsequently secured forty-nine signatures. After this first public display of opposition the committee sought to co-ordinate the Conservative opposition during the two-day debate on the EEC in the Commons on 2–3 August. Days earlier Macmillan had privately threatened that he would resign if thirty or more Conservatives abstained on the government motion.[134] It was a threat that went unheeded. When the House divided on 3 August, according to *The Times*, 24 Conservatives abstained on the Labour amendment and 29 abstained on the main government motion, with Anthony Fell actually cross-voting with the 4 Independent Labour Party MPs.[135] Throughout the negotiations the committee sought to maintain the pressure on the government by tabling a series of EDMs that highlighted its concerns. Thus a series of EDMs, on 21 March and 13 December 1962, argued the case for the Commonwealth, whilst the motions of 26 July 1961 and 30 July 1962 pointed to concern about the implications for British sovereignty. At the 1961 Brighton conference the committee prepared a carefully worded amendment, which Turton moved, calling upon the government to hold to its earlier pledges on agriculture and the Commonwealth and not to accept any diminution of British sovereignty. Members of the committee felt themselves to be in a difficult position. If they adopted too soft an approach they risked seeing Britain 'slipping into a federal Europe under the most damaging conditions'; equally, if they were too vigorous in their condemnation they risked undermining Ted Heath's attempts to negotiate satisfactory safeguards.[136]

Although the membership of the Common Market Committee was decimated by the elections of 1964 and 1966 (half lost their seats, mainly in 1964), the core of the group remained; 10 of the remaining 21 joined 16 other Conservatives and voted against their own whips and the Labour government in two divisions on 10 May 1967. From the late 1960s, after the failure of the second EEC bid, aware that they could no longer advocate purely no membership, a number of Tories became involved in the cross-party Atlantic Free Trade Area parliamentary group from 1968 to 1970.[137] This group saw its role as to 'seek every opportunity ... to question the advisability of Britain's entry into the Common Market'. This ranged from challenging the BBC over its perceived pro-European bias, to tabling parliamentary questions and intervening in parliamentary debates. In July 1969 the group decided that it should downplay the idea of an Atlantic Free Trade Area and move to wholesale opposition to EEC membership.[138]

Derek Walker-Smith also convened the 1970s Group, a discussion group receiving official sanction from the whips' office and nicknamed 'Derek's

Diner'. Neil Marten became one of the leading lights, with John Biffen acting as its informal whip. This group requires some comparison with the 'Fresh Start' group that opposed the passage of the European Communities (Amendment) Bill 1992–3. Their name was taken from the June 1992 early day motion that called for a 'fresh start' on the issue of Europe. Chaired by Michael Spicer, the group operated with an informal whip organised by Christopher Gill and James Cran with support from Teresa Gorman and Roger Freeman. They had the use of Lord McAlpine's Great College Street House, and claimed a membership of eighty. During the Maastricht Bill Richard Ryder, the chief whip, regularly had meetings with its leaders, thereby conforming to the concept of loyal dissent.[139] This has parallels to 1972 when Francis Pym, the then chief whip, kept in close touch with the 1970 Group, even to the extent of being told how many they expected to rebel. Rumours that they were preparing to become a general purpose faction grouping proved baseless. The extremely poor reception experience by John Major when addressing the group in June 1995 was one of the factors that encouraged his decision to initiate the 1995 leadership election contest.[140] The comparison rests upon the point that during the two most recent occasions when the Conservatives have operated with a small majority that overall majority has been threatened each time by an internal anti-European grouping. There were some important distinctions. By the 1990s Euroscepticism was securing funding from sources external to the party, which allowed critics to raise the charge that they were becoming a party within a party. Observers noted that the Fresh Starters were ideologically driven, and as much driven by their hostility towards Major as a betrayer of Thatcher as they were by their hostility to Europe.[141] Such ungentlemanly treachery would have been unthinkable to Walker-Smith, Marten or even Biffen.

In frustration at the pro-Common Market literature being produced by Central Office in 1971 Roger Moate created the Conservative Anti-Common Market Information Service to disseminate material on Europe that Central Office was unwilling to distribute.[142] There were other public expressions of Conservative hostility. For example, Conservatives were prominent on the National Common Market Petition Council, chaired by the Conservative activist and author Arthur Bryant (ten Conservative MPs on the council), that was launched in June 1968.[143] The aim of this organisation was to secure signatures for a petition to the queen that asked that she use her royal prerogative to prevent Britain joining the EEC. It was finally presented on 2 May 1972 with 764,107 signatures.[144] The important point to observe about all of these groups is the overlap in membership, and that often resources and premises were shared.

Apart from activities in the lobby and discussion groups, other parliamentary tactics were in operation. The use of EDMs was widespread. Prior to and during the first application a series of EDMs were tabled by the Common Market Committee aimed at reminding Macmillan of the concerns amongst the parliamentary party about entry and any terms that might be negotiated.[145] During Maastricht one of most notorious was the 'Fresh Start' EDM, on 3 June 1992, tabled immediately after the Danish referendum 'No' vote. It secured eighty-six signatures. EDMs are not intended for debate but are meant as a gauge of parliamentary support for a given topic. Parliamentary questions have proved another useful tactic, indeed 'one of the most important tasks'. The aim has been to use these to illicit official information, sometimes on the most innocuous of issues, about matters European and then, with the credibility of being a parliamentary answer, use the detail to bolster the sceptic argument and 'probe ... on inconsistencies'.[146] During the referendum campaign it was the deliberate aim 'when quoting figures ... [to] ... use parliamentary answers'.[147] In addition attempts were made to move anti-Marketeers into places of influence on party committees, such as getting Neil Marten selected in November 1961 as a vice-chairman of the Conservative Foreign Affairs Committee; similarly in the 1990s attempts were made to capture the European Affairs Committee. Of course this attempt to pack party committees was countered by the pro-European elements of the party. The anti-Marketeers used the full plethora of party committees to ensure their perspective was heard. Party managers kept a watchful eye, but could do little to prevent the articulation of such views.[148] During the first application, whenever the Foreign Affairs Committee discussed the matter the Eurosceptics dominated matters.[149] Similarly, following de Gaulle's second veto sceptics tried, in vain, to persuade the Foreign Affairs Committee to reconsider the original arguments for the EEC and consider possible alternatives.[150] In July 1993, on the eve of the vote on Labour's amendment to force the government to accept the Social Chapter, the Eurosceptics pointedly absented themselves from the 1922 Committee meeting which Major was addressing.[151]

The tactics during the Maastricht debate utilised a combination of all the above. The sceptics wished to delay the bill whilst hoping for an external saviour, such as French '*Non*' referendum vote. Second, they intended to force the government to put the matter to a referendum, and finally during the 210 hours that the bill was debated they hoped by the extensive tabling of amendments that they could wreck the bill. Some sceptics freely admit that the committee stage of the Maastricht Bill, with the continuous points of order, was too tedious, and that despite their best intentions they played no part in the debate, although they attended divisions.[152] Tactically there were two important differences between this ratification debate and the 1971–2 accession debate. This was with regard to the position of the Labour Party. Whereas in 1971–2 Labour was deeply divided over Europe and Heath was able to rely on the support of Labour pro-Marketeers like Roy Jenkins, in 1992–3 Labour was reasonably unified around its leadership's pro-Europeanism. Also, the situation in Northern Ireland had an impact on the arithmetic in the lobby. Although in 1971–2 many of the Ulster Unionists were sceptical about EEC entry they were technically still in receipt of the Conservative whip. The government brought pressure to bear on them by reminding them 'that they may need friends at some time in the future. ... The Ulster Members have used this argument to put pressure on the Government concerning Ulster but it is a two-edged sword'.[153] By 1992 the Unionist movement had splintered into several different factions, each a separate entity from the Conservative Party, and because of the Good Friday Agreement and the Major government's dialogue with Sinn Fein the support of the Unionists was volatile – not that the unionists tactics were much changed from the 1970s, when they were perfectly willing to use their parliamentary votes as bargaining chips to lever concessions from the government about the Irish peace process.[154]

## The message

Over the years the focus of the anti-Marketeer message changed. Roughly it can be categorised as follows: 1961–2 emphasis was upon the problems EEC membership posed for the Commonwealth and EFTA and to question whether the application was even necessary; then towards the end of 1962 came the beginning of calls for the government to consider alternatives; 1963 saw a shift towards emphasising the risks of political and economic union; 1970–3 saw the emphasis move towards the costs of EEC membership (food, pensions, etc.) and the risks to sovereignty; finally, with the referendum campaign sovereignty became the main issue. Between 1975 and 1980 there was considerable uncertainty over what the message should be. It was generally accepted that now that there had been both parliamentary and public approval for entry it was difficult to maintain the opposition, but developments such as direct elections still needed to be monitored to ensure nothing detrimental to British interests was imposed. From the 1980s the inequalities of CAP and the British budgetary contribution were worthy causes, with the argument that Britain was yet to see the promised economic returns on its membership; however, the much heralded implementation of Thatcherism in Europe through the Single European Act rather appeared to weaken the sceptics' arguments. By the 1990s the Eurosceptics were successfully arguing (or rather presenting) the idea that in joining the EEC they thought Britain had joined a free trade area, that there had been no discussion of further unity or integration. Because of this the sceptics began championing the need for a referendum, first to confirm support for Maastricht and thereafter to sanction any governmental decision to join the single currency. From 1997, with the Conservative Party relieved of the duties of office, the Eurosceptic message became official party policy, which obliged ruling out British membership of the euro and campaigning to 'save' the pound. The demand for a referendum has now become a basic demand of the Conservative leadership for every European initiative. Therefore, as the European Union, under the presidency of the Italians and then the Irish, sought to secure agreement for a European Constitution the Conservatives launched a petition demanding a referendum on the matter. There has been a small, but growing Conservative voice advocating total withdrawal from the EU, but this has not become a leadership-sanctioned view.[155]

## The alternatives?

The key problem for the anti-Marketeers was what alternative to EEC membership could they promote?[156] An EDM laid down on 13 December 1962 attracted the support of forty-seven Conservatives and urged the government 'to formulate as soon as possible an alternative policy based on a major Commonwealth initiative'.[157] This was the first definite plea for the government to consider the possibility of the failure of the first application and therefore prepare alternative options, whilst the ACML resolved that it should avoid promoting alternatives and 'concentrate on opposing adherence to the Treaty of Rome'.[158] Others did try to formulate a response. These tended to be variations on three ideas: EFTA, Commonwealth preference or NAFTA. Each, though, was problematic and the pro-Europeanists were confident from 1962 that there was 'little new ammunition' in the anti-Marketeers' arguments.[159]

EFTA was hindered by its inability to expand, although it was suggested that Eastern Europe might prove viable if its markets were liberalised. Peter Walker argued in the early 1960s that if the Commonwealth nations reached an economic agreement with EFTA, the leverage the combination of raw materials/manufacturing goods and market share would give would allow the enlarged EFTA to tell the EEC: 'if you put up tariffs against us, we will retaliate and put up tariffs against you and cut off raw material supplies.'[160] As the 1960s progressed it became apparent that Commonwealth preference was realistically restricted only to the 'White' dominions since the Asian and African markets were considered too volatile. The 1968 party conference saw twelve pro-NAFTA resolutions but NAFTA was never viable without US interest, and that was lukewarm. Furthermore, there was a concern that a NAFTA-type arrangement would result in the US sending exports to Britain whilst giving the EEC capital and technology. This led one anti-Marketeer to conclude that 'there are no very obvious alternatives to membership of the Common Market' and therefore Britain should concentrate economically on seeing Europe as 'the natural domestic market' without accepting the necessity of joining.[161] This was symbolic of the problem: that they were unable to challenge the economic rationale of joining, and instead had to reply on the 'fear' factor.

The idea of a North Atlantic Free Trade Area has enjoyed two periods of promotion: 1967–9, 1995–2000. With de Gaulle's second veto the question of whether there was an alternative option to EEC membership was raised. Although Heath did not seriously entertain any other course than EEC membership he was prepared to sanction internal consideration of the viability of NAFTA. This had a dual purpose: it enabled Heath to counter

critics who felt that the party had not been given the opportunity to consider
alternatives and, second, it distracted the attentions of the anti-Marketeers,
who now channelled their energies into making the case for NAFTA. The
forum for the debate was the Conservative Foreign Affairs Committee and a
sub-committee under the chairmanship of Lord Balniel and Richard Wood.
The divisions during the debate split between the anti-Marketeers, who saw
considerable merit in the proposals, and the pro-Europeanists, who considered it impractical and a distraction from the real objective of EEC
membership. The Conservative Research Department had begun consideration of an Atlantic Free Trade Area in February 1967. Previously it had
been assigned 'unspeakable alternatives' status. Within the CRD there
appears to have been some disagreement about whether such an arrangement would exclude Britain from subsequently joining the EEC.[162] The
pro-Europeanists were clearly worried that if the party started debating
NAFTA it would 'let down our many European friends'.[163] The matter had
come before the Foreign Affairs Backbench Committee in December 1967,
with Turton and Marten pushing for proper consideration. Both accepted
that the project 'might take sometime to realise' but thought the forthcoming American presidential elections meant this was an appropriate time
to consider it.[164] This was always the weakness with NAFTA, namely the
'very meagre support' from America.[165] As St John Stevas declared, 'If the EEC
were a dead duck, NAFTA was no more than an embryo duck'. The Foreign
Affairs Committee heard from Sir Michael Wright, chair of the Atlantic
Trade Study Group, that NAFTA had 'attractive possibilities', but it is
evident that the committee had concerns that the US would be the principal
beneficiary and that it meant abandoning Europe.[166] Proponents countered that language, customs and law made the UK closer to the US and
that meant 'much less sovereignty would be surrendered'. Further, the
problem of Britain's balance of payments and the risk of world recession
made it an urgent proposition. Others speculated whether it might actually
strengthen any subsequent EEC application. 'Our leaders', suggested
Harmar Nicholls, 'should not give the impression of being so wedded to
Europe that they were unable even to consider other possibilities'. However,
even amongst the anti-Marketeers support for NAFTA was by no means
universal. Biggs-Davison was concerned that if Britain turned its back on
Western Europe it would increase the risks of Russian domination of
Europe.[167] The conclusion for the shadow foreign secretary was that it was
too full of 'ifs' and Heath's Europe advisors were of the opinion that it
combined a 'rather sophisticated economic argument' with 'a good deal of
political naivety'.[168]

If presenting an alternative to joining the EEC proved difficult, once
Britain actually became a member state the problem became more acute. It
has become the Achilles heel of the Eurosceptic case as it struggles to articulate a viable alternative to British membership of the European Union. This
difficulty had been privately acknowledged by sceptics, with Marten warning

during the referendum campaign that 'we must be much clearer in our answer to the "alternatives" question'. That message had obviously failed to get through, as a CPC report from 1992 showed that although many activists had serious reservations about Maastricht they would support it for the lack of an alternative.[169] In 1975 the message was withdrawal, but there was vagueness about what Britain should replace it with. The idea of a free trade area was fraught with difficulties given that Britain had abandoned EFTA to join the EEC, whilst any ideas of an Atlantic Free Trade Area were impossible without active American commitment, which was not forthcoming. Marten thought perhaps the best solution was to talk about 'suitable trading arrangements and emphasis that the anti-Marketeers opposed exclusivity in a single market'.[170] The European movement has been able to counter the withdrawal argument by playing the fear factor and emphasising the risks of leaving the EU. Since the 1975 referendum sceptics have been wary of advocating total withdrawal from the Community. Even under the leadership of William Hague it was thought 'totally fraudulent' that the Conservative vision of Europe equated with withdrawal.[171] It is noticeable that small elements within the party since the mid-1990s have begun to argue that withdrawal might be advantageous. Norman Lamont was one of the first to do so at a fringe meeting at the party conference in 1994.[172] Although dismissed as 'siren voices' by Malcolm Rifkind, there has been a serious attempt to consider the implications of withdrawal.[173] Furthermore there was evidence after 1997 that the idea was taking hold amongst the parliamentary party.[174] William Waldegrave, who had previously taken the view that Britain could only secure a global leadership role through Europe, in November 1997 advanced idea of a 'sort of European Canada'. Britain would seek EU withdrawal, but would remain in its shadow, free of central economic control, yet benefiting from proximity to its markets.[175] Roger Helmer aired a similar line about the economic impact of withdrawal in September 2000:

> The truth is that, in trade terms, withdrawal would be broadly neutral, while in fiscal and regulatory terms, it would be highly to our advantage. We in the Conservative Party argue for reform rather than withdrawal, but I am in no doubt that unless radical reform is achieved the pressure for withdrawal will become irresistible.[176]

In April 2006 the Freedom Association launched the 'Better Off Out' campaign, urging withdrawal. Philip Davies, the MP elected for Shipley in 2005, fronted much of the media publicity, and was supported by fellow 2005 entrants Douglas Caswell (Harwich) and Phillip Hollobone (Kettering), plus long-term sceptics Nicholas and Ann Winterton, Eric Forth and Bob Spink.[177] The risk that the calls for withdrawal might place unbearable pressures on the party was clearly on the minds of the 1990s leadership. The idea of a NAFTA arrangement has again secured support, not least from the likes of Redwood and Thatcher.[178] Addressing an American audience in June 1991, she proposed the extension of the newly formed North Atlantic Free Trade Area (combining USA, Canada and Mexico) to include Europe (both Western and Eastern) to form a single Atlantic Economic Community.[179] NAFTA has become a particular theme of Thatcher's since leaving office, but has been dismissed by John Major as a 'sugar coated turnip'.[180] The weakness of NAFTA was always the lack of American interest in the project; therefore Eurosceptics made much of the proposition of American Senator Phil Gramm, who proposed that Britain could join the newly formed NAFTA. As one sceptic wrote, Gramm 'has performed a valuable service by reminding us that there may indeed be an alternative to the officious, protectionist, union-dominated, anti-democratic, socialist-minded Europe that threatens both our prosperity and our liberties'.[181] Publication of Thatcher's *Statecraft* took the debate a stage further, with her arguing that Britain should engage in a fundamental renegotiation of her EU membership and when that failed withdrawal would be the only option, with membership of NAFTA the preferred outcome.[182] Such a suggestion went beyond everything the Conservative leadership had argued since at least 1961. The potential consequences were profound, and threatened schism. Teddy Taylor was warning in late 1992 that advocacy of either withdrawal or NAFTA would 'require the formation of a new political party. There may well be the need to create such a party in the fullness of time'.[183] These pressures would channel into the creation of UKIP and Goldsmith's Referendum Party.

The linguistic discourse of the European debate has been recognised by participants as an important and impressionistic area. Just as for many decades Conservative politicians would refer to 'the Socialists' rather than the Labour Party because it conjured images of the Bolshevik bogeyman, so the nomenclature in the Europe debate carries specific meaning. From the creation of the EEC through into the 1980s, sceptics consistently referred to it as the Common Market. This was both a deliberate ploy to downgrade its status and deny it a legitimacy and also because it implied a restrictive trading bloc. Similarly during the 1970s they liked to refer to the European Parliament as an 'Assembly'. Again this was a desire to avoid giving it a legitimacy and because they had no wish to confer it with any legislative powers at the expense of the Westminster parliament. When discussing the matter of sovereignty sceptics have been warned to avoid expressions such as 'pooling' sovereignty or 'taking our decisions in common': 'they are honeyed words to express loss of sovereignty.'[184] Just as some Eurosceptics would prefer to see themselves labelled 'Euro-realists' to reinforce the positive nature of their opposition to the European Union, their opponents have been happy to equate scepticism with a narrow 'Little Englander' vision. The label is seen as insulting by Eurosceptics.[185] Rather, they would see themselves as patriots defending 'Britishness'.[186] Nick Hawkins (Blackpool South) said during the Maastricht debates: 'I regard myself as sceptical about the ambition of various Commission officials to move towards a more federal state and to subsume Britain's independence.'[187] This theme of defending 'Britishness' can be found in the calls for the 'repatriation' of the European Court of Justice, a familiar theme from when Michael Howard was home secretary. This line of argument also plays to the British 'uniqueness' argument by implying that this continental form of justice is detrimental to the traditions of British law and by implication makes out that Britain is the only EU member to have been slighted or harmed by its rulings, which belies the reality. The judgements of the European Court of Justice must also be placed in a party political context, as for example during the BSE crisis when the court ruled that France had acted illegally in banning British beef. France chose to ignore the judgement, which undermined the legitimacy of the European Union. The theme of national survival is a central message of the sceptic argument. It can manifest itself in relatively trivial forms. Take as an example Gillian Shephard, who as education minister urged the BBC to adopt a 'rousing' English work for its theme tune for its coverage of the football Euro '96 competition instead of Beethoven's 'Ode to Joy'.[188]

Behind all of this there is also a presumption of British uniqueness, historic, economic and political, which means that somehow the continental experience was different and consequently they had a different regard for sovereignty. Anthony Nutting, a former Foreign Office junior minister, summed this up: the attachment of the Six to a supranational solution could be explained because they no longer believed in national sovereignty, 'as we do', because it had let them down in two world wars.[189] This represented a fundamental incompatibility which meant that Britain had nothing to gain from joining an 'alien' system that was geared to achieving the aims of the continental Europeans. Derek Walker-Smith, looking to history, thought that the 'continental and collective' political development of Europe was incompatible with Britain's 'insular and imperial' past.[190] A similar view was expressed by Enoch Powell in February 1971: 'the sovereignty of our Parliament is something other for us than what your assemblies are for you.'[191] Thatcher felt that for the UK 'European democracy is remote resting on very different traditions'.[192] Reggie Maudling and Rab Butler were broadly sceptical during the first application that British interests would be served by any European solutions to Britain's economic situation.[193] This was the critique used by Hague against EMU, when he sought to emphasise the 'uniqueness' of the British position, which stressed that the British economy lacked convergence with the European economies: Britain had a larger financial services sector, home ownership and pension provision than European counterparts, which when combined with Britain's flexible labour market, low taxation and trade with non-EU nations meant Britain could be more influential outside the euro zone.[194] This line of argument could, and often did, mutate into anti-Europeanism: a patriotic nationalism that belittled the Europeans and appealed to the lowest common denominator, and which has served the populist media well.

Generally the sceptics have been keen to portray their international and European credentials in order to deflect the criticism that they are xenophobic and to allow them to develop a theme that Europe is something more than the EU. It is the mode of unity rather than any sense of anti-foreigner that drives their position. Hence James Cran's view:

> I do not regard myself as a Eurosceptic. I am very much in favour of Europe. I do not say that we should pull up the anchor and take the United Kingdom somewhere else. We are part of Europe and we must stay part of Europe. I am concerned only about the kind of Europe that we will have.[195]

Similarly, Iain Duncan Smith's maiden speech on 20 May 1992: 'I am not by any means anti-European. After all Europe is a geographical expression. Therefore, being in the centre of Europe or supporting Europe is neither here nor there.'[196] The message is to emphasise that it's not Europe but the mode of integration that causes the disquiet. Enoch Powell, speaking in Lyon in 1971, felt it necessary to declare that he spoke 'as a European among Europeans'. He continued: 'I have always argued that Britain's commitment to the alliance with her continental neighbours is second only in importance to the commitment to the air and maritime defence of her own islands.'[197] Made at a point in the Cold War, this prioritisation of the primacy of the defence of Britain is a classic affirmation of limited liability, a strategic doctrine preferred by the 1930s national governments until March 1939.

## The Eurosceptic media

One significant factor has been the attitude of the press, which has taken an increasingly Eurosceptic tone. This attitude has been displayed at all levels from proprietors to editors to individual journalists. The *Sun*, *The Times* and the *Daily Telegraph*, along with the *Daily Mail*, all opposed the single currency. It was not purely the editorial and proprietarily stances that were important, but also the contribution of individual sceptical journalists like Simon Heffer, Matthew d'Ancona, Boris Johnson and Christopher Booker. History is not important; it is the telling that counts. Consequently, these journalists have willingly participated in the construction of the myth. As Ken Clarke lamented, the 'Conservative press is almost without exception edited by way-out Eurosceptics'.[198] This is all the more important if it is noted that the circulation of the anti-single currency press is almost double that of those newspapers in favour.[199] The support of the 'Conservative' print media for the Eurosceptic cause since the 1990s has made it a significant pillar within the broader 'elite' Eurosceptic establishment. This contrasts very vividly with the situation in the 1970s and 1960s.

The antis campaign during the 1960s was greatly assisted by the press empire of Beaverbrook. His *Daily Express* had a circulation of 4.3 million and was frequently the most cited reason for the electorate's hostility to entry.[200] As one agent complained to Central Office, 'we are losing by default against a well-sustained and somewhat unscrupulous attack'.[201] The *Express'* emotive campaign played upon the latent prejudices of its readership, portraying the Europeans as Catholic, undemocratic and unclean. Through the use of guest commentators, such as the historian A.J.P. Taylor, the paper portrayed itself as the epicentre of Euroscepticism. As David Price, MP for Eastleigh, observed, 'opinion has hardened considerably against our entry. ... The campaign in the Beaverbrook press has had its impact'.[202] The direct personal interest of the proprietor, Lord Beaverbrook, made matters more complicated for the government. They recognised that it was useless making appeals to individual journalists on the paper and that they could only deal directly through Beaverbrook.[203] An example of this is the personal appeal of Peter Walker to Beaverbrook to support the Conservative candidate, Charlie Morrison, in the 1964 Devizes by-election. Beaverbrook wanted to know Morrison's views on Europe but was satisfied enough by the assurance that the candidate was a farmer, of a distinguished family and enthusiastic about the British empire and agriculture.[204] The *Daily Express'* reaction to the collapse of negotiations in January 1963 was gloating: 'Glory, Glory Hallelujah! It's all over.'[205] However, the majority of the British press was favourable to entry. *The Times* swung behind entry, but with reservations, from early 1961. Central Office even reprinted one of the paper's leader columns from 14 June 1961, 'Common Sense', which 'was quite a helpful comment on the Prime Minister's statement in the House'.[206] The letters columns of the broadsheets have proved one of the main forums for the sceptics to air their arguments. The editor of *The Times* admitted to 'receiving very heavy post bags' on the matter,[207] but the problem is that the audience for these arguments was largely confined to the educated elites of British society and have failed to translate into a wider audience in the way in which headlines like the *Sun's* 'Up Yours Delors' have.[208] During the 1960s and 1970s the sceptics were concerned that they were failing to get sufficient coverage for their views in both the print and TV media. The brief boost of *The Daily Telegraph* adopting an anti-Europe stance, during the last year of Maurice Green's editorship, was negated by the appointment as editor of former minister, and pro-European, Bill Deedes in 1974. Some sections of the local press, at particular moments in time, adopted sceptical stances: *Inverness Courier*, *Ayrshire Post* and *Shetland News* (1961–2), *Nottingham Guardian Journal* (1962–3), *Western Gazette* (1973–5). The Atlantic Free Trade Area (AFTA) Parliamentary Group wrote to the BBC in 1969 'protesting at the amount of coverage given to Common Market enthusiasts and the lack of coverage given to the AFTA concept' and received what they considered to be a 'rather unsatisfactory' reply.[209] Neil Marten secured a minor triumph when he forced Lord Hill of Luton, the BBC chairman, to concede in July 1970 that 'it is broadly true that over the last few months the case for Britain not joining the Common Market has not had much of a hearing' and to promise that the antis' argument would be represented in future current affairs programmes.[210] However, by the early 1970s even the forum of the *Daily Express* was lost to the sceptics, causing exasperated protests.[211] Then the 1975 referendum revealed that lack of wide-ranging support for the antis' message, and this would prove to be one of the enduring lessons the sceptics would take with them into the 1980s.[212] A further burden was that the pro-European cause was better funded and therefore had the means to monitor the output of the media and if necessary bring pressure to bear. During the November 1962 South Dorset by-election campaign Conservative Central Office brought legal pressure to bear on Southern TV to abandon a live four-way discussion amongst the main candidates so as to starve the Debenham campaign of vital exposure and similarly complained to the BBC's *Panorama* about a feature on the campaign which included a sequence, with voice-over, of Hinchingbrooke and Debenham.[213] Likewise, the Britain in Europe campaign complained the to the Independent Broadcasting Authority (IBA) about anti-EEC comments made by George Gale, a former *Daily Express* journalist and then editor of the *Spectator*, on his local radio programme and extracted the 'promise' that on the issue of Europe he would be gagged.[214] The lack of media exposure was one of the main lessons the 'No' campaign drew in its post-mortem of the 1975 European referendum.[215]

# 7   Conservatives in Europe

## 'The concern of a private army'?

A caricature exists of the Conservative Party that is insular and nationalistically chauvinistic. Although historically British Conservatism does not have a strong 'internationalist' strain, unlike the Labour Party, either ideologically or organisationally there has since 1945 been a willingness on the part of Conservative politicians and activists to engage with their European counterparts.[1] This helps account for the party's label as the European party, which it successfully carried for forty years. It is not a recent phenomenon solely restricted to Members of the European Parliament and to senior Conservatives as ministers attending meetings of the Council of Ministers, but dates back to the immediate post-war years when Conservatives first participated in the Council of Europe at the Hague and subsequently became involved in organisations such as the Western European Union and NATO. The question that must be asked is to what extent have these European contacts helped foster the European ideal?

### Inter-European party liaison

From the very moment that British Conservatives began participating in European political structures, such as the Council of Europe, the question arose as to whether it was necessary to ally with their European counterpart parties. The extent of liaison took place on a number of levels from individual to organisational, from *ad hoc* to formal. Within continental European politics, the three main political groupings were the Christian Democrats, the Liberals and the Socialists, plus a plethora of smaller groups, such as the Communists. If involvement in Europe were to signal a revival of British leadership, then given the tendency of European politics to be conducted around coalitions the Conservatives would be obliged to seek and build alliances. The problem the Conservatives faced was that they 'had no such natural affiliation' with any of these groups, not even the Christian Democrats.[2] This stemmed from the 'complete isolation of the British political system from Europe'.[3] Nevertheless, the fact that the Conservative Party had been a mass party since the nineteenth century and had been integrated into the democratic process for most of its history suggested in one respect, at least, a commonality with continental Christian Democrat parties.[4] The Conservative apathy towards the Christian Democrats was, and remains, multifaceted. The dependency of Christian Democracy on trade union support and the willingness of these parties to contemplate coalitions with parties of the left was anathema to the 'anti-Socialist' Conservative Party. The spectre of the Christian Democratic commitment to federalism also played its part and, finally, the origins of these parties, with their association with Roman Catholicism, caused disquiet to an essentially secular party. Furthermore, the emphasis on ideas of social responsibility and the family in contrast to individualism was a key ideological distinction. Consequently the matter of liaison has proved a thorny matter that has still not been satisfactorily resolved over six decades later. The matter has raised problems for Conservative ideological, organisational and financial concerns. The structural organisation of the Conservatives was often very different from that of its continental counterparts, which caused problems whenever too prescriptive a liaison structure was proposed.[5] Between 1949 and 1950 Young Conservative representatives had been sent to the youth wing of the Christian Democrat Nouvelles Equipes Internationales (NEI). However, by 1950 the representative Anthony Nutting was seeking permission to withdraw because he felt the NEI 'was running a policy in Europe with which the great majority of the Conservative Party fundamentally disagree, i.e. federalism'.[6] This difference in policy objectives was because the political parties of continental Europe shared a different ideological heritage to the Conservative Party of Winston Churchill and Margaret Thatcher. This was nowhere more clearly evident than in the CAP, which paid 'lip-service' to the commitment to free trade and was instead used 'quite shamelessly, but legally, to distort fair competition'.[7] More often than not, the continuation of these liaisons has been reliant upon the enthusiasm of individuals, rather than due to any particular institutional Conservative zeal. Whilst this might appear to apportion blame to the party's leadership, this would be to exclude the factor of how the Conservative Party was received by its European partners. On the continent the word 'Conservative' drew negative connotations because of its association with fascism. Consequently this could act as a hindrance in Conservative attempts to formulate alliances in a manner it perceived to be beneficial. At various times there were suggestions that the Conservatives in Europe might re-brand themselves as European Unionists or European Democratic Centrists, but these ideas were firmly rejected at the highest levels.[8] But even as the war years became a distant memory to the new generation of European political leaders, the Conservative Party, because of its commitment to secular liberal values and free trade, especially during the 1980s and 1990s, remained equally unattractive to the Christian Democrats.

During the 1940s, 1950s and 1960s responsibility for the party's links with European parties rested with the Conservative Overseas Bureau (COB). Initially it had been instructed to rule 'out any question of formal alliance with kindred parties at the [Council of Europe] Assembly'.[9] In terms of the party's priorities Europe was low down the rankings, with policy research preference being given to domestic issues, and despite platitudes from senior figures COB had to survive on a very restricted budget.[10] Money was always a constant issue. A familiar complaint was that individual Conservatives hosted overseas political visitors at their own expense and were unable to 'afford to reciprocate lavish hospitality they have been granted abroad'.[11] For pro-Europeans it suggested that the leadership's rhetoric of the Conservatives as the party of Europe was not being matched in practical terms. Party treasurers countered that the money they raised was given to help the party win votes and elections: inter-European party links achieved neither of these objectives. This desire to keep a rein on financial expenditure further explains why COB was required to seek approval from the parliamentary Foreign Affairs Committee prior to sending party delegates to overseas European gatherings, an approval system that was tightened to required ministerial acquiescence after the party's return to office in 1951.[12] When later in the 1950s a plea was made for increased funding for COB's activities this led to further demands for tightened oversight since it is 'essential that such activities should be co-ordinated and controlled at a high level'.[13] The strength of the Overseas Bureau was the contacts it established within the European political establishment, though these links were as much with individuals as they were with political parties.[14] COB was also responsible for overseeing Conservative links with a much broader range of peripheral European organisations, such as the European Union of Women and the United European Movement,[15] the rationale being that it was important to provide a 'Conservative' counterweight to the Socialists within such groups.

Macmillan's 1961 application gave added impetus to the search for links with continental partners. Prior to that date the relationships could be best described as 'tentative liaisons'.[16] A specific party committee was established in December 1962 and co-ordinated by party chairman Iain Macleod to consider this issue.[17] At this time the Conservative delegates to the Council of Europe were allied to the 'Independent Representatives', a grouping that had emerged in 1958 although which carried no commitment to vote together. After 1962 a 'useful liaison' had been established with the Christian Democrats and Liberals through the attendance of Conservative observers at their meetings, but the committee concluded that the party had more to gain if they remained as independents. Although this weakened their influence in committees and the Council Chamber, it meant that their votes were sought, and could prove decisive in narrow divisions, whilst if de Gaulle vetoed the British application the 'Independents' might gain new support from those French delegates opposed to de Gaulle.[18] One consequence of the 1963 French veto was that it gave a temporary stimulus to those who thought the Conservatives should exploit European sympathy. During 1963 there were various initiatives such as an abortive proposal that the Conservatives might rejoin the Christian Democrat NEI and a series of exchange meetings with the German Christian Democrats (CDU).[19] The financial question was never far from the surface, with the NEI proposal being vetoed because the burden of membership would have fallen upon Conservative coffers, whilst it was agreed that the Conservative/CDU meetings could only occur if the cost alternated between London and Bonn. Of the various continental Christian Democrat parties the German CDU was the most amenable towards British Conservatism, and would later be behind many of the initiatives that tried to ally the Conservatives with the wider Christian Democrat movement. With an eye on the potential enlargement of the EEC, the CDU was anxious to ally itself with parties from countries which had no Christian Democrat heritage to form a broader non-collectivist majority within the European Parliament. But many of the initiatives rested upon personal commitment. The case of Peter Smithers, MP for Winchester from 1950, who had been chair of the Overseas Bureau from 1956 to 1960, is illustrative. When he was appointed to the Foreign Office he carried forward these contacts and was at the fore of Foreign Office proposals to extend the Conservatives' links in Europe.[20] It also fell to Smithers to try and rescue the Conservative/CDU talks when Macleod was dismissed from the party chairmanship. This was greeted with 'some consternation' in Bonn, where they were fearful that it meant 'a setback'. Smithers was anxious that Macleod's successor, John Hare, should immediately reassure his CDU counterpart and commit at least a full day's attendance at the cross-party gathering scheduled for later in the month in Bonn.[21] That these exchanges continued, and were encouraged, under Heath's leadership was evidenced by a senior Conservative delegation, led by Alec Douglas-Home and Michael Fraser, that attended the Second European Christian Democrats Conference in Stockholm in May 1968: 'The personal contacts were extremely close and useful ... particularly as many had met before at one of the previous meetings, at the Council of Europe or elsewhere'.[22] The importance of these personal contacts should not be underestimated, although it is hard to measure the effect of personal chemistry. However, it is evident that respect, even friendship, with European counterparts has smoothed negotiations.[23]

In fact the exchange visits with the German CDU mark a turning point in the Conservatives' views towards its relationship with Christian Democracy. This shift was motivated by a number of factors. Although ideologically there was suspicion of where the CDU parties stood on the means and methods of European integration, there was a realisation that they tended to be the controlling group within the Council of Europe and the European Parliament. If Britain was to join the EEC, then Conservatives would be expected to participate in the European Parliament, where business was conducted in a different manner to the Council of Europe and Western European Union Assemblies. Whereas in these two later forums seating arrangements were alphabetical by party, within the European Parliament seats were arranged by group affiliation. Therefore, whilst the Conservatives remained affiliated to the Independents they ran the risk of being an isolated national grouping if and when they secured accession to the EEC. This would mean a consequential loss of influence, as the means to secure positions within the various committees and Chamber were often carved up by the larger groups.

Once a Conservative delegation was dispatched to the European Parliament in 1973 the challenge was to find allies. Party activists had expressed hope that the party would seek co-operation with other centre-right parties.[24] The outcome was mixed, not least because the Conservative name was a hindrance. Nevertheless, Douglas Dodds-Parker, as the delegation's leader, was under firm instructions to 'keep the label "Conservative" and demonstrate to our like-minded counterparts by our actions that we are not intolerably right-wing'.[25] In fact, the Danish Conservatives were similarly concerned about the need for allies and approached the British Conservatives, via Hugh Rossi, suggesting an alliance in advance of their respective delegations taking their seats in 1973. The initial response was 'cautious', partly because of concerns about nomenclature but also for fear of upsetting Christian Democratic 'susceptibilities'.[26] In the event both groups did ally together, naming themselves the European Conservative Group (ECG). In reality this was little more than a 'national' grouping since there were only two Danish Conservative delegates.[27] The problem was that ECG 'credibility as a force in the European Parliament suffers by virtue of their small size as well as the mono-national character'.[28]

Whilst relations with the German CDU had consistently improved during the 1960s and early 1970s, the Christian Democrat parties in Italy, Belgium and Holland were not as willing to ally themselves with the Conservatives. All had participated alongside the Conservatives in inter-party conferences since 1967. It was agreed in 1975 amongst a conference of ten party leaders to develop the European Democratic Union (EDU), an umbrella group of like-minded centre-right parties from Scandinavia, Germany, Austria and a number of other European countries inside and outside the Community. The Italian, Belgium and Dutch Christian Democrat parties opted out, preferring to fight the up and coming European elections alongside other Christian Democrat parties in the European People's Party (EPP). This EDU coalition received the approval of the 1975 Conservative conference.[29] For Thatcher the anti-Socialist nature of the EDU was central and given that the alliance was a loose umbrella organisation it was easy to promote the areas of commonality. 'Each of us, in our own countries', Thatcher declared in Hanover in May 1976,

> have our different problems. But many problems – of maintaining free economies, of combating threats to our way of life both from within and from without – we hold in common. It is to solve those problems and meet these threats that we should bring ourselves closer together.[30]

Thomas Jansen, a German Christian Democrat, has suggested that the Conservative's motivation derived from their desire to seek 'a new order, one consonant with the adversarial nature of their system of government – an order which pooled together anti-Socialist forces'. The EDU's constitution was agreed at Munich in October 1977 and formally established at Salzburg on 24 April 1978. However, the signatory parties to the EDU were alert to Christian Democratic sensibilities. Their alternative grouping, the EPP, considered the creation of the EDU to have a 'negative, divisive effect' on their image. EPP signatories were warned that dual membership of both the EPP and the EDU was 'bigamy'.[31] Conscious of this 'ill feeling', the launch of the EDU was delayed until after the EPP's First Congress.[32] This ill will would only be dispelled, warned Henrig Wegener of the CDU, with 'patient, painstaking explanation'.[33] For the Conservatives, thereafter, relations with the EPP were conducted on an *ad hoc* basis, but helped considerably by the party's 1976 *Right Approach* manifesto, which clarified the Conservatives' ideological position for their European counterparts and because they supported the election of the Italian Christian Democrat Emilio Colombo, who served as president of the Parliament from 1977 to 1979. This was a compliment that would be repaid in 1986 when Lord Plumb was elected the first Conservative president of the European Parliament.

The French were also a notable absence from the EDU. Since de Gaulle's first veto, the Conservative Party had found it difficult to forge meaningful relations with the major French parties. During the EEC accession debate the Conservative Group for Europe (CGE) had tried to sustain these links given that the 'government was muzzled and the party unable to come out into the open'. However, the CGE felt it had neither the resources nor the guidance to continue these liaisons.[34] Nor did the party machine seem any keener after 1973 to undertake these tasks. As Chris Patten, director of the Conservative Research Department, admitted:

> I do not really understand the point of these liaisons meetings but I dare say that they do not do any harm provided they are kept in a very low key and that the 'Euro-nuts' on our side are kept on a tight rein.

'Pointless' was the agreeing minute from the party chairman, Peter Carrington.[35] Heath might have persuaded the party to enter the EEC, but the 'Europeanisation' of the party was going to be resisted.

Following the first direct elections to the European Parliament in 1979 one of the first actions of the newly appointed leader of the Conservative Group, Scott-Hopkins, was to change the name of the Conservatives alliance with the Danish Conservatives to European Democratic Group (EDG).[36] This was an affirmation of the Conservative commitment to the European Democratic Union. It was also intended to satisfy the concerns of those who felt that the title 'Conservative' carried too much negative baggage for potential European allies. There was continued *ad hoc* collaboration between the Conservative Group and the EPP. It would still have been a step too far to formally ally with this grouping because the federalist and corporatist themes which were so central to European Christian Democracy held no appeal to mainstream Conservative thinking, and because of initial animosity, caused by the EDU's creation. Nevertheless there was pressure from some quarters for such an arrangement since 'it is difficult to maintain that we are really [a] European party so long as we remain in European terms a small isolated group outside the main currents of European political thought'.[37]

It was not until the late 1980s, in the twilight of Thatcher's leadership, that the Conservatives formally applied to join the EPP. Christopher Prout, then leader of the Conservative MEPs, made the application on behalf of the EDG immediately after the 1989 European elections. The EPP secretary-general, Thomas Jansen, believes that 'Conservative MEPs understood, before their party friends in Westminster or in Central Office, that Britain's future is "at the heart of Europe"'.[38] It was also a numerical matter after the 1989 elections since with only thirty-four members in a 518-member Parliament the EDG lacked any hope of effective influence.[39] However, the EPP's executive, led by Jacques Santer, decided 'the time was not yet ripe' and proposed revisiting the application in two years time. One of the reasons for this was the perceived hostility of Margaret Thatcher. However, there were also ideological issues. Would Conservative entry into a Christian Democrat organisation dilute Christian Democrat identity? There were elements within the EEP, notably the German CDU, who felt the EPP needed to establish a foothold in those countries that had no Christian Democrat tradition, especially with the proposed enlargement of the European Union.[40] This was not a universal view. These internal divisions ensured that there was no dialogue or attempts at co-operation between the EDG and the EPP from 1989 until 1991, although from 1990 party chairman, Kenneth Baker, was in discussions with Volker Ruhr about how to ease the Conservatives into the EPP.[41] A special meeting of the EPP in April 1991 specifically discussed these problems. Thatcher was no longer Conservative leader and her successor John Major appeared more willing to adopt a European role. This meeting confirmed the core values of Christian Democracy and reaffirmed the EPP commitment to federalism, but it signalled the opportunity for co-operation with parties of 'a similar social project, and with the same goals in terms of their European policy'.[42] The Conservative application was now to be reconsidered and a decision made by the end of the year. During the summer of 1991 Wilfried Martens acted as the liaison with the EDG and Chris Patten, Conservative party chairman.

The formal alliance between the EPP and the Conservative Allies was announced on 1 May 1992. In the view of one seasoned Strasbourg watcher it was 'primarily a marriage of practical convenience rather than the result of any ideological imperative'. This 'marriage of convenience' thesis was accentuated by the decision of the president of the EPP/Christian Democrat Group in the Council of Europe Assembly to rule out any such similar merger on 'ideological grounds'.[43] It reinforced the EPPs and Socialists oligarchical grip on patronage within the European Parliament. Whilst this alliance was not as formal as appearances implied, it was controversial nevertheless. Whereas all EPP member parties were committed to fighting European elections on a common manifesto, the Conservative Party was not bound by any such commitment. Instead, individual Conservative MEPs were allied to the EPP, which allowed both sides to paper over the significant differences over the Social Chapter and single common currency. Attempts were made to embarrass the Conservatives over their links with the EPP. In both the 1994 and 1999 European elections Labour sought to portray the Conservatives as fully signed up to the EPP manifesto with its federalist, pro-Euro commitments. In 1994 the Conservatives enlisted the support of Wilfried Martens as group chairman of the EPP to confirm their independence and in 1999 Hague countered that his party was not a signatory to the manifesto.[44] However, this was 'Labour's one clear hit' of the 1999 European election campaign.[45]

What this did was reignite the internal party debate about the merits of allying with the EPP. A lively exchange of correspondence on the letters page of the *Daily Telegraph* typified the debate, with many former MEPs springing to the defence of the arrangement with the EPP. These correspondents reminded the paper's largely Eurosceptic readership, as well as the party leadership, that the European Parliament made its decision by a majority of all members (present or not) which meant compromise between the two largest groups (the EPP and the Socialists) over legislation: 'The politics', explained Michael Welsh, an MEP until 1994, 'lie in shaping the consensus during the negotiations that take place in committee and before the final vote'. The Conservatives were now the second largest national delegation in the largest political group and in a powerful position to exert influence. They also held the balance of power, because without them the EPP would lose its position as the largest group. The largest group gets the pick of the committee chairmanships and other key posts: 'Our experience clearly shows', argued Lord Inglewood, also an MEP until 1994, 'that this [influence] is best achieved by being part of them. To leave the EPP Group means relinquishing the greatest tool at our disposal to achieve results'.[46] Put another way by John Taylor, an MEP from 1979 to 1984, 'there was a bias in favour of being bigger. It was not merely better to be bigger. It was much better to be bigger'.[47] This advice was heeded when Hague, Maples and Macmillan-Scott reaffirmed the party's affiliation until 2009 of its thirty-six MEPs to the group of the EPP and Conservative Allies.[48] Wilfried Martens, EPP chairman, confirmed, in exchange, that Conservative MEPs were free to vote differently from the majority of the group and were not committed to its manifesto.[49] Common sense played its part. The 1999 Euro-elections left the Conservatives in their strongest position since the first elections of 1979. The Centre for Policy Studies (CPS) did publish a paper in 2001, which advocated the Conservatives leaving the EPP and forming a new alliance with anti-European MEPs.[50] This was greeted angrily by MEPs like Christopher Beazley, who were horrified at proposals that they should ally themselves with politicians from Central and Eastern Europe with distinctly dubious right-wing policies just because they were Eurosceptic: 'a successful party of the right must continue to recruit its strength from the centre. Once it begins to shrink into itself like a snail it will be doomed.'[51] The CPS's advice was disregarded by the new Conservative leader, Michael Howard, who in advance of the June 2004 European elections reaffirmed the EPP relationship. However, the success of UKIP in these elections, and the debate about the European Constitution, allowed the Eurosceptics to continue to challenge the issue. The election of David Cameron as leader in December 2005 has added to the challenge. During the leadership contest he offered a pledge, one of the very few specifics of his campaign, to withdraw from the EPP, and has since tasked his shadow foreign secretary, William Hague, with the task of negotiating the withdrawal. This has provoked considerable disquiet amongst sections of the party's MEPs, with reports suggesting that as many as one-quarter would disregard any order to leave the EPP.[52]

## The Council of Europe

Regardless of whether Winston Churchill was, or was not, a positive European, he nevertheless left one important legacy. His 1946 Zurich speech began a process which led to the creation of the Council of Europe with the encouragement of his son-in-law Duncan Sandys and the United European Movement. Churchill's rally call saw an important coterie of young Conservative politicians ride to his standard. These so-called Tory Strasbourgers, men like Harold Macmillan, David Eccles and Robert Boothby, signed up to the European Movement and embraced the idea that Western Europe was only too willing to accept British leadership. Via the Assembly debating chamber and the committee rooms of the Council of Europe these politicians found themselves able to do business with the impenetrable continental mind, and were exposed to the European mode of political practice. The experience tended to confirm these individuals' pro-European position and enabled them to judge issues in other than strictly national terms. Their presence at Strasbourg helped transform the Council of Europe from an intergovernmental debating forum into a venue of polit-ical integration. The Churchillian rhetoric about a parliamentary assembly 'gave an impression that the Conservative Party was broadly in support'.[53] This appeared to be confirmed by the level of Conservative support for an EDM welcoming the Council of Europe.[54] In reality a large proportion of the Conservative Party was uneasy about the whole concept.[55] The resulting internal debate, within the forum of the Conservatives' backbench parlia-mentary committees, about the Council of Europe confirmed that the zeal for European unity was not shared by the majority of Conservatives.[56]

Partly because of its association with Churchill throughout the 1950s and 1960s, Conservatives looked to the Council of Europe as an avenue for enhancing British interests in Europe. But in equal measure there was unease about the form that European unity was taking. The pro-Europeanists were alert to their party's concerns and this probably explains why they sponsored a moderate EDM on Western union on 23 February 1949.[57] With the failed 1961 and 1967 EEC applications it is noticeable that proposals were made each time for some sort of reform of the Council, which would once more enhance its reputation and help promote Conservative European credentials.[58] Since the creation of the EEC the Council of Europe 'had been out of the political limelight', but this was 'deceptive' since it was the only 'large scale European institution to show a capacity for growth both as regards range of functions and increasing its membership'.[59] Part of the attraction of the Council was its inclusivity. After 1957 it was a forum that gave an opportunity to hear views of those Europeans outside the EEC.[60] Some Conservatives argued it was the forum in which Britain could exercise European leadership which would 'off-set' the Six's tendency 'to concentrate interest in the European Parliament'.[61] To this day the Council of Europe has remained out of the limelight and since the advent of the European Parliament many electors have been unable to distinguish between the two, if indeed they admitted to knowing of its existence. Harold Macmillan, returning to the Strasbourg Assembly to deliver a ministerial address in July 1955, felt that although it had evolved differently to expectations the fact that potential co-operation was possible was 'tremendous': 'The problem is to re-state the precise function of the Council of Europe in all this.' He thought it had two functions: to review and discuss the political aspects of the European organisations, and to debate, as the only parliamentary European forum, the 'great questions of the day. In addition, it represents the concept of Europe as a whole; even tho' now divided ideologically, Europe is a historical and cultural whole'.[62] Some Europeanists, though, were more sceptical, believing that the Churchill government from 1951 did its utmost to undermine the Council of Europe, particularly with Eden's refusal to participate in a European army. Leading continental politicians, like Spaak and Monnet, recognising the moribund nature of the Council without active British participation, determined to find an alternative means of securing European unity.[63]

The British 'delegates'[64] to the Council of Europe were from 1949 selected by the prime minister of the day, responding to the advice of the whips from each of the parties. Robert Boothby secured his place on the recommendation of the Conservative chief whip Patrick Buchan-Hepburn, who considered that 'he is most keen ... and has said that he wants to make this United Europe his major interest. Mr Sandys said he talks with much more knowledge about it all than any other Conservative MP'.[65] Support for European integration could be one reason for selection; another was an ability with foreign languages. Harold Macmillan, a delegate from 1949 to 1951 as a result of his time as minister resident in North West Africa in 1942–5 knew many French and Italian politicians and was fluent in French, making him confident enough to ditch the translation headphones 'except to listen to the bad French of the Italians and Turks. When the French speak, it is generally easy to understand'.[66] It was also thought politic to include an Ulster Unionist representative to counter any accusations of neglect of the province.[67] The delegation could comprise both peers and MPs and would also include a whip. Delegates to the Council, as well as the Western European Union, in fact comprised all strands of Conservative European thought, from those like John Eden who were anti-Marketeers in principle, to Russell, whose opposition was based upon Commonwealth preference, to those like Maitland who were pro-entry provided there were adequate agricultural safeguards. There were confederalists like Scott-Hopkins and Mayhew and federalists like Kirk and Ridley. Churchill decided to lead the first Conservative delegation himself, with Harold Macmillan as deputy, supported by Eccles, Maxwell-Fyfe, Boothby, Ronald Ross and with John Foster and Lord Birkenhead as 'substitutes'. Duncan Sandys, who was still out of Parliament, acted as Churchill's chief of staff, using his role in the United Europe Movement to particular effect.

During the Council's first decade a total of sixty-one Conservative MPs and ten peers, serving just over an average of two years each, participated in the party's delegation. Although, in contrast to Labour delegates, a number of Conservatives did serve considerably longer periods, notably Lord Goschen (ten years), Robert Boothby (seven years), John Foster (six years), Julian Amery and Sir J. Hutchinson (both five years).[68] Several reasons explain the turnover: pressures of parliamentary work and a concern that work for the Council of Europe should not impinge upon a delegate's Westminster role. Also, there was a sense that the opportunity to experience the Assembly should be given to as many as possible. Whilst the first Conservative delegation might have been deemed 'heavyweight', solely because of Churchill's presence, it is evident thereafter that those selected for Strasbourg duty lacked seniority – the *deuxième cru*, as Julian Critchley labelled them.[69] Appointment to the delegation could be a sign that a MP was being tested for junior political office. Could they demonstrate their mettle and not turn 'native' once surrounded by the continentals? Ursula Branston, who acted as secretary to the Strasbourg delegation, was inclined to agree that the quality of the Conservative delegates diminished during the 1950s and that 'the Europeans themselves were disappointed'. However, Ted Heath, as chief whip, took the view that 'the more people we can send who are not stars but likely to become interested in Europe in the future, the better'.[70] This was borne out during the 1961–3 application when the majority of Council of Europe and WEU delegates favoured entry, and from the backbenches of Westminster provided Macmillan with a reliable source of support. The leadership of these delegations also lacked gravitas. As Critchley acidly observed:

In my day the delegates came to be led by Sir John Rodgers, who never missed a party; Sir Simon Wingfield Digby, whose idea of Europe was Antibes; and Sir Frederic Bennett, who collected foreign decorations. Europe was put on the backburner.[71]

It is worth comparing this with the composition of the Conservative group in the European Parliament.[72] Half of the 1973 Conservative MEP delegates had experienced the Council of Europe or sat on the Assembly of the Western European Union, which eased the process of adjustment and which meant that many already had established personal contacts amongst continental European politicians.[73] One MEP has suggested Conservative candidates are often selected because of their perceived European suitability, which can be as trivial as having a foreign-born spouse or wide foreign travel experience.[74] Another perception was that MEPs were rejects from the Westminster selection process.[75] However, this delegation and the directly elected Conservative Group from 1979 suffered too from a paucity of senior party figures, especially when compared to other national groups that included former prime ministers and senior ministers or party leaders. The 1979–84 Conservative group contained three ex-junior ministers and a few individuals like Fred Catherwood, Henry Plumb and David Nicholson who had substantial business or administrative experience. Ten per cent of Conservative European candidates in 1979 were either present or former delegates to the Strasbourg Parliament, whilst Community institutions had previously employed seven of them. At a Europe-wide level, of those MEPs elected in 1979 20 per cent had previous experience of the Strasbourg Parliament, 25 per cent had previous experience of another European assembly such as the Council of Europe or Western European Union, whilst 45 per cent were former or current national parliament representatives.[76] However, one of the new intake, although hardly an impartial source, was impressed by the calibre of the British Conservatives, considering them 'the most eclectically talented group of people that I have ever had the privilege to belong to'.[77]

From the very beginning of the Council of Europe idea, concern was being expressed about whether those who were to attend on behalf of the Conservative Party were to act as delegates of the party or as individuals. This proved to be the dress rehearsal for arguments that are still repeated over five decades later about the extent to which Conservative Members of the European Parliament should reflect the views of the Westminster parliamentary party. There is clear historical pedigree in the ability of Conservative representatives in Europe to successfully embarrass the party at home by their actions and words. This was apparent following the first Council of Europe session when a significant number of Conservative backbenchers expressed concern about the Conservative delegates' positive contributions to the calls for European unity. Some, like Oliver Stanley, himself serving on the executive of the United European Movement, wished to see delegates take 'a party view' and warned that Europe 'could no longer be the concern of a private army'.[78] Macmillan was forced to admit that this debate reflected a 'certain amount of anxiety' within the party 'about the implications of United Europe'.[79] The consequence of these discussions was that the subsequent nomination of party delegates required the approval of the backbench Foreign Affairs Committee, and then, after a return to government, ministerial approval as well.[80] The experience of attending the Council of Europe, and whether it confirmed or developed delegates' support for European unity, will be considered later.

The Strasbourg experience was not restricted to parliamentarians; party activists were able to join as observer delegations sent to attend European conferences. The rationale of party managers was simple: it enabled members to make contacts and observe leading European figures at first hand. The political benefits of these study visits were illustrated, as one internal party document noted, by the fact that they enabled these activists 'to inspire others to venture politically beyond the narrow seas, at any rate, to grasp the significance of urgent developments outside our coasts'.[81] Yet in real terms the value the party placed upon this approach was indicated by its allocation of a mere £750 for the budgetary year 1954–5, which was hardly 'an excessive amount for a great imperial party to spend on external relations', especially when compared with Labour's £10,500 for 1952 and £4,600 for 1953.[82] Money was always the issue and the bold declarations of the positive benefits of such study visits were really aimed at trying to loosen the party's purse strings. That these visits continued for over a decade into the 1960s suggests that the party hierarchy considered there to be some benefit. From reading these reports a sense emerges of the changing perspectives of the Conservative activists towards the European experiment. These observers perceived that Britain's role, and especially that of the Conservative participants, was one of leadership:

> The Council, partly because of British Conservative tenacity, had shown a resilience which promised better things for the pan-European ideal, and encouraged our own members in their enthusiastic but realistic interest.[83]

Revealing too is a comparison of the 1961 and 1962 reports. In 1961 the hostility of the French towards Britain is clearly flagged up and, as negotiations for British entry to the EEC have just begun, there is confidence that the Six 'value the Commonwealth' and appreciate the legitimacy of problems this poses for Britain, but as the negotiations stall the 1962 report is quick to blame the Six and accuse them of ignorance of what the Commonwealth means to Britain.[84]

## Members of the European Parliament

With British accession to the European Community, Britain was invited to send delegates to the European Parliament. Although Labour initially vetoed the participation of their members, a Conservative delegation of eighteen led by Peter Kirk, a junior minister in the Ministry of Defence, took their seats in the Strasbourg European Parliament in January 1973.[85] As Tom Normanton observed, this was one of the two greatest moments in his life: 'we were gladiators back from Gaul.'[86] The pro-European elements within the party were anxious that 'our delegation' should secure the necessary funding to continue to promote the European message. Central Office was reluctant to be the source of these funds, so the City was looked to. As Michael Fraser explained, 'some fairly major exercise in money raising for the various European parts of the Party is quite essential in view of the relative uselessness of the European Movement in this field at the present time'. Ambitious plans were hatched to secure donations of up to £20,000 from the chairmen of fifty invisible export companies, but Heath was unwilling to act as a figurehead. In the event the donations fell substantially below the expectation and there ensued a battle between Central Office and the European Representation Fund over how this money should be spent. Carrington wanted to use the monies to relieve Central Office of financing activities in connection with Europe, whilst the Europeanists wanted to use it to promote Europe through political activities.[87]

At this stage there was no provision for direct elections to the European Parliament, therefore those sent were 'delegates' of the British government, as with the Council of Europe. Conservative Central Office chose the Conservatives with attention to geographical and political balance. Pro-Europeanists were quick to encourage Heath to send the strongest possible delegation to Strasbourg, drawing upon the body of experienced Europeanists who had seen service on the Council of Europe. Indeed over half of the Conservative 1973 delegation had served on either the Council of Europe or the Western European Union Assembly. This need for experience was deemed necessary because of 'the great challenge [in refining the EEC's institutions], even beyond the economics', argued Dodds-Parker. 'We will need strong delegates – from the chair and the table and constitutional lawyers as well as from practising politicians in both Houses'.[88] The old problem of whether a Member of Parliament could combine their Westminster duties with serving on a European Assembly again raised its head. This was made all the more pressing because the European Parliament sat for 100 days per annum, considerably longer than the Council of Europe. One internal party evaluation concluded that the use of sitting MPs would prove unpopular with constituents and no MP was 'likely to wish to endanger his seat' by taking the dual mandate.[89] This explains why once direct elections had been agreed it was decided to 'discourage' dual membership of the House of Commons and European Parliament.[90] However, there was some ambiguity. One candidate received a letter of support from the chief whip which agreed that the dual mandate was not the preferable option but declared:

> I believe there should be certain exceptions. ... There is certain to be a major problem in establishing a positive Conservative identity for this new Group ... any of them will not have been involved in any party political activity prior to their election. As a Party, we are determined that this Group will give complete loyalty to both the Conservative Party and to its principles.[91]

In the end four successfully secured the dual mandate: Jim Spicer, Elaine Kellett-Bowman, Tom Normanton and Brandon Rhys-Williams. The European delegation had been favourable to this arrangement and actually voted against banning dual mandates in the January 1975 Plenary of the European Parliament.[92] The unhappiness of the grassroots activists with the prospect of a dual mandate is clearly shown by the list of those who failed to gain a Euro-nomination in 1979: from existing MEPs, individuals like Charles Fletcher-Cooke, Derek Walker-Smith, John Osborn and John Corrie; and from MPs, Paul Channon, Eldon Griffith, John Page, Kenneth Warren, John Hunt, John Rodgers and Frederick Bennett.[93] In 1973 the narrowness of Heath's majority also suggested that the absence of Conservative parliamentarians might prove awkward and unpopular. Add to this the relatively poor air communications, at that time, between Britain and the key cities of the EEC, Strasbourg, Luxembourg and Brussels, and the lack of financial reward for serving at the European Parliament, and some thought it would be difficult to secure volunteers.[94]

The other challenge for the party was how to 'manage' this new breed of Conservative delegate. The operations of the European Parliament and its physical distance from Westminster posed potential problems. This was exemplified when in February 1978 the Conservatives narrowly lost a House of Commons division, 160 to 149, on a motion to secure voting rights in European elections for British citizens resident in Europe. Had dual-mandate Conservative MEPs managed to make it back for the vote, it would have been won.[95] It would prove a matter of simmering discontent that non-parliamentarian MEPs felt as though they were treated as second-class citizens, as exemplified by their lack of reciprocal rights to use facilities at the House of Commons until 1980, twelve months after originally being elected.[96] Because these delegates were not part of the parliamentary party there was concern that MEPs would 'not feel any significantly greater ties to the Westminster party than, say, members of the Conservative Group on a local council'. This raised the likelihood of the party suffering embarrass-ment 'by conflicting views expressed in the European Parliament and in Westminster'.[97] To this end, from the beginning it was thought 'very impor-tant' to have a Westminster whip assigned to the European delegates to ease liaison.[98] Proposals were also put forward to help overcome the potential divisions between MPs and MEPs. There would have been a 'Standing Committee for European Affairs' that would have been open to both MPs and MEPs and which would provide 'an important forum for vigorous debate'.[99] This idea was ultimately not carried through but is one that still remains popular with some Conservative MEPs.[100]

It would not, though, have prevented periods of tension between the Westminster leadership and MEPs. For example, in February 1984, against Thatcher's wishes, twenty-one Conservatives MEPs voted for the draft European Union Treaty, with six abstaining and a further twenty-eight absenting themselves from Strasbourg. This was one of a number of examples during the period 1982–4 when Conservative MEPs refused to yield to the demands of Downing Street. To those back at Westminster it confirmed the long-held suspicions that a European Parliament could be used to embarrass, and undermine, national governments and that the physical distance between London and Strasbourg made it all the more difficult to impose the normal means of party discipline.[101] To Thatcher it was proof that MEPs 'were a residue of Heathism'.[102] The MEPs' defence was that as a group they only represented 63 votes out of 434. The different operational mode of the European parliament dictated the need to trade co-operation for influence. As a consequence there would be occasions when they had to support motions which might be unpopular back at Westminster if they were to retain any influence. This was exemplified by the 1984 Vredleing proposals on workers' rights to access to information about their company. Downing Street was openly hostile to these proposals, but Conservative MEPs adopted a more conciliatory approach to try and water the regulations down.[103] Relations generally with Thatcher were difficult, especially during the period 1979–84 and again after 1989. They proved little better during the 1992–3 period under John Major's leadership. Each was suspicious of the other. Thatcher suspected the MEPs of having gone 'native' and having elevated themselves to a station above their position, and increasingly saw the European Parliament as an irrelevance, whilst the MEP group generally thought Thatcher's belligerence towards Europe was counterproductive and implied a 'little Englander' mentality.[104] However, during the 1990s relations between MEPs and the Westminster party improved through the evolution of a series of *ad hoc* measures. There has been increased MEP involvement in the drafting of Euro-election manifestos. MEPs have been given positions in the National Union of Conservative Associations (National Convention from 1997) and the party's Board of Management. At the same time the right to attend and speak at backbench committee meetings, including the 1922 Committee, has been granted.[105]

It is difficult to judge how much of an impact the British delegation made between 1973 and 1979. Contemporary accounts suggest that individual Conservative delegates did make an impression, especially given that the total numbers of MEPs at this time was relatively small: people like Michael Shaw and Rafton Pounder on the budget committee and Peter Kirk, who from 1975 was rapporteur on the Political Affairs Committee.[106] In 1975 Kirk drafted a paper on the European Parliament's powers. It made two proposals. One suggested that MEPs could have the power of initiative to introduce draft legislation, which if it secured approval from a plenary session could be sent to the Commission. The second was for a 'conciliation procedure' for all Community legislation. However, Kirk's unexpected death in 1977 and the decision to move to direct elections undermined the momentum for reform. Nevertheless, two internal reforms that saw the establishment of a 'Control' Sub-committee of the Budget Committee and the commitment to hold public hearings for all European Parliament committees could be counted as successes.[107] The decision to seek directly elected national representatives for the European Parliament gave renewed expectation to those who hoped that the Parliament might prove a vehicle for reversing the Community's democratic deficit.

The idea of direct national elections to the European Parliament, floated in 1969, was agreed in principal at the 1974 Paris Summit, with the European Council of Ministers agreeing the process in December 1975. The first elections were held Europe-wide in 1979. The Conservatives did well, securing 60 of the 81 seats available. This made the Conservatives the third-largest grouping in the Parliament and meant that the centre-right had a majority over the left of 216 MEPs to 156. The difference in national electoral procedures to the European Parliament has produced distortions in the composition of the Parliament. It has provoked large national differences in the necessary electoral threshold required to enter the Parliament, ranging from 2 per cent to as much as 15 per cent in the British case.[108] Once directly elected representatives were sent to Strasbourg the nature of the European Parliament changed. James Spicer, who acted as the MEPs chief whip in 1979, reported quite dramatic changes and

> did not find it to be sensible to be in both parliaments unless I could be paired as we always had been between 1975 and 1979. As far as the Whips were concerned, one has to remember that we did have a very substantial majority [at Westminster] in that particular period and they only ever called us back when absolutely necessary.[109]

The leadership of the Conservative MEPs has proved a problematic matter, revealing the tensions between the Westminster and Brussels parties and the limitations of central interference. Kirk was a reluctant choice of delegate and leader. He was an experienced Europeanist, having previously served as chair of the General Affairs Committee of the Western European Union. As a former diplomat he was a skilled linguist and had established European contacts. However, he consider the appointment to be a sideways move and feared it would be detrimental to his Westminster career. Nevertheless, he quickly adapted to his new position. The Conservative delegation arrived at the European Parliament stirred by a belief that its very presence would help reinvigorate this institution and, with the correct British leadership, help initiate reforms that would both rectify the democratic deficit of the EEC and help curb its federalist tendencies. Peter Kirk's first speech emphasised the need for reform. He explained that Conservative policy was

> a simple one – power to the Parliament. Our rules must be shaped with that and that alone in mind. There must be power of the Commission first because that is implied in the Treaty. But we must examine our relations with the Council [of Ministers] as well. ... By this means the Parliament will live and the peoples will clamour to be directly represented in it.

Peter Kirk ran his delegation like a cabinet and allocated each member a specialism and a member country to shadow. Whilst the European Parliament was in session he insisted on daily meetings of the delegation and also called regular meetings back in Britain. Given the relatively small size of the delegation compared to the potential numbers, once direct elections were introduced this made direct oversight possible and manageable.[110]

When Kirk died in April 1977 his deputy, Scott-Hopkins, was passed over by Thatcher in preference for Geoffrey Rippon, an ex-Cabinet minister and accession negotiator in 1971–2. He faced difficulties from his Hexham Conservative Association, which was resentful of the dual mandate. With direct elections pending, Rippon tried to secure a Euro-nomination and when that failed he announced his resignation.[111] Attempts by Central Office to have a 'suitable' replacement leader imposed on a nomination paper failed when Essex North East rejected the former junior minister Paul Channon. This might have suggested activist concern about dual mandates, but more likely highlighted a desire to retain autonomy over candidate selection. In the event, Thatcher was reluctantly obliged to appoint Scott-Hopkins as leader designate on 28 March 1979, after he secured nomination for Hereford and Worcester.[112] He had previously served on the Council of Europe from 1960 and been appointed by Heath as a European Parliament delegate in 1973. Regarded as a moderate Europeanist, Scott-Hopkins' leadership was during a formative time, as MEPs sought to define their role in the European Parliament and in terms of relations with the Westminster party. Amongst themselves there were also significant personal and ideological divisions and Conservative MEPs found it hard to act as a single unit, a problem that remains today. Equally, the leader of a delegation lacked the powers of patronage, which can be used to maintain discipline. It is suggested that the chairmen of the various policy committees have greater power than a group leader. One MEP lamented that 'too many members of our group have a stripe on their arm for there to be much scope for sergeants'. Scott-Hopkins was deposed as leader in July 1982 after he ignored the advice of his group and offered himself as a candidate for the presidency of the European parliament. His fellow MEPs blamed him for splitting the vote and allowing the Dutch Socialist Pieter Dankert to triumph over the German Christian Democrat Egon Klepsch. Scott-Hopkins' successor was the former National Farmers' Union president Sir Henry Plumb. However, he lacked any national profile which could have helped project the workings of the European Parliament to the British electorate. Nevertheless he enjoyed 'amiable' relations with Conservative Central Office.[113] Plumb also successfully brought the Spanish Partido Popular into the European Democratic Group which made the EDG the third-largest grouping in the Parliament – half as large as the EPP. However, after 1989 the Partido Popular withdrew from the EDG, citing Thatcher's anti-European rhetoric as the reason. Christopher Prout, who succeed Plumb, was one of the motivating figures behind trying to join the EPP, and was credited by colleagues with having been successful at making informal changes to the procedures of the Parliament that enhanced its role of scrutiny.[114]

What does a Member of the European Parliament do? This was the question that the consumer magazine *Which?* posed in late 1983, prior to the 1984 European elections.[115] MEP Fred Tuckman's response was that he saw his most important functions as being able to influence and shape opinion, an ability to reach agreement with other member nations, to counteract the EEC's 'inevitable' bureaucratic tendencies and to 'show that being good European and sound British are not in conflict'.[116] That *Which?* felt it necessary to run an article on MEPs suggests the failure of the European Parliament to project itself onto the consciousness of the British electorate, and the tone of the article was quite negative about Britain's relations with Europe. Even by the mid-1990s MEPs were prone to observe that their constituents perceived them as the option of last resort. They did notice that their postbag grew ever larger as work from local authorities doubled and single-issue groups, particularly the animal welfare sector, began to lobby the Parliament. For those MEPs with several parliaments' service behind them there was also a belief that their powers of scrutiny had been enhanced.[117] But even more concerning is that twenty years later the question that *Which?* set still remains valid.

## The European experience

It is necessary to consider whether the experience of attending the Council of Europe and the European Parliament confirmed, or developed substantially, delegates' support for European unity. It has been argued that the leading figures of the first Council of Europe delegation were 'passionate "Europeans"'.[118] Nick Ridley, a Eurosceptic of the late 1980s, who was a Strasbourg delegate from 1962 to 1966, freely admits that he went native 'and became converted to a much more federalist point of view'.[119] This reveals the expectations of delegates as well as providing useful counterpoints to their previous political experience.

With the creation of the Council of Europe there was a sense of utopian zeal in the early days amongst the party's pro-Europeans. On learning he had been appointed a delegate, Robert Boothby observed that '[t]he Council may come to nothing – or everything. But I am convinced it is the main – perhaps the only – hope of European civilisation'.[120] Similarly, shortly after arriving at the European Parliament Tufton Beamish felt able to record his belief that after just six months the Conservative delegation had 'made a good start – having a major impact on procedure' – and extol his confidence that the parliament could advance its own position. However, initial euphoria, for both forums, was soon dampened. On returning to the Council as foreign secretary in 1955 Macmillan admitted, 'it hasn't all worked out quite as we had hoped, yet in one way or another, tremendous steps have been taken towards practical co-operation in European affairs. The instruments have varied; NATO, WEU, OEEC and so on. But the work has been done'.[121] Similarly, Tufton Beamish was soon bemoaning that the British contribution 'was not coming through to the British public via the media'.[122] By the end of the year his confidence had been seriously knocked, with his reporting that the experience 'had been disappointing because hopes had been pitched too high, and impossible targets set'.[123]

The constraints imposed on the Council of Europe Assembly by its statutes meant that it was never really to be anything more than a talking shop. To suggest that the Council of Europe is no longer important, whilst true in political and economic terms, overlooks its importance as a conditioner of experience for Conservative politicians. Harold Nicolson observed when his son, Nigel, became a delegate in 1956 that it 'is meaningless but valuable. It is a lot of eye-wash: Optrex, it is. But it is valuable in giving backbench MPs diplomatic experience';[124] whilst on a light-hearted note one former leader of British delegation to the Council felt able to quip, 'the food, dear boy, is much better than in England, and the oratory largely incomprehensible'.[125] There was certainly a sense that Strasbourg was a 'jolly'. Evidently the whole Strasbourg experience was very different to that which they had known at Westminster. Harold Macmillan admitted that 'one of the agreeable features … is that when anything interesting or exciting has happened – you adjourn, for drink, gossip and repose'.[126] However, since the Assembly had 'no majority; no government; no opposition; no whips', '[y]ou have to rely on persuasiveness and the weight of argument to carry a point. It strikes some of us as very queer and rather alarming!'[127] Furthermore, 'it is clear that *humour* is no good here – *Wit*, yes; but not British school-boy or public-house "chaff"'.[128] The continental aversion to adversarial politics made acclimatising a drawn-out experience for British politicians. When Herbert Morrison and Winston Churchill fell into an argument in the Chamber about an allowance for one of the Conservative reserve delegates, '[t]he French and other foreigners were amazed'.[129] Nor was it particularly well received in Britain, even by Conservatives.[130]

Aside from the main forum of the Assembly smaller-issue specific committees were established. David Maxwell-Fyfe, with his legal background and experience as a prosecutor at the Nuremberg trials, presided over the Human Rights Committee, whilst David Eccles was the representatives on the Economics Committee, with Macmillan and Boothby sitting on the Political (or General) Committee. The experience of sitting on these committees was also different to the Westminster committee stage. Macmillan found the method 'interesting, though rather slow. The chairman and rapporteur are expected to be impartial (or more or less impartial) and do not guide the debate as much as a chairman would do with us'. Conservatives have had to adjust to the European nature of conducting politics.[131] 'The secret of success in European politics', observed Bill Newton Dunn, 'is to make alliances, to give and take, but not to demand everything. It is a lesson that the Commons does not teach'.[132] There is evidence that once exposed to the Strasbourg experience a sense grows amongst MEPs that they do have a positive role to play.[133] Early analysis of Conservative experience suggested that the Parliament's structure, especially its emphasis on committees rather than adversarial Chamber debates, made the experience 'more satisfying and worthwhile than membership of the House of Commons', whilst the openness of the Community bureaucracy gave rise to a belief that MEPs could be more influential at the pre-legislative stage than a Westminster MP and were more than mere lobby fodder.[134]

When considering whether the experience of the European Parliament confirmed the Conservative European outlook, it must be balanced against the observation that a significant proportion of the 1979 intake had shown no previous interest in European affairs. The sceptic Harmar Nicholls, who stood 'in order to understand the ramifications' of European integration, felt his MEP experience confirmed his belief that the Parliament was 'not likely to pass the test of time, on the grounds that the one ingredient which is vital for its success did not exist – that ingredient was "a natural affinity between the Member States"'.[135] Butler and Marquand reached the conclusion in 1981 that there was 'no evidence' that membership of the European Parliament 'changed their attitudes'. They did consider it telling that of those Conservatives sitting in the Parliament during 1978–9 nearly all sought the nomination for the direct elections. However, they caution against this being interpreted as a sign of Euro-enthusiasm; rather, they sensed amongst Conservative candidates a belief that they were more valuable as MEPs.[136] A witness seminar of current MEPs in 1995 concurred with this view and noted that ex-MEPs who entered the House of Commons appeared to abandon their former Europeanism.[137] Certainly after the SEA there was a growing belief that the European Parliament was increasing in prestige, which encouraged some Westminster-based MPs, like Edwina Curry, to seek nomination.[138] What is evident is that amongst those first elected in 1979 there was a range of ideological standpoints, something that has remained the case since. Whilst generally Conservative MEPs might be categorised as 'pro-European', this ranged from the extreme of William Newton-Dunn, an unreconstituted federalist, to the moderates, typified by Scott-Hopkins and Plumb, to those sceptical about the need for further integration, dubbed the 'H-block', who tended to be right-wingers and included Harmer Nicholls, John Marshall, Eric Forth and Sheila Roberts, amongst others. This partly explains why the Conservative MEPs had a tendency to split during key European Parliamentary votes, as when twenty-two voted for the Spinelli (Draft Treaty) Report in February 1984, with twenty-eight absent, and three voted in favour of Britain's veto being overridden in the Farm Council in May 1982, or when they split twenty-six to twenty-two over criticism of the Athens Summit to freeze the British and German rebates in December 1983.[139] It should be noted that the EDG still endured fewer splits than its Labour Group counterparts. However, because of these internal divisions Bill Newton Dunn believed that 'they punch below their weight and fail to obtain a due share of key rapporteurships on the committees'.[140] Ideological differences do not solely explain the voting splits. Whilst the Conservative group have their own whips they lack the potential moral leverage in comparison with their Westminster counterparts: the knowledge that each vote might be decisive in passing or blocking legislation or ending a government. Also, caution should be exercised when considering the abstention figures. The nature of the Parliament's voting procedures, in conjunction with the weak whipping procedures, helps explain the high levels of abstention, non-participation and absence. Participation for activists and backbenchers in the various parliamentary assemblies of Europe may have offered an insight into the European mentality for conducting politics, but suggests little about the nature of the EU's institutions. This is the preserve of ministers and their civil servants. What has been their experience? And how does the party perceive these institutions?

## Conservatives and the EU's institutions

### The European Parliament

Formed from Article 108.3 of the 1957 Treaty of Rome and based in Brussels and Strasbourg, the European Parliament generally has, since Maastricht, equal powers (or 'co-decision') with the Council of Ministers over legislation.[141] It agrees the EU budget and scrutinizes expenditure. The size of the European Parliament's membership has expanded with each phase of enlargement, from 198 in 1973 (36 British) to 410 in 1979, to the level of 826, of whom 87 are British. The enlargement of May 2004 has meant a further expansion of the total numbers of MEPs but saw, from the June 2004 elections, a reduction in the size of the British parliamentary delegation to 78. Since 1979 the average European turnout in elections to the European Parliament has fallen steadily, from 63 per cent in 1979 to 49 per cent (despite compulsory voting in three of these countries). In Britain the decline is even more pronounced, falling to 24 per cent in 1999 but recovering to its highest turnout level of 38.2 per cent in June 2004. The Conservatives have on three occasions (1979, 1984, 2004) secured the largest number of seats, but their percentage share of the vote has steady declined, from 51 per cent in 1979 to 27 per cent in 2004.

The constant evolution of the European Parliament's powers has been of concern to Conservatives since the 1960s, with the fear that this was an institution with the potential to develop its role beyond its mandate under the Treaty of Rome. This has horrified Eurosceptics, who fear the ability of the European Parliament to advance the cause of federalism by usurping the sovereignty of national parliaments by holding the Council of Ministers to account and potentially developing the ability to influence national taxation and budgetary issues.[142] Neil Marten warned in 1970:

> It will be strengthened ... it will go on. It will get budgetary power and so on, it will be directly elected and in the end it will vote on a majority vote. It will have a common foreign policy, a common defence policy, common social, money and even now they're talking of a common education policy. So in the end this is what will rule this country and the British parliament will be reduced, and I do not say that this is exaggeration, it will be reduced to the status of a County Council as we know it.[143]

For Conservative Europhiles the reverse has been argued. Instead they have suggested that reform of the Parliament's procedures to assist it in its scrutiny of the Commissioners and Council of Ministers means that the 'democratic deficit' of the European Union can be reversed, and the abuses of the Community, such as the CAP and the budget, can be restrained and used to promote a genuine free market. The internal debate about the European Parliament has characterised the Conservative's European debate. One camp has suggested that interdependence, when combined with new notions of sovereignty sharing, can work to Britain's advantage, with the Parliament offering the mechanism to fulfil democratic procedures. Their opponents have opposed this vision, arguing that despite interdependence Britain should seek to exert domestic control over key policy areas and that the European Parliament just represents an alien institution to the British electorate. The party leadership was being warned as early as 1961 that on entry Britain would face a 'difficult problem' in choosing between increasing scrutiny of the Council of Ministers, which was responsible only to national parliaments, and boosting the ability of the European Parliament to scrutinise the European Commission.[144] But the ability of the European Parliament to act as a scrutiny body would depend upon whether there was 'a desire' from those who sat, something that would require 'elected representatives' rather than delegates.[145] During Britain's first application, when the European Parliament was still a fledgling institution, one party committee speculated whether the European Parliament, rather than national governments, might become the driving force of future political union. They thought that the opportunity 'might stimulate' the Parliament 'to go beyond their mandate in the Treaty of Rome, as the Council of Europe went beyond its original statute'.[146] In fact it was the perception that the Treaty of Rome 'appears confused in its conception of the role for the European Parliament' that encouraged those who thought it could be remodelled to suit British interests.[147] The reality is that the Parliament is not a legislature. Its powers of co-decision have gradually expanded since the Single European Act.[148]

Under the Amsterdam Treaty (1997), which came into effect in 1999, the European Parliament was handed co-decision powers in 80 per cent of EU policy and law-making areas. This means legislation must have two readings each from MEPs and the Council of Ministers, and if there is a failure to agree a final conciliation meeting to negotiate the precise wording of the EU directive must be agreed; if that fails, the directive fails. For many of the participants in the Parliament this is evidence that their powers have increased and that the Parliament is no longer a talking shop. To support this it is noteworthy that nearly 70 per cent of the European Parliament's amendments on second readings are ultimately included in legislation. Lord Cockfield has cautioned those whom might feel indignant at the limitations imposed upon the Parliament's ability to initiate legislation, observing that domestically the British government is 'brutal' at restricting the ability of Westminster backbenchers to introduce and enact legislation that they, rather than the executive, favour.[149]

One of the key reforms during the 1960s and early 1970s was the matter of direct elections, an issue particularly favourable to the Italians and Belgians, who were keen to weaken the hegemony of the French and Germans, and an issue that had 'quite a lot [of] steam' behind it.[150] Direct elections to the Parliament renewed concerns about the potential for the European Parliament to usurp Westminster's sovereignty. This was especially the case amongst Conservative backbenchers, who in the view of the shadow minister for Europe, had 'not taken the various opportunities open to them to discuss the matter in backbench committees' and consequently misconceived the Parliament's powers. There was a genuine fear that the European Parliament was brought into being with powers that national parliaments had taken centuries to gain: power over the budget, power over legislation, power over the executive. Whilst it was likely a directly elected European Parliament would seek to improve its prestige and power, in reality this could only happen if the Council of Ministers approved, where Britain retained a veto. Direct elections would not be 'authorising a leap into federalism'. Quite the contrary:

> The powers of the European Parliament are not powers filched from the House of Commons. They do not in anyway diminish our ability or our responsibility to challenge or stimulate British ministers representing Britain on the Council of Ministers or to examine Community legislation as it effects this country.[151]

In a sense the manner of the European Parliament's workings bore closer relation to those of an English county council, with the commitment to committees and monthly plenaries of the full council.[152] It was recognised too that the European Parliament offered the potential for the opposition to use it as a forum to attack a sitting national government, and ultimately try to infringe on that government's traditional monopoly of domestic policy-making by supporting the transfer of power to Brussels. The potential of a European assembly to embarrass a sitting government was not far fetched. The Conservatives had after all used the Council of Europe in 1949–50 to good effect to harass Attlee's Labour government. The ability of their own MEPs to embarrass had been evident since Bill Newton Dunn tabled an amendment in May 1982 which called for a majority vote in the Council on the farm price settlement after the Thatcher government had vetoed farm price increases.

Since the implementation of direct elections the Parliament has existed distinct from national parliamentary assemblies. For pro-Europeans this has been problematic; as Kellett-Bowman explained, 'it is crucial that the two parliaments do not get off at a tangent – we need to cog them in together'.[153] One suggested remedy to this came from Leon Brittan, who advocated the creation of a 'Committee of Parliaments' consisting of representatives from each national parliament. His argument was that if voters felt their local MPs were part of the European legislative process it would serve the dual purpose of enhancing the EU's democratic processes and enhance its credibility. The proposal ultimately floundered at the Maastricht negotiations.[154] In reality this suggestion was for a Council of Europe mark II. But with the acceptance of the subsidiarity principle some pro-Europeans have returned to the idea of a second European chamber, arguing that it could apply the principle, '"policing" the responsibilities of the EU and determining which decisions really need to be taken at the European level'.[155]

### The European Commission

Conservatives have always viewed the European Commission, and the Commissioners, with suspicion. The Commission, which is the executive arm of the Community, has three functions: the right to initiate legislation; to act as guardian of the treaties; and to undertake the day-to-day management responsibility for the Community. 'It is both lawmaker, policeman and prosecutor', bemoaned Nick Ridley.[156] It is the full-time civil service and 'government' of the EU. After enlargement in May 2004 there are now twenty-four commissioners plus the president of the Commission: each has a specific portfolio and is appointed for a five-year tenure. Their apparent lack of accountability has been the principle concern. Even before British entry to the EEC senior Conservatives were bemoaning the activities of the Commission. Douglas-Home, in a private briefing, labelled the then Commission president, Hallstein, 'an Empire-building bureaucrat' and warned colleagues that 'one of the real problems will be how to curb this tendency while providing that the Commission will be controlled in the future'.[157] The answer amongst pro-Europeanists has been to suggest an increase in the powers of the Council of Ministers and the European Parliament.[158] As Edwina Curry recorded, 'if we are to clip the Commission's wings, then increasing the power of Euro MPs to check and balance the action of the Council of Ministers seems wisest'.[159] When these reforms have been suggested by other leading European politicians there has been hesitancy amongst Conservatives, but as one leading pro-Europeanist observed, 'some of their ideas seem close to ours'.[160]

This desire to reverse the democratic deficit has never been fully reconciled with the more general Conservative reluctance to see any increase in the powers of the European parliament for fear that it would encourage the federalist agenda. The counter to this catch-22 situation has been the right of British governments to select two commissioners to serve in Brussels. This has led to succession of senior Conservatives being dispatched to Brussels: Christopher Tugendhat (1977–84), Lord Cockfield (1985–8), Leon Brittan (1989–99), and Chris Patten (1999–2004). This has been to the appointing government's advantage. In 1984 Thatcher engineered the removal of Christopher Tugendhat as commissioner and replaced him with her former Cabinet minister Lord Cockfield, who would be charged with seeking to implement Thatcherism in Europe. However, relations between Conservative governments and their national commissioners have often soured amid accusations that once in Brussels the Conservative commissioners have gone native.[161] This stems from the desire of these national commissioners to act independently and, whilst prepared to seek the views of London, not to take direct orders. As one Commissioner observed, 'while this did not endear me to some elements in London, it was an invaluable asset in dealing with other Members States'.[162] Another, Leon Brittan, suggests his pro-European views were well known since his Cambridge days, and blamed Thatcher for failing to do her homework on his views.[163] Brittan has for many years favoured reducing the number of commissioners to one per country, a view most recently articulated in the Conservative Group for Europe report on *The Future of Europe*.[164] This was accepted by the intergovernmental conference negotiating the Maastricht Treaty, but the specifics of the treaty left it over as a matter for further consideration, and again it was not resolved at the Nice Treaty negotiations in 2000. Former commissioner Cockfield does not consider the total numbers to be a real issue but believes that the distribution of the workload between the existing commissioners needs to be more even, and offers the suggestion that a system similar to the British Cabinet system be adopted, with a commissioner being appointed to a particular portfolio and then supported by a group of fellow commissioners in the manner of junior ministers.[165]

The ability of the Commission to issue directives that oblige implementation into British law, but without the option of scrutiny by Parliament, has become a particular irritation to Eurosceptics. Typical was the response of Winston Churchill Jr to the Commission's 'fifties Kremlin mentality', which had in his view resulted in 26,000 regulations and directives being imposed upon Britain.[166] When Commission president Romano Prodi suggested that he should become responsible for the recruitment and retention of commissioners the Conservative Eurosceptic response was predictable in its negativity, as they feared that this would change the president's role from 'head of a glorified secretariat into a fully fledged president of a Euro-cabinet'.[167] The suggestion that commissioners are civil servants clearly grates with the office holders, who remind their critics that they are an institution of the European Union.[168]

In May 2001 the theme of reforming the Commission, which had formed part of the party's 1999 Euro-election manifesto, was developed further by the suggestion that the Commission should be reduced to 'an impartial civil service' with its rights to initiative constrained.[169] The desire to reform the Commission had been given added impetus by the resignation of the Santer Commission in 1999 after a damning report into fraud and mismanagement. It confirmed Conservative suspicions that the Commission was little more than a self-perpetuating oligarchy. In addition there was the fear that the Commission was seeking to advance a federalist agenda. As David Heathcote-Amory explained following his resignation from John Major's Cabinet, 'The European Commission is not the servant of the participating states; it is rather the engine of European statehood'.[170] Cockfield accepts that during the 1990s, on occasion, the Commission 'adopted too aggressive a role', but believes the hostility of the Conservative Party is 'primarily a reflection of internal difficulties' and 'an attempt to find a scapegoat to divert attention and deflect criticism from its own supporters'.[171] This thesis finds confirmation in the proposals by the Conservative Group for Europe that because of enlargement 'a strong Commission will be of greater rather than less importance'. This should not be achieved through a greater range of powers but rather through strengthening its existing powers.[172]

### The Council of Ministers

If the European Commission has the role of initiator, then the Council of Ministers is the forum that can aid or reject its plans. It is composed of government ministers, one from each state appropriate to the subject under discussions, such as foreign policy or agricultural policy. The chairmanship rotates between member states, in line with the six-month rotation of the presidency of the European Council.[173] In practice, committees of officials or working groups take most decisions. The power of the national veto consequently remains an important weapon in the domestic arsenal. The relationship between the Commission and the Council of Ministers has long been one open to potential reform. There has always been a latent Conservative suspicion that Commission presidents were keen to seek the aggrandisement of their role at the expense of the Council, but had felt able to reassure themselves that the 'reality of politics dictates ... that the Council of Ministers will have the last word for a long time'.[174] Indeed, the Council of Ministers has, in a sense, reinforced the idea of the national interest such that reform cannot, will not, be allowed to interfere: 'in truth all the Heads of Government had a common interest in maintaining their own joint and special authority, as represented by the powers of the European Council.'[175] In May 2001 Francis Maude did put forward proposals to reform both the Council of Ministers and the Commission. He wished to see a reduction in the Commission's powers, making it little more than a civil service with reduced powers of initiative, and to strengthen the role of the Council. It was envisaged that member states would appoint senior ministers to the Council who would be directly responsible for EU negotiations. This would oblige these ministers to be based part time in Brussels. To ensure no diminution of Westminster's sovereignty a British minister for Europe would be directly accountable to Parliament and the powers of the Westminster parliament would be given primacy, ensuring that no minister could approve proposals in the Council without the necessary Westminster scrutiny and approval.[176] This suggestion of greater Council ministerial accountability to national parliaments met with the approval of some pro-Europeans, whom one MEP has likened to 'behaving like rulers in North Korea or Beijing'.[177] The secret discussions of the Council of Ministers, in the eyes of many pro-Europeans, seriously undermine the democratic accountability of the EU. It is a frequently mooted suggestion that the Council proceedings should be conducted in public, with the ministerial votes being published.[178] However, the issue of enlargement has brought to the fore the question of whether qualified majority voting within the Council, in specific areas, is a means of speeding up the Council of Minister's decision-making process. Not surprisingly this suggestion has horrified Eurosceptics, who see it as a further degradation of their national sovereignty.

The Council of Ministers 'experience' is hardly a positive one for participants, and has encouraged Conservative calls for reform. Alan Clark's encounter with an all-day Foreign Affairs Council was not untypical: 'Quite extraordinarily draining and repetitive', an experience he likened to afternoon gambling, which 'reinforces the painful sense of waste and unnatural exhaustion'.[179] It is notable that many former Conservative ministers in their memoirs attribute their growing sense of Euroscepticism to having attended Council sessions and witnessed the pursuit of national self-interest, particularly from the French, and observed the extension of Community powers to areas for which it had no responsibility.[180] John Major reportedly said of European foreign ministers, 'if they stab you in the chest ... that is because they have missed their target which was your back'. Yet he always found his finance ministerial counterparts convivial.[181] Leon Brittan sensed that ministers spending hour upon hour listening to each other's pre-written speeches was too much, and fears that the experience will be exacerbated by enlargement. That decisions as important as setting annual farm prices or allocating the third world aid budget should be reached in this manner was lunacy: the decisions should be reached 'on the basis of balanced negotiation, not on stubbornness and stamina',[182] a phenomenon Thatcher would attribute either to 'talkative males' or to 'garrulous Europeans'.[183] This negativity was not universal. Norman Tebbit, who later became a staunch Eurosceptic, confessed he 'enjoyed the challenge of negotiation and dealing inherent in the Community system and first became aware of the extent to which Ministers and officials were benefiting from the cross fertilisation of ideas and experience'.[184]

### The European Court of Justice

Under Section 2 of the 1972 Treaty of Accession, European law secured primacy over British law.[185] It is clear that many politicians, and the wider electorate, were oblivious to this at the time. The fear for sceptics by 2004 was that the proposed European Constitution would make the European Court of Justice the supreme court of all the citizens of the EU, in other words the legal apparatus of a European state supported by the EU Charter of Fundamental Rights.[186] However, as the European Court of Justice has ruled against the British government on a number of occasions, so the hackles of the Eurosceptics have been raised as they perceive the judgement of the European Court of Justice to be 'unjust, odious, obnoxious and unfair'.[187] However, some elements of the party appeared perfectly alert during the 1960s to the implications for British law if Britain joined the EEC. Indeed, they appeared to be anticipating the rationale of the 1986 Single European Act by advocating the uniformity of law, both with regard to company and trade unions laws, which was absolutely necessary if fair competition and equality of rights were to be promoted throughout the EEC.[188] Some, such as Robert Jackson, have argued that the European Court of Justice blended supranational and national elements of law; supranational in the sense that judgements were final, but also national because its judges were nominated by national governments.[189] The problem has been that the European Court of Justice's remit is expected to take account of the law-makers' intentions in a manner foreign to those used to the English law tradition.

Whilst Michael Howard was home secretary, from 1993 to 1997, the European Court of Justice was seen as a legitimate target to enable the Major government to demonstrate its Eurosceptic tendencies. This frustrated many Europhiles in the party, who thought this hostility weakened the sympathy for the British proposals to reform the court. Leon Brittan was clear that the government needed to make 'an objective assessment of the extent to which the court has promoted Britain's interests'.[190] This obliged Conservative sceptics to appreciate that it was not just Britain that the

European Court of Justice ruled against. This was not an analysis that David Heathcote-Amory felt able to accept when he resigned from Major's government. He saw the EU as a 'dynamic legal system, which encroaches daily into the way we govern ourselves'. The European Court of Justice was advancing a federalist agenda and undermining political agreements, such as Britain's opt-outs from Maastricht, by seeking to extend and make European law.[191] An example was the 1995 ruling that health was a service which could be traded, therefore public health was covered by single market legislation. This is the crux of the issue for Conservatives: who governs Britain? The concept that the Westminster Parliament is sovereign goes to the core of many Conservatives' values, and so the ability of the European Union to circumvent this sanctity by imposing legal judgements and directives which must be implemented into British law is difficult to accept. Until Conservatives accept the diminished, but evolving, sovereignty of the Westminster Parliament there is little hope of them becoming reconciled to the European Union. Under Hague the Conservatives continued Major's theme of European Court of Justice reform. It was proposed that the court should be prevented from extending the powers of other EU institutions through its legal judgements. Those European Court of Justice judgements, which offer a different interpretation to the original intention of legislation, should be immediately amended. That the court's ability to impose liability for damages on member states should be restricted to only the most serious cases. Iain Duncan Smith unsuccessfully tried to launch a Private Member's Bill to give Parliament the power to overturn the rulings of the European Court of Justice.[192]

# Conclusion

Ideological oscillation by a political party is a feature of democratic politics. It can be exacerbated by periods of opposition and constrained when in government. The Conservative Party has at varying times been scornful of continental concepts of 'European union', at others indifferent, and for much of the 1960s and early 1970s its leadership was an enthusiastic cheerleader. Measuring the party's contribution to European unity is more problematic. In many cases the significance rests with individuals rather than the wider party. This is not just the high-profile figures like Churchill, Heath and Macmillan, but those behind the scenes who actively participated in European events: individuals like Douglas Dodds-Parker, Ursula Branston, Diana Elles and Tufton Beamish. Sceptics like Neil Marten, Derek Walker-Smith and Bill Cash have contributed too, in that they have sought to publicise the debate about the consequences of the EC, and tried to persuade the electorate to reject the chosen pathway for Britain's relationship with the continent. It must be remembered too that the EU is only one organisational component of European unity and that Conservative experiences of Europe are just as likely to have occurred through alternative structures such as Western European Union or the Council of Europe or through pan-European organisations such as the European Women's Union.

Winston Churchill's rhetoric encouraged the development of the Council of Europe, yet the majority of his party were at best indifferent, at worst hostile to this. Indifference again classifies the party's response to the Schuman Plan of 1950. The Eden government's apathy to the Messina Conference in 1955 meant that the European Community emerged as a real, if unpalatable, fact, without any British input to its forms or aims. This has proved costly for the party. For the next fifteen years, Macmillan and then Heath sought to rectify this deficiency and succeeded in persuading the majority of the grass roots, largely in grudging acquiescence, to believe that there was no alternative. As Ludlow's analysis of the 1961–3 negotiations has shown, the British application forced the Six to consider precisely where, and by what means, they wished to evolve. The consequence was that Britain was obliged to join the club on terms and conditions that were very much skewed against it.[1] After the 1975 referendum it appeared as though the issue might have exhausted itself. But the need for Thatcher to use 'Europe' as a tool in her domestic statecraft to deflect from the difficulties at home, with the emphasis on 'them' versus 'us', began to reinforce a message of British uniqueness and exceptionalism. Furthermore, many of the issues about the EC that affronted Conservatives, such as CAP and the moves towards monetary union, were legacies of decisions taken before Britain joined the Community. It placed the leadership's consensus on Europe under strain in a manner as never before. There has never been unanimity amongst the senior leadership about the merits of European union, but those with doubts, at least until 1988, were prepared to set aside their concerns in the belief that the wider Conservative project justified the means; whether it was EFTA or ERM.[2] Thatcher's Bruges speech transformed that. It brought Euroscepticism into the mainstream. This was not some obscure backbencher lambasting the EU: it was the party's leader and most successful prime minister in recent living memory. What Thatcher had done was put public voice to doubts that many had held privately, but dared not speak for fear that it threatened the party's ethos of loyalty and silence. Although the Europeanists succeeded in maintaining the ascendancy in Cabinet until the early 1990s, doubts were growing amongst the wider party. This was significant because many of these had previously been agnostic about matters European, or else privately harboured their doubts. So why this transformation?

Until EC entry in 1973, 'Europe' was an issue about Britain's external relations. Although it was often conceived as an economic issue it was not one that actually impinged on British governmental policy-making, except for matters relating to defence. As many anti-Marketeers had forewarned, and some ministers were prepared to concede, entry meant that European policy became intertwined with other domestic policy issues: taxation, national and regional planning, public ownership, monetary policy, agricultural and fisheries policy, to name a few. They now were subsidiaries of European policy. What was dangerous about the debates of the 1990s was that Europe linked together domestic and international politics in a manner that bore similarity to the Conservative crises of 1846 and 1906. They left the party arguing amongst themselves over state intervention versus the free market. This helps explain why opposition to closer European integration is a not a phenomenon exclusively of the Conservative right. Alongside this the emphasis of European ideas has changed. Once there had been agreement about the need to combine economic intervention and social welfare with a degree of transnational co-operation. Now the emphasis was towards the 'threats' Europe posed to the state, nation and British democratic tradition. Ideology has crept into the equation for the first time. The modern Eurosceptics sense that they are engaged in a battle to save the post-1979 Conservative project. This need to 'rescue' the party has meant a willingness to disregard the conventions of party loyalty. The evocations to act as the descendants of Churchill's anti-appeaser tradition are telling: it is envisaged as a country-before-party issue. The sceptics might have won the argument of ideas, but the price has been high: consigning the party to opposition since 1997. In allowing ideology to dominate, the Conservatives since the 1990s have shown the reasons why pragmatism and loyalty were held as such prized virtues by their predecessors. Where the Eurosceptics of the 1990s have been particularly successful is in perpetuating the idea that parliamentarians and the British public had been kept in the dark in the 1970s about the wider implications of entry. At the parliamentarian level this is a falsehood. Issues of sovereignty were discussed from the earliest days. Internal party planning, whether in committees or research briefings, was alert to the harmonisation implications of membership, and parliamentary debates ranged across the issues. Ministers in 1971–2 could at times have been more explicit, but the anti-Marketeers did ensure discussion of the key issues. The governments of Macmillan and Heath were more economic with the truth with the wider party. There was clearly a desire to keep the debate restricted to parliamentarians and the political establishment. The activists did not help their position by constant calls for simpler explanations of policy. This just encouraged the leadership in their belief that the complexity of the issues meant this could only be understood by the political elites. Further, they feared that any misunderstanding of policy would only fuel the perceived hostility of the wider party base. Again this was a mistaken assumption. The grass roots were often not opposed to entry, just confused. If Europeanist activists were struggling to explain their rationale, then what hope for the average association member?

Piers Ludlow has observed that had Macmillan in 1961 made Britain's application unconditional, and agreed to resolve the issues of EFTA, agriculture and the Commonwealth from within the EEC, the French would never have been able to veto the bid.[3] But as Ludow, Milward and others have suggested, Macmillan could not do so because he felt hampered by what he thought the Conservative Party felt and wanted to hear.[4] The same has applied ever since at every moment when a Conservative leader has been obliged to negotiate a new treaty arrangement with Europe. What this study has shown is that the Conservative leadership mistook party ignorance for 'hostility'. The difficulty, then, is that the party comes to expect its views to be accounted for, so that even when, as Major ensured at Maastricht, the British conditions are accepted by Europe, the party's reaction may not be so positive.

The need to understand the views of activists is important and has been taken seriously by the leadership over the decades. They define the parameters of acceptable policy. Yet more often the leadership's understanding of the activists' views has become increasingly intuitive rather than scientific. Since the 1950s the party's membership has rapidly contracted and aged. At the same time 'key' organisational features that were designed to facilitate the linkage between the party's periphery and centre have broken down. There has been a steady decline in the numbers of Conservative associations employing agents: from 535 in 1959, to 233 in 1987 and a modest revival of 310 in 1997. The fall has been due to declining association revenues and falling memberships, which means that there are many without an agent, or sharing, or which only appoint agents in the run-up to a general election. The consequence of this is that the party has lost a significant conduit for filtering 'intelligence' from the frontline back to Central Office. Local constituency officials and agents have historically performed an important role in providing analysis of public or party opinion, both for MPs and Central Office. Further, since the late 1960s cutbacks have seen a reduction in staff levels in the party's regional offices, and a subsequent reduction in the numbers of area offices, with the decision taken in July 1998 to close all of them. Previously area agents were based in these provincial offices and again provided an important channel for intelligence analysis. Central Office might argue that the Conservative Political Centre's contact and discussion groups allow the leadership to gauge grassroots opinion, but those who participate tend by nature to be either the most loyal or at least the most 'active' of members.

The presumption has been that ideologically these activists are more to the right than the national leadership. Yet this is often a caricature.[5] In terms of European policy the activists were often waiting to have the merits of the cause explained. There was a sense during the 1960s that the leadership's obsession with Europe was distracting attention from the real issues of the economy and social policy. Europe is an issue that seems to excite only those on the extremes of the debate; the majority are indifferent. Even with the growing parliamentary Euroscepticism of the 1990s, it is not clear that this transferred itself to the grass roots. They seem to be largely immune to ideological groundswells: their primary concern is that the Conservatives are electable. Consequently, whilst appeals to their sense of nationhood do encourage their natural prejudicial values, a sense of proportion makes them realise that matters of taxation, education and National Health Service (NHS) provision are more important issues to the electorate. What the Europeanist cause appears to have lost is the claim to being the patriotic cause – this is now solely the preserve of Euroscepticism.

It has been suggested that the adoption of Euroscepticism after 1997 marked a new departure for the Conservative Party. This is based upon a post-1945 interpretation of the party's history. Taking a longer view across the twentieth century, a case can be made to argue that in fact 1997 marks a return to the 'limited liability' tradition of Conservative thinking that held ascendancy during the inter-war years. This suggests there are two ideological strands of thinking on Britain's relationship with continental Europe, each struggling for supremacy within the party. What exists is a history of Conservative debate over foreign economic policy, in which attempts have been made to revise Conservative ideologies and economic strategies to take account of the constraints of economic interdependence and increased globalisation.[6]

Thus the debates of 1903 about tariff reform sparked by Joe Chamberlain were concerned with the problems of managing an overextended empire whilst sustaining social harmony and industrial competiveness in the face of

German and US competition. By the 1930s the arguments over British foreign policy were how to contain the growing German threat without crippling the British economy, destroying the empire and losing yet more economic ground to the US and Japan whilst managing the internal risks from Bolshevism or fascism. From the 1950s, with the retreat from empire the issue was whether Britain wished to ally with a federal Europe and thus accept the progressive pooling of sovereignty, economically, socially and politically; or whether a looser association with Europe would allow Britain greater latitude as a free agent to pursue imperial preference or develop the Atlanticist relationship. The consistent theme running throughout is sense of British decline and how to minimise or reverse that trend.[7]

The ideological difficulties stemmed back to the free trade/protectionist debates of the 1840s and 1850s and the empire 'question' associated with Joseph Chamberlain's defection to the Conservatives with the Liberal Unionists in the 1880s. Rhetorically they brought a sense of empire primacy that emphasised the links between mother country and the White Dominions. In a world of growing US and German economic challenge the empire offered to preserve Britain's place in the world economy. Julian Amery's 1951 biography of Joseph Chamberlain drew comparisons between the tariff reform campaign and participation in the European movement, and sought to claim Joe for the European camp, likening the cause of imperial tariff reform to a modern vision of a greater European empire.[8] By the 1950s many of the Imperial Preferrers believed in a mixture of domestic and imperial policies, which made any thought of association with a European common market unpalatable. Free trade was not an attractive prospect, especially as in 1957, 1961 and again from the 1990s few were able to articulate a vision of free trade that satisfied either their concerns or those of Europe. During the inter-war years the Chamberlainite view splintered, in a manner akin to the breakdown of the Thatcherite alliance, from which emerged two 'traditions'. The point of divergence was their acceptance, or not, of 'interdependence'. This interlinked with issues of collectivism and the extension of the state, as well as that of imperialism.[9] For those Conservatives who looked more willingly to continental Europe, and who accepted the 'continental commitment' thesis, a preparedness to participate in a 'Concert of Europe' and ally themselves with, especially, the French was a key element behind their thinking. Linked to this is an appreciation of European culture and a belief that Britain had much to learn as well as to give. It was a recognition that Britain could be *a* leader in Europe. Finally, the economics of a closer association with Europe would enable Britain to assert her independence of the United States. There was a sense that the world trading order that was increasingly being imposed by the US after 1918 limited Britain's room for manoeuvre, consequently making it in Britain's 'national' interest to build partnerships with other (non-US) nations.[10] The counter limited liability 'tradition' looked to the empire to secure British 'greatness' in the economic, prestige and military spheres. As head of the empire and Commonwealth, Britain could continue to act as one of the world powers. It was a pre-eminence that drew upon Britain's diplomatic tradition and experience. The empire allowed Britain to assert her independence of the US politically and economically. Furthermore, there was a suspicion of the economic motives of her rivals, particularly the US and Japan. With the demise of empire, an alternative vehicle, such as NAFTA, has been sought but not found. Finally, a sense of Anglo-Saxon superiority meant that the European continent was viewed with suspicion and a belief that it spawned political systems alien to the Westminster tradition.

Much in the differences revolved around an interpretation of the balance of power. As a way of illustrating these differing historic 'traditions' the views of Austen and Neville Chamberlain are worth consideration. Austen represented the 'continental commitment' thesis. He considered that Britain's proximity to the continent made it impossible not to be entwined in Europe's affairs. He thus declared that the Rhine was Britain's frontier, a view that would be repeated during the 1930s by the likes of Baldwin. For Austen, Britain could not afford to retreat into isolation. He claimed to be taking a long-term perspective that anticipated a revived Germany some decades in the future. As he told the King in 1925, 'I am working not for today or tomorrow but for some date like 1960 or 1970'.[11] Austen's view was that there was no likelihood of peace unless Britain was prepared to mediate between France and Germany. Britain was therefore the European power-broker: 'If we withdraw from Europe I say without hesitation that the chance of permanent peace is gone.'[12] What is more, Britain had to work economically from within Europe to help constrain Germany's economic might. This last point would be articulated by Macmillan and Thorneycroft in the late 1950s and early 60s with the Cabinet discussion about EFTA and then about the first EEC application.

Neville Chamberlain was less enthusiastic than Austen about the French favouring the limited liability thesis. During the 1930s he began to subscribe to the view that France's intransigence was only antagonising Germany and threatening the stability of Europe.[13] For most of his premiership, Neville did his utmost to ensure the French were Britain's junior partner, always left uncertain as to whether they would receive British military assistance in the event of war. In many ways Neville's 24 March 1938 statement to the House of Commons is the classic exposition of his world-view and appeasement rationale.[14] His approach to European affairs was guided by five principles that were prioritised:

1   that Britain avoids continental alliances except with the Low Countries and France;
2   that there should be an emphasis on empire and world trade;
3   that defence costs should be capped to ensure sound finance and a strong British economy;

4    that the priorities of defence should be home defence, naval and commercial and not require a continental field force;

5    that Britain should diplomatically retain a free hand in order to maintain the balance of power either by leading or controlling allies and have the freedom to avoid others' quarrels.

As his personal diplomacy during 1938–9 showed, he was not averse to diplomatic intervention in Europe, but it stemmed from a different perception of the balance of power. Britain should seek to avoid direct European entanglements, instead sustaining an aloofness that would allow Britain to pick and choose the level of intervention and to concentrate upon her role as an economic and imperial world power. Paul Kennedy has suggested this strain of appeasement is 'traditional' British foreign policy, a tradition that only ended with Britain's 1939 guarantee to Poland. For Chamberlain the consequences of British involvement in a continental war would be potentially catastrophic: a bankrupt and empireless Britain, with Europe subservient to Bolshevism.[15]

Many of those who became leading figures in Britain's moves to join Europe had during the late 1930s established for themselves credentials as opponents of Neville Chamberlain's foreign policy, individuals like Churchill, Boothby, Macmillan, Sandys and Heath. This suggests that they had subscribed to a particular world-view in the 1930s and now in the post-war era were evolving that view to account for the new circumstances. They favoured intergovernmental co-operation over federalism. During the inter-war years they had been willing to surrender a degree of British sovereignty to the League of Nations, and were prepared to do so in the post-war period to the United Nations, NATO and Western European Union. For them the 'pooling' of sovereignty was acceptable. Broadly speaking, they saw the countries of continental Europe as being economically, and in some cases politically, in a state of ruin or collapse. The United States appeared to be on the verge of repeating what it had done in 1918 and retreating to its isolationist position, and the Soviets were threatening Western Europe with most of the East under their subjugation. Britain appeared to be Europe's natural leader, not least because she had won the war. A united Europe also offered a potential solution to Franco-German hostilities and offered hope to Eastern Europe under the Communist yoke. But for all the apparent acceptance of the European movement the reality remained until 1971 that continental commitment retained its meaning since Elizabethan times, a strategic obligation, not a form of political or economic union.[16]

Although the Conservative electoral disaster of 1945 had wiped out many former supporters of Neville Chamberlain, there remained a significant rump within the parliamentary party. One academic analysis of those sceptical of closer British association with Europe in the 1945–50 parliament calculates that thirty-five of these had supported the prime minister in May 1940, compared to only two for Churchill.[17] Furthermore, many of those associated with the anti-Marketeer movement, either in or out of Parliament, such as Maurice Petherick, Somerset de Chair, Robin Turton and Derek Walker-Smith, had been Chamberlainites. These 'sceptics' thought that a Europe associated with the British Commonwealth under British leadership would restore European economic prosperity. They felt that the value of British institutions had been reconfirmed by their baptism and survival in war. They also subscribed to a view that twice in the past fifty years Britain had been deeply embroiled in the continent, each time with disagreeable results. In other words, a continental commitment would cost Britain more than it would benefit her. They held a conviction that the empire and Commonwealth were the mainstay of Britain's world power status, and once that alternative had gone they should look to NAFTA as their new saviour.

It was amongst the party's grass roots that the 'isolationist imperial' tradition held sway. Many subscribed to the view that Britain had achieved her great power status by remaining aloof from the continent – using her sea power to acquire an empire whilst her rivals fought costly continental wars against one another. They accepted the vision articulated by Disraeli and adapted by Joseph Chamberlain of a group of English-speaking colonies linked in imperial federation, and now felt that once again British involvement in the continent had been detrimental to British imperial interests.

As the Yorkshire deputy area agent reported in 1962, 'Conservatives have been brought up for so long on the Disraeli maxims that even the more open minded find that it goes against the grain to think of Britain as a part of Europe'.[18] The support for this could be seen in activists' support for imperial preference, a 'cardinal principle of the party' in the view of Birmingham Conservatives.[19]

## The future?

What is apparent is that the continuing Conservative divisions over Europe are a reflection of the fact that successive Conservative governments have failed to find a satisfactory position for Britain within Europe. The strident nationalism that has become associated with the debate, and the desire to defend British interests against any perceived threat from Brussels, has taken hold within the Conservative Party and the British population more generally, especially amongst the tabloid-*Sun*-reading majority. This has left an important legacy, namely a reluctance to pursue overtly European policies by the post-1997 Blair administration.

Where will the Conservative Party go from here? Can it ever regain its reputation for unity? Looking at Europe long term also offers insights into the issue of 'rebellion' within the party. On first inspection it looked as if from 1992 the rise of ideology and the growing numbers of implacable opponents of the EEC would result in a party split potentially as damaging as that which occurred following the 1846 Corn Laws. In the event this has not happened. Opposition to Europe did not transfer into a wider party rebellion, even if the revolts over coalmine closures and Post Office privatisation during the Major years perhaps suggested that on first inspection. Although eleven former Conservative MPs were by 2006 members of UKIP this is not evidence of a wider schism. Despite the significance of the issue, Europe has still not reached the proportions of 'country before party' on any significant scale. Over time only a few parliamentarians have declined office, such as Neil Marten or James Cran, because of their views on Europe, or resigned ministerial positions solely because of Europe, as in the cases of Jasper More, Teddy Taylor and Derek Heathcote-Amory. Many sceptics have been prepared to set aside their concerns and accept preferment. Whilst most in the party, of either Europhile or Eurosceptic persuasion, still feel able to set aside their concerns for the greater Conservative project, then Europe will remain a matter of passion, but also one for tendencies.

The election of David Cameron has meant that current policy is still pretty fluid and it noticeable that he has avoided making any specific pledges, save for his promise to review the relationship with the EPP. What will happen if the Conservative Party is returned to office? If the party continues to use the rhetoric employed since 1997 it would appear that the Conservatives are committed to a re-evaluation of Britain's relationship with the EU. There would be two probable routes: either a treaty renegotiation leading to withdrawal – but this would be dependant on other EU member states acquiescing – or they could seek to establish some form of 'associated' relationship with the EU. Yet before either can be achieved the party needs to establish an alternative political economy framework to that which has sustained the party since 1961. That the Eurosceptics have failed to create a credible alternative in over forty years of trying suggests there are serious limitations to this pathway. Ultimately the fact that the Conservative Party is now a Eurosceptic party is an admission of failure: a failure of successive Conservative governments to satisfactorily find a relationship for Britain with Europe. Yet what is more likely is a fudge whereby the pragmatism that is associated with holding office will once more encourage the party's head to overrule its heart and convince itself that leadership and economic strength from association with Europe will require its grudging participation in the continuing European project.

# Notes

## Introduction

1 For the best 'historical' overviews of the integration project, see: J.W. Young *Britain and European Unity 1945–99* Basingstoke: Macmillan, 2000; S. Greenwood *Britain and European Integration since the End of the Second World War* Manchester: Manchester University Press, 1996; S. George *Awkward Partner: Britain in the European Community* Oxford: Oxford University Press, 2nd edn, 1994.

2 A.S. Milward *Rise and Fall of a National Strategy* London: Frank Cass, 2002.

3 D. Butler and U. Kitzinger *The 1975 Referendum* London: Macmillan, 1976 and A. King *Britain Says Yes: 1975 Referendum on the Common Market* Washington: AEI Press, 1977.

4 S. George *Britain and European Integration since 1945* Oxford: Blackwells, 1991, p. 71.

5 J. Buller *National Statecraft and European Integration* London: Pinter, 2000.

6 A. Geddes 'Europe' in K. Hickson (ed.) *The Political Thought of the Conservative Party since 1945* Basingstoke: Palgrave, 2005, p. 126.

7 H. Thompson *British Conservative Government and the European Exchange Rate Mechanism: 1979-94* London: Pinter, 1996.

8 Cyprus, Czech Republic, Estonia, Hungary, Latvia, Malta, Poland, Slovakia and Slovenia joined in 2004.

9 J. Baylis *The Diplomacy of Pragmatism: Britain and the Formation of NATO* Basingstoke: Macmillan, 1993; E. Fursdon *The European Defence Community* London: Macmillan, 1980; Chatham House *Britain in Western Europe: WEU and Atlantic Alliance* London: RIIA, 1955.

10 D. Charlton *The Price of Victory* London: BBC, 1995; R. Denman *Missed Chance: Britain and Europe in the Twentieth Century* London: Cassell, 1996; George *Awkward Partner*.

11 E. Dell *The Schuman Plan and the British Abdication of Leadership in Europe* Oxford: Oxford University Press, 1995, p. 5.

12 R. Broad *Labour's European Dilemma* Basingstoke: Palgrave, 2001, p. 31.

13 A. Milward *The European Rescue of the Nation-State* London: Routledge, 1992, p. 433.

14 L. Brittan *A Diet of Brussels: The Changing Face of Europe* London: Little Brown, 2000, p. 191.

15 F. Pym *The Politics of Consent* London: Hamish Hamilton, 1984, p. 74.

16 *The Independent*, 19 September 1996, Heath, Howe, Hurd, Whitelaw *et al.* to editor.

17 A. Seldon 'The Churchill Administration 1951–55' in P. Hennessy and A. Seldon (eds) *Ruling Performance: British Governments from Attlee to Thatcher* Oxford: Blackwells, 1987, pp. 63–97.

18 E.g. J. Young *Britain, France and the Unity of Europe* Leicester: Leicester University Press, 1984.

19 E.g. A. Milward *The Reconstruction of Western Europe 1945–51* London: Routledge, 1984.

20 N. Beloff *The General Says No: Britain's Exclusion from Europe* Harmondsworth: Penguin, 1963; M. Camps *Britain and the European Community 1955–63* London: Oxford University Press, 1964; U. Kitzinger *Diplomacy and Persuasion: How Britain Joined the Common Market* London: Thames and Hudson, 1973.

21 Camps *Britain, passim.*

22 W. Kaiser *Using Europe, Abusing the Europeans: Britain and European Integration 1945–63* Basingstoke: Macmillan, 1996; J. Tratt *The Macmillan Government and Europe: A Study in the Process of Policy Development* Basingstoke: Macmillan, 1996; J. Ellison *Threatening Europe: Britain and the Creation of the European Community 1955–58* Basingstoke: Macmillan, 2000.

23 H. Parr *British Policy towards the European Community: Harold Wilson and Britain's World Role 1964–67* London: Routledge, 2005; O. Daddow (ed.) *Harold Wilson and European Integration* Newbury: Frank Cass, 2003; J. Toomey 'The Velvet Veto: Harold Wilson, Charles de Gaulle and Britain's 2nd EEC Application 1964–1967', unpublished PhD, University College Dublin, 2004.

24 H. Young *This Blessed Plot: Britain and Europe from Churchill to Blair* London: Macmillan, 1998; P. Stephens, *Politics and the Pound: The Tories, the Economy and Europe* London: Macmillan, 1996; A. Forster *Euroscepticism in Contemporary British Politics: Opposition to Europe in the British Conservative and Labour Parties since 1945* London: Routledge, 2002.

25 E.g. N. Davies *Europe: A History* Oxford: Oxford University Press, 1996; E. Chryos, P. Kitromidldes and C. Svolopoulos (eds) *The Idea of European Community in History* Athens: National University of Athens, 2003.

26 P. Kennedy *Realities behind Diplomacy: Background Influences on British External Policy 1865–1980* London: Fontana, 1985; D. Reynolds *Britannia Overruled: British Policy and World Power in the Twentieth Century* Harlow: Longman, 2nd edn, 2000; W. Kaiser. and G. Staerck (eds) *British Foreign Policy 1955–64* Basingstoke: Macmillan, 1999.

27 S. Ball 'The National and Regional Party Structure' in S. Ball and A. Seldon *Conservative Century* Oxford: Oxford University Press, 1994; R. Frasure and A. Kornberg 'Constituency Agents and British Politics' *British Journal of Political Science* 5, 1975; R. Kelly *Conservative Party Conference: The Hidden System* Manchester: Manchester University Press, 1989; M. Pinto-Duschinsky *British Political Finance 1830–1980* Washington, AEI, 1981; J. Fisher 'Political Donations to the Conservative Party' *Parliamentary Affairs* 47(1), 1994; J. Ramsden *The Making of Conservative Party Policy* London: Longman, 1980; Arnold Beichman 'Hugger-Mugger in Old Queen Street: The Origins of the Conservative Research Department' *Journal of Contemporary History* 13(4), 1978; J. Kellas 'The Party in Scotland' in S. Ball and A. Seldon (eds) *Conservative Century*; S. Kendrick and D. McCrone 'Politics in a Cold Climate: The Conservative Decline in Scotland' *Political Studies* 37, 1989; S. Ball 'Local Conservatism and the Evolution of the Party Organisation' in S. Ball and A. Seldon (eds) *Conservative Century*; P. Whitely, P. Seyd and J. Richardson *True Blues: The Politics of Conservative Party Membership* Oxford: Clarendon Press, 1994; P. Seyd and, P. Whitely 'Conservative Grassroots: An Overview' in S. Ludlam and M. Smith (eds) *Contemporary British Conservatism* Basingstoke: Macmillan, 1996; R. Morris *Tories: From Village Hall to Westminster* Edinburgh: Mainstream, 1991. J. Holroyd-Doveton *Young Conservatives* Edinburgh: Pentland, 1996; D. Baker, A. Gamble and S. Ludlam 'More "Classless" and Less "Thatcherite"? Conservative MPs after the 1992 Election'

*Parliamentary Affairs* 45, 1992; P. Norton 'The Parliamentary Party and Party Committees' in S. Ball and A. Seldon (eds) *Conservative Century* Oxford: Oxford University Press, 1994; Bryon Criddle 'Members of Parliament' in S. Ball and A. Seldon *Conservative Century*; J. Ramsden *The Age of Churchill and Eden* London: Longman, 1994; J. Ramsden *Winds of Change: Macmillan to Heath* London: Longman, 1996; R. Shannon *The Age of Salisbury 1881–1902: Unionism and Empire* London: Longman, 1996; R. Stewart *The Foundations of the Conservative Party* London: Longman, 1978; R. Shannon *The Age of Disraeli: The Rise of Tory Democracy* London: Longman, 1992; M. Francis and I. Zweiniger-Bargielowska *The Conservatives and Society 1880–1990* Cardiff: University of Wales Press, 1996.

28  G. Stewart *Burying Caesar: Churchill, Chamberlain and the Battle for the Tory Party* London: Weidenfeld and Nicolson, 1999; Hickson (ed.) *The Political Thought of the Conservative Party since 1945*; E.H.H. Green *Ideologies of Conservatism: Conservative Political Ideas in the Twentieth Century* Oxford: Oxford University Press, 2002; N. McCrillis *The British Conservative Party in the Age of Universal Suffrage: Popular Conservatism 1918–29* Columbus, OH: Ohio State University Press, 1998; J.A. Ramsden *An Appetite for Power: A History of the Conservative Party since 1830* London: HarperCollins, 1998; A. Gambles *Protection and Politics: Conservative Economic Discourse 1815–1852* Woodbridge: Royal Historical Society/Boydell Press, 1999; M. Jarvis *Conservative Governments, Morality and Social Change in Affluent Britain 1957–64* Manchester: Manchester University Press, 2005; J. Barr *The Bow Group: A History* London: Politicos, 2001.

29  J. Critchley and M. Halcrow *Collapse of the Stout Party: The Decline and Fall of the Tories* London: Gollancz, 1997; I. Gilmour and M. Garnett *Whatever Happened to the Tories* London: Fourth Estate, 1997; J. Ramsden *'Britain is a Conservative Country that Occasionally Votes Labour': Conservative Success in Post-war Britain* London: CPC, 1997.

30  S. Ball 'Bibliography' in S. Ball and A. Seldon (eds) *Conservative Century* Oxford: Oxford University Press, 1994.

31  E.g. J. Moon *European Integration in British Politics 1950–63: A Study of Issue Change* Aldershot: Gower, 1985; Buller *National Statecraft*; N. Ashford 'The European Economic Community' in Layton-Henry, Zig (ed.) *Conservative Party Politics* London: Macmillan, 1980, pp. 95–125; D. Baker *et al.* '1846 … 1906 … 1996? Conservative Splits and European Integration' *Political Quarterly*, 1993, pp. 420–34; D. Baker *et al.* 'Whips or Scorpions? The Maastricht Vote and the Conservative Party' *Parliamentary Affairs* 46(2), 1993, pp. 151–66; G. Howe *Conflict of Loyalty* London: Macmillan, 1994; M. Thatcher, *Downing Street Years* London: HarperCollins, 1993; A. Seldon *Major: A Political Life* London: Weidenfeld and Nicholson, 1997.

32  S. Onslow *Backbench Debate within the Conservative Party and Its Influence on British Foreign Policy 1948–57* Basingstoke: Macmillan, 1997.

33  Green *Ideologies of Conservatism*, pp. 188–90.

34  J. Turner *The Tories and Europe* Manchester: Manchester University Press, 2000, p. 260.

35  Forster *Euroscepticism*, quotation, p. 142.

36  Thompson *British Conservative Government and the European Exchange Rate Mechanism*.

37  Buller *National Statecraft and European Integration*.

38  Particularly the work of the Members of Parliament Project involving David Baker, Andrew Gamble, Steve Ludlam and David Seawright. See D. Baker *et al.* 'Backbenchers with Attitude', paper presented to the European Consortium for Political Research Conference, Bordeaux, 1995.

39  Secretary Conservative Foreign Affairs Cttee, January 1956, cited in Onslow *Backbench*, p. 1.

40 A. Seldon *Churchill's Indian Summer: The Conservative Government 1951–55* London: Hodder and Stoughton, 1981.

41 R.A.C. Parker *Chamberlain and Appeasement* Basingstoke: Macmillan, 1994, p. 343.

42 J. Bulpitt 'The European Questions: Rules, National Modernisation and the Ambiguities of *Primat der Innenpolitik*' in D. Marquand and A. Seldon (eds) *The Ideas that Shaped Post-war Britain* London: Fontana, 1996, p. 229.

43 S.J. Ball 'Harold Macmillan and the Politics of Defence' *Twentieth Century British History* 6, 1995, pp. 78–100; see, pp. 97–98 for this point being made. This article provoked R. Lowe 'Archival Report: Plumbing New Depths: Contemporary Historians and the Public Record Office' *Twentieth Century British History* 8(2), 1997, pp. 239–65.

44 S. Ball *Baldwin and the Conservative Party* London: Yale University Press, 1988; N.J. Crowson *Facing Fascism: The Conservative Party and the European Dictators 1935–40* London: Routledge, 1997.

45 The Thatcher Foundation, www.margaretthatcher.org.

46 P. Morris 'The British Conservative Party' in J. Gaffney *Political Parties and the European Union* London: Routledge, 1996, p. 125.

47 Bulpitt 'The European Questions', pp. 214–56, quotation, p. 215.

48 M. Cowling *The Impact of Hitler: British Politics and British Policy, 1933–1940* London: Cambridge University Press, 1975.

49 Cowling *Hitler*, *passim*.

50 Butler Mss: Rab to Annie Chamberlain, 22 November 1940, Trinity College, Cambridge.

51 Young *Britain and European Unity*, p. 2.

52 Macmillan *Tides of Fortune*, p. 159.

53 Conservative Central Office press release: Michael Ancram speech 'Building true partnerships', 9 May 2002, www.conservatives.com/news.

54 E.g. Conservative Party Archive: M. Niblock to D. Hurd, 29 October 1968, CRD3/10/39, Bodleian Library, Oxford.

55 A. Chamberlain 'Great Britain as a European Power' *Royal Institute of International Affairs*, March 1930, pp. 180–8, quotation, p. 181.

56 *Hansard*, vol. 270, col. 632, 10 November 1932.

57 Rhys Williams Mss: minutes, Management Cttee, UK Council of the European Movement, comments of Maurice Macmillan, 1 November 1961, J/7/1/1, BLPES; Winchester CA, James Spicer *Hampshire Chronicle*, 18 June 1971, 73M86W/43, Hampshire Records Office.

58 *The Times*, 22 January 1998, p. 18, William Hague 'Why Tories Should Call Blair's Bluff'.

59 Daniel Hannan *Sunday Telegraph*, 18 December 2005; Richard Body *The Breakdown of Europe* ch. 7.

60 Milward *Rise and Fall*, p. 272.

## 1 Conservative moves towards Europe, 1945 – 75: 'like chasing a girl'

1 Phrase used by Geoffrey Rippon, January 1971, press conference, Copenhagen: Marten Mss: MS.Eng.hist.c.1138 f. 238, Bodleian Library, Oxford.

2 J.W. Young 'Churchill's "No" to Europe: The "Rejection" of European Union by Churchill's Post-war Government 1951–52' *Historical Journal* 28(4), 1985, pp. 923–37.

3 For Sandys' influence, see: M. Charlton *The Price of Victory* London: BBC, 1983, p. 133; R. Boothby *Recollections of a Rebel* London: Hutchinson, 1978, p. 216; P. Henri-Spaak *The Continuing Battle: Memoirs of a European 1936–1966* London: Weidenfeld and Nicolson, 1971, p. 202.

4 Cited H. Macmillan *Tides of Fortune* London: Macmillan, 1969, p. 156.

5 Lord Kilmuir *Political Adventure: The Memoirs of the Earl of Kilmuir* London: Weidenfeld and Nicolson, 1964, p. 175.
6 H. Young *This Blessed Plot: Britain and Europe from Churchill to Blair* London: Macmillan, 1998, p. 20.
7 R.R. James *Bob Boothby* London: Hodder and Stoughton, 1991, p. 346.
8 Original signatories were: Belgium, France, Luxemburg, Holland, Britain, Ireland, Italy, Denmark, Norway and Sweden. Signed Treaty of London 5 May 1949.
9 A. Nutting *Europe Will Not Wait* London: Hollis and Carter, 1960, p. 24.
10 I am grateful to Lady Gloria Hooper for this phrase.
11 Spaak *Battle*, p. 221; Conservative Party Archive [hereafter CPA]: memo 'Strasbourg Study Visit 21–28 September 1952' R. Milne, 24 October 1952, COB21/1/2, Bodleian Library, Oxford.
12 Con O'Neill cited in Charlton *Price of Victory*, p. 40.
13 R. Churchill (ed.) *Europe Unite* London: Cassell, 1950, p. 494. Churchill attributes Labour's attitude to Europe to 'personal jealousies and party rancour'; see also CPA: Foreign Affairs Committee 21 April 1948 Peter Roberts, CRD2/34/1, the Commons debates on political union would reveal 'a conflict of opinion within the socialist party.'.
14 Young 'Churchill's "No"', p. 924.
15 R. Broad *Labour's European Dilemma* Basingstoke: Palgrave, 2001, p. 11.
16 See comments of Churchill's principal private secretary, Jock Colville, in Charlton *Price*, p. 129.
17 A.S. Milward *The Rise and Fall of a National Strategy* London: Frank Cass, 2002, ch. 2.
18 *Conservative Party Conference Report* 1949 Macmillan, p. 65. *Archives of the British Conservative Party* [hereafter *ABCH*] microfiche card no. 5.
19 H. Macmillan *Riding the Storm* London: Macmillan, 1971, p. 65.
20 Birmingham Conservative Association: Officers' sub-cttee, 15 February 1946, f. 4, central council 2 June 1947, f. 115 Birmingham Central Library; Northern Area: AGM, 29 May 1948, NRO3303/2, Northumberland Record Office; CPA: Home Counties finance and general purposes cttee, 21 April 1953, ARE8/1/10; Accrington Conservative Association: executive 4 July 1961, Acc/AV, John Rylands Library, Manchester.
21 Woolton Mss: Woolton to Churchill n.d. box 21, Bodleian Library, Oxford. See also J. Ramsden *The Age of Churchill and Eden 1940–57* London: Longman, 1995, p. 106.
22 Macmillan addressing the Consultative Assembly of the Council of Europe 15 August 1950, cited P. Beswick 'The Tory Strasbourgers and the Evolution of Conservative Party Debate over Europe 1945–61' unpublished MPhil, University of Birmingham, 2001, p. 51.
23 Cited A.S. Milward *The European Rescue of the Nation-State* London: Routledge, 1992, p. 432.
24 *Conservative Party Conference* report 1949, pp. 52–60 *ABCP* microfiche card no. 5.
25 A. Seldon *Major: A Political Life* London: Weidenfeld and Nicolson, 1997, p. 486.
26 P. Kennedy *Realities behind Diplomacy* London: HarperCollins, 1991, p. 335. In 1958 trade with the Commonwealth would represent 35 per cent of total UK exports; by 1969 this had declined to 22 per cent, CPA: P. Thomas to N. Marten, 22 February 1961, CCO20/32/4.
27 Figures from W. Kaiser *Using Europe, Abusing the Europeans* Basingstoke: Macmillan, 1998, p. 8.
28 J. Moon *European Integration in British Politics* Aldershot: Dartmouth, 1985, p. 87; S. Onslow *Backbench Debate in the Conservative Party on Foreign Policy* Basingstoke: Macmillan, 1997, p. 56.

29  E. Dell *The Schuman Plan and the British Abdication of the Leadership in Europe* Oxford: Clarendon Press, 1995; Milward *Rise and Fall*, ch. 5.

30  See limited comment by S. Ball (ed.) *In the Age of Attlee and Churchill: The Diaries of Cuthbert Headlam* Cambridge: Royal Historical Society Camden Series, 2001, 16 May 1950, p. 628.

31  The rebels were Henry Legge-Bourke, Enoch Powell, Gerald Nabarro, Stephen McAdden, A.V. Harvey and John Mellor.

32  Legge-Bourke Mss: notes for speech, n.d. [1961] MS 742/737 ff. 1–8, Brotherton Library, University of Leeds.

33  North Wiltshire Conservative Association AGM 15 April 1950 2436/2 Wiltshire Record Office; *Newcastle Evening News* 1 July 1950 1633/17/2 Tyne and Wear Archives.

34  Onslow *Backbench*, p. 59.

35  P. Routledge *Public Servant, Secret Agent* London: Fourth Estate, 2002, p. 201. Speaking House of Commons 8 July 1950.

36  E. Heath *Course of My Life* London: Hodder and Stoughton, 1999, p. 144.

37  CPA: Foreign Affairs Committee brief Ursula Branston 13 June 1950 cited in Onslow *Backbench*, p. 65.

38  E.g. BOAPAH, interview with Lord Muirshiel, BLPES; Macmillan *Tides*, pp. 156–7.

39  Macmillan *Tides*, p. 195. Eighty attended, twenty-three spoke in favour and three against.

40  Woolton Mss: Woolton to Churchill n.d. [July 1948], box 21.

41  Yorkshire Area AGM 28 March 1948 cited in N. Ashford 'The Conservative Party and European Integration 1945–75' unpublished PhD, University of Warwick, 1983, p. 73.

42  Onslow *Backbench*, p. 49.

43  *Conservative Conference Report 1949*, pp. 60–5 *ACBH* microfiche card no 5.

44  R. Boothby *About Western Union* London: CPC, 1949.

45  Ashford *Conservative*, pp. 71–2.

46  J. Rhys Williams Mss: Boothby to J.R. Williams 23 September 1953, J/9/1/1; minutes of Executive UK Council of European Movement 17 October 1963 (Boothby), J/7/1/1, BPLES.

47  1949 CPC Western Union report cited Ashford *Conservative*, pp. 71–2.

48  For detailed analysis of the British government response, see Milward *Rise and Fall*, ch. 4.

49  R. Jenkins *Churchill* London: Macmillan, 2001, pp. 854–5.

50  Quote Macmillan *Tides*, p. 463; Kilmuir *Political Adventure*, p. 187.

51  Spaak *Battle*, p. 221.

52  Macmillan Ministerial Mss: Macmillan to Bonham Carter 20 April 1955, MS.Macmillan.dep.c.302 f1.

53  Macmillan Mss: diary 3 January 1951, MS.Macmillan dep.d.8.

54  E.g. CPA: Strasbourg study visit 1952 R.D. Milne, COB21/1/2.

55  Rhys Williams Mss: Boothby to J. Rhys Williams 23 September 1953, J/9/1/1.

56  Crookshank Mss: speech, Ashridge 5 December 1952, MSS.Eng.hist.c.603 ff 188–204, Bodleian Library, Oxford.

57  See also Ursula Branston *Britain and European Unity* London: CPC, 1953. For further reading on West German rearmament, see A. Deighton *The Impossible Peace: Britain, the Division of Germany, and the Origins of the Cold War* Oxford: Clarendon Press, 1993; S. Dockrill *Britain's Policy for West German Rearmament 1950–55* Cambridge: Cambridge University Press, 1991; J.W. Young 'German Rearmament and the European Defence Community' in J.W. Young (ed.) *The Foreign Policy of Churchill's Peacetime Administration 1951–55* Leicester: Leicester University Press, 1988, pp. 81–108; S. Mawby *Containing Germany: Britain and the Arming of the Federal Republic* Basingstoke: Macmillan, 1999.

58 A. Deighton 'Last Piece of the Jigsaw: Britain and the Creation of Western European Union 1954' *Contemporary European History* 7(2), 1998, pp. 181–97.
59 Macmillan Mss: diary 4 September 1954, MS.Macmillan.dep.d.20.
60 E. Fursdon *The European Defence Community* London: Macmillan, 1980.
61 CPA: 'The Council of Europe' 28 September 1954, COB21/1/2.
62 BOAPAH, interview with Lord Muirshiel, BLPES.
63 K. Lindsay *European Assemblies: The Experimental Period* London: Stevens and Sons, 1960, p. 27.
64 P. Catterall (ed.) *The Macmillan Diaries 1950–57* London: Macmillan, 2003, entry for 10 June 1955, p. 435.
65 Macmillan *Riding*, p. 246.
66 D. Dutton *Anthony Eden: A Reputation and Life* London: Arnold, 1998, p. 306.
67 Onslow *Backbench*, p. 82, citing Peter Smithers.
68 Catterall *Macmillan Diaries*, entry for 24 October 1954, p. 363.
69 N. Piers Ludlow *Dealing with Britain* Cambridge: Cambridge University Press, 1997, p. 19.
70 Nutting *Europe*, p. 78.
71 June 1960 John Profumo (minister of state at the Foreign Office) spoke of his desire to 'consider anew' proposals for UK to join Euratom and ECSC, cited J. Moon *European Integration in British Politics 1950–63: A Study of Issue Change* Aldershot: Gower, 1985, p. 38.
72 CPA: Foreign Affairs Committee minutes, 27 February 1963, CRD3/10/15.
73 CPA: Foreign Affairs Committee minutes 3, 27 February, 13 March 1963, CRD3/10/15.
74 Ludlow *Dealing*, p. 227.
75 Milward *Rise and Fall*, pp. 194–204.
76 Rushcliffe Conservative Association: *Rushcliffe Review* No. 112, June 1957, p. 8, DD.PP.1/3/10, Nottinghamshire Record Office.
77 Northern Area: council 15 February 1958, NRO3303/3.
78 CPA: Eastern Area Agricultural Advisory Cttee, 29 November 1957, ARE7/12/1; Tuckman Mss: Bow Group press release 14 February 1961, MS270/A921/4/1 Folder 2, University of Southampton Special Collections.
79 Cited Milward *The European Rescue of the Nation-State*, p. 432.
80 Edinburgh CA: clipping *Scottish Daily Mail* 6 January 1959 Acc.198. The view about the need to rethink attitudes was echoed by chairman North Wilts CA: report on Llandudno, 1956, 2436/10, Wiltshire Record Office.
81 W. Kaiser *Using Europe, Abusing the Europeans* Basingstoke: Macmillan, 1996, chs 3–4 for discussion of the FTA and EFTA negotiations.
82 Macmillan Mss: Martin Redmayne to Macmillan 9 August 1959, MS.Macmillan. dep.c.311 f. 54.
83 Legge-Bourke Mss: 'Imperial Red Herring' 17 July 1957, including *Economist* clipping 13 July 1957, MS742/739/1.
84 Waterhouse Mss: I.M. Lishman to Charles Waterhouse 16 January 1957, private possession.
85 CPA: Wales and Monmouthshire YCs 'Report on Britain and Europe' CCO506/14/15.
86 Rushcliffe CA: David Eccles in *Rushcliffe Review* No. 109 March 1957, p. 10, DD.PP.1/3/10.
87 E.g. Northern Area Council 15 February 1958, NRO3303/3.
88 CPA: Eastern Area Agric. Advisory Cttee, 29 November 1957, ARE7/12/1.
89 Reigate CA: Exec 10 July 1959, 353/4/2/1; Northern Area council 15 February 1958, NRO3303/3; North Wilts CA 24 April 1957, 2436/10.
90 Heath *Course*, pp. 202–3.
91 Accrington CA: Exec. 15 January 1957 Acc/AV.

92  CPA: ACP minutes 15 March 1957, ACP2/1; Shoreham CA, Exec 24 June 1958, CO/1SH/1/1/1.

93  Kaiser *Europe*, p. 102.

94  Catterall *Macmillan Diaries*; J. Tratt *The Macmillan Government and Europe: A Study in the Process of Policy Development* London: Macmillan, 1996; Milward *Rise and Fall*, ch. 11; K. Steinnes 'The European Challenge: Britain's EEC Application in 1961' *Contemporary European History* 7(1), 1998, pp. 61–80.

95  BOAPAH: Edward Boyle Interview, BLPES.

96  See, for example, joint meeting of the Conservative trade and industry cttee and the Agriculture committee 13 June 1961. Macmillan Mss: Knox Cunningham's notes, MS.Macmillan.dep.c.354.ff31–32.

97  S. George *An Awkward Partner: Britain in the European Community* Oxford: Oxford University Press, 2nd edn, 1994, p. 33 citing the *Guardian*.

98  *Hansard*, 5th series, vol. 645, col. 928–41 (Macmillan) 31 July 1961; see Penryn and Falmouth CA: Exec. 7 July 1961, DDX551/17 motion on EEC for a typical resolution calling for safeguards.

99  S. Heffer *Like a Roman: The Life of Enoch Powell* London: Weidenfeld and Nicolson, 1998, p. 340.

100  M. Mendoza 'Thirty-one Years on: May–August 1961' *Contemporary Record* 6(3), 1992, p. 574.

101  *The Times*, 4 August 1961. Although it doesn't name all the abstainers its list includes: J. Barlow, J. Biggs-Davison, F.W. Farey-Jones, J. Farr, R, Grimston, Hinchingbrooke, J. Hollingworth, G.R. Howard, R. Jenkins, J.C. Jennings. H.B. Kerby, A.A. Marlowe. D. Marshall, J. More, R.S. Russell, R.H. Turton, P. Walker, D. Walker-Smith, P. Williams and A.R. Wise (these were all members of the Common Market Committee and signatories of the 27 July EDM); the list also includes B. Baxter, who signed the 27 July EDM and had attended the 25 July Common Market Committee meeting but did not attend any thereafter. P. Norton *Dissension in the House of Commons* London: Macmillan, 1975, p. 190, also notes that L. Lucas, having voted in the first division, was absent from the second. In all likelihood this should be counted as an abstention given that Lucas was a signatory of the 27 July EDM and subsequently started attending meetings of the Common Market Committee. A. Fell, who cross-voted on the government motion, was also a member of the committee. S.J. McAdden should be added to the abstainers since he attended a meeting of the Common Market Committee on 3 August. For activities of the Common Market Committee, see Hinchingbrooke Mss: D/MAP263.

102  Macmillan Mss: Macmillan to Martin Redmayne, 5 August 1961 MS. Macmillan.dep.c.312 ff. 233–34.

103  A view shared by other Tories: CPA: V.B. Petherick to COO 6 September 1962 CCO 500/31/4, following constituency tour fears 'a complete split in the Party ... whatever the terms.'.

104  Cited J. Ramsden *Winds of Change: Macmillan to Heath 1957–1975* London: Longman, 1996, p. 152.

105  Moon *European*, pp. 164–5.

106  See Ludlow *Dealing* for details of the negotiations.

107  E.g. Lord Home to Conservative Foreign Affairs Cttee 28 February 1962 and Edward Heath to the same committee 16 May 1962. Macmillan Mss: Knox-Cunningham's notes for Macmillan MS.Macmillan.dep.c.354 ff. 196–97, 218–19.

108  M. Kandiah 'British Domestic Politics, the Conservative Party and Foreign Policy-making' in W. Kaiser and G. Staerck (eds) *British Foreign Policy 1955–64* Basingstoke: Palgrave, 1999, pp. 61–88.

109  See various reports filed CPA: CCO500/31/3.

110  Edinburgh North CA, Secretary's report 1962, Acc 198.

111  Conservative Party conference report 1962, p. 51 *ABCP* microfiche card no. 24.

112 See, for example, the reports from J.T. Lacy to COO 7 September 1962, BT Powell to COO 7 September 1962, P. Goldsworthy to COO 10 September 1962, BT Slim to COO 10 September 1962, CCO500/31/4, quotation from Conrad Corfield to Iain Macleod 22 January 1963 CCO2/6/15; see also CPA: North West Area Council minutes 24 November 1962 ARE3/1/6.

113 CPA: Macleod to Macmillan 6 June 1962 CCO20/8/5.

114 R.J. Leiber *British Politics and European Unity: Parties, Elites and Pressure Groups* Berkeley: University of California Press, 1970, p. 207; A. King and R. Wybrow (eds) *British Political Opinion 1937–2000: The Gallup Polls* London: Politicos, 2001, ch. 15.

115 D. Dutton 'Anticipating Maastricht: The Conservative Party and Britain's First Application to Join the European Community' *Contemporary Record* 7(3), 1993, pp. 527–8.

116 Ronald Butt 'The Common Market and Conservative Party Politics' *Government and Opposition* 2(3), 1967, p. 384.

117 E.g. CPA: 'confidential memorandum' I. Macleod to H. Macmillan, 24 September 1962, CCO20/8/5.

118 R. Shepherd *Iain Macleod* London: Hutchinson, 1994, p. 286.

119 Macmillan Ministerial Papers: P. De Zulueta to Macmillan 28 May 1962, MS.Macmillan.dep.c.310 f. 49.

120 J. Ramsden *Making of Conservative Party Policy* London: Longman, 1980, p. 212.

121 I am grateful to David Richardson for bringing this to my attention. PREM11/4230, 30 November 1962, letter from Philip de Zulueta.

122 See, for example, Vaughan-Morgan MP address to Reigate Conservative Association executive 18 September 1962, 353/4/2/1, Surrey Record Office.

123 Macmillan Ministerial Papers: Knox Cunningham to Bligh reporting conversation with Dudley Williams, 13 September 1962, MS.Macmillan.dep.c.354 f167.

124 C. Cook and J. Ramsden *By-elections in British Politics* London: UCL Press, 1997; D. Dutton *History of the Liberal Party in the Twentieth Century* Basingstoke: Palgrave, 2005.

125 J. Turner *Macmillan* Harlow: Longman, 1994; CPA: S. Curtis to COO 11 September 1962, reported that in Eastbourne three branches were refusing to canvas, 'saying that they are getting too many angry questions on the doorstep'. CCO500/31/4.

126 See N.J. Crowson 'Lord Hinchingbrooke, Europe and the November 1962 South Dorset By-election' *Contemporary British History* 17(3), 2003.

127 Macmillan Ministerial papers: Macmillan to Wyndham, 21 October 1962, MS.Macmillan.dep.c.353 ff. 337–38.

128 Moon *European*, p. 165.

129 CPA: Macleod to Macmillan 25 January 1963 CCO20/8/6; and Parliamentary Group on the Common Market minutes 28 January 1963 CRD2/42/8.

130 Heath *Course*, pp. 229–36.

131 See, for example, John Biggs-Davison's comments to Conservative Foreign Affairs Committee, 6 February 1963 CRD3/10/15; see also TNA, CAB 128/37 CCO5 and CAB 128/37 CCO7.

132 *Conservative Campaign Guide 1964*, p. 468 *ABCP* microfiche card no. 463; Conservative Party Report 1963, p. 88 (Meyer) *ABCP* microfiche card no. 27.

133 CPA: Macleod to Macmillan 25 January 1963, CCO20/8/6.

134 CPA: minutes Parliamentary Group on the Common Market, 4 February 1963, CRD2/42/8.

135 CPA: Ursula Branston 'The party's role after Brussels' 4 March 1963, CCO20/32/1.

136 CPA: Minutes Conservative Foreign Affairs Committee 6 February, 27 February, 13 March 1963 CRD3/10/15.

137 TNA: CAB128/37 10 January 1963, need to 'enlist the support of member countries other than France'.

138 Macmillan Mss: diary 16 July 1963 MS.Macmillan dep.d .49; TNA: CAB128/37 CC59, 8 October 1963; FO371/169 126, 11 June 1963 memo Paris Embassy to Foreign Office.

139 CPA: Minutes Conservative Foreign Affairs Committee 29 May 1963, CRD/3/10/15.

140 Macmillan Ministerial Mss: Knox Cunningham's notes on foreign affairs committee 16 May, 23 July 1962, MS.Macmillan.dep.c.354 ff. 180–81, 196–97.

141 R. Shepherd *The Power Brokers: The Tory Party and Its Leaders* London: Hutchinson, 1991, ch. 6.

142 R. Shepherd *Enoch Powell: A Biography* London: Pimlico, 1996, p. 302; Heffer *Like a Roman*, pp. 390–1.

143 N. Ashford 'The EEC' in Z. Layton Henry (ed.) *Conservative Party Politics* London: Longman, 1980, p. 103.

144 H. Parr *British Policy towards the European Community: Harold Wilson and Britain's World Role 1964–67* London: Routledge, 2005; O. Daddow (ed.) *Harold Wilson and European Integration: Britain's Second Application to Join the EEC* London: Frank Cass, 2003.

145 CPA: G. Pears, 'Debate on the application to join Common Market', 4 May 1967, CRD3/10/10.

146 CPA: G. Pears to Sewill, 5 June 1967, outlining Heath's intended tactics CRD3/10/10.

147 Dodds-Parker Mss: 'report on the prospects and position of Sterling' Jt Cttee from Cttee on Europe and the Commonwealth and Europe Group, March 1967, MC:P2/7/32/1, Magdalen College Archives, Oxford.

148 CPA: John Stevens to Du Cann 30 August 1967, CCO20/70/1.

149 CPA: Douglas Hurd to Heath, 6 November 1967, CRD3/10/11.

150 CPA: 'Brief for debate on Europe' [n.d. November 1967] CRD3/7/8/1.

151 CPA: minutes Leader's Consultative Committee, 17 July 1967, LCC(67). This, not surprisingly, was the anti-Marketeers' view. See, for example, Marten Mss: Marten to Alex Douglas-Home, 14 November 1967, MS.Eng.hist.c.1137 ff 55–57.

152 Dodds-Parker Mss: CRD brief 'Atlantic Political and Economic Ties', 21 February 1967, MC:P2/7/3C/5.

153 CPA: 'Paper 3 – general social articles in a treaty of association', 30 September 1967, CRD3/10/9.

154 CPA: Gordon Pears to Russell Lewis, 5 December 1967, CCO150/2/1/6.

155 CPA: minutes Foreign Affairs Committee, 5 December 1967, CRD3/10/16.

156 Marten Mss: Marten to Heath, 29 November 1967, MS.Eng.hist.c.1137 ff. 67–69.

157 E.g. Dodds-Parker Mss: Dodds-Parker to Richard Wood, 15 December 1967, MC:P2/7/3MS/1.

158 Dodds-Parker Mss: Dodds-Parker to Richard Wood, 17 January 1968, MC:P2/7/3C/1.

159 Dodds-Parkers Mss: Eldon Griffiths to Dodds-Parker, 20 December 1967, MC;PS/7/3C/1. The letter was signed by Griffiths, Parkers, Beamish, Kirk, Peel and Walters and published 1 January 1968, *Frankfurter Allgemeine Zeitung, Corriere della Sera, Le Monde, Die Welt, Tijd*; TNA: PREM 11/4220, cited in R. Lamb *The Macmillan Years 1957-63: The Emerging Truth* London: John Murray, 1995, pp. 199–200.

160 Dodds-Parker Mss: Dodds-Parker to Richard Wood, 15 December 1967, MC:P2/7/3MS/1.

161 Marten Mss: memo 8 March 1968: report of 7 February 1968 meeting of Committee on Europe, MS.Eng.hist.c.1137.

162 For example: 'Next step after the veto' by Jock Bruce-Gardyne, 'The New Zealand economy and the Common Market' by Tufton Beamish, 'Other ways

into Europe' and 'Other relationships' by Gordon Pears and a paper by Nicholas Ridley outlining tactics for achieving the objective of EEC membership. Marten Mss: MS.Eng.hist.c.1137.

163 CPA: Gordon Pears to Brian Reading, 1 March 1968, CRD3/7/8/1.

164 *Hampshire Chronicle*, 18 June 1971, James Spicer.

165 E.g. Marten Mss: Derek Walker-Smith to Tufton Beamish, 18 March 1971, MS.Eng.hist.c.1138 f. 323.

166 E.g. CPA: D. Hurd to E. Heath, 6 November 1967, CRD3/10/11; B. Reading to E. Heath, 15 July 1969, CRD3/7/8/1.

167 Dodds-Parker Mss: Dodds-Parker to Richard Wood, 17 January 1968, MC:P2/7/3C/1.

168 There were widely divergent views about the potential increase in food prices that might result from CAP. At the extremes were: CPA: 'European Policy' Michael Niblock, CRD, 27 June 1969, LCC(69)244, suggested 20 per cent; *Common Market and British Agriculture*, 11 March 1966, CRD3/2/9, predicted 1 per cent; 'Europe' memo by Douglas-Home, 18 July 1969, LCC(69)252, forecast a maximum increase of 14 per cent; 'Britain, the EEC and the Commonwealth', Gorrell Barnes, April 1966, CRD3/10/9, estimated between 3 and 4.5 per cent.

169 CPA: 'European policy', M. Niblock, 27 June 1969, LCC(69)244.

170 Dodds-Parker Mss: Dodds-Parker to Richard Wood, 17 January 1968, MC:P2/7/3C/1; quotation from Marten Mss: 'Britain and Europe', John Biffen, 28 December 1967, MS.Eng.hist.c.1137 ff 114–16.

171 Boyle Mss: memo 'Common Added-Value Tax System', Gordon Pears, CRD, 17 February 1969, MS660/23023/1.

172 Marten Mss: press release of Heath speech, 5 May 1970, MS.Eng.hist.c.1138 ff22–31. Marten underlined this quoted passage.

173 CPA: Foreign and Commonwealth Affairs cttee, 12 November 1970, CRD3/10/16.

174 Cited C. Lord *British Entry to the European Community* Aldershot: Dartmouth, 1993, p. 40.

175 CPA: minutes Foreign and Commonwealth Affairs Cttee, 12 November 1970, CRD3/10/16.

176 *The Times*, 15 July 1971, pp. 1, 6.

177 CPA: Opinion Research Centre (ORC) 'Britain and the Common Market' 5–9 August 1970, 'Speedsearch' 17–21 February 1971, poll 30 June–4 July 1971 CCO180/13/1/2–3, CCO180/13/1/6.

178 M. Garnett and I. Aitkens *Splendid! Splendid! The Authorised Biography of William Whitelaw* London: Cape, 2002, pp. 96–7.

179 CPA: Nigel Forman to Mrs Peck, 25 June 1971, CCO20/32/6.

180 D. Hurd *End to Promises* London: Collins, 1979, p. 66.

181 CPA: 'Interim report', 19 October 1971, CCO20/32/7.

182 This was larger than some insiders had been predicting. See Hurd *Promises*, p. 68, thought 33.

183 Lord *British Entry*, p. 23.

184 S. Ball and A. Seldon (eds) *The Heath Government: A Reappraisal* London: Longman, 1996.

185 Heffer *Like a Roman*, pp. 698–709.

186 J. McKay 'Labour Party's Attitudes to European Integration 1945–75' unpublished PhD, University of Birmingham, 2006, pp. 239–40.

187 R. Broad *Labour's European Dilemma* Basingstoke: Macmillan, 2000, pp. 100–6.

188 *Hansard*, 5th series, vol. 889, cols 821–961, 1020–1189, 1243–1371, 7–9 April 1975.

189 Britain in Europe (hereafter BIE) Mss: Minutes 16th mtg Europe Co-ordinating Cttee, 24 March 1975, BIE/1/49, House of Lords Records Office.

190 Cited Routledge *Public Servant*, p. 267.
191 D. Hurd *Memoirs* London: Little Brown, 2003, p. 236.
192 Thatcher Foundation Archive: Leader's Consultative Committee, 26 February 1975, www.margaretthatcher.org.
193 Thatcher Foundation Archive: Leader's Consultative Committee, 26 March 1975, www.margaretthatcher.org.
194 BIE Mss: minutes 16th mtg Europe Co-ordination Committee, 24 March 1975, BIE/1/49.
195 Hurd *Memoirs*, p. 236.
196 BIE Mss: minutes 16th mtg Europe Co-ordination Committee, 24 March 1975, BIE/1/49.
197 Thatcher Foundation Archive: Leader's consultative Committee, 11 April 1975, www.margaretthatcher.org.
198 See B. Castle *The Castle Diaries 1974–6* London: Weidenfeld and Nicolson, 1980, entry for 30 May 1975, p. 402: 'I feel frustrated in having to work through an umbrella organization over which we have no real control.'
199 Castle *Diaries*, entries for 28–31 May 1975, pp. 401–3.
200 Garnett and Aitkens *Splendid!*, p. 222.
201 Hinchingbrooke Mss: ACML Executive, 16 July 1975.
202 D. Butler and U. Kitzinger *The 1975 Referendum* London: Macmillan, 1976, pp. 281–2.
203 BIE minutes 9th mtg Europe co-ordinating Committee, 20 January 1975, BIE/1/49.
204 BIE: minutes 24th mtg Europe Co-ordinating Committee, 12 May 1975, BIE/1/49.
205 Thatcher Foundation Archive: Leader's Consultative Committee, 24 March 1975, www.margaretthatcher.org.
206 Marten Mss: Whitelaw to CA chairmen, 30 January 1975, MS.Eng.hist.c.1131 f 230; CPA: Thorneycroft to CA chairmen, May 1975, CCO4/10/263.
207 Thatcher Foundation Archive: Leader's Consultative Committee, 26 March 1975, www.margaretthatcher.org.
208 See CD-ROM *Complete Public Statements of Margaret Thatcher, 1945–90* Oxford: Oxford University Press, 1998.
209 BIE Mss: 'European Campaign December 1974' BIE/1/49.
210 BIE Mss: Minutes Referendum Campaign, 21 April 1975, BIE/14/1.
211 N.J. Crowson *Facing Fascism: The Conservative Party and the European Dictators 1935–40* London: Routledge, 1997, pp. 52–4.
212 D.S. Birn *The League of Nations Union* Oxford: Clarendon Press, 1981, pp. 143–54; M. Ceadel 'The First British Referendum: The Peace Ballot, 1934–35' *English Historical Review* 95, 1980, pp. 810–39.
213 *Warwick Advertiser*, 18 April 1975.
214 Marten Mss: Cyril Black to Marten, 13 June 1975, MS.Eng.hist.c.113 ff 174–75.
215 BIE Mss: minutes 10th mtg Europe Co-ordinating Group, 27 January 1975, BIE/1/49.
216 Butler and Kitzinger *Referendum*, p. 110.
217 Marten Mss: Cyril Black to Marten, 13 June 1975, MS.Eng.hist.c.113 ff 174–5.
218 A. King *Britain Says Yes* Washingston: AEI, 1977, p. 123.
219 Hurd *Memoirs*, p. 237.
220 Thatcher Foundation Archive: Leader's Consultative Committee, 11 April 1975, www.margaretthatcher.org.

## 2  From EEC to EU, 1975 – 2006: 'in Europe, but not run by Europe'?

1 N. Ridley *My Style of Government* London: Hutchinson, 1991, p. 136. Claims there were no policy groups. But see Conservative Party Archive (hereafter

CPA): 'Policy Group on Direct Elections to the European Parliament' chaired by Anthony Royle, CCO20/32/10.

2 Manifesto 1979 can be consulted, www.psr.keele.ac.uk/area/uk/man.htm; see also *Hansard: The Debates of the House of Commons*, 5th series, 13 March 1979, vol. 964, cols 455–56. M. Thatcher *Downing Street Years* London: HarperCollins, 1993, p. 339, claims this was just opportunism as the Official Opposition.

3 CPA: 'The problem of direct elections to the European Parliament', n.d. [1976], CCO20/32/10.

4 Thorneycroft Mss: 92nd National Union Conference, 7–10 October 1975, Official Programme MS278/A962/2/2, University of Southampton Special Collections.

5 Marten Mss: Marten to editor *Monthly News*, 3 March 1975, MS.Eng.hist.c. 1141 f. 312, Bodleian Library, Oxford.

6 For the tactics following this, see Margaret Thatcher Foundation: 'European Assembly Elections Bill' Howell and Hurd, 13 January 1978, www.margaret-thatcher.org.

7 N. Lamont *In Office* London: Little Brown, 1999, p. 450.

8 CPA: James Douglas to Thatcher, 15 April 1977, CCO20/32/11; for quotation, see Memo 'The British Representation in the European Parliament', S. Wingfield Digby, n.d., CCO20/32/6.

9 CPA: 2nd report by policy group on Direct Elections to European Parliament, 18 May 1976, CCO20/32/10.

10 CPA: Angus Maude to Peter Thorneycroft, 2 July 1976, CCO20/32/10.

11 E. Heath *Course of My Life* London: Hodder and Stoughton, 1998, p. 697.

12 *Select Committee on Direct Elections to the European Parliament 2nd Report*, 1976, memo from CGE, appendix 15, p. 42. It is worth noting that under cross-examination by William Clark, himself a member of CGE, Jim Spicer admitted that this report had not been widely circulated and had been agreed by a meeting of the General Purposes Committee where '4 or 5 people out of 14 who were there said they wanted it'. *Minutes of Evidence to Select Committee on Direct Elections*, 22 July 1976, para. 612, p. 161.

13 D. Hurd *Memoirs* London: Little Brown, 2003, p. 244; Thatcher Foundation: speech to Conservative Group for Europe, London, 24 November 1976, www.margaretthatcher.org.

14 CPA: James Douglas to Thatcher, 15 April 1977, CCO20/32/11.

15 J. Campbell *Margaret Thatcher: I: The Grocer's Daughter* London: Jonathan Cape, 2000, p. 417.

16 D. Butler and D. Marquand *European Elections and British Politics* London: Longman, 1981, p. 41.

17 CPA: 2nd report by policy group on Direct Elections to European Parliament, 18 May 1976, CCO20/32/10.

18 Hurd *Memoirs*, p. 245.

19 CPA: correspondence between Edward Du Cann, Baroness Young and Peter Thorneycroft, 7 December 1977 to 3 January 1978, CCO20/32/11; Thatcher Foundation: H. Atkins to Thatcher, 6 December 1978, www.margaretthatcher.org.

20 F.W.S. Craig *Europe Votes 1: European Parliamentary Results 1979* Chichester: PRS, 1980.

21 E.g. Derek Prag, Bow Group European Liaison Committee, in written evidence to a 1976 Select Committee wrote: 'The Community has achieved little enough since its enlargement, and its lack of achievement is striking in all fields.' *Select Committee on Direct Elections to European Assembly 2nd Report*, July 1976, appendix 16, p. 45.

22 Based upon per head of population. Information from J.W. Young *Britain and European Unity, 1945–92* Basingstoke: Macmillan, 1993, p. 130; see D. Butler

and G. Butler *Twentieth Century British Political Facts* Basingstoke: Macmillan, 2000, p. 512, for figures of net UK payments to EC 1973–99.

23　H. Young *One of Us* London: Pan, 1990, pp. 185–7, referring to advice of Peter Middleton.

24　J. Buller *National Statecraft and European Integration* London: Pinter, 2000, pp. 53–4.

25　Thatcher Foundation: Thatcher speech, 'Youth for Europe' rally, NEC, Birmingham, 2 June 1979, www.margaretthatcher.org.

26　Thatcher Foundation: Thatcher press conference, Dublin Castle, 30 November 1979, www.margaretthatcher.org.

27　M. Thatcher *Downing Street* London: HarperCollins, 1993, p. 81.

28　H. Young *This Blessed Plot: Britain and Europe from Churchill to Blair* London: Macmillan, 1998, p. 314.

29　For a private articulation of this view, see Thatcher Foundation: Nigel Lawson to Thatcher, 30 October 1978, www.margaretthatcher.org.

30　B. Cartledge 'Margaret Thatcher: Personality and Foreign Policy' in S. Pugliese (ed.) *The Political Legacy of Margaret Thatcher* London: Politicos, 2003, p. 159; Young *This Blessed Plot*, p. 318, confirms this verdict, although he notes that officials' views of her methods cover the spectrum from reluctantly agreeing to bullish enthusiasm.

31　Thatcher Foundation: speech at dinner in honour of Chancellor Schmidt, 10 May 1979; press conference with Chancellor Schmidt, answer to Andrew Roth question, 11 May 1979, www.margaretthatcher.org.

32　Thatcher Foundation: speech 'Europe as I See It' to Centro Italona di studi per la Concillazione Internazionale, Rome, 24 June 1977, www.margaretthatcher.org.

33　Hurd *Memoirs*, p. 244.

34　E.g. Thatcher Foundation: Thatcher press conference, Dublin Castle, Thatcher's answer to Stephen Milligan, *Economist*, 30 November 1979, www.margaret thatcher.org.

35　A. King and R. Wybrow (eds) *British Political Opinion: 1937–2000: Gallup Polls* London: Politicos, 2001, pp. 191–2.

36　*Hansard*, 5th series, vol. 975, cols 29–31 (Thatcher), 3 December 1979; Buller *National Statecraft*, p. 95.

37　F. Pym *The Politics of Consent* London: Hamish Hamilton, 1984.

38　Lord Carrington *Reflect on Things Past* London: Collins, 1988, p. 319.

39　I. Gilmour *Dancing with Dogma* London: Simon and Schuster, 1992, p. 240.

40　G. Howe *Conflict of Loyalty* London: Macmillan, 1994, p. 184.

41　J. Dickie *Inside the Foreign Office* London: Chapmans, 1992.

42　Thatcher *Downing Street*, pp. 309–10.

43　D. Kavanagh *Thatcherism and British Politics* London: Macmillan, 1990, p. 268.

44　Young *This Blessed Plot*, p. 311.

45　*The Times*, Edward Heath, 'Where Are Today's Action Men?', 5 April 1983, p. 10; Francis Pym 'Problems that Can Be Talked Away', 19 November 1983, p. 8.

46　Thatcher Foundation: Howe to Thatcher, 31 October 1978; see also minutes of meeting on 'The EMS', 27 October 1978, www.margaretthatcher.org.

47　Howe *Conflict*, p. 111.

48　Thatcher Foundation: Leader's Consultative Committee, 15 November 1978, www.margaretthatcher.org.

49　Thatcher Foundation: Nigel Lawson to Thatcher, 30 October 1978, www.margaret thatcher.org.

50　Thatcher Foundation: minutes of meeting on 'The EMS', 27 October 1978; Howe to Thatcher, 31 October 1978; Leader's Consultative Committee, 15 November 1978, www.margaretthatcher.org.

51　Howe *Conflict*, p. 456.

52 Thatcher *Downing Street*, pp. 63, 554; J. Campbell *Margaret Thatcher: Iron Lady, Volume Two* London: Jonathan Cape, 2002, pp. 227–8.

53 Young *Blessed Plot* chp 9.

54 See statement on London European Council, *Hansard*, 6th series, vol. 107, col. 21, 8 December 1986.

55 Buller *National Statecraft*, p. 88.

56 The 'Europeanisation' statecraft thesis is developed by Buller *National Statecraft*. For the 1984 White Paper see also, pp. 69–70.

57 Cockfield *The European Union* London: Wiley Chancery Law, 1994.

58 *Hansard*, 6th series, vol. 63, cols 934–40, 10 July 1984 (Teddy Taylor); vol. 93, cols 346–50 (Anthony Kershaw), 5 March 1986; see also vol. 96, cols 324–25 (Michael Knowles), cols. 358–61 (George Gardiner), cols 378–79 (Bill Cash), 23 April 1986.

59 For 149, against 43; Young *This Blessed Plot*, pp. 334–5; A. Forster *Euroscepticism in Contemporary British Politics* London: Routledge, 2001, p. 67.

60 *Hansard*, 6th series, vol. 100, col. 490, 26 June 1986, Edward Du Cann.

61 *Hansard*, 6th series, vol. 63, col. 890, 10 July 1984, G. Howe; vol. 81, col. 466, 20 June 1985, Rifkind.

62 N. Ashford 'The Political Parties' in S. George (ed.) *Britain and the European Community: The Politics of Semi-detachment* Oxford: Oxford University Press, 1992, p. 134.

63 *Hansard*, 6th series, vol. 93, col. 346 (Anthony Kershaw), 5 March 1986.

64 Gilmour *Dancing*, p. 188.

65 P. Morris 'The British Conservative Party' in J. Gaffney *Political Parties and the European Union* London: Routledge, 1996, p. 133; Campbell *Iron Lady*, p. 227.

66 Buller *National Statecraft*, p. 136.

67 Howe *Conflict*, p. 533.

68 Forster *Euroscepticism*, p. 74; Young *This Blessed Plot*, p. 334, passage of act, pp. 349–53.

69 Thatcher Foundation: Thatcher speech to College of Europe, Bruges, 20 September 1988, www.margaretthatcher.org.

70 P. Riddell 'Margaret Thatcher: The Lady Who Made the Weather' in S. Pugliese (ed.) *The Political Legacy of Margaret Thatcher* London: Politicos, 2003, p. 12.

71 Lawson *View*, p. 923.

72 Forster *Euroscepticism*, p. 78.

73 Buller *National Statecraft*, p. 121.

74 For further details, see P. Stephens *Politics and the Pound: The Tories, the Economy and Europe* London: Macmillan, 1996; Campbell *Iron Lady*, pp. 600–18; Howe *Conflict*, chs 38–43; Lawson *View*, chs 74, 76, 77.

75 Thatcher *Downing Street*, pp. 759–60.

76 Thatcher *Downing Street*, p. 752.

77 See R. Shepherd *Powerbrokers: The Tory Party and Its Leaders* London: Hutchinson, 1990, especially chs 1–4.

78 Howe *Conflict*, p. 643.

79 'I Can Remain No Longer', Radio 4 documentary on Howe resignation, broadcast 22 February 2004, http://bbc.co.uk/news/westminster_hour. See also K. Baker *Turbulent Years* London: Faber and Faber, 1993, p. 379, for the final Cabinet meeting. Although Baker in his memoirs does not mention Thatcher's aside in the chamber, he does record her observing, 'I didn't think he would do something like that', p. 386.

80 Christopher Gill *Whips' Nightmare: Diary of a Maastricht Rebel* Spenneymore: Memoir Club, 2003, p. 31; see also P. Cowley 'How Did He Do that? The Second Round of the 1990 Conservative Leadership Election' in D. Broughton (ed.) *British Election and Parties Yearbook, 1996* London: Frank Cass, 1996. Cowley sees European policy as the determining ideological variable in the contest.

81  Young *This Blessed Plot*, p. 387.
82  A. Seldon *Major: A Political Life* London: Weidenfeld and Nicolson, 1997, pp. 166–8.
83  Thatcher Foundation: Thatcher speech, Foreign Relations Council of Chicago, 17 June 1991, www.margaretthatcher.org.
84  Cited Seldon *Major*, p. 243.
85  *Hansard*, vol 199, cols 269–81 (Major); rest of debates cols 281–390 (20 November 1991) and cols 436–519 (21 November). Division split (Div. No. 15) was 351–250; Major's majority was 101, with only 6 Conservatives voting against and a further 9 abstaining.
86  Seldon *Major*, p. 245.
87  N. Lamont *In Office* London: Little Brown, 1999; Major *Autobiography*, ch. 12; As an example of a positive journalistic reaction see *Daily Telegraph*, Boris Johnson, 11 December 1991, editorial 12 December 1991; *The Times*, 12 December 1991.
88  Seldon *Major*, p. 244; for the attack, see *Hansard*, vol. 199, cols. 290–98, Thatcher, 20 November 1991; this was followed by an interview on ITN on 22 November.
89  D. Butler and D. Kavanagh *The British General Election of 1992* Basingstoke: Macmillan, 1993.
90  Hurd *Memoirs*, p. 423.
91  *Hansard*, vol. 203, cols. 230–55, European Communities budget debate, 4 February 1992.
92  *Hansard*, 21 May 1992, vol 204, cols. 509–600.
93  Hurd *Memoirs*, p. 423.
94  These words were attributed to him by the No. 10 Press Office, Seldon *Major*, p. 248; For optimistic assessments, see *Daily Telegraph*, 12 December 1991, 13 December 1991.
95  Seldon *Major*, pp. 251, 293.
96  M. Spicer *A Treaty too Far: A New Policy for Europe* London: Fourth Estate, 1992, p. 165. Those who withdrew were Hartley Booth, David Evans, Lady Maitland and Michael Shersby.
97  Hurd *Memoirs*, p. 424, diary entry for 5 June.
98  Seldon *Major*, pp. 293–6.
99  This has in part been considered by M. Sowemimo 'The Conservative Party and European Integration 1988–95' *Party Politics* 2(1), 1996, pp. 77–97.
100  *Daily Telegraph*, 19 September 1992, p. 7.
101  *The European*, 8–11 October 1992, p. 8.
102  Spicer *Treaty*, pp. 203–4 for full wording of EDM and list of signatures.
103  *Daily Telegraph*, 10 June 1993, p. 10, report of resignation speech; *The Times*, 16 September 1993, Lamont article for anniversary of Black Wednesday; Lamont article, 23 June 1995, p. 18.
104  *Daily Telegraph*, 19 September 1992, p. 7.
105  *Daily Telegraph*, 7 October 1992, p. 1.
106  *Daily Telegraph*, 19 September 1992, p. 7.
107  Hurd *Memoirs*, p. 428.
108  C. Gill *Whips' Nightmare*, p. 57. This was borrowing an idea suggested by Knud Pederson of the Danish 'No' campaign.
109  Hurd *Memoirs*, p. 432.
110  *Sunday Times*, 14 February 1993, p. 1.20.
111  *Sunday Times*, 18 April 1993, p. 1.24.
112  D. Baker *et al.* 'Backbenchers with Attitude' paper to European Consortium for Political Research Conference, Bordeaux, 1995, Table 1, p. 14, records the number of times individual MPs recorded dissenting votes on the European Communities (Amendment) Bill 1992/3.

113 *Hansard*, vol. 204, cols 581–89 (R. Shepherd), Div. No. 90, 21 February 1992. The second reading secured 46 votes to 3, but was not carried due to an insufficient majority being present. Immediately accusations of dirty tricks were made, claiming that the division bells had been switched off, col. 650.

114 *Hansard*, vol. 229, cols 519–611, 22 July 1993, Div. No. 358 (317 votes to 317, with the speaker taking the casting vote and defeating the amendment); Div. No. 359 (316 votes to 24, defeating the Social Chapter).

115 *Hansard*, vol. 229, cols 610–11 (Major), 22 July 1993; cols 625–723, vote won 339 to 299.

116 Major told Michael Brunson, 'You can think of ex-ministers who are going round causing all sorts of trouble. We don't want another three more of the bastards out there', 27 July 1993. M. Brunson *A Ringside Seat* London: Hodder and Stoughton, 2000, pp. 197–200.

117 See Macmillan's comments: PREM11/1831B, record of mtg 9 March 1957 with Guy Mollet.

118 Legge-Bourke Mss: Legge-Bourke to R.E. Hooper, 8 November 1971, MS.742/910/1.

119 *Hansard*, vol. 240, col. 802, March 1994.

120 *Sunday Times*, 20 March 1994, p. 1.26.

121 Major *Autobiography*, pp. 603–7; Seldon *Major*, pp. 544–5.

122 Gill *Whips' Nightmare*, p. 124.

123 K. Alderman, 'The Conservative Party Leadership Election of 1995' *Parliamentary Affairs* 49(2), 1996, pp. 316–32.

124 E.g. see *The Times*, 10 March 1996.

125 David McKay *Federalism and European Union* Oxford: Oxford University Press, 1999, p. 3.

126 *Daily Telegraph*, 12 February 1995.

127 EDM No. 581, 8 February 1995, 102 signatures, http://edmi.parliament.uk/edmi/; see also *Daily Telegraph*, 10 February 1995, pp. 1–2.

128 *Hansard*, vol. 255, cols 1060–74, quotations cols 1068, 1071 (Major), 1 March 1995; see also *Daily Telegraph*, 2 March 1995, p. 1.

129 *The Times*, Norman Lamont article, 23 June 1995, p. 18.

130 *Daily Telegraph*, 21 March 1995, p. 14, Tebbit addressing European Foundation rally.

131 *The Times*, letters to editor, 21 June 1995, p. 17.

132 *Daily Telegraph*, 21 March 1995, p. 14.

133 *The Times*, Quentin Davies plus 14 other MPs to editor, 21 October 1996, p. 21.

134 *The Independent*, letter to editor, 19 September 1996 and 5 January 1998.

135 *Daily Telegraph*, letters to editor, 20 September 1996, p. 25.

136 S. Ludlam 'The Spectre Haunting Conservatism' in S. Ludlam and M.J. Smith (eds) *Contemporary British Conservatism* Basingstoke: Macmillan, 1996, p. 100.

137 *Daily Telegraph*, 14 September 1996.

138 *The Sunday Times*, 16 March 1997.

139 www.psr.keele.ac.uk/area/uk/man.htm.

140 K. Alderman 'The Conservative Party Leadership Election of 1997', *Parliamentary Affairs* 51(1), 1998, pp. 1–17.

141 *Daily Telegraph*, 31 October 1997.

142 *The Times*, 22 January 1998, p. 18, Hague article.

143 *Daily Telegraph*, 3 November 1997, p. 20.

144 *Daily Telegraph*, John Stevens MEP to editor, 29 September 1997, and the response of Norman Tebbit to editor, 30 September 1997.

145 *The Independent*, 5 January 1998, p. 12; *Daily Telegraph*, 1 November 1997, speech by Leon Brittan to Roxburgh and Berwickshire Tories.

146 *Daily Telegraph*, 4 June, 16 August 1999.

147 *Daily Telegraph*, 6 October 1998, Budgen article.

148 Nigel Dudley 'Britain, the Tories and the Euro-Zone' *Reformer Magazine*, Spring 1999.
149 *Daily Telegraph*, 25 September 1998, Lord Younger to editor, and 26 Conservative MPs to editor, p. 29.
150 Statistics taken from *Daily Telegraph*, 6 October 1998.
151 *Daily Telegraph* 6 October 1998.
152 *Daily Telegraph* Tom Spencer to editor, 25 September 1998, p. 29.
153 *Daily Telegraph* 9 July 1999 reporting Hague's speech to Congress for Democracy, London.
154 *Daily Telegraph* 20 May 1998, p. 13.
155 *Daily Telegraph*, 21 May 1998, p. 18; 13 October 1999, p. 13.
156 E.g. CCO press release, 24 May 2001 'Our vision for Europe', Francis Maude, www.conservatives.com/news.
157 CCO press release, 26 May 2001 'Six Days to save the pound', www.conservatives.com/news.
158 Thatcher Foundation: speech to Conservative election rally in Plymouth, 'The Mummy Returns', 22 May 2001, www.margaretthatcher.org. S. Walters *Tory Wars: Conservatives in Crisis* London: Politicos, 2001, ch. 15, portrays the difficulties this speech presented the Hague camp with.
159 *The Times*, 28 July 1999, p. 18.
160 Walters *Tory Wars*, *passim*.
161 Conservative percentage share of vote in European elections: 1979 48 per cent, 1984 39 per cent, 1989 34 per cent, 1994 27 per cent.
162 E.g. *Daily Telegraph*, 2 October 2000, reporting on monthly Gallup poll for the paper.
163 *Daily Telegraph*, Grant to editor, 16 June 1999, p. 23.
164 See, for example, the Tory Reform Group evaluation, 'Lessons from the 2001 General Election: Winning Back the Missing Conservatives', 11 June 2001, www.trg.org.uk/publications.
165 *The Times*, 12 May 2001, p. 1. A historical parallel could be drawn with Churchill's infamous 1945 'Gestapo' radio election broadcast implying this was the likely outcome of a Labour reforming government.
166 For an explanation of the new rules, see N.J. Crowson *The Longman Companion to the Conservative Party since 1830* Harlow: Pearsons, 2001, p. 8.
167 Derived from K. Alderman and N. Carter 'The Conservative Party Leadership Election of 2001' *Parliamentary Affairs* 55(4), 2002, pp. 569–85; see also P. Cowley and J. Green 'New Leaders, Same Problems: The Conservatives' in A. Geddes and J. Tonge (eds) *Britain Decides: The UK General Election 2005* Basingstoke: Palgrave, 2005, pp. 47–50.
168 *Daily Telegraph*, 1 July 2002.
169 CCO press release: Michael Ancram, 'Building true partnerships', speech 9 May 2002 to EEP group, www.conservatives.com/news.
170 The convention convened for first time on 28 February 2002 at the European Parliament.
171 Lord Brittan *et al. The Future of the EU: A Positive Conservative Approach.* Other signatories included Ian Taylor (chairman, European Movement and Tory European Network), Robert Walter (chair, Positive European Group), Michael Welsh (COE, Action Centre for Europe) and Giles Marshall (chair, Tory Reform Group), quote from, p. 18 of document. www.cge.org.uk/links.
172 CCO press release, Heathcote-Amory, 'Europe of Democracies', 30 May 2003, www.conservatives.com/news. See also David Heathcote-Amory *The European Constitution and What It Means for Britain* London: Centre for Policy Studies, June 2003.

173 Howard's adverts in national press, e.g. *Daily Telegraph*, 2 January 2004; see also CCO press release, 'Michael Howard's personal credo', 2 January 2004, www.conservatives.com/news.
174 CCO press release, Michael Howard, 'A new deal for Europe', 12 February 2004, www.conservatives.com/news.
175 E.g. Centre for Policy Studies press release, 'Tidying Up?', www.cps.org.uk; see also CCO press releases: 'Michael Howard promises EU constitution overhaul', 24 March 2004; 'First step to common EU criminal code', Michael Ancram, 26 March 2004, www.conservatives.com/news.
176 *Daily Telegraph*, 26 April 2006, p. 10.

## 3 The issues and debates: 'head versus heart'

1 Alexander Cadogan.
2 C. Lord *British Entry into the European Community under the Heath Government* Aldershot: Dartmouth, 1993, pp. 16–17.
3 Daniel Hannan, *Sunday Telegraph*, 18 December 2005, p. 32.
4 Birmingham CA, officers sub-committee, 15 February 1946, AQ329.94249CON f. 4, Birmingham Central Library; Legge-Bourke Mss: Legge-Bourke to George Gale, 21 December 1970, MS.742 f.793/1–2, Brotherton Library, University of Leeds.
5 CPA: S.T. Ward (Chair, Ely CA) to Macleod, n.d. [April 1962], CCO1/14/380; P. Goldsworthy to COO, 10 September 1962, CCO500/31/4; Boyle Mss: H. Shires (agent) to Boyle, 28 December 1962, MS660/12204; North Wiltshire Conservative Association: executive, 10 June 1963, 2436/10, Wiltshire Record Office.
6 Heath has suggested retrospectively that this speech fuelled doubts about Eden's potential suitability as party leader. E. Heath *Course of My Life* London: Hodder and Stoughton, 1998, p. 204.
7 Thatcher Foundation: speech to College of Europe, 20 September 1988, www.margaretthatcher.org.
8 CPA: V.B. Petherick to COO, 6 September 1962, CCO500/31/4; Horton to COO, 23 August 1962, CCO500/31/2.
9 Boyle Mss: 'Summary of electors comments' week ending 31 August 1962, MS660/20553, Brotherton Library, University of Leeds.
10 CPA: 'Strasbourg Study visit 21–28 September 1952', R.D. Milne, 24 October 1952, COB21/1/2; 'Common Market and Public opinion', S. Eastern Area, 27 August 1962, CCO500/31/2; P.G. Gower to COO, 5 September 1962, CCO500/31/4; Tynemouth CA: Irene Ward speech, *Newcastle Evening News*, 1 July 1950, 1633/17/2; and Irene Ward speech, 26 January 1962, 1633/17/5, Tyne and Wear Archives; *Independent*, 12 October 1994, p. 19, Lamont addressing Selsdon Group.
11 CPA: 'The Council of Europe', Ursula Branston, 28 September 1954, COB21/1/2; Cab Conclusions, 14 January 1958; Sheffield Ecclesall CA, newscutting, 16 November 1946, LD2117, Sheffield City Archives.
12 Cited Peter Catterall 'Macmillan and Europe' paper presented to WCBS, Houston, 2000.
13 Cab 128/32 conclusions, 14 January 1958.
14 Thatcher *Downing Street* London: Harper Collins, 1993, pp. 792–6, 813–15, she admits this was the one area of her foreign policy that met with 'unambiguous failure', p. 813; J. Campbell *Margaret Thatcher: Iron Lady* London: Jonathan Cape, 2003, pp. 628–29, 632–41, 704; H. Young *This Blessed Plot: Britain and Europe from Churchill to Blair* London: Macmillan, 1998, pp. 357–62.
15 *Spectator*, 12 July 1990; for reaction of Eurosceptics, see *Independent*, 14 July 1990, p. 3.
16 CPA: Parliamentary Group on the Common Market, minutes, 10 December 1962, Maurice Macmillan, CRD2/42/8; North Edinburgh CA: newsclippings,

Harold Macmillan cited in *Scottish Daily Mail*, 5 January 1959, Acc. 198, Edinburgh City Archives.

17  CPA: Foreign Affairs Committee, minutes, 26 March 1968, Peter Kirk, CRD3/10/16; Some suggested that fear of the threat to the primacy of French as the language of diplomacy was behind much of the French resistance: Con O'Neill *Britain's Entry into the European Community: Report on the Negotiations of 1970–72* London: Whitehall History Publishing/Frank Cass, 2000, ch. 33, para 19, p. 337; CPA: Frederick Corfield to Mrs Peck, 22 June 1971, CCO20/32/6.

18  Dodds-Parker Mss: Simon Digby to Dodds-Parker, 8 November 1971, MC:P2/7/3MS/5.

19  CPA: 'Strasbourg Study Visit 22–30 September 1961', COB58/2; Foreign Affairs Committee, 6 February 1963, 18 February 1969, 22 July 1969, CRD3/10/15–16; 'Europe', A. Douglas-Home, 18 July 1969, LCC(69)252; 'European Policy', M. Niblock, 27 June 1969, LCC(69)244; Marten Mss: MS.Eng.hist.c.1141 ff. 73–78.

20  North Wiltshire CA: AGM, 15 April 1950, 2436/2, Wiltshire Record Office.

21  CPA: 'The Council of Europe', U. Branston, 28 September 1954, COB21/1/2.

22  Lord *British Entry*, p. 47.

23  Macmillan Mss: Redmayne to Macmillan, 9 August 1959, MS.Macmillan.dep.c. 311 ff. 57–58.

24  CPA: minutes, foreign affairs committee, 29 May 1963, CRD3/10/15.

25  Dodds-Parker Mss: D.-P. to Richard Wood, 17 January 1968, MC:P2/7/3C/1, as an example of a pro-European anxious not to allow closer integration to become anti-American.

26  *Daily Telegraph*, 11 October 1995, p. 8.

27  CCO press release: Michael Ancram, 'Building true partnerships', 9 May 2002, www.conservatives.com/news.

28  CPA: P. Goldsworthy to COO, 10 September 1962, CCO500/31/4; 'Common Market and Public opinion S.E. Area', 27 August 1962, CCO500/31/2; J. Varley to COO, 24 August 1962, CCO500/31/2; Boyle Mss: H. Shires (agent) to Boyle, 28 December 1962, MS660/12204; 'Summary of electors comments', week ending 31 August 1962, MS660/20553.

29  Waterhouse Mss: C. Waterhouse to H.C. Fairbrother, 12 December 1956, in private possession.

30  Birmingham CA: officers sub-cttee 15 February 1946.

31  Young *Blessed Plot*, p. 376.

32  CPA: see CCO500/31/1–4.

33  P. Walker *Staying Power: An Autobiography*, London: Bloomsbury, 1991, pp. 30–1.

34  CPA: 'European Policy', M. Niblock, 27 June 1969, LCC(69)244.

35  CPA: Peter Thomas to Neil Marten, 22 February 1971, CCO20/32/4.

36  Tuckman Mss: Bow Group press release, 14 February 1961, MS270/A921/4/1 Folder 2; CPA: 'Common Market Basic Facts', Gordon Pears, CRD, September 1967, CCO150/2/1/6.

37  CPA: ORC poll, 5–9 August 1970, CC0180/13/1/2.

38  E. Curry *Diaries* London: Little Brown, 2000, entry for 16 May 1989, p. 131.

39  North Edinburgh Conservative Association: *Scottish Daily Mail*, 6 January 1959, interview with Selwyn Lloyd, Acc 198; CPA: Foreign Affairs Committee, 3 February 1963 (Peter Kirk), 29 May 1963, CRD3/10/15–16.

40  S. Ball (ed.) *In the Age of Attlee and Churchill: The Cuthbert Headlam Diaries* Cambridge: Royal Historical Society, 1999, entry for 16 February 1949, pp. 573–4.

41  CPA: 'Report of ACML meeting', 7 November 1962, reporting Hinchingbrooke's speech, CCO500/31/3.

42  CPA: 'Report on Britain and Europe', Wales and Monmouth Young Conservatives, n.d., CC0506/14/15; Foreign Affairs Committee, 13 March 1963 (Julian

Critchley), CRD3/10/15; see also E. Fursdon *The European Defence Community* London: Macmillan, 1980.

43 Macmillan Diary, entry for 3 January 1951, cited Catterall 'Macmillan and Europe'.

44 Ball *Headlam Diaries*, entry for 19 March 1949, p. 579.

45 *Sunday Telegraph*, 12 February 1995, reporting Rifkind's speech to Belgian Royal Institute of International Affairs.

46 *Daily Telegraph*, 2 March 1995, p. 2.

47 *Daily Telegraph*, 1 July 1996, p. 34.

48 CPA: Foreign Affairs Committee, 27 February, 13 March (quotation Smithers), 29 May 1963, CRD3/10/15.

49 Marten Mss: press release Heath speech, Paris, 5 May 1970, MS.Eng.hist.c.1138 f. 27.

50 A. Forster *Euroscepticism in Contemporary British Politics* London: Routledge, 2002, p. 94.

51 *Daily Telegraph*, 15 January 1998, p. 6.

52 CCO press release: Michael Ancram, 'Building true partnerships', 9 May 2002, www.conservatives.com/news.

53 *Hansard*, vol. 457, col. 1410 (Maxwell-Fyfe), 31 October 1948.

54 European Movement *European Movement and Council of Europe* London: Hutchinson, n.d., p. 142.

55 CPA: OPC 'Attitudes to Europe', April 1967, CCO500/31/5; minutes, Foreign Affairs Cttee, 21 October 1969, CRD3/10/16.

56 Marten Mss: G. Rippon to Marten, 7 January 1971, MS.Eng.hist.c.1138 ff231–32.

57 Marten Mss: Douglas-Home to Marten, n.d. [?late 1972], MS.Eng.hist.c.1141 f. 41.

58 CPA: minutes, Foreign and Commonwealth Affairs Committee, 12 November 1970, CRD3/10/16.

59 CPA: 'Europe', Douglas-Home, 18 July 1969, LCC(69)252.

60 Marten Mss: Marten to Heath, 12 August 1971, MS.Eng.hist.c.1141 f. 221.

61 CPA: Foreign Affairs cttee, 19 January 1971, Rippon, CRD3/10/17; see also Legge-Bourke Mss: H. L.-B. to R.E. Hooper, 8 November 1971, MS.742/910/1.

62 CPA: 'Britain in Europe', July 1976, West Midlands Ycs, CCO20/32/10.

63 Randolph Churchill (ed.) *Europe Unite* London: Cassell, 1950, p. 465.

64 *The Times*, Meyer to editor, 11 October 1996, p. 21.

65 Cited Lord *British Entry*, p. 38.

66 *Hansard*, vol. 645, cols 1507–14, 2 August 1961.

67 CPA: complied from CCO500/31/2, quotations from S.R. Newman (Home Counties) to COO, 28 August 1962, and P.K. Livingston (Northern Area) to COO, 6 September 1962, CCO500/31/4.

68 CPA: ORC poll, 30 June–4 July 1971, CCO180/13/1/6.

69 CPA: Strasbourg study visit, R.D. Milne, 24 October 1952, COB21/1/2.

70 *The Times*, 23 June 1995, p. 18, Lamont article.

71 Avon Mss: Avon to Chandos, 30 October 1962, AP23/17/63B, University of Birmingham Special Collections.

72 Macmillan Ministerial Mss: Dilhorne to Macmillan, 24 July 1962, MS.Macmillan.dep.c.311 f22, Bodleian Library, Oxford.

73 D. Dutton 'Anticipating Maastricht: The Conservative Party and Britain's First Application to Join the European Community' *Contemporary Record* 7(3), 1993, p. 536.

74 D. Hurd *Memoirs* London: Little Brown, 2003, pp. 237–8.

75 Boyle Mss: Gordon Pears to Edward Heath, 17 February 1969, MS660/23023/1.

76 PREM11/1831B record of mtg, 9 March 1957, Macmillan and Mollet.

77 France, Belgium and Luxembourg favoured the former, whilst West Germany, Netherlands and Italy took the reverse. This is why the Werner Committee was established in March 1970.

78 CPA: Michael Niblock to Brian Sewill, 'The Future of Sterling', 24 January 1969, CRD3/7/8/1.
79 Marten Mss: A Douglas-Home to Neil Marten, 29 October 1969, MS.Eng.hist.c. 1134 f145.
80 CPA: Michael Niblock, 'Thinking European', 4 February 1972, CRD3/10/14.
81 *Daily Telegraph*, Teddy Taylor to editor, 21 January 1997.
82 *Hansard*, vol. 831, col. 650 (Howe), cols. 743–52 (Heath), 17 February 1972.
83 E.g. CPA: Foreign Affairs Cttee, 19 January 1971, Rippon, CRD3/10/17.
84 CPA: M. Niblock to J. Cordle, 3 December 1968, CRD3/10/39.
85 See, for example, F.H. Hinsley *Sovereignty* Oxford: Alden Press, 1966; A. James *Sovereign Statehood* London: Allen and Unwin, 1986; A. Milward *et al. The Frontier of National Sovereignty: History and Theory* London: Routledge, 1993; R. Bellamy (ed.) *Constitutionalism, Democracy and Sovereignty* Aldershot: Avebury, 1996; S. Krasner *Sovereignty: Organised Hypocrisy* Princeton, NJ: Princeton University Press, 1999; Lord *British Entry*, ch. 3.
86 S. Benn 'The Uses of Sovereignty' *Political Studies* 3(2), 1955, pp. 109–22; See W.N. Medlicott *British Foreign Policy since Versailles* London: Methuen, 1967, p. xix, on appeasement.
87 E.g. *Hansard*, vol. 2021, cols 1526–1624, 9 February 2005, debate on referendum bill.
88 W. Kaiser *Using Europe, Abusing the Europeans* Basingstoke: Macmillan, 1996, p. 138.
89 See P. Williamson *Stanley Baldwin* Cambridge: Cambridge University Press, 2001, pp. 12–18, for a persuasive articulation of this view.
90 See Young *This Blessed Plot*, pp. 332–8, for the impact of the Single European Act on Conservative thought.
91 P. Whiteley, P. Seyd and J. Richardson *True Blues: The Politics of Conservative Party Membership* Oxford: Clarendon, 1994, p. 57. It is worth noting that 67 per cent also agreed that Britain should remain in the European Exchange Rate Mechanism, this aspect of the loss of sovereignty clearly not being opposed by the majority.
92 E.g. YouGov/*Sunday Times*, 18–19 June 2004; YouGov/*Sun*, 15–17 April 2004.
93 E.g. J. Redwood *Our Currency, Our Country* Harmondsworth: Penguin, 1997, p. 13.
94 *Daily Telegraph*, Winston Churchill to editor, 11 July 2000, p. 19.
95 *The Times*, 15 July 1971, p. 6.
96 E.g. *Yes to Europe: Conservative Campaign Notes* No. 1, 19 May 1975, filed with Newcastle West Conservative Association, 1579/42, Tyne and Wear Archives. For the official referendum leaflets prepared and distributed at the government's expense in late May 1975, see D. Butler and U. Kitzinger *The 1975 Referendum* London: Macmillan, 1976, pp. 291–304. *Hansard*, vol. 831, col. 743, 17 February 1972.
97 Buller *National Statecraft*, p. 46.
98 *Daily Telegraph*, Teddy Taylor to editor, 21 January 1997.
99 M. Garnett and I. Aitkens *Splendid! Splendid! The Authorised Biography of William Whitelaw* London: Cape, 2002, p. 96.
100 Marten Mss: 'No to the Common Market' [April 1975], MS.Eng.hist.c.1130 ff357–60.
101 J. Critchley and M. Halcrow *Collapse of the Stout Party* London: Gollancz, 1997, p. 284.
102 Thatcher Foundation Archive: speech Finchley, 14 October 1961, www.margaretthatcher.org.uk.
103 Marten Mss: press release for Heath speech, Paris, 5 May 1970, MS.Eng. hist.c.1138 f.27.
104 J. Campbell *Edward Heath* London: Pimlico, 1993, pp. 341–2.

105 Chris Patten 'Letter from Europe' *Reformer Magazine*, Winter 2001.
106 Howe *Conflict*, p. 631.
107 Marten Mss: 'Some thoughts on the referendum campaign', MS.Eng.hist.c. 1131 f. 185.
108 CPA: minutes, 13 June 1950, ACP2/1.
109 Winchester CA: *Hampshire Chronicle*, 12 November 1960, 73M86W/41; further examples CPA: minutes, Parliamentary Group on Common Market, 12 November 1962, CRD2/42/8.
110 Tynemouth CA: clipping, 26 January 1962, 1633/17/5.
111 Lord *British Entry*, p. 37.
112 *Hansard*, vol. 883, col. 1911, 19 December 1974.
113 D. McKay *Federalism and European Union* Oxford: OUP, 1999, p. 75.
114 Howe *Conflict*, p. 631.
115 Balfour in 1911 moved a clause in the Parliament Bill; in 1930 Stanley Baldwin pledged a referendum prior to the possible introduction of taxes on non-empire foods; and Churchill in 1945 failed to persuade Attlee that the wartime parliament should be extended until the end of the war with the Japanese by means of a referendum. Thatcher Foundation: 'Report of the Conservative Party committee on the referendum', 5 July 1978, submitted to LCC, www.margaretthatcher.org.uk. This committee recommended that the party support referendums for constitutional changes and that a referendum commission be established.
116 CPA: M. Fraser to Peter Thomas, 12 January 1971, CCO20/32/4.
117 N.J Crowson *Facing Fascism: The Conservative Party and the European Dictators, 1935–40* London: Routledge, 1997, pp. 53–4.
118 E.g. CPA: Gwen Jones (Sec. Gerrans branch, Truro CA) to R. Butler, 4 October 1961; area agents reported similar calls, CPA: S.R. Newman (Home Counties North) to COO, 28 August 1962, CCO500/31/2, and B.T. Powell (Eastern Area) to COO, 7 September 1962, CCO500/31/4.
119 Winchester CA: press cutting, *Hampshire Chronicle*, 3 November 1962, 73M86W/41.
120 CPA: Francis Pym to Peter Thomas, 4 January 1971, CCO20/32/4.
121 See, for example, CPA: minutes, Leader's Consultative Committee, 23 February 1970, CCO20/70/2.
122 CPA: ORC poll, 5–9 August 1970, CCO180/13/1/2; Marten Mss: Marten to Heath, 12 August 1972, MS.Eng.hist.c.1141 f. 221.
123 I. Gilmour *Dancing with Dogma* London: Simon and Schuster, 1992, p. 188.
124 Marten Mss: Press release, Heath's speech, 5 May 1970, MS.Eng.hist.c.1138 f 30. My emphasis, although Marten had underlined this entire passage himself.
125 *Harborough Mail*, 24 June 1971, article reporting Heath's objections to a referendum. He suggested MPs should consult constituents, but ultimately voting was their decision.
126 Hurd *Memoirs*, p.184.
127 Marten Mss: Marten to E. Heath, 12 August 1972, MS.Eng.hist.c. 1141 f221.
128 *Daily Telegraph*, S. Scammell to editor, 24 February 1995.
129 CPA: 'Report and analysis of the state of the party', n.d. [Feb. 1971], CCO20/32/28.
130 E.g. Aston CA, 17 February 1970, CPA, Clyde Hewlett to Home, 4 March 1970, CCO20/70/2, and East Ham CA, 24 March 1971, Clyde Hewlett to Rippon, 5 April 1971, CCO20/70/4.
131 *Hansard*, vol. 279, Div. No. 139.
132 *Sunday Times*, 18 April 1993, p. 1.24.
133 *The Times*, letter to editor, 27 June 1995.
134 *Daily Telegraph*, 22 June 1995, p. 2.
135 *Daily Telegraph*, letter to editor, 20 September 1996.
136 A. Meyer 'What's Wrong with the Tories?' *Reformer Magazine*, Winter 2001.

137  R. Boyson *Speaking My Mind* London: Peter Owen, 1994, p. 231.
138  D. Heathcote-Amory *The European Constitution* London: CPS, June 2003, p. 36.
139  Spaak addressing European movement: Rhys Williams Mss: notes of discussion 28 September 1950, 7/1/1.
140  Northern Area Council, 15 February 1958, NRO3303/3.
141  North Wiltshire CA: 24 April 1957, 2436/10.
142  CPA: minutes, Foreign Affairs Cttee, 27 February 1963, Heath, CRD3/10/15.
143  CPA: Wales and Monmouth YCs, 'Report on Britain and Europe', CCO506/14/15; Margaret Thatcher Foundation Archive: speech to Finchley Conservatives, Finchley, 18 August 1961, www.margaretthatcher.org.
144  CPA: minutes, Foreign Affairs Ctee, 13 March 1963, Peter Kirk, CRD3/10/15; Marten Mss: paper by Robin Turton, 31 January 1968, MS.Eng.hist.c.1137 ff122–24; CPA: 'Strasbourg Study Visit 21–28 September 1962', COB57/1.
145  Legge-Bourke Mss: letter to editor, *The Times*, 22 September 1956, MS.742 f. 762.
146  Tynemouth CA: views of C. Norton, Northern area agent, scrapbook, 22 May 1958, 1633/17/4.
147  Birmingham CUA: Central Council, 2 June 1947, f. 115.
148  Legge-Bourke Mss: n.d. notes for speech [1961?], MS.742/737; CPA: report on economic conference of UEM, April 1949, CCO3/1/47.
149  Winchester CA: AGM press cutting, *Winchester Chronicle*, citing Gordon Pears, 12 November 1960, 73M86W/41.
150  Rushcliffe CA: *Rushcliffe Review* No. 109, March 1957, p. 10, DD.PP.1/3/10.
151  T. Bromund 'Whitehall, the National Farmers' Union and Plan G, 1956–57' *Contemporary British History* 15(2), 2001.
152  *The Times*, 9 July 1962.
153  Graham Wilson *Special Interests and Policymaking: Agricultural Policies and Politics in Britain and the United States of America* London: Wiley, 1977, pp. 22, 27.
154  Macmillan Ministerial Mss: Butler to Macmillan, 1 September [1961], MS.Macmillan.dep.c.310 ff. 226–27.
155  CPA: Eastern Area Agricultural Advisory Committee, minutes, 28 June 1957, ARE7/12/1.
156  CPA: ACP2/1 minutes, 13 November 1957.
157  J. Ramsden *The Making of Conservative Party Policy* London: Longman, 1980, p. 212.
158  Wilson *Special Interests*, p. 22, citing Andrew Roth.
159  CPA: minutes, Parliamentary Group on the Common Market, 26 November 1962, CRD2/42/8.
160  CPA: B.A. Cobb to COO, 27 August 1962, CCO500/31/2.
161  CPA: minutes, Leader's Consultative Committee, 3 November 1969, LCC(69).
162  CPA: Eastern Area Agricultural Advisory Committee, 6 May 1961, ARE7/12/1.
163  E.g. Tuckman Mss: Bow Group press release, 'Priorities for Agricultural Policy', 14 February 1961, MS270/A291/4/1/Folder 2.
164  CPA: 'Europe' by A. Douglas-Home, 18 July 1969, LCC(69)252.
165  CPA: ORC polls, April 1967, CCO500/31/5; ORC poll, 17–21 February 1971, CCO180/13/1/3; ORC poll, 30 June–4 July 1971, CCO180/13/1/6.
166  Dodds-Parker Mss: memo 'Themes for Europe', 9 October 1970, MC:P2/7/3MS/2.
167  CPA: Mrs I. Peck to CCO, 17 June 1971, CCO20/32/6.
168  E.g. Southampton Itchen CA, exec., 24 November 1971.
169  CPA: Peter Thomas to Geoffrey Rippon, 23 December 1970, CCO20/32/4.
170  CPA: 'Common Market and British Agriculture', 11 March 1966, CRD3/2/9. My emphasis.
171  J. Rhys Williams Mss: John Penton to Juliet Rhys Williams, 5 July 1956.
172  CPA: Foreign Affairs Cttee, 22 July 1969, CRD3/10/16.

173 M. Heseltine *The Challenge of Europe: Can Britain Win?* London: Weidenfeld and Nicolson, 1989, p. 49.
174 Marten Mss: MS.Eng.hist.c.1141 ff 73–78.
175 James Hill, 1985, *Daily Telegraph*, obituary, 18 February 1999.
176 Heseltine *Challenge*, p. 49.
177 M. Ball *The Conservative Conference and Euro-sceptical Motions, 1992–5* London: Bruges Group Occasional Paper no. 23.
178 N. Ridley *My Style of Government*, pp. 136–37; quotation R. Body *Europe of Many Circles* London: NEP, 1990, p. 87.
179 Heseltine *Challenge*, p. 51.
180 CCO press release, 11 January 2001, 'Hague urges target dates for enlarged EU', www.conservatives.com/news.
181 Heathcote-Amory *The European Constitution*, p. 4.
182 *Sunday Times*, 2 August 1992, p. 1.11.
183 76 per cent opposed. D. Baker *et al.* 'Backbenchers with Attitude', p. 10, paper presented to European Consortium for Political Research Conference, Bordeaux, 1995.
184 CPA: 'Questions of Policy', No. 10, 9 March 1966, CRD3/2/9.
185 Boyle Mss: memo 'Common Added-Value Tax System', Gordon Pears, CRD, 17 February 1969.
186 CPA: B. Reading to E. Heath, 15 July 1969, CRD3/7/8/1.
187 CPA: 'Britain, the EEC and the Commonwealth', Gorell Barnes, April 1966, CRD3/10/9.
188 Legge-Bourke Mss: notes for speech, n.d. [?1961], MS742/737 ff 1–8.
189 CPA: Question of policy: CRD briefing for general election, CRD3/2/9.
190 CPA: minutes, Foreign Affairs Committee, 12 November 1970, CRD3/10/16.
191 CPA: 'Thinking European', Michael Niblock, 4 February 1972, CRD3/10/14.
192 *Sunday Times*, 2 August 1992, p. 1.11.
193 Heseltine *Challenge*.
194 Boyson *Speaking*, p. 234.
195 *Independent*, 14 July 1990, p. 3.
196 See Buller *National Statecraft*, p. 131, for an explanation of the Euro-ratchet effect.
197 House of Lords parliamentary answer, 13 January 2003, cited Heathcote-Amory *The European Constitution*, p. 11.
198 Paragraph based upon Forster *Euroscepticism*, pp. 74–5.
199 Margaret Thatcher in *The European*, 8–11 October 1992, p. 8.
200 D. Baker *et al.* 'Backbenchers with Attitude', p. 10.
201 S. Walters *Tory Wars: Conservatives in Crisis* London: Politicos, 2001, *passim*.
202 E.g. *Daily Telegraph*, letters to editor, R. Helmer MEP and thirteen other Conservative MEPs, 4 May 2000; eleven Tory MEPs to editor, 8 July 2000, p. 23.
203 *Daily Telegraph*, 20 May 1998, p. 13, reporting Hague's Fontainebleau speech.
204 *Daily Telegraph*, 15 January 1998, p. 6, reporting Portillo's first speech since the loss of his Enfield seat in May 1997.
205 Compare *Daily Telegraph*, Howard Flight to editor, 4 November 1997, with *Independent*, K. Clarke *et al.* to editor, 30 November 1998.
206 N. Lamont *Sovereign Britain* London: Duckworth, 1995; J. Redwood *Our Currency Our Country* Harmondsworth: Penguin, 1997.
207 *Daily Telegraph*, 24 November 1997, Waldegrave article 'Freedom v. Empire'.
208 Leon Brittan described Waldegrave's proposal as 'the most honest Conservative argument for disengagement from Europe', Tory Reform Group 1999 International Lecture, 21 July 1999, www.trg.org.uk/publications/proeuropeanpolicy.html.
209 Views of Ken Clarke, *Guardian*, 21 March 1995, p. 1; Ted Heath in *Daily Telegraph*, 21 March 1995, p. 14.
210 A. Milward *The European Rescue of the Nation-State* London: Routledge, 1992.

211 *Daily Telegraph*, 10 February 1995, pp. 1–2, 6; John Stevens MEP to editor, 29 September 1997.
212 *Hampshire Chronicle*, 18 June 1971, James Spicer.
213 R. Jackson *The Powers of the European Parliament*, p. 38.
214 *Guardian*, 9 July 1996, p. 3.
215 *Guardian*, 26 March 1996.
216 *The Times*, article by Hague, 22 January 1998, p. 18.
217 CCO press release, 11 January 2001, 'Hague urges dates for enlarged EU', www.conservatives.com/news.
218 CCO press release, 24 May 2001, 'Our vision for Europe', www.conservatives.com/news.
219 Leon Brittan 'A Pro-European Policy for Conservatives' Tory Reform Group 1999 International Lecture, 21 July 1999, www.trg.org.uk/publications/proeuropeanpolicy.html.

## 4 The Conservative Europeanist

1 One survey from 2000 found that only twelve prospective parliamentary candidates from the 170 most winnable seats were prepared to admit to being 'Europhile'. *Daily Telegraph*, 6 September 2000, p. 10.
2 D. Baker *et al.* 'Mapping Conservative Fault Lines: Problems of Typology' in P. Dunleavy and G. Stayner (eds) *Contemporary Political Studies 1994* Exeter: Exeter University Press, 1994; P. Norton 'The Conservative Party: In Office but Not in Power' in A. King *et al.* (eds) *New Labour Triumphs: Britain at the Polls* Chatham NJ: Chatham House, 1998; R. Hague and H. Berrington 'Europe, Thatcherism and Traditionalism' in H. Berrington (ed.) *The Politics of Paradox* Newbury: Frank Cass, 1998; T. Heppell 'The Ideological Composition of the Parliamentary Conservative Party 1992–97' *British Journal of Politics and International Relations* 4(2), 2002, pp. 299–324.
3 J. Turner *The Tories and Europe* Manchester: Manchester University Press, 2001, pp. 189, 214. Turner calculates that 6 per cent of the 1992–7 parliamentary party could be termed Loyalist Europhiles; after 1997 this had fallen to 3 per cent.
4 Turner *Tories*, p. 214; Heppell 'Ideological Composition', p. 312.
5 E.g. Conservative Party Archive [hereafter CPA]: 'Speakers List', November 1967, CCO150/2/1/6, Bodleian Library, Oxford, lists speakers by 'special interests' and excludes shadow and front bench spokesmen. This has 55 out of 225 listed MPs interested in Europe (24 per cent). That they have no wish to use anti-Marketeers on this subject is apparent from absences of names like Derek Walker-Smith. Similarly in 1948 sixty Conservative MPs (28 per cent of parliamentary party) signed a pro-federal EDM.
6 See R. White 'The Europeanism of Coudenhove-Kalergi' in P.M.R. Stirk (ed.) *European Unity in Context: The Interwar Period* London: Pinter, 1989, pp. 23–40.
7 See J. Pinder 'Federalism in Britain and Italy: Radicals and the English Liberal Tradition' in P.M.R. Stirk (ed.) *European Unity in Context: The Interwar Period* London: Pinter, 1989, pp. 201–23; and R. Grayson *Austen Chamberlain and the Commitment to Europe: British Foreign Policy 1924–9* London: Frank Cass, 1997.
8 C.H. Pegg *Evolution of the European Idea 1914–32* Chapel Hill, NJ: University of North Carolina Press, 1983, pp. 5–6, 36, 40, 44, 53, 65.
9 Pegg *Evolution*, p. 150.
10 A view supported by S. Onslow *Backbench Debate within the Conservative Party and Its Influence on British Foreign Policy* Basingstoke: Macmillan, 1997, p. 13.
11 Austen Chamberlain 'Britain as a European Power' *RIIA* 1930.
12 CPA: Foreign Affairs Committee, 17 November 1964, CRD3/10/15.
13 Onslow *Backbench*, pp. 79–80.

14 J. Young *Britain and European Unity 1945–1999* Basingstoke: Macmillan, 2nd edn, 2000, p. 114.
15 *Daily Telegraph*, 'Sir Edward Dies at 89', 'Tory Son of Manual Worker Who Steered Britain into Choppy European Waters', 'Obituary', 18 July 2005.
16 CPA: Foreign Affairs Committee, 18 February 1970, St John Stevas, CRD3/10/16.
17 E. Heath *Course of My Life* London: Hodder and Stoughton, 1998; J. Campbell *Edward Heath* London: Pimlico, 1994.
18 Norwood CA, executive, 26 October 1962, IV/166/1/18, Lambeth Archives; Macmillan Ministerial Mss: Knox Cunningham's notes for FAC 16 May, 23 July 1962, MS.Macmillan.dep.c.354 ff 180–81, 196–97; CPA Peter Horton to COO, 29 September 1961, CCO500/31/2.
19 BOAPAH, Edward Boyle interview, BPLES.
20 CPA: Gordon Pears to Richard Wood, 9 November 1967, CRD3/10/11; Gordon Pears to Sewill, 5 June 1967, CRD3/10/10.
21 CPA: John Stevens (Heath's private office) to Du Cann, 30 August 1967, CCO20/70/1; 'Motion to be debated ... ', 18 October 1967, CRD3/10/11.
22 CPA: D. Hurd to M. Fraser, 15 July 1971, CCO20/32/6; see also Young *This Blessed Plot*, p. 223.
23 See Chapter 5 for discussion of the methods.
24 CPA: National Union: Central Council report, NUA2/2/26.
25 Peter Walker *The Ascent of Britain* London: Sidgwick and Jackson, 1977, p. 114; Lord Walker, correspondence with author.
26 Legge-Bourke Mss: Henry Legge-Bourke to Lord Gladwyn, 30 May 1962, MS.742 ff. 766/1–2; notes for speech, n.d., MS742/737 ff1–8.
27 Onslow *Backbench*, p. 113, for a character sketch and ch. 6 for the Suez Group.
28 Legge-Bourke Mss: Henry Legge-Bourke to J.C. Dagless, 19 July 1971, MS.742/859; Legge-Bourke to Heath, 18 October 1971, MS.742/881 ff. 1–2.
29 Legge-Bourke Mss: 1971 correspondence MS.742/814–70; *Hansard*, vol. 823, cols 989–96, 21 October 1971.
30 U. Kitzinger *Diplomacy and Persuasion* London: Thames and Hudson, 1973, p. 149.
31 *The Times Magazine*, 6 July 1996, pp. 11–15.
32 M. Garnett and I. Aitkens *Splendid! Splendid!* London: Cape, 2002, p. 33.
33 *Daily Telegraph* obituary for Percy Grieve (MP for Solihull 1964–83).
34 BOAPAH: Maclay interview; Dodds-Parker Mss: D.-P. to Heath, 29 November 1967, MC:P2/7/3C/1.
35 Boyle Mss: 'Summary of electors comments', week ending 31 August 1962, MS660/20553.
36 S. Onslow *Backbench*, p. 235; *Guardian*, 22 March 1994, p. 11.
37 Legge-Bourke Mss: H.L.-B. to D.M. Hutchins, n.d. [July 1971], MS.742/857; Dodds-Parker Mss: D.-P. to Heath, 29 November 1967, MC:P2/7/3C/1.
38 N.J. Crowson 'Conservative Parliamentary Dissent over Foreign Policy during the Premiership of Neville Chamberlain: Myth or Reality?' *Parliamentary History* 14(3), 1995, p. 315.
39 See N.J. Crowson *Facing Fascism: The Conservative Party and the European Dictators 1935–40* London: Routledge, 1997, *passim*.
40 *Reformer Magazine* 'Britain in Europe', Autumn 1999.
41 Chris Patten *Britain, Asia and Europe: A Conservative View*, London: Conservative Political Centre, 1995, p. 13.
42 BOAPAH: Edward Boyle interview, BPLES; North Wiltshire Conservative Association, executive, 24 April 1957, David Eccles, 2436/10, Wiltshire Record Office.
43 CPA: Foreign Affairs Committee minutes, 17 November 1964, CRD3/10/15.
44 J. Rhys Williams: Boothby to J.R.W., 23 September 1953, J/9/1/1.

45  E.g. Julian Amery *The Life of Joseph Chamberlain*, vol. 6, pp. 1,051–2; BOAPAH, Muirshiel interview, BPLES; developed by historians since: D. Charlton *The Price of Victory* London: BBC, 1983, pp. 136, 139–40; D. Carlton *Anthony Eden: A Biography* London: Allen Lane, 1981, p. 314.

46  See D. Dutton *Anthony Eden*, pp. 293–302, 311–13.

47  Kilmuir *Political Adventure: The Memoirs of the Earl of Kilmuir* London: Weidenfeld and Nicolson, 1964, pp. 146, 186; Macmillan *Tides of Fortune* London: Macmillan, 1969, p. 468. Eden was not averse to the recourse to law to protect his reputation; see P. Beck 'Politicians versus Historians: Lord Avon's "Appeasement Battle" against "Lamentably, Appeasement-Minded" Historians' *Twentieth Century British History* 9(4), 1998, pp. 396–419.

48  D. Hurd *An End to Promises* London: Collins, 1978, p. 59.

49  A. Nutting *Europe Will Not Wait* London: Hollis and Carter, 1960.

50  CPA: A.N. Banks to COO, 7 February 1961, CCO2/6/14.

51  C. Lord *British Entry to the European Community under the Heath Government* Aldershot: Dartmouth, 1993, p. 38. Hugo Young saw these lectures at Harvard as 'the working out, in opposition, of new and distinct priorities'. Young *This Blessed Plot*, p. 221.

52  *Independent*, Howe, Brittan, Carrington, Clarke, Curry, Gummer, Heseltine, Patten, Taylor, Tudengdhat and Younger to editor, 5 January 1998, p. 12.

53  *Sunday Times*, 1 November 1992, p. 2.4.

54  Patten *Britain, Asia and Europe*, pp. 13–14.

55  *Daily Telegraph*, Critchley to editor, 20 September 1996, p. 25.

56  Michael Portillo, cited *Sunday Times*, 1 November 1992, p. 2.4.

57  Shoreham CA: Divisional Exec., 27 July 1971, CO/ISH/1/1/2.

58  North Edinburgh CA, newsclipping, 29 June 1971, Acc 198.

59  CPA: 'The Common Market: Conservative Policy', n.d. [1967], CCO20/32/2.

60  *Daily Telegraph*, Raymond Whitney to editor, 11 July 2000, p. 19.

61  CPA: 'Thinking European', Michael Niblock, 4 February 1972, CRD3/10/14.

62  S. Lloyd *Suez 1956: A Personal Account* London: Jonathan Cape, 1978; S. Kelly and A. Gorst (eds) *Whitehall and the Suez Crisis* London: Frank Cass, 2000; W.S. Lucas (ed.) *Britain and Suez: The Lion's Last Roar* Manchester: Manchester University Press, 1996; W.S. Lucas (ed.) *Divided We Stand: Britain, the US and the Suez Crisis* London: Hodder and Stoughton, 1991.

63  See R. Shepherd *The Power Brokers: The Tory Party and Its Leaders* London: Hutchinson, 1991.

64  CPA: Foreign Affairs Committee, 14 April 1948, CRD2/34/1.

65  see CPA: 'Common Market public opinion S. Eastern Area', 27 August 1962, CCO500/31/2.

66  R. Aldous and S. Lee (eds) *Harold Macmillan's World Role* Basingstoke: Macmillan, 1996, p. 142.

67  Cited C. Lord *British Entry to the European Community under the Heath Government*, p. 23.

68  CPA: Foreign Affairs Committee minutes, 26 March 1968, David Howell, CRD3/10/16; FAC, 14 March 1956, Robert Boothby, CRD 2/34/2, for an earlier example.

69  TNA: CAB128/37, 8 October 1963; FO371/169126, 11 June 1963, memo, Paris embassy to Foreign Office.

70  P. Routledge *Public Servant, Secret Agent* London: Fourth Estate, 2002, p. 245.

71  CPA: Brian Reading to Heath, 2 January 1970, CRD3/7/8/1.

72  CPA: 'Report of the Policy Group on Foreign Affairs', 6 August 1965, ACP (65)20.

73  Northern Area: council, 15 February 1958, NRO3303/3; CPA: 'Report on Britain and Europe', Wales and Monmouth Young Conservatives, n.d., CCO506/14/15; Winchester CA: news clipping, *Hampshire Chronicle*, 25 July

1961, 73M86W/41; CPA: Foreign Affairs Committee, 27 February 1963, CRD3/10/15; *Daily Telegraph*, R. Whitney MP to editor, 11 July 2000, p. 19.

74 Winchester CA: newsclipping, *Hampshire Chronicle*, 25 July 1961, 73M86W/41.

75 Shoreham CA, executive, 27 July 1971, CO/ISH/1/1/2.

76 Tynemouth CA: scrapbook clipping, 26 January 1962, 1633/17/5.

77 CPA: Frederick Corfield to Mrs Peck (Sec. Northville ward, Bristol CA), 22 June 1971, CCO20/32/6.

78 See CPA: Richard Body to Peter Thomas, 6 April 1971, CCO20/32/4; Marten Mss MS.Eng.hist.c.1138 ff338–39.

79 CPA: Foreign Affairs Committee minutes, 18 February 1970, see Ian Lloyd contribution, CRD3/10/16.

80 Dodds-Parker Mss 'Themes for Europe', 9 October 1970, MC:P2/7/3MS/2.

81 B. Castle *The Castle Diaries* London: Weidenfeld and Nicolson, 1980, entry for 29 May 1975, p. 402.

82 *Sunday Times*, 1 November 1992, p. 2.4.

83 *Sunday Times*, 5 February 1995, Heseltine article.

84 Patten *Britain, Asia and Europe*, p. 14.

85 Macmillan Mss: diary, 3 September 1954.

86 CPA: Foreign Affairs Committee, 2 May 1956, CRD2/34/2.

87 CPA: 'Report of the Policy Group on Foreign Affairs', 6 August 1965, ACP(65)20.

88 CPA: minutes, 13 June 1950, ACP2/1; Winchester Conservative Association: *Hampshire Chronicle*, 12 November 1960, 73M86W/41; Tynemouth Conservative Association: clipping, 26 January 1962, 1633/17/5; CPA: Parliamentary Group on the Common Market minutes, 12 November 1962, CRD2/42/8; Chris Patten 'Letter from Europe' *Reformer Magazine*, Winter 2001.

89 *Hansard*, vol. 96, cols 665–67 (Gummer), 28 April 1986.

90 P. Norton 'The Parliamentary Party and Party Committees' in S. Ball and A. Seldon (eds) *Conservative Century* Oxford: OUP, 1994, pp. 97–144.

91 CPA: Gordon Pears to Richard Wood, 9 November 1967, CRD3/10/11.

92 Macmillan Ministerial Mss: Knox Cunningham notes, MS.Macmillan.dep.c.354.

93 CPA: Foreign Affairs Committee, 9 February 1965, 13 March 1963, CRD3/10/15.

94 Marten Mss: papers re. Committee on Europe, MS.Eng.hist.c.1137 f. 121.

95 CPA: Gordon Pears to Richard Wood, 9 November 1967, CRD3/10/11.

96 Marten Mss: various papers re. Committee on Europe, MS.Eng.hist.c.1137.

97 Membership included Richard Wood, Nick Ridley, Gordon Pears, John Biggs-Davison, John Biffen and Jock Bruce Gardyne. CPA: Foreign Affairs Committee minutes, 26 March 1968, 23 July 1968, CRD3/10/16.

98 CPA: Foreign Affairs Committee, 17 December 1968, CRD3/10/16.

99 CPA: 'Membership list 1966: Commonwealth and Europe group', CRD3/10/9.

100 CPA: Gordon Pears to Richard Wood, 9 November 1967, CRD3/10/11.

101 CPA: Commonwealth and Europe Group minutes, CRD3/10/9.

102 CPA: minutes joint working party on monetary problems, 25 July 1966, CRD3/10/9.

103 Dodds-Parker Mss: Gorell Barnes to D.-P., 3 May 1967, MC:P2/7/3MS/1.

104 Dodds-Parker Mss: Dodds-Parker to John Harvey, 15 August 1967, MC:P2/7/3MS/1; CPA: Gorell Barnes to Michael Fraser, 14 December 1967, CRD3/10/9.

105 J. Ramsden *Making of Conservative Party Policy* London: Longman, 1980, pp. 212–13.

106 Macmillan Ministerial Mss: HM to Amery, 29 June 1955 MS.Macmillan.dep.c.301.

107 See J. Rhys Williams Mss: Boothby to J.R.W., 23 September 1953, J/9/1/1; J.R.W. to Boothby, 16 March 1956, J/9/1/1.

108 CPA: 'report on economic conference of UEM', Pat Hornsby-Smith, 30 April 1949, CCO3/1/47.

109  CPA: Maxse to Hopkinson, 3 May 1949, CCO3/1/47.
110  D.S. Birn *The League of Nations Union* Oxford: Clarendon Press, 1981.
111  U. Kitzinger *Diplomacy and Persuasion*, pp. 190–93.
112  *The Times*, 24 July 1969, p. 4.
113  D. Butler and U. Kitzinger *The 1975 Referendum* London: Macmillan, p. 77.
114  Butler and Kitzinger *The 1975 Referendum*, pp. 74–5.
115  *The Times*, 28 July 1999, p. 18.
116  *The Express*, 3 August 1999.
117  E.g. *Reformer Magazine* special edition on Britain and Europe, Summer 1998; 'Britain, the Tories and the Euro-Zone', Spring 1999; 'Britain in Europe', Autumn 1999.
118  E.g. *Independent*, letters to editor, 19 September 1996, 5 January 1998.
119  See CPA: CCO500/31/2–4.
120  A quarter of delegates to the 1962 conference were Young Conservatives and many wore 'Yes' badges. Nigel Ashford 'The European Economic Community' in Z. Layton-Henry (ed.) *Conservative Party Politics* London: Macmillan, 1980, p. 101.
121  J. Ramsden *Winds of Change*, p. 169.
122  E. Curry *Diaries*, entry for 16 May 1989, p. 131; Macmillan Ministerial Mss: Knox Cunningham to Bligh, 13 September 1962, citing views of Dudley Williams (MP for Exeter), MS.Macmillan.dep.c.354 f.167.
123  J. Ramsden *Winds of Change*, p. 404.
124  J. Barr *The Bow Group: A History* London: Politicos, 2001, p. 59.
125  Tuckman Mss: minutes Bow Group council, 20 June 1961, 23 May 1962, MS270/A291/4/2 Folder 1.
126  D. Thompson *The Rome Treaty and the Law* London: Bow Group, July-September 1962.
127  Barr *Bow Group*, p. 60.
128  Barr *Bow Group*, pp. 26, 44; CPA: Horton to COO, 7 September 1961, CCO500/31/3.
129  Tuckman Mss: minutes, 20 June 1961; Barr *Bow Group*, p. 74.
130  CPA: 'List of Conservative supporters of the campaign', n.d. [1969], CCO150/5/1/12.
131  Beamish Mss: CLW1/8/6, CLW1/5/22; *The Times*, 'New Pro-Market Group Sponsored by Tories', 16 August 1969, p. 2.
132  Kitzinger *Diplomacy* pp.160–1.
133  CPA: John Cope to Peter Thomas, 11 September 1970, CCO20/32/4.
134  CPA: Report and Analysis of the State of the Party, n.d. [Feb. 1971], CCO20/32/28.
135  Out of the parliamentary party of 326, 127 joined by February 1971; this had risen to 202 by August. CPA: CCO20/32/28, plus *Minutes of Evidence to Select Committee on Direct Elections to the European Parliament* London: HMSO, p. 156, para. 582; p. 158, para. 596.
136  CPA: W. Clark to Peter Thomas, 10 March 1971, CCO20/32/4.
137  *Minutes of Evidence to Select Committee on Direct Elections*, 22 July 1976, pp. 160–1, para 606–10. Spicer countered: 'certainly every member of the Conservative Party who was not either an agnostic or an unbeliever was a member of the Conservative Group for Europe.'
138  CPA: Report and Analysis of the State of the Party, n.d. [Feb. 1971], CCO20/32/28.
139  CPA: St John Stevas to Peter Thomas, 25 August 1970, CCO20/32/4.
140  C. King *Diaries 1964–70* London: Cape, 1972, entry for 25 July 1965, p. 24.
141  Kitzinger *Diplomacy*, p. 173; see fn. 1 for an example of using a parliamentary question to impart rather than elicit information.

142 CPA: Committee on Europe minutes, 19 January 1971, CCO20/32/4; Beamish Mss: 'New Targets for Members', *Tory European*, Autumn 1972 CLW1/5/22.
143 Kitzinger *Diplomacy*, p. 161.
144 Dodds-Parker Mss: Tufton Beamish to Anthony Royle, 16 December 1971, MC:P2/7/3MS/5; Beamish Mss: Beamish's article, *Tory European*, Autumn 1972, CLW1/5/22.
145 See Kitzinger *Diplomacy*, p. 161; and CPA: minutes, 'Money for European Activities mtg', 16 July 1973, CCO20/32/8.
146 Britain in Europe Mss: 'A Conservative campaign for Europe', Jim Spicer, 8 November 1974, BIE/1/49.
147 A. Meyer 'What's Wrong with the Tories?' *Reformer Magazine*, Winter 2001.
148 BIE Mss: Spicer to E. Wistrich, 12 December 1974; 10th mtg, Europe Co-ordinating Group, 27 January 1975, BIE/1/49.
149 www.cge.org.uk.
150 A. Seldon *Major: A Political Life* London: Weidenfeld and Nicolson, 1997, p. 370.
151 *Daily Telegraph*, 17 February 1999, 23 March 1999.

## 5 Selling Europe: 'a pretty big thing to undertake'

1 Macmillan Mss: Macmillan to Martin Redmayne, 5 August 1961, MS.Macmillan.dep.c.312 f232, Bodleian Library, Oxford.
2 Conservative Party Archive [hereafter CPA]: J.T. Lacy to COO, 7 September 1962, CCO500/31/4, Bodleian Library, Oxford.
3 Supporting this claim of uncertainty amongst the majority, see: Marten Mss: Michael Fidler to Peter Thomas, 26 March 1971, MS.Eng.hist.c.1138 f. 331–32, Bodleian Library, Oxford; CPA: J.T. Lacy to COO, 7 September 1962, CCO500/31/4.
4 Speaking to *Daily Mail*, cited in Ritchie *Enoch Powell on 1992* London: Anaya, 1989, pp. 12–13.
5 S. Walters *Tory Wars* London: Politicos, 2001, pp. 52–4.
6 R.R. James (ed.) *Complete Speeches of Winston Churchill*; also J.W. Young 'Churchill's "No" to Europe: The "Rejection" of European Union by Churchill's Post-war Government 1951–52' *Historical Journal* 28(4), 1985, pp. 923–37.
7 This was Macmillan's position. J. Turner *The Tories and Europe* Manchester: Manchester University Press, 2001, p. 49.
8 CPA: memo 'Strasbourg study visit 21–28 September 1952', R.O. Milne, 24 October 1952, COB21/1/2.
9 Churchill Mss: Leo Amery to Duncan Sandys, 20 September 1946, cited P. Beswick 'Tory Strasbourgers and the Evolution of Conservative Party Debate over Europe' unpublished MPhil, University of Birmingham, 2001, pp. 12–13.
10 Birmingham Conservative Association: Central Council, 24 September 1948, AQ329.94249CON ff. 237–38, Birmingham Central Library; CPA: 'Report on Britain and Europe', Wales and Monmouth Young Conservatives, n.d., CCO506/14/15.
11 A. Milward *The European Rescue of the Nation-State* London: Routledge, 1994, pp. 424–5.
12 David Eccles addressing North Wiltshire Conservative Association executive, 24 April 1957, 2436/10, Wiltshire Record Office; CPA: Foreign Affairs Committee, 13 March 1963 (Anthony Kershaw), CRD3/10/15.
13 CPA: Foreign Affairs Cttee, 25 May 1960, Selwyn-Lloyd, CRD2/34/4.
14 CPA: Foreign Affairs Cttee, 7 May 1958, Horburgh, CRD2/34/3.
15 CPA: joint meeting Trade and Industry Cttee, Foreign Affairs Cttee and Agriculture Cttee, 5 July 1960, CRD2/34/4; Foreign Affairs Cttee, 22 June 1960, CRD 2/34/4.

16   CPA: 'Britain, the EEC and the Commonwealth', Gorrell Barnes, April 1966, CRD3/10/9; Macmillan Ministerial Mss: Paul Channon to Knox Cunningham, 25 July 1962, MS.Macmillan.dep.c.354 f. 176; CPA: Frederick Corfield MP to Mrs I. Peck (Sec. Northville ward, Bristol CA), 22 June 1971, CCO20/32/6; *Rising Standards in Europe* London: Conservative Central Office, 1971.

17   CPA: Foreign Affairs Cttee, 11 November 1959, CRD2/34/4.

18   Rushcliffe Conservative Association: Robert Tilney (chairman), *Rushcliffe Review* 112, June 1957, p. 8, DD.PP.1/3/10.

19   Tynemouth Conservative Association: clipping, *Newcastle Evening News*, 16 October 1957, reporting speech by Irene Ward MP, 1633/17/3; Winchester Conservative Association: *Hampshire Chronicle*, 25 July 1961, reporting Peter Smithers addressing Alresford Conservative fete, 73M86W/41.

20   Macmillan told the Cabinet in early 1961 that political union 'would be unwelcome to us; and, as President De Gaulle was himself opposed to such a development; it might be to our advantage to reach a settlement in Europe while he was still in power'. I am grateful to David Richardson for drawing my attention to this quotation.

21   CPA: Macleod to Prime Minister, 25 January 1963, CCO20/8/6; see also TNA, FO 371/169114.

22   *Conservative Campaign Guide*, 1964, p. 469, *Archives of British Conservative Party* [hereafter *ABCP*] microfiche card no. 43.

23   See: CPA: Gordon Pears to Brian Sewill, 5 June 1967, CRD3/10/10; CPA: minutes, Leaders Consultative Committee, 17 July 1967, LCC (67); CPA: 'Brief for debate on Europe', n.d. [November 1967], CRD3/7/8/1.

24   CPA: 'Memorandum on Britain and the Commonwealth', n.d. [Sept. 1970], Norman St John Stevas; see also C. Ramsden (chair, Bridlington CA) to John Taylor, 16 March 1971, CCO20/32/4.

25   E.g. Derek Prag, Bow Group European Liaison Committee written evidence to *Select Committee on Direct Elections to European Assembly 2nd Report* London: HMSO, 1976, Appendix 16, p. 45.

26   CPA: 'Memorandum on Britain and the Common Market', n.d. [September 1970], N. St John-Stevas, CCO20/32/4.

27   CPA: Minutes, money for European activities mtg, 16 July 1973, CCO20/32/8.

28   Conservative Political Centre *Our Voice in Europe* London: CPC, March 1976, p. 16.

29   Hinchingbrooke Mss: Hinchingbrooke to Robin Williams, 14 February 1983, D/MAP86; For Thatcher the mixed EEC response to the war suggested the need to enhance the organisation to ensure future support for a 'troubled' member nation. M. Thatcher *Downing Street Years*, p. 548.

30   G. Brandreth *Breaking the Code: Westminster Diaries* London: Weidenfeld and Nicolson, 1999, entry for 17 February 1997, p. 464–5; C. Gill *Whips' Nightmare: Diary of a Maastricht Rebel* Spenneymore: Memoir Club, 2003, p. 213; A. Seldon *Major: A Political* Life London: Wiedenfeld and Nicolson, 1997, p. 702.

31   CPA: Anthony Royle to Secretary of State, FCO, 15 September 1970, CCO20/32/4.

32   R. Jackson *Rebels and Whips* London: Macmillan, 1968; T. Renton *Chief Whip* London: Politicos, 2004.

33   Michael Cockrill *Westminster's Secret Service: The Whips Office*, BBC 2, 21 May 1995; see also CPA: Derek Walker-Smith to Peter Thomas, 20 July 1971, CCO20/32/6.

34   D. Hurd *Memoirs*, p. 430.

35   Hinchingbrooke Mss: 'Note of conversation with PM in Smoking Room of House of Commons 18 July 1961', D/MAP265.

36 Macmillan Ministerial Mss: Macmillan to Andrew, Duke of Devonshire, 29 July 1961, MS.Macmillan.dep.c.311 f.5.

37 Gill *Whips' Nightmare*, p. 40.

38 S. Onslow *Backbench Debate within the Conservative Party and Its Influence on British Foreign Policy* Basingstoke: Macmillan, 1997, pp. 96–7.

39 Macmillan Ministerial Mss: Macmillan to Wyndham, 21 October 1962, MS.Macmillan.dep.c.353 ff 337–38.

40 Kitzinger *Diplomacy*, p. 163n.

41 Marten Mss: Marten to Royle, 9 December 1970, MS.Eng.hist.c.1138 f 359.

42 14 October 1999, 'Britain in Europe' campaign relaunched, with Heseltine and Kenneth Clarke joining Blair on the platform for a high-profile media launch.

43 BOAPAH: Edward Boyle interview.

44 Marten Mss: Marten to M. Fraser, 24 May 1971, MS.Eng.hist.c.1138 ff. 401–2.

45 Anthony Howard *Rab: The Life of RA Butler*, p.295.

46 Macmillan Mss: diary, 21 August 1962.

47 Moon *European Integration in British Politics 1950–63: A Study of Issue Change* Aldershot: Gower, 1985, p. 165.

48 CPA: Parliamentary Group on the Common Market, 10 December 1962, CCO2/42/8.

49 E.g. 'Common Market Basic Facts', CCO150/2/1/6.

50 CPA: Britain and Europe Reading List', October 1967, CCO150/2/1/6.

51 CPA: minutes, Tactical Committee, 6 July 1971, CCO20/32/6; M. Cockrill *Westminster's Secret Service: The Whips' Office* BBC 2, 21 May 1995.

52 CPA: Philip Goodhart to Francis Pym, 18 December 1970; Michael Fraser to Peter Thomas, 12 January 1971; Geoffrey Rippon to Francis Pym, 25 January 1971; all CCO20/32/4.

53 CPA: Michael Fraser to Peter Thomas, 29 July 1971, CCO20/32/6.

54 CPA: Gordon Pears to Richard Wood, 9 November 1967, CRD3/10/11.

55 CPA: A. Royle to Secretary of State, FCO, 15 September 1970, CCO20/32/4.

56 R. Kelly *Conservative Party Conferences* Manchester: Manchester University Press, 1989.

57 CPA: Tactical Committee minutes, 6 July 1971, CCO20/32/6.

58 *1962 Conservative Conference Report (Verbatim)*, p. 51, *ABCP* microfiche card no. 24.

59 *Sunday Times*, 20 March 1994, p. 1.26.

60 CPA: John Stevens (Heath's private office) to Du Cann, 30 August 1967, CCO20/70/1.

61 Howard *Rab*, p. 296.

62 CPA: Alan Green to Michael Fraser, 20 July 1960, ACP1/11.

63 CPA: COO to Duncan Sandys, 2 August 1961, CCO150/5/1/7.

64 Macmillan Ministerial Mss: Macmillan to Wyndham, 21 October 1962, MS.Macmillan.dep.c.353 ff. 337–38.

65 CPA: minutes, Parliamentary Group on the Common Market, 5, 19 November 1962, CRD2/42/8.

66 Macmillan Ministerial Mss: Macmillan to Wyndham, 21 October 1962, MS.Macmillan.dep.c.353 ff. 337–38. It was a tactic repeated in 1971, CPA: Tactical Committee minutes, 6 July 1971, CCO20/32/6.

67 CPA: Parliamentary Group on Common Market, CRD2/42/8: comprised of Bill Deeds (chair), W.T. Atkin, Tufton Beamish, C.F.H. Gough, Stephen Hastings, Lionel Heald, Marcus Kimball, Peter Kirk, Gilbert Longden, Maurice Macmillan, Robert Mathew, Gerald Nabarro, James Prior, W.L. Roots and Guy Haley as secretary.

68 CPA: minutes, Parliamentary Group on the Common Market, 4 February 1963, CRD2/42/8.

69 CPA: N. Ridley to various, 4 May 1967, CRD3/10/10.

70  CPA: Gordon Pears to Richard Wood, 9 November 1967, CRD3/10/11; Lord
     Balneil to Gordon Pears, 15 February 1967, CRD3/10/4; minutes, 14 June 1967,
     CRD3/10/10.
71  Hurd *An End to Promises*, p. 66.
72  *The Times*, 13 July 1971, p. 1 (for quotation), 21 July 1971, p. 8; *Hansard*, 20
     July 1971.
73  Hurd *An End to Promises*, p. 67, citing diary entry.
74  *The Times*, 15 July 1971, pp. 1, 6.
75  CPA: minutes, Tactical Committee, 6 July 1971, CCO20/32/6.
76  See S. Ball and A. Seldon (eds) *The Heath Government* London: Longman,
     1996; J. Ramsden *Winds of Change: Macmillan to Heath 1957–1975* Harlow:
     Longman, 1996, ch. 6.
77  CPA: ORC polls, 17–21 February 1971, 30 June–4 July 1971, CCO180/13/1/3,
     CCO180/13/1/6.
78  E.g. Winchester CA held four meetings: 1 June, Winchester Guildhall (200
     present); 30 July, same venue (67 present); 4 August, Crossfield Hall, Romsey
     (38 present); and 16 September, Alresford Community Centre (170 present):
     Finance and General Purposes Committee, 9 November 1971, 73M86W/7.
79  CPA: minutes, Tactical Cttee, 6 July 1971, CCO20/32/6.
80  CPA: P. Goodhart to Peter Thomas, 8 October 1971, CCO20/32/7.
81  CPA: J. Rickes (chair, Wrenkin CA) to Peter Thomas, 12 August 1971; B.
     Cunliffe (chair, Clitheroe CA) to Peter Thomas, 7 June 1971; G. Whicker
     (agent, Weston-super-Mare) to Peter Thomas, 23 June 1971, CCO20/32/6.
82  R. Pearce (ed.) *Patrick Gordon Walker: Political Diaries 1932–1971* London:
     Historian's Press, 1991, entry for 7 July 1971, p. 327.
83  CPA: '3rd report and analysis on the state of the party', N. St John Stevas,
     CCO20/32/82.
84  BIE Mss: campaign committee, 14 February 1975, BIE/14/1.
85  Newcastle West CA: Referendum file 1579/42.
86  Seldon *Major*, p. 390; Major claims that he was not referring to serving Cabinet
     ministers, but rather to former Cabinet ministers who were now leading the
     Eurosceptic challenge from the backbenches or the House of Lords. J. Major
     *The Autobiography* London: HarperCollins, 1999, p. 343.
87  CPA: 'Notes for the record', 10 May 1963, CCO20/8/7.
88  CPA: 'Memorandum on Britain and the Common Market', n.d. [Sept. 1970],
     CCO20/32/4.
89  Crowson 'South Dorset', p. 54.
90  CPA: minutes, Tactical Committee, 6 July 1971, CCO20/32/6.
91  Britain in Europe Mss: minutes, 11th meeting, Europe Co-ordinating Cttee, 3
     February 1975, BIE1/49.
92  Britain in Europe Mss: minutes 17th meeting, Europe Co-ordinating Cttee, 17
     March 1975, BIE1/49.
93  E.g. Seldon *Major*, p. 250.
94  CPA: F.E. Stride (Hon. Sec., Poole CA) to Peter Thomas, 12 July 1971,
     CCO20/32/7; similarly, Clyde Hewlett (chair Maccesfield CA) to Peter Thomas,
     29 March 1971, CCO20/32/4.
95  Marten Mss: M. Fidler to P. Thomas, 26 March 1971, MS.Eng.hist.c.1138 ff
     331–2.
96  See, for example, Macmillan Ministerial Mss: Macmillan to Wyndham, 21
     October 1962, MS.Macmillan.dep.c.353 ff. 337–38.
97  CPA: Peter Thomas to M. Fraser, 8 June 1971, CCO20/32/6; Swindon CA:
     General Council, 30 July 1971, MB14/3.
98  Sam Younger, chair of the Electoral Commission, told a conference on 24
     November 2004 that the government should not be allowed to use any
     taxpayers' movement to promote a 'Yes' vote for ten days before a referendum

on the European constitution. See Andrew Sparrow 'Referendum Spending Rules "Unfair to No Vote"', *Daily Telegraph*, 25 November 2004, p.10.

99 CPA: Anthony Royle to Secretary of State, FCO, 15 September 1970, CCO20/32/4.

100 HM Ministerial Mss: HM to Wyndham, 21 October 1962, MS.Macmillan.dep.c. 353 ff. 337–38.

101 BOAPAH: John Maclay interview.

102 Chelmsford CA: Finance and General Purposes Cttee, 23 June 1961, D/Z 96/11, Essex Records Office.

103 CPA: General Purposes Cttee, 3 May 1962, NUA5/2/1.

104 *Sunday Times*, 18 April 1993, p. 1.24.

105 CPA: V.B. Petherick to COO, 6 September 1962, CCO500/31/4.

106 CPA: CCO500/31/4.

107 E.g. CPA: minutes, FCA Cttee, 12 November 1970, views of Rippon, CRD3/10/16.

108 E.g. CPA: 'Paper 3: General Social Articles in a Treaty of Association', 30 September 1967, CRD3/10/9.

109 See party's own polling, Boyle Mss: CRD poll summaries, 2 April 1969, MS660/22761.

110 CPA: CPC to Duncan Sandys, 2 August 1961, CCO150/5/1/7.

111 CPA: Ian Deslandes to Peter Thomas, 26 March 1971, CCO20/32/4. Between April and June meetings were held in London, Cambridge, Leeds, Bristol, Birmingham and Manchester, each addressed by a senior party figure. Note there were no meetings in either Scotland or Wales.

112 CPA: Caryle to M. Fraser, 22 February 1971. A maximum of £1,500 was allocated to these seminars with the proviso that total expenditure for Special Projects 1971/2 did not exceed £5,000.

113 CPA: 'Report and Analysis of the state of the Party', n.d. [February 1971], CCO20/32/28.

114 CPA: Gordon Pears to Richard Wood, 9 November 1967, CRD3/10/11; 'Britain and Europe', March 1967, CCO506/14/16.

115 CPA: 'Common Market', Gordon Pears, September 1967; and 'Britain and Europe Reading List', October 1967, CCO150/2/1/6.

116 CPA: Gordon Pears to Sewill, 5 June 1967, CRD3/10/10; see also 'Paper 3: General Social Articles in a Treaty of Association', 30 September 1967, CRD3/10/9.

117 CPA: Gordon Pears to Russell Lewis, 5 December 1967, Pears to Howell 16 January 1968, CCO150/2/1/6.

118 CPA: Brendon Sewill to Russell Lewis, 16 November 1967, CCO150/2/1/6.

119 P. Norton 'The Role of the Conservative Political Centre 1945–98' in S. Ball and I. Holliday (eds) *Mass Conservatism: The Conservatives and the Public since the 1880s* Newbury: Frank Cass, 2002, pp. 183–99.

120 CPA: 'Interim report on CPC discussions on the Common Market', 19 October 1971, CCO20/32/7: 308 groups expressed 'yes to entry', 15 'no' and 31 were either divided, abstained or were undecided.

121 CPA: Brian Cunliffe (chair, Clitheroe CA) to Peter Thomas, 7 June 1971, CCO20/32/6.

122 Conservative Political Centre *Our Voice in Europe*.

123 *Sunday Times*, 18 April 1993, p. 1.24, CPC report on Maastricht.

124 CPA: Gerry Wade (chair, Greater London YCs) to Peter Thomas, 7 January 1971, CCO20/32/4.

125 CPA: Michael Fraser to Peter Thomas, 12 January 1971, CCO20/32/4.

126 *Sunday Times*, p. 2.5, 15 November 1992; *The Times*, 23 June 1995, p. 11.

127 Kitzinger *Diplomacy*, p. 155; see also Legge-Bourke Mss: Henry Legge-Bourke to T.W. Scarr, 28 June 1971, MS742/837.

128 Kitzinger *Diplomacy*, p. 156. The government costed these 'free' publications at £461,000.
129 Kitzinger *Diplomacy*, p. 157.
130 Lord Windlesham *Communication and Political Power* London: Cape, 1966, pp. 186–7.
131 Windlesham *Communication*, pp. 186–7.
132 CPA: minutes, Tactical Cttee, 6 July 1971, CCO20/32/6; Swindon CA, General Council, 30 July 171, MB14/3. The association ordered 1,000 copies of the White Paper; these had been provided free to Central Office by the European movement. CPA: Peter Thomas to M. Fraser and Webster, 8 June 1971, CCO20/32/6.
133 CPA: Peter Thomas to Geoffrey Finsberg, 30 September 1971, CCOP20/32/7; similar complaint during first application, 'Current issues in Eastleigh', David Price, 1 May 1962, ACP1/13; I.A. Coventon (Wembley CA) to I. Macleod, 20 May 1962, CCO1/14/95.
134 Marten Mss: David Mudd (Western Area CPC) to Marten, 7 September 1971, MS.Eng.hist.c.1139 f. 172.
135 Windlesham *Communication*, p. 178n.
136 Marten Mss: G. Gardiner to Marten, 3 March 1975, MS.Eng.hist.c.1141 f313.
137 Kitzinger *Diplomacy*, p. 190.
138 Windlesham *Communication*, pp. 175–8.
139 CPA: Peter Lasttimer (agent, East Herts CA) to B.T. Powell (agent, Eastern Area), 27 September 1961; and B.T. Powell to COO, 28 September 1961, re. East Hertfordshire CA and Walker-Smith. See also Ramsden *Winds of Change*, pp. 152–4. Similarly, for the accession debates, see: Legge-Bourke Mss: H.L.-B. to J.E. Dagless, 19 July 1971, MS.742.859, Brotherton Library, Leeds University; Marten Mss: Marten to President of Banbury CA, 12 December 1973, MS.Eng.hist.c.1134 ff. 209–13; South Bucks CA, executive, 19 July 1971; Finance and General Purposes Committee, 16 June 1975, D1631/2 and D163/2/3/1, Buckinghamshire Records Office.
140 CPA: North West Provincial Area, minutes, F&GP Committee, 28 September 1962, ARE3/1/6. Liverpool CA reproduced parts of the preamble of the Treaty of Rome and combined it with visual aids.
141 CPA: minutes, Cttee on Europe, 19 January 1971, CCO20/32/4.
142 CPA: Ashley Shute (aent, N. Dorset CA) to Peter Thomas, 8 July 1971, CCO20/32/6.
143 CPA: Jack Friswell (chair, Banbury CA) to Peter Thomas, 6 October 1971, CCO20/32/7.
144 All post-1945 manifestos can be accessed online, www.psr.keele.ac.uk/area/uk/man.htm; see also I. Dale (ed.) *Conservative Party Manifestos 1945–2000* London: Routledge, 1999.
145 www.psr.keele.ac.uk/area/uk/man.htm.
146 J. Ramsden *Winds of Change*, p. 335; D. Butler and M. Pinto-Duschinsky *The General Election of 1970*, London: Macmillan, pp. 440, 444.
147 CPA: 'Britain and the Common Market', Norman St John Stevas, n.d. [September 1970], CCO20/32/4.
148 TNA PREM11/4412. I am grateful to David Richardson for drawing my attention to this.
149 CPA: 'Summary of discussions … discussion of constituency chairmen Wessex Area 12–19 March 1964', CCO2/6/15.
150 CPA: 'The party's role after Brussels', 4 March 1963, CCO20/32/1.
151 www.psr.keele.ac.uk/area/uk/man.htm.
152 D. Butler and A. King *The British General Election of 1966* London: Macmillan, 1966, p. 103. This compared to a figure of 11 per cent in 1964.

153  A. King and R. Wybrow (eds) *British Political Opinion 1937–2000: The Gallup Polls* London: Politicos, 2001.
154  J. Young *Britain and European Unity*, pp. 90–1.
155  CPA: 'Summary of discussion ... East Midlands Area Annual Meeting', 13 June 1966, CCO2/7/5.
156  CPA: R.A Millard (chair, Bromsgrove CA) to Anthony Barber, 14 April 1969, CCO20/70/2; Harrogate CA Contact Programme Group Report, 22 May 1967, CCO1/14/259.
157  *Conservative Party Conference Report*, 1962, p. 53, ABCP card no. 24.
158  J. Ramsden *Winds of Change*, p. 338.
159  King and Wybrow (eds) *British Political Opinion 1937–2000*, pp. 264–73.
160  Winchester CA: press cutting, *Hampshire Chronicle*, 3 November 1962, 73M86W/41.
161  Young *This Blessed Plot*, p. 506.
162  'Britain and Strasbourg' witness seminar held 23 February 1995, ICBH, 2002, www.icbh.ac.uk/icbh/brussels/, p. 104.
163  Young *This Blessed Plot*, pp. 489–9.
164  G. Brandreth *Breaking the Code: Westminster Diaries* London: Weidenfeld and Nicolson, 1999, entry for 29 September 1992, p. 121.
165  Rhodes Boyson *Speaking My Mind* London: Peter Owen, 1994, p. 231.
166  Heath *et al.* 'Between First and Second Order: A Comparison of Voting Behaviour in European and Local Elections in Britain' *European Journal of Political Research* 35(3), 1999, pp. 389–414; Turnout: 1979 (32.7 per cent), 1984 (32.6 per cent), 1989 (36.8 per cent), 1994 (36.8 per cent), 1999 (24.1 per cent); 2004 (38.4 per cent).
167  1979 manifesto, www.psr.keele.ac.uk/area/uk/man.htm.
168  D. Butler and D. Marquand *European Elections and British Politics* Harlow: Longman, 1981, p. 72; D. Butler and P. Jowett *Party Strategies in Britain: A Study of the 1984 European Elections* Basingstoke: Macmillan, 1985, pp. 48–9; G. Howe *Conflict of Loyalty* London: Macmillan, 1994, p. 571.
169  *The Times*, 1 June 1984, David Howell.
170  E. Curry, *Diaries 1987–1992* London: Little Brown, 2000, entry for 15 June 1989, p. 136; N. Lawson *View from Number 11: Memoirs of a Tory Radical* London: Bantam Press, 1992, p. 922. It may also explain why Leon Brittan chose to call his 2000 book on Europe *A Diet of Brussels: The Changing Face of Europe* London: Little, Brown, 2000.
171  *The Sunday Times*, 20 March 1994, p. 1.26, citing a CPC report based on the views of 3,400 activists; *Guardian*, 22 March 1994, p. 11.
172  D. Butler and M. Westlake *British Politics and the European Elections 1999* Basingstoke: Macmillan, 2000, p. 56.
173  In 2005 the manifesto emphasised that Britain was a 'net' contributor to the EU, that the party championed enlargement, was emphatically opposed to the constitution and the euro, and sought a more flexible, liberal and decentralised Europe.
174  D. Baker *et al.* 'MPs and Europe' *British Elections and Parties Review* Newbury: Cass, 1999, vol. 9, pp. 170–85; P. Norton 'Electing the Leader' *Politics Review* 7(4), 1998, pp. 10–14.
175  D. Butler and D. Kavanagh *The British General Election of 1997* Basingstoke: Macmillan, 1997.
176  P. Lynch ' The Conservatives and Europe, 1997–2001' in Garnett and Lynch (eds) *The Conservatives in Crisis*, p. 158.
177  See A. Meyer 'What's Wrong with the Tories' *Reformer Magazine*, Winter, 2001.

## 6 The Conservative sceptic: 'a confederacy of zealots and lurchers'?

1   H. Young *This Blessed Plot: Britain and Europe from Churchill to Blair* London: Macmillan, 1998, p. 386.
2   *Hansard*, vol. 645, cols 1507–14, 2 August 1961.
3   Macmillan Mss: diary, 5 August 1961, MS.Macmillan dep.d.43 f. 17, Bodleian Library, Oxford.
4   D. Walker-Smith and P. Walker *A Call to the Commonwealth* London: published privately, 1962.
5   R. Butt 'The Common Market and Conservative Party Politics' *Government and Opposition* 2(3), 1967, p. 379.
6   N.J. Crowson 'Lord Hinchingbrooke, Europe and the November 1962 South Dorset by-election' *Contemporary British History* 17(4), 2003, pp. 43–64.
7   Hinchingbrooke Mss: Hinchingbrooke to Major Lane, 30 October 1962, D/MAP273.
8   Hinchingbrooke Mss: R.W. [Bill] Elliott (vice-chairman, Standing Advisory Cttee on Candidates) to Hinchingbrooke, 20 May 1971. The letter has been torn into four and stuck back together with sellotape!.
9   Hinchingbrooke Mss: V. Montagu to Robin Williams, 14 February 1983, D/MAP86.
10  Macmillan Mss: diary, 5 August 1961, MS.Macmillan dep.d.43 f. 17.
11  Avon Mss: Avon to R. Turton, 30 June 1960, AP23/64/25A.
12  Avon Mss: Avon to Chandos, 30 October 1962, AP23/17/63B.
13  Macmillan Ministerial Mss: Dilhorne to Macmillan, 24 July 1962, MS.Macmillan. dep.c.311 f. 22.
14  D. Dutton 'Anticipating Maastricht: The Conservative Party and Britain's First Application to Join the European Community' *Contemporary Record* 7, 1993, p. 536.
15  Hinchingbrooke Mss: ACML executive, 6 July 1971, D/MAP87; Hinchingbrooke to Lord Clitheroe, 1 February 1972, D/MAP Series C, Subject 'C', General.
16  A. Aughey 'The Party and Foreign Policy' in P. Norton (ed.) *The Conservative Party* London: Prentice Hall, 1996, p. 208.
17  Marten Mss: Marten to editor, *Monthly News*, 3 March 1975, MS.Eng.hist.c.1137 ff. 114–16.
18  Marten Mss: Marten to Edward Heath, 12 August 1971, MS.Eng.hist.c.1141 f. 221.
19  P. Norton *Conservative Dissidents: Dissent within the Parliamentary Conservative Party 1970–74* London: Temple Smith, 1978, p. 80.
20  B. Castle *The Castle Diaries 1974–76* London: Weidenfeld and Nicolson, 1980, entries for 22, 29 May 1975, pp. 401–2. Mrs Joan Marten went with Castle to Brussels shopping to highlight the expense to the housewife of the EEC.
21  S. Heffer *Like a Roman: A Life of Enoch Powell* London: Weidenfeld and Nicolson, 1998, p. 420; in contrast, Hinchingbrooke Mss: Francis d'Aft to Hinchingbrooke, 19 June 1973, D/MAP86.
22  CPA: correspondence between Michael Fraser and J.P. Friswell, July–August 1971, CCO20/32/6; Marten Mss: press release, 'Banbury constituency', 25 June 1971, Marten to president, Banbury CA, 12 December 1973, MS.Eng.hist.c.1136 ff203–4, 209–13.
23  E.g. Marten Mss: May 1977 EDMs on Euro-passports, MS.Eng.hist.c.1136.
24  Between 1970 and 1974 Powell voted against the Conservative whip on 113 occasions. D. Baker *et al.* 'Backbenchers with Attitude' paper presented to the European Consortium for Political Research Conference, Bordeaux, 1995, p. 2.
25  Hinchingbrooke Mss: Francis d'Aft to Hinchingbrooke, 19 June 1973, D/MAP86.
26  Legge-Bourke Mss: Legge-Bourke to Mr and Mrs Voice, 21 July 1971, MS.742/863.

27 R. Shepherd *Enoch Powell: A Biography* London: Pimlico, 1997, p. 415.
28 Hurd *End to Promises*, p. 69.
29 Young *This Blessed Plot*, p. 377; *Daily Telegraph*, Boris Johnson, 3 March 1995, p. 4.
30 There appears to be some confusion about this figure: A. Forster *Euroscepticism in Contemporary British Politics*, p. 44, credits Biffen with 78 rebellions to Powell's 80; Hugo Young suggests otherwise: Biffen 'voted more often against the European Communities Act 1972 than any other Tory. He even beat his hero, Enoch Powell, on the count', Young *This Blessed Plot*, p. 376; whilst Heffer says Powell rebelled on *all* 104, see *Dictionary of National Biography*, www.oxforddnb.co,/view/article/69398.
31 Marten Mss: John Biffen speech to Denbigh Conservatives, Abergele, 22 January 1971, MS.Eng.hist.c.1138 f. 238.
32 Heffer *Like a Roman*, p. 384; Young *This Blessed Plot*, pp. 376–7.
33 Marten Mss: 'Britain and Europe', John Biffen, 28 December 1967, MS.Eng.hist.c.1137 ff. 114–16.
34 Eleven Conservatives voted against the government, including the former Chancellor's PPS, Tony Favell, who had resigned earlier over the issue. See *Hansard*, vol. 183, cols 316–19, 19 December 1990, Biffen.
35 The November rebels were: Biffen, N. Winterton, Browne, Shepherd, Body and Fairburn. Abstainers: were Tebbit, Taylor, Cran, Jessel, Gill, Cash, A. Winterton, Favell. Seven Conservatives rebelled in December (Biffen, Tebbit, Budgen, Favell, Browne, Walker and Shepherd); three abstained (Thatcher, Howarth, Gorman). Overall government majority eighty-six. *The Times*, 20 December 1991.
36 Baker *et al.* 'Backbenchers with Attitude', p. 14, Table 1.
37 A. Seldon *Major: A Political Life* London: Weidenfeld and Nicolson, 1997, p. 458.
38 D. Baker, A. Gamble and S. Ludlam '1846, 1906, 1996? Conservative Splits and European Integration' *Political Quarterly* 64, 1993, pp. 420–34.
39 *Daily Telegraph*, Bill Cash to editor, 19 October 1999, p. 27.
40 M. Sowemimo 'Conservative Party and European Integration 1988–95' *Party Politics* 2(1), 1996, pp. 77–97; and J. Turner *Tories and Europe* Manchester: Manchester University Press, 2000.
41 M. Spicer *Treaty*, p. 168.
42 *Hansard*, vol. 201, cols 505–7, 19 December 1991.
43 E.g. see CPA: S.R. Newman to COO, n.d. [August 1962], CCO500/31/2.
44 J.A. Ramsden *Age of Churchill and Eden* London: Longman, 1995, p. 196.
45 CPA: J.A. Mellsop to R. Horton, 11 May 1962, CCO500/31/3.
46 CPA: 'Report and Analysis of the State of the Party', n.d. [February 1971], CCO20/32/28.
47 Legge-Bourke Mss: H.L.-B. to editor, *The Times*, 22 September 1956, Brotherton Library, University of Leeds.
48 Norton *Conservative Dissidents*, pp. 81–2.
49 Norton *Conservative Dissidents*, p. 80; U. Kitzinger *Diplomacy and Persuasion: How Britain Joined the Common Market* London: Thames and Hudson, 1973, pp. 401–5. The detail of Kitzinger's analysis reveals that he must have been shown a 'confidential' copy of the 'Report and Analysis of the State of the Party' by Norman St John-Stevas cited above. This was circulated to only nine individuals, including St John-Stevas.
50 *Daily Telegraph*, 6 June 2000, p. 4.
51 Douglas Hurd as a pro-European was urged to withdraw from the selection process. See Hurd *Memoirs*, p. 200.
52 Hinchingbrooke Mss: George Gardiner to Hinchingbrooke, 13 November 1974, D/MAP90; Marten Mss: Marten to G. Gardiner, editor, *Monthly News*, 3

March 1975, MS.Eng.hist.c.1141 f 312; *Daily Telegraph*, obituary, 18 November 2002, p. 23.

53 *Hansard*, vol. 96, cols 358–61 (Gardiner), 23 April 1986.

54 CPA: Richard Body to Peter Thomas, 4 May 1971, CCO20/32/4.

55 CPA: Richard Body to Peter Thomas, 6 April 1971, CCO20/32/4.

56 See, for example, Richard Body *Europe of Many Circles: Constructing a Wider Europe* London: NEP, 1990.

57 Cited Crowson ' South Dorset', p. 59.

58 N. Ridley *My Style of Government* London: Hutchinson, 1991; see also *Sunday Times*, 7 March 1993, p. 2.1, Thatcher tribute to Ridley.

59 *Daily Telegraph*, 18 November 2002, p. 23, obituary.

60 *Daily Telegraph*, 25 March 1998, p. 25, obituary. Fell was the only Tory to vote against the 1961 application.

61 M. Westlake *Britain's Euro-elites* Aldershot: Dartmouth, 1994, pp. 73–4n.

62 D. Butler and D. Marquand *European Elections and British Politics* London: Longman, 1981, p. 27.

63 *Daily Telegraph*, obituary, 13 October 1994, p. 21.

64 Based upon CPA: CCO20/32/28, 1st, 2nd, 3rd reports on 'State of Party', February, May, August 1971, by St John Stevas, Francis Pym to N. St John Stevas, 3 February 1971; Hinchingbrooke Mss: 'Memo: House of Lords peer voting 28/10/71', n.d.; Hinchingbrooke to Lord Clitheroe, 1 February 1972, D/MAP86; Marten Mss: minutes, CACMIS, 8 May 1972, MS.Eng.hist.c.1130 ff 114–16.

65 Baker *et al.* 'Backbenchers with Attitude', pp. 9–10.

66 CPA: 'Report and Analysis of the State of the Party', n.d. [February 1971], CCO20/32/28.

67 C. Gill *Whips' Nightmare: Diary of a Maastricht Rebel* Spenneymore: Memoir Club, 2003, p. 106.

68 Gill *Whips' Nightmare*, p. 106.

69 Figures derived from Norton *Conservative Dissidents* and Baker *et al.* 'Backbenchers with Attitude', p. 6, 16. In 1971–2 92 Conservative MPs cast a dissenting vote, compared to 206 in 1992–3.

70 E.g. Nick Budgen, see *Daily Telegraph*, obituary, 27 October 1998, p. 27.

71 P. Whitely, P. Seyd and J. Richardson *True Blues: The Politics of Conservative Party Membership* Oxford: Oxford University Press, 1994, p. 57.

72 Spicer *Treaty too Far*, p. 166.

73 Butt 'The Common Market and Conservative Party Politics 1961–62' *Government and Opposition* 2(3), 1967, pp. 380, 385.

74 Of the 69 unqualified: 12 were 'supporting', 14 'welcoming', 22 'congratulating' and the remainder 'applauding'.

75 M. Ball *The Conservative Conference and Eurosceptical Motions 1992–5* London: Bruges Group Publication, 1996.

76 CPA: 'Report and Analysis of the state of the party', n.d. [February 1971], CCO20/32/28.

77 Norwood Conservative Association: executive, 15 July 1960, 21 July 1961, Special General Meeting, 4 July 1963, IV/166/1/18, Lambeth Archives.

78 Accrington Conservative Association executive, 4 July 1961, 20 September 1961, Acc/AV.

79 He fought his contests 'with very good reports, but we have heard little from him since'. CPA: Paul Bryan to Chairman, 25 October 1961, CCO1/14/68/1. He would remain chairman until his death from a heart attack in June 1969. In August 1962 he was obliged to resign from Mobil because of his political activities. This so incensed one supporter that they donated £35,000 towards a press advertising campaign. Lord Windlesham *Communication and Political Power* London: Cape, 1966, p. 176. Nor did he give up trying to secure a Conservative seat. He was interviewed for Orpington in November 1961 and secured three

votes, but was considered 'a frightful liability' by the majority of the selection panel. CPA: A.N. Banks to Paul Bryan, 7 November 1961, CCO1/14/68/1.

80  Walker *Staying Power*, pp. 30–1.
81  This appears to have been a consistent theme throughout Walker's political life. Although his memoirs make no mention of the ACML, his later refusal to consider a defection to the SDP in 1981 was for the same reasons. See Walker *Staying Power*, pp. 134–5.
82  Windlesham *Communication*, pp. 171–2.
83  One informant was Ian Greer, who declined the offer of becoming the ACML's national organising secretary. He had been approached by Roger Moate and invited to meet with John Paul on 1 September, but declined. He also reported that the official launch would be 4 October, who the main speakers would be and that *The Times* personal column would be utilised. CPA: A.A. Hammond to COO, 1 September 1961, CCO500/31/3. Also, elements of the Young Conservatives were reporting 'rumours' from August/September 1961: Horton to A.A. Hammond, 7 September 1961, CCO500/31/3.
84  Marten Mss: 'Statement by Neil Marten', 7 January 1975, MS.Eng.hist.c.1131 ff. 150–51. After the failure of the referendum campaign the ACML reformed and continued operations into the early 1980s but with ever-declining fortunes. Hinchingbrooke Mss: ACML executive minutes, 13 August 1975, D/MAP86.
85  See www.bullen.demon.co.uk/cibacml.htm. This site contains quarterly newsletters from the ACML.
86  Hinchingbrooke Mss: ACML executive, 26 January 1973, D/MAP86.
87  J. Ramsden *Winds of Change*, p. 153. Other examples would be CPA: Greater London Young Conservatives Conference, 18 March 1967, G. Pears to E. Heath, 20 March 1967, CRD3/10/10.
88  Windlesham *Communication*, p. 175.
89  Windlesham *Communication*, p. 178.
90  CPA: A.N. Banks to COO, 27 August 1962, CCO500/31/2; the wording of this quiz can be found Windlesham *Communication*, p. 274.
91  R.J. Leiber *British Politics and European Unity: Parties, Elites and Pressure Groups* Berkeley: University of California Press, 1970. This view is challenged by M. Kandiah 'British Domestic Politics, the Conservative Party and Foreign Policy-making' in W. Kaiser and G. Staerck *British Foreign Policy 1955–64* Basingstoke: Macmillan, 1999, pp. 61–88.
92  For example, at the 1971 party conference the Monday Club undertook to distribute ACML literature.
93  See various reports filed CPA: CCO500/31/3.
94  CPA: BA Cribb to COO, 27 August 1962, CCO500/31/2.
95  CPA: memos from Richard Webster to COO, autumn 1962, CCO500/31/3. Anthony Fell was a particular culprit, although other ACML speakers did take the precaution of seeking the permission of the local sitting MP before addressing a meeting in their constituency; see CPA: B.T. Powell to COO, 27 August 1962, CCO500/31/2.
96  CPA: Macleod to Macmillan, 27 November 1962, CCO20/8/5. Other attempts to intervene were spectacularly unsuccessful, e.g. John Paul in Bexley in the 1964 election polling only 2.4 per cent of the vote and losing his deposit. See also N.J. Crowson 'Lord Hinchingbrooke, Europe and the November 1962 South Dorset by-election' *Contemporary British History* 17(4), 2003, pp. 43–64.
97  Walker *Staying Power*, p. 32, although he mistakenly suggests that Hinchingbrooke was actually the candidate.
98  Hinchingbrooke Mss: Hinchingbrooke to John Paul, 12 April 1964, D/MAP87.
99  Hinchingbrooke Mss: ACML executive, minutes, 5 September 1972, D/MAP86.
100 Windlesham *Communication*, p. 174; Hinchingbrooke Mss: ACML executive, minutes, 12 June 1972, D/MAP86.

101 Hinchingbrooke Mss: Robin Turton to Hinchingbrooke, 11 May 1972, D/MAP87.

102 Hinchingbrooke Mss: correspondence C. Horsfield and V. Montague 5, 22 March 1972; minutes 2nd mtg, Kingston Conservatives against the Common Market, 14 March 1972, D/MAP, Series C, Subject Files 'C', General.

103 Hinchingbrooke Mss: ACML executive, minutes, 6 July, 5 October 1971, D/MAP86.

104 E.g. CPA: A.N. Banks to COO, 'Common Market and Public Opinion: South Eastern Area', 27 August 1962, CCO500/31/2.

105 Marten Mss: 'Some thoughts on the referendum campaign', MS.Eng.hist.c. 1131 f. 185.

106 CPA: B.A. Cribb to COO, 27 August 1962, 'Common Market and Public Opinion S. Eastern Area Report', A.N. Banks, 27 August 1962, CCO500/31/2; S. Curtis to COO, 11 September 1962, CCO500/31/4; 'Report on ACML meeting Cardiff', 7 November 1962, anon., CCO500/31/3.

107 Britain in Europe [hereafter BIE] Mss: minutes, 9th mtg, Europe Co-ordinating Group, 20 January 1975, BIE/1/49.

108 See, for example, CPA: E.A. Walker (chairman, Falmouth and Camborne CA) to Peter Thomas, 23 September 1971; Hinchingbrooke Mss: 'Memo House of Lords peers voting against EEC', D/MAP86; CPA: correspondence between Michael Fraser and J.P. Friswell, July–August 1971, CCO20/32/6.

109 CPA: Marten to Peter Thomas, 27 January 1971, CCO20/32/4; Marten Mss: Peter Thomas to Marten, 2 February 1971, MS.Eng.hist.c.1138 f.247. Not to be deterred, Marten again tried in May 1971; Marten and Thomas correspondence, CPA: CCO20/32/4, 24, 27 May 1971.

110 Marten Mss: Marten to editor, *Monthly News*, 3 March 1975, MS.Eng.hist.c. 1141 f 312.

111 CPA: minutes, Tactical Cttee, 6 July 1971, CCO20/32/6.

112 Gill *Whips' Nightmare, passim.*, for his frequent run-ins with Lightbown; quotation, p. 11. See also G. Brandreth *Breaking the Code: Westminster Diaries 1990–1997* London: Weidenfeld and Nicolson, 1999, entry for 4 November 1992, p. 129.

113 CPA: D. Walker-Smith to Peter Thomas, 20 July 1971, CCO20/32/6.

114 Gill *Whips' Nightmare*, pp. 40.

115 CPA: 'Report and Analysis of the state of the party', n.d. [February 1971], CCO20/32/28.

116 CPA: R.E. Smith to Peter Thomas, 19 July 1971, CCO20/32/6.

117 CPA: Peter Lattimer (agent) to B.T. Powell (area agent), 27 September 1961, CCO500/31/2.

118 CPA: Marten to Thomas, 24 August 1971, CCO20/32/7.

119 Marten Mss: David Mudd to Marten, 7 September 1971, MS.Eng.hist.c.1139 f 172.

120 *Harborough Mail*, 8 July 1971.

121 J. Ramsden *Winds of Change*, pp. 335–6.

122 Hinchingbrooke Mss: Alan Clark to Hinchingbrooke, 24 April 1975, D/MAP89.

123 D. Baker *et al.* 'Whips or Scorpions? The Maastricht Vote and the Conservative Party' *Parliamentary Affairs* 46(2), 1993, p. 155.

124 Gill *Whips' Nightmare*.

125 For examples from another period, see N. J. Crowson *Facing Fascism: The Conservative Party and the European Dictators, 1935–40* London: Routledge, 1997, pp. 79–80, 85–7, 102–6, 112–13.

126 E.g. South Buckinghamshire CA: AGM agenda, 26 March 1956, D163/1/3; Finance and General Purposes Committee, 16 June 1975, D163/2/3/1.

127 Marten Mss: press release, 25 June 1971, MS.Eng.hist/c/1136 ff 203–4; for other examples, see *Harborough Mail*, 12 June 1975, for views of John Farr; Legge-Bourke Mss: letter to J.E. Dagless, 19 July 1971, MS.742/859.

128 BIE Mss: 13th mtg, Europe Coordinating Cttee, 17 February 1975, BIE/1/49.
129 Rhodes Boyson *Speaking My Mind*, p. 230; Gill *Whips' Nightmare*, p. 60, considered this a betrayal.
130 Gill *Whips' Nightmare*, p. 60.
131 Marten Mss: 'United to Win', MS.Eng.hist.c.1131 ff.194–95.
132 E.g. Marten Mss: Hinchingbrooke to Marten, 23 October 1969.
133 See Michael Cockrill *Westminster's Secret Service*, BBC 2 documentary on whips' office broadcast on 21 May 1995.
134 According to Harold Evans' *Downing Street Diary* London: Hodder and Stoughton, 1981, entry for 29 July 1961, p. 155: Harold Macmillan had been assured by the whips that there was no risk of defeat but that 'he goes on himself pretending that there is a serious possibility that a backbenchers' revolt will cause the Government to fall'. Evans thought this belief was, in part, due to Macmillan's poor performance in the recent economics debate, which had weakened his confidence.
135 See Chapter 1, note 101, for list of the abstainers.
136 Avon Mss: Turton to Avon, 20 November 1962, AP23/64/14; For more on the Common Market Committee, see Hinchingbrooke Mss: D/MAP283. Hinchingbrooke acted as the secretary.
137 Conservative participants were: Turton, Nicholls, Marten, Clark Hutchinson, Du Cann, Walker-Smith, Wall and Fraser. Marten Mss: MS.Eng.hist.c.1134, Bodliean Library. Labour members were: Jay, Morris, Tuck, Short, Page, Royle; and for the Liberals, Bessell.
138 Marten Mss: MS.Eng.hist.c.1134 ff 1–5, quotation f. 2, Bodleian Library.
139 Seldon *Major*, p. 369. This challenges the claims of Forster *Euroscepticism*, p. 87.
140 Brandreth *Breaking the Code*, p. 326.
141 Young *This Blessed Plot*, p. 396.
142 Marten Mss: MS.Eng.hist.c.1130: Turton (president); Walker-Smith, Marten (vice-presidents) and Moate (chairman).
143 These were: Ronald Bell, Cyril Black, Eric Bullus, John Jennings, Harmar Nicholls, Ronald Russell, Edward Spears, Edward Taylor, Robin Turton, Derek Walker-Smith.
144 Kitzinger *Diplomacy*, p. 243.
145 Hinchingbrooke Mss: D/MAP283 for list of EDMs and names of signatories.
146 Marten Mss: minutes, Atlantic Free Trade Area Parliamentary Group, 17 June 1969, MS.Eng.hist.c.1134 ff. 3–4.
147 Marten Mss: 'Some thoughts on the referendum campaign', MS.Eng.hist.c.1131 f. 185.
148 Macmillan Mss: Knox Cunningham notes on party committees, e.g. MS.Macmillan dep.c.354 ff.168–73, 31 July 1962.
149 Macmillan Mss: Knox Cunningham notes on Foreign Affairs Committee, 16 May, 23 July 1962, MS.Macmillan.dep.c.354 ff 196–97, 180–81.
150 CPA: minutes, Foreign Affairs Committee, 26 March 1968, CRD3/10/16, contributions from Neil Marten, Robin Turton and Hugh Fraser.
151 Seldon *Major*, p. 387.
152 Rhodes Boyson *Speaking My Mind*, p. 230.
153 CPA: *3rd Report and Analysis of the State of the Party*, 1 August 1971, CCO20/32/82.
154 Seldon *Major*, pp. 386–7, based upon an interview with Ulster Unionist Party (UUP) leader Jim Molyneaux, dismisses these claims, suggesting that the UUP's switch to Major on 22 July 1993 was based on Labour's decision to use the Social Chapter as a means of defeating the government.
155 E.g. *Daily Telegraph*, 26 April 2006, p. 10.
156 The difficulty can be seen in Marten Mss: 'Some thoughts on the referendum campaign', 7 January 1975, p. 3, MS.Eng,hist.c.1131 f. 187.

157 Butt 'The Common Market', p. 386.
158 Hinchingbrooke Mss: ACML executive, 22 October 1970, D/MAP86.
159 Macmillan Ministerial Mss: Knox Cunningham's notes on Foreign Affairs Committee, 16 May 1962, MS.Macmillan.dep.c.354 ff. 196–97.
160 Walker *Staying Power*, p. 30.
161 Marten Mss: 'Britain and Europe', John Biffen, 28 December 1969, MS.Eng.hist.c. 1137 ff. 114–16.
162 Compare CPA: 'The case for AFTA', Peter Blaker, 25 April 1967, CRD3/10/10; with Dodds-Parker Mss: 'Atlantic political and economic ties', 21 February 1967, MC:P2/7/3C/5.
163 Dodds-Parker Mss: D.P. to Richard Wood, 15 December 1967, MC:P2/7/3MS/1.
164 CPA: Foreign Affairs Committee, 5 December 1967, CRD3/10/16.
165 CPA: joint meeting, Foreign Affairs Cttee and Commonwealth Affairs Cttee, 23 July 1968 (Richard Wood), CRD3/10/16.
166 CPA: Foreign Affairs Committee, 23 January 1968, CRD3/10/16.
167 CPA: Foreign Affairs Committee, 5 December 1967, 23 January, 12 March, 26 March, 23 July 1968, CRD3/10/16.
168 CPA: M. Niblock to E. Heath, 21 October 1968, CRD3/10/39.
169 *Sunday Times*, 18 April 1993, p. 1.24.
170 Marten Mss: 'Some thoughts on the referendum campaign', 7 January 1975, MS.Eng.hist.c.1131 f. 185.
171 *Daily Telegraph*, article by William Hague, 20 October 1999.
172 *Sunday Times*, 16 October 1994.
173 *Daily Telegraph*, Rifkind interview with Boris Johnson, 6 January 1997, p. 30.
174 A 1998 survey found that 26 per cent of parliamentary party thought Britain should withdraw. D. Baker *et al.* 'MPs and Europe' *British Elections and Parties Review* 9, 1999, pp. 170–85.
175 *Daily Telegraph*, 24 November 1997, William Waldegrave, 'Freedom versus Empire'.
176 *Daily Telegraph*, Helmer to editor, 2 September 2000, p. 21.
177 *Daily Telegraph*, 26 April 2006, p. 10; 27 April 2006, p. 16.
178 J. Redwood *Stars and Strife* London: Palgrave, 2001.
179 J. Campbell *Margaret Thatcher: Iron Lady, Volume Two*, pp. 762–3.
180 *Guardian*, 23 April 1993, reporting Major's speech to the Conservative Group for Europe.
181 *Daily Telegraph*, W.S. Churchill Jr to editor, 11 July 2000, p. 19.
182 M. Thatcher *Statecraft: Strategies for a Changing World* London: Harper Collins, 2003.
183 *Guardian*, 7 September 1992, p. 19.
184 Marten Mss: 'Some thoughts on the referendum campaign', MS.Eng.hist. c.1131 f. 185.
185 *Daily Telegraph*, Taylor, Body and Shepherd to editor, 20 September 1996, p. 25.
186 Marten Mss: Marten to editor, *The Times*, 17 February 1975, MS.Eng.hist.c. 1131 f. 256.
187 *Hansard*, vol. 208, cols 564–6 (N. Hawkins), 20 May 1992.
188 Young *This Blessed Plot*, p. 499.
189 Cited D. Dutton *Anthony Eden* London: Arnold, 1997, p. 301.
190 Young *This Blessed Plot*, p. 154.
191 Ritchie *Enoch Powell on 1992*, p. 12.
192 Thatcher Foundation.
193 J. Barnes and R. Cockett 'Factions and Ideology' in S. Ball and A. Seldon (eds) *Conservative Century* Oxford: OUP, 1994, p. 350; see also L. Baston *Reggie: The Life of Reginald Maudling* Thrupp: Sutton, 2004, p. 190.
194 *Daily Telegraph*, 9 July 1999, reporting Hague's speech to Congress for Democracy, London.

195 *Hansard*, Maastricht debate, vol. 208, cols 441–4 (J. Cran), 20 May 1992.

196 *Hansard*, vol. 208, cols 353–7 (Duncan Smith), 20 May 1992.

197 Ritchie *Powell*, p. 68.

198 P. Stephens *Politics and the Pound* London: Macmillan, 1996, p. 330, citing *Today* interview, BBC Radio 4, 25 April 1996.

199 Forster *Euroscepticism*, p. 111.

200 CPA: 'Common Market and Public Opinion', 27 August 1962, CCO500/31/2, and various reports in CCO500/31/4.

201 CPA: S. Curtis to COO, 11 September 1962, CCO500/31/4.

202 CPA: 'Current issues in Eastleigh', David Price MP, 1 May 1962, ACP1/13.

203 CPA: 'Notes for the record', 10 May 1963, CCO20/8/7.

204 Walker *Staying Power*, p. 33.

205 Leiber *British Politics*, p. 223.

206 CPA: R.A. Butler to Otto Prior-Palmer, 15 June 1961, CCO4/8/94.

207 Legge-Bourke Mss: *The Times* to Legge-Bourke, October 1962, MS.742 f. 768.

208 *Sun*, 1 November 1990; the next line ran: the *Sun* 'today calls on its patriotic family of readers to tell the filthy French to FROG OFF'.

209 Marten Mss: AFTA Parliamentary Group minutes, 13 May, 17 June 1969 MS.Eng.hist.c.1134 ff. 1–4.

210 Marten Mss: Lord Hill to Marten, 14 July 1970, MS.Eng.hist.c.1138 f. 77.

211 Marten Mss: Victor Montagu to Max Aitken, 2 July 1971, MS.Eng.hist.c.1139 f. 121.

212 B. Castle *The Castle Diaries*, entry for 30 May 1975, p. 402: 'These NRC press conferences are not like press conferences at all, but public meetings with an overtly hostile audience. The spleen of some of the reporters that anyone should dare to oppose their precious Community is almost ungovernable.'

213 Crowson 'Hinchingbrooke', p. 54.

214 BIE Mss: minutes, 11th mtg, Europe Co-ordinating Cttee, 3 February 1975, BIE1/49.

215 Marten Mss: Sir Cyril Black to Marten, 13 June 1975, MS.Eng.hist.c.1132 ff. 134–35. For the press during the campaign, see Butler and Kitzinger *Referendum*, pp. 214–45.

## 7 Conservatives in Europe: 'the concern of a private army'?

1 That said, Labour organisationally was reluctant to establish links with European socialist parties. See J. McKay 'Labour Party Attitudes to European Integration 1945–75' unpublished PhD, University of Birmingham, 2006, pp. 225–9.

2 Conservative Party Archive [hereafter CPA]: 'Role of organised political groups in the European Parliamentary Assemblies', 15 January 1962, CCO20/32/1, Bodleian Library, Oxford. See B. Girvin *The Right in the Twentieth Century: Conservatism and Democracy* London: Pinter, 1994, ch. 4.

3 Robert Jackson, 'Britain and Strasbourg' witness seminar held 23 February 1995, ICBH, 2002, www.icbh.ac.uk/icbh/brussels/, p. 113.

4 See A. Aughey and P. Norton *Conservatives and Conservatism* London: Temple Smith, 1981.

5 E.g. CPA: CDU visit, 19–20 July 1963, CCO20/15/2.

6 CPA: Overseas Cttee minutes, 3 April 1950, COB.

7 N. Ridley *My Style of Government* London: Hutchinson, 1992, pp. 136–61, quotation p. 137.

8 E.g. CPA: correspondence Lady Elles and party chairman, August 1973, CCO20/32/8.

9 CPA: Overseas Cttee minutes, 19 July 1949, 'Rab' Butler, COB.

10 CPA: 'External relations', 19 January 1955, CCO4/6/364.

11 CPA: Geoffrey Stewart-Smith to Peter Thomas, 27 July 1971, CCO20/32/6.
12 CPA: 'Contacts with Continental Right-wing Parties', n.d., CCO4/5/328.
13 CPA: 'External relations', 19 January 1955, general director to chairman, Woolton, CCO4/6/364.
14 CPA: 'Our current relations with European centre/right parties', n.d. [1967], CCO20/15/3.
15 E.g. CPA: 'Brief notes on the origin and growth of EUW', 18 February 1960, COB52/2; European Union of Women: British Section, 4 May 1960, COB33/1/1.
16 CPA: Strasbourg Study Visit 1962, n.d., COB57/1.
17 Macleod (chair), Aldington, Robert Allan, William Urton, Peter Smithers, Tufton Beamish, Stephen Hastings, Crathorne, Emmet, Michael Fraser, plus whip in attendance. The committee fell into abeyance after the collapse of the Brussels negotiations in 1963.
18 CPA: Committee on Links with Europe, CCO20/32/1.
19 For a history of the Nouvelles Equipes Internationales, see T. Jansen *The European People's Party* Basingstoke: Macmillan, 1998, chs 4–5. See also M. Gehler and W. Kaiser 'Transnationalism and Early European Integration: The *Nouvelles Equipes Internationales* and the Geneva Circle 1947–57' *Historical Journal* 44(3), 2001, pp. 773–98.
20 CPA: Smithers/Macleod correspondence, 29 April 1963, CCO20/15/2.
21 CPA: Peter Smithers to John Hare, n.d., CCO20/15/2.
22 CPA: 'Report on 2nd European-Christian Democrat conference', John Cope, 13 May 1968, CCO20/15/3.
23 G. Shepherd *Shepherd's Watch* London: Politicos, 2000, p. 161; P. Walker *Staying Power* London: Bloomsbury, 1991, p. 104; N. Tebbit *Upwardly Mobile* London: Weidenfeld and Nicolson, 1998, p. 169.
24 Six resolutions on the subject were received for the 1972 party conference.
25 CPA: Europe Committee, reporting letter Carrington sent to Dodds-Parker, 27 November 1972, CCO20/32/7.
26 CPA: Europe Committee, 27 November 1972, CCO20/32/7.
27 A member of the Danish Centre Democrat Party also joined in 1974.
28 CPA: 'Direct elections and the relationship between the Conservative Party and the European Conservative Group', James Douglas, 8 February 1977, CCO20/32/11.
29 Thorneycroft Mss: Conservative Conference Resolutions 1975, MS278/A962/2/2.
30 Thatcher Foundation Archive: 'The European Democratic Union', Douglas Hurd, 12 April 1978, www.margaretthatcher.org.uk.
31 Jansen *European People's Party*, pp. 68–9, citing the resolution from First EPP Congress and the view of Walloon PSC leader, C.F. Northomb.
32 Thatcher Foundation: Thatcher speech to CDU conference, Hanover, 25 May 1976, www.margaretthatcher.org.uk.
33 Jansen *European People's Party*, p. 69.
34 Dodds-Parker Mss: Tufton Beamish to Anthony Royle, 16 December 1971, MC:P2/7/3MS/5, Magdalen College Archives, Oxford.
35 CPA: Chris Patten to Peter Carrington, 10 January 1974, CCO20/32/9.
36 *Daily Telegraph*, obituary, Scott-Hopkins, 14 March 1995; J. Taylor *Please Stay to the Adjournment* Studley, Brewin Books, 2003, p. 63.
37 CPA: 'Direct elections and the relationship between the Conservative Party and the European Conservative Group', James Douglas, 8 February 1977, CCO20/32/11.
38 Jansen *European People's Party*, p. 116.
39 D. Butler and M. Westlake *British Politics and the European Elections 1994* Basingstoke: Macmillan, 1995, p. 29.
40 Jansen *European People's Party*, pp. 86–7.
41 K. Baker *Turbulent Years* London: Faber and Faber, 1993, p. 351.

42 Jansen *European People's Party*, p. 87.
43 M. Westlake *Britain's Emerging Euro-elites* Aldershot: Dartmouth, 1994, p. 271.
44 Butler and Westlake *British Politics and the European Elections 1994*, p. 102; *Financial Times*, Christoper Prout to editor, 26 February 1994, p. 11; *Guardian*, Christopher Prout to editor, 3 March 1994, p. 23.
45 D. Butler and M. Westlake *British Politics and the European Elections 1999* Basingstoke: Macmillan, 2000, p. 131.
46 *Daily Telegraph*, M. Welsh to editor, 17 June 1999, p. 29; Inglewood to editor, 24 June 1999, p. 27.
47 Taylor *Adjournment*, p. 63.
48 Macmillan-Scott interview, *Today* programme, BBC Radio 4, 30 January 2006.
49 *Daily Telegraph*, 1 July 1999, p. 2.
50 Gawain Towler *Bloc Tory* London: Centre for Policy Studies, 2001. The author was a prospective parliamentary candidate in June 2001 and an advisor to Conservative MEPs.
51 Christopher Beazley 'Blockhead views on *Tory Bloc*' *Reformer Magazine*, Autumn, 2001.
52 *Daily Telegraph*, 10 December 2005, p. 2; 12 December 2005, p. 10; Bill Cash to editor, 12 December 2005, p. 19; David Hannan, 'At the header of Europe', *Sunday Telegraph*, 18 December 2005, p. 32; *Daily Telegraph*, 30 January 2006.
53 CPA: Foreign Affairs Committee, 3 June 1948, CRD2/43/1.
54 H. Berrington *Backbench Opinion in the House of Commons* Oxford: Pergamon, 1973, p. 169. Sixty-five signed.
55 CPA: minutes, Foreign Affairs Committee, Manningham-Buller, 3 June 1948, CRD2/43/1.
56 P. Beswick 'The Tory Strasbourgers and the Evolution of the Conservative Party Debate over Europe, 1945–61' unpublished MPhil, Birmingham University, 2001, p. 24. See also S. Ball (ed.) *Parliament and Politics in the Age of Churchill and Attlee: The Headlam Diaries 1935–51* Cambridge: Royal Historical Society Camden Series, 1999, 17 May, 12 August, 3 September, 22 December 1949, pp. 589, 599, 600, 612.
57 S. Onslow *Backbench Debate within the Conservative Party* Basingstoke: Macmillan, 1997, p. 44.
58 CPA: Foreign Affairs Committee, minutes, 13 March 1963, CRD3/10/15; Rhys Williams Mss: minutes, Executive UK Council of European Movement, views of Boothby, 17 October 1963, J/7/1/1, British Library of Political and Economic Science (BPLES).
59 CPA: Commonwealth and Europe Group, 20 July 1966, CRD3/10/9.
60 CPA: Europe (Co-ordinating) Committee, 28 November 1973, CCO20/32/8.
61 CPA: Foreign Affairs Committee, 7 May 1958, Peter Kirk, CRD2/34/3.
62 P. Catterall (ed.) *The Macmillan Diaries* London: Macmillan, 2003, entry for 4 July 1955, pp. 444–5.
63 Robert Boothby *Recollections of a Rebel* London: Hutchinson, 1978, pp. 220–3; R. Rhodes James *Bob Boothby* London: Hodder and Stoughton, 1991, p. 347.
64 This is a deliberate choice of word so as to avoid any suggestion that they are representatives of the House of Commons.
65 Beswick *Strasbourgers*, p. 30n.
66 Macmillan Mss: Harold to Dorothy, 22 August 1949, letter 2, MS. Macmillan.dep.c.11/1 ff. 37–38.
67 Onslow *Backbench*, p. 96.
68 J. Blondel 'United Kingdom' in K. Lindsay (ed.) *European Assemblies: The Experimental Period 1949–59* London: Stevens and Sons, 1960, p. 137.
69 J. Critchley and M. Halcrow *Collapse of the Stout Party: The Decline and Fall of the Tories* London: Gollancz, 1997, p. 284.
70 Onslow *Backbench*, pp. 96–7.

71  Critchley and Halcrow *Collapse*, p. 284.
72  Butler and Marquand *European Elections and British Politics*, p. 78.
73  Derived from *Who's Who, Dod's, Vacher* entries.
74  Bill Newton Dunn, 'Britain and Strasbourg' witness seminar held 23 February 1995, ICBH, 2002, www.icbh.ac.uk/icbh/brussels/, p. 99.
75  A. Clark *Diaries* London: Weidenfeld and Nicolson, 1993, entry for 6 March 1986, p. 143.
76  M. Westlake *Britain's Emerging Euro-elites*, pp. 20–1.
77  Taylor *Adjournment*, p. 64.
78  CPA: minutes, joint meeting, Foreign Affairs and Imperial Affairs Committees, 1 November 1949, CRD2/34/1.
79  Macmillan to Churchill, 25 April 1950, cited Beswick *Strasbourgers*, p. 32.
80  CPA: 'Contacts with continental right-wing parties', n.d., CCO4/5/328.
81  CPA: 'Strasbourg Study Visit 21–28 September 1952', R.D. Milne, COB21/1/2.
82  CPA: 'External relations', 19 January 1955, G.D. to chairman, CCO4/6/364.
83  CPA: 'Group Report: 2nd Strasbourg Study Visit 20–27th Sept 1953, CCO4/5/328.
84  CPA: Strasbourg Study Visit reports, 1961, 1962, COB58/2, COB57/1.
85  The British delegation also included two Liberals.
86  Cited Butler and Marquand *European Elections and British Politics*, p. 7.
87  CPA: correspondence, July–August 1973, CCO20/32/8; Carrington-Selsdon correspondence, 1973–4, CCO20/32/9.
88  Dodds-Parker Mss: Parker to Douglas Hurd, 3 November 1971, MC:P2/7/3MS/5.
89  CPA: memo, 'The British representatives in the European Parliament', n.d., S. Wingfield Digby, CCO20/32/6.
90  CPA: 2nd report by Policy Group on Direct Elections to the European Parliament, 18 May 1976, CCO20/32/10. A CPC discussion pamphlet, March 1976: 'there must be some doubt whether it will be physically possible for anybody to do both jobs effectively … it would, however, be unreasonable and unduly authoritarian to suggest that British MPs should be prevented by law from standing for election'. Conservative Political Centre *Our Voice in Europe* London: CPC, 1976, p. 14; Similarly, a memo by D. Hurd on behalf of the party, *Select Committee on Direct Elections to the European Assembly 2nd Report* London: HMSO, 1976, 15 July 1976, Appendix 3, p. 16.
91  Butler and Marquand *European Elections and British Politics*, p. 72.
92  Peter Kirk evidence on behalf of ECG to European Parliament, *Select Committee on Direct Elections to the European Assembly 2nd Report*, pp. 40–1.
93  Butler and Marquand *European Elections and British Politics*, p. 77; The nomination experience is described in Taylor *Adjournment*, pp. 59–62.
94  CPA: memo, 'The British representatives in the European Parliament', n.d., S. Wingfield Digby, CCO20/32/6.
95  Butler and Marquand *European Elections and British Politics*, p. 41; 'Britain and Strasbourg' witness seminar held 23 February 1995, ICBH, 2002, www.icbh.ac.uk/icbh/brussels/.
96  Butler and Marquand *European Elections and British Politics*, p. 5; see also Anthony Meyer *Stand Up and Be Counted*, pp. 99–100.
97  CPA: 'Direct elections and the relationship between the Conservative Party and the European Conservative Group', James Douglas, 8 February 1977, CCO20/32/11.
98  Dodds-Parker Mss: Parker to Humphrey Atkins (chief whip), 29 March 1974, MC:P2/7/3C/5.
99  CPA: 'Your voice in Europe', Royle Policy Group, n.d., CCO20/32/10. This is articulated in a Conservative Political Centre discussion pamphlet *Our Voice in Europe*, March 1976, p. 14.

100 'Britain and Strasbourg' witness seminar held 23 February 1995, ICBH, 2002, www.icbh.ac.uk/icbh/brussels/, pp. 106, 107–8.
101 *The Times Guide to the European Parliament 1984* on the Spinelli vote: 'This divided approach to a resolution which incorporated three key proposals to which Mrs Thatcher and her Government were bitterly opposed – ending the veto, adding to Parliament's powers, and the Community raising taxation – was not warmly welcomed in London.'
102 Thatcher *Downing Street*, p. 749.
103 D. Butler and P. Jowett *Party Strategies in Britain: A Study of the 1984 European Elections* Basingstoke: Macmillan, 1985, p. 21; see also *The Times*, Tom Spencer MEP to editor, 12 July 1984, p. 15.
104 Ridley *My Style*, p. 141; Butler and Jowett *Party Strategies*, pp. 26–7.
105 Butler and Westlake *British Politics and European Election 1994*, pp. 30–1.
106 Butler and Marquand *European Elections and British Politics*, p. 9.
107 Butler and Marquand *European Elections and British Politics*, pp. 21–2.
108 J. Lodge *The 1994 Elections to the European Parliament* Aldershot: Pinter, 1996, p. 1.
109 M. Westlake *Britain's Emerging Euro-elites*, p. 115n.
110 Derived from Butler and Marquand *European Elections and British Politics*, pp. 8–10, quotation p. 10; *The Times*, obituary, Peter Kirk, 18 April 1977, p. 14.
111 He initially resigned in February 1979 but was persuaded to remain until after the election in June.
112 Butler and Marquand *European Elections and British Politics*, pp. 72–3.
113 Butler and Jowett *Party Strategies in Britain*, p. 24.
114 Peter Price, 'Britain and Strasbourg' witness seminar held 23 February 1995, ICBH, 2002, www.icbh.ac.uk/icbh/brussels/, p. 101.
115 'The European Parliament 84', *Which?*, 1984, pp. 265–7.
116 Tuckman Mss: correspondence V. Graham to Tuckman, October 1983, MS270/A291/6/3/3.
117 Bill Newton Dunn, 'Britain and Strasbourg' witness seminar held 23 February 1995, ICBH, 2002, www.icbh.ac.uk/icbh/brussels/, p. 104.
118 Young *This Blessed Plot*, p. 42.
119 Ridley *My Style*, p. 139.
120 James *Boothby*, p. 347.
121 Macmillan diary, entry for 4 July 1955, cited P. Catterall 'Macmillan and Europe' paper presented to WCBS, Houston, 2000.
122 CPA: minutes, Europe (Co-ordinating) Committee, 26 July 1973, CCO20/32/8.
123 CPA: minutes, Europe (Co-ordinating) Committee, 30 January 1974, CCO20/32/9.
124 N. Nicolson (ed.) *Diaries and Letters of Harold Nicolson 1945–62*, H.N. to Phillippa Nicolson, 22 October 1956, p. 311.
125 *Daily Telegraph*, Wingfield Digby obituary, 26 March 1998, p. 31.
126 Macmillan Mss: Harold to Dorothy, 22 August 1949, MS.Macmilllan.dep.c.11/1 f. 10.
127 Macmillan Mss: Harold to Dorothy, 22 August 1949, MS.Macmilllan.dep.c.11/1 f. 32.
128 Macmillan Mss: Harold to Dorothy, 24 August 1949, MS.Macmillan.dep.c.11/1 ff. 54–55.
129 Macmillan Mss: Harold to Dorothy, 22 August 1949, MS.Macmillan.dep.c.11/1 ff. 22–23.
130 Ball *Headlam Diaries*, entry for 12 August 1949, p. 599.
131 Taylor *Adjournment*, p. 66.
132 Bill Newton Dunn 'Letter from Europe' *Reformer Magazine*, Autumn, 2000.
133 Taylor *Adjournment*, p. 55.

134 Butler and Marquand *European Elections and British Politics*, p. 27–8; see also Curry *Diaries*, pp. 238–9.
135 Westlake *Euro-elites*, pp. 52, 73n.–74n.
136 Butler and Marquand *European Elections and British Politics*, pp. 27–8.
137 'Britain and Strasbourg' witness seminar held 23 February 1995, ICBH, 2002, www.icbh.ac.uk/icbh/brussels/.
138 Curry *Diaries*, entry for 21 February 1991, p. 238.
139 Butler and Jowett *Party Strategies in Britain*, pp. 19, 20, 24.
140 Bill Newton Dunn 'Letter from Europe' *Reformer Magazine*, Autumn, 2000.
141 For an explanation of 'co-decision' see Leon Brittan *Europe: The Europe We Need* London: Hamish Hamilton, 1994, p. 235.
142 Ridley *My Style*, pp. 68–9.
143 Speaking on Thames Television programme *Europe the Great Debate*, 11 August 1970, cited M. Holmes 'The Conservative Party and Europe' Bruges Group paper No. 17, 1994, p. 12.
144 CPA: Strasbourg Study visit 22–30 September 1961, COB58/2.
145 Rhys Williams Mss: minutes, Management Committee, UK European Movement, 1 November 1961, J/7/1/1.
146 CPA: Report for Committee on Links with Europe, 15 January 1962, CCO20/32/1; see also R. Jackson *The Powers of the European Parliament* London: CPC, n.d. [1978], pp. 10–11; but he concludes this 'is hardly realistic'.
147 CPA: 'Direct elections and the relationship between the Conservative Party and the European Conservative Group', James Douglas, 8 February 1977, CCO20/32/11.
148 A development welcomed by Conservative MEPs, see 'Britain and Strasbourg' witness seminar held 23 February 1995, ICBH, 2002, www.icbh.ac.uk/icbh/brussels/.
149 Cockfield *The European Union*, p. 99.
150 CPA: 'Europe', Douglas-Home, 18 July 1969, LCC(69)252.
151 CPA: 'Direct elections to the European Parliament', Douglas Hurd, 25 February 1976, CCO20/32/10.
152 Taylor *Adjournment*, p. 66.
153 *Daily Telegraph*, 2 June 1979, cited Westlake *Euro-elites*, p. 73n.
154 Brittan *Europe*, pp. 226–7.
155 Chris Patten 'Letter from Europe' *Reformer Magazine*, Winter, 2001.
156 Ridley *My Style*, p. 141.
157 CPA: 'Europe' by Douglas-Home, 18 July 1969, LCC(69)252.
158 Rhys Williams Mss: minutes, Management Cttee, UK Council of the European Movement, Maurice Macmillan, 1 November 1961, J/7/1/1.
159 Curry *Diaries*, entry for 10 June 1991, p. 267.
160 Dodds-Parker Mss: D.-P. to Hurd, 3 November 1971, MC:P2/7/3MS/5.
161 W. Wyatt *Journals of Woodrow Wyatt: Thatcher's Fall and Major's Rise*, vol. 2, ed. S. Curtis London: Macmillan, 1999, Thatcher to Wyatt, 12 February 1989, p. 30.
162 Cockfield *The European Union*, p. 110.
163 Brittan *A Diet of Brussels* London: Little Brown, 2000, pp. 182–3.
164 Leon Brittan *et al. The Future of the EU: A Positive Conservative Approach*, p. 14.
165 Cockfield *The European Union*, p. 106; these ideas were also incorporated into Brittan *The Future of the EU*.
166 *Daily Telegraph*, Churchill to editor, 11 July 2000, p. 19. In fact according to a House of Lords Parliamentary question on 13 January 2003 the UK has been subject to 102,567 EU directives since entry in 1973. *Hansard: House of Lords Debates*, 13 January 2003.
167 *Daily Telegraph*, Bill Cash to editor, 19 October 1999, p. 27.
168 Cockfield *The European Union*, p. 108.

169 Conservative Central Office press release, 3 May 2001, 'Conservatives unveil EU reform plans', www.conservatives.com/news.
170 *Daily Telegraph*, 23 July 1996, p. 16.
171 Cockfield *The European Union*, p. 115.
172 Brittan *et al. The Future of the EU*, pp. 12–14.
173 Home thought the Council overly bureaucratic and believed six-monthly rotations of the presidency gave insufficient time to settle into the job. D.R. Thorpe *Alec Douglas-Home* London: Sinclair-Stevenson, 1996, p. 419.
174 CPA: 'Europe' by Douglas-Home, 8 July 1969, LCC(69)252.
175 Howe *Conflict*, p. 455.
176 Conservative Central Office press release, 3 May 2001, 'Conservatives unveil EU reform plans', www.conservatives.com/news.
177 Chris Patten 'Letter from Europe' *Reformer Magazine*, Winter, 2001; quotation Bill Newton Dunn 'Letter from Europe' *Reformer Magazine*, Autumn, 2000.
178 Roy Perry 'Just how Democratic is the EU' *Reformer Magazine*, Spring, 2002; Brittan *et al. The Future of the EU*, p. 8.
179 Clark *Diaries*, entry for 26 October 1988, p. 233.
180 J. Nott *Here Today Gone Tomorrow* London: Politicos, 2002, pp. 152–4; K. Baker *Turbulent Years* London: Faber and Faber, 1993, p. 443; M. Parris *Chance Witness* London: Viking, 2002, p. 151; Ridley *My Style*, pp. 141–2.
181 J. Cole *As It Seemed to Me* London: Weidenfeld and Nicolson, 1995, p. 347.
182 Brittan *Europe*, p. 223.
183 Howe *Conflict*, p. 454.
184 Norman Tebbit *Upwardly Mobile* London: Weidenfeld and Nicolson, 1988, p. 168.
185 A House of Lords Law Ruling in 1996 on the Factortame case overturned for the first time an Act of Parliament for being incompatible with Community obligations. The case had been brought by a Spanish fishing company objecting to the restrictions imposed on its fleet by the 1988 Merchant Shipping Act.
186 David Heathcote-Amory *The European Constitution* London: CPS, June 2003, pp. 3, 5.
187 *Sunday Telegraph*, 14 September 1996, citing Lord Tebbit addressing YC Rally, Southport.
188 E.g. CPA: Wales and Monmouthshire YCs report on 'Britain and Europe', n.d., CCO506/14/15.
189 Jackson *The Powers of the European Parliament*, p. 10.
190 *Daily Telegraph*, 14 September 1996.
191 *Daily Telegraph*, 'Why Europe has made me resign', 23 July 1996, p. 16.
192 *Hansard*, vol. 96, cols 378–9 (Duncan Smith), Div. Nos. 202–3; main motion secured 66 Conservative votes, and was lost by 77 to 83. Six Conservatives voted against; see Gill *Whips Nightmare*, p. 189.

## Conclusion

1 N. Piers Ludlow *Dealing with Britain: The Six and the First UK Application to the EEC* Cambridge: Cambridge University Press, 1997.
2 A.S. Milward *The UK and the EC, volume 1: The Rise and Fall of a National Strategy 1945–63* London: Frank Cass, 2002, pp. 272–3; J.Buller *National Statecraft and European Integration: The Conservative Government and the European Union* London: Pinter, 2000, pp. 127–31.
3 Ludlow *Dealing*, p. 246.
4 Milward *Rise and Fall*, p. 356–7.
5 P. Seyd and P. Whiteley 'Conservative Grassroots: An Overview' in S. Ludlam and M.J. Smith (eds) *Contemporary British Conservatism* Basingstoke: Macmillan, 1996, pp. 63–85.

6 This is essentially the theme, although for an earlier period, of J. Charmley *Splendid Isolation: Britain and the Balance of Power 1874–1914* London: Hodder and Stoughton, 1999.

7 This latter point is made by D. Cannadine *In Churchill's Shadow* London: Allen Lane, 2002.

8 J. Amery *The Life of Joseph Chamberlain*, vol. 6, London: Macmillan, 1951, pp. 1,050–5.

9 J. Barnes 'Ideologies and Factions' in S. Ball and A. Seldon (eds) *Conservative Century* Oxford: Oxford University Press, 1994, pp. 315–46.

10 For this latter point I am drawing upon E.H.H. Green *Ideologies of Conservatism* Oxford: Oxford University Press, 2002, p. 189.

11 Austen Chamberlain Mss: A.C. to King, 9 February 1925, AC52/378, cited R. Grayson *Austen Chamberlain and the Commitment to Europe: British Foreign Policy 1924–29* London: Cass, 1997, p. 41.

12 Paragraph based upon D.Dutton *Austen Chamberlain: Gentleman in Politics* Bolton: Ross Anderson, 1985, pp. 238–40, quotation p. 239.

13 E.g. N.C. Mss: N.C. to Hilda, 6 December 1931, in R. Self (ed.) *The Neville Chamberlain Diary Letters: Volume Three* Aldershot: Ashgate, 2002, pp. 295–8.

14 *Hansard*, vol. 333, 24 March 1938.

15 J. Charmley *Chamberlain and the Lost Peace* London: Hodder and Stoughton, 1989.

16 P. Kennedy *Realities behind Diplomacy: Background Influences on British External Policy 1865–1980* London: Fontana, 1985, p. 371.

17 S. Onslow *Backbench Debate within the Conservative Party and Its Influence on British Foreign Policy 1948–57* Basingstoke: Macmillan, 1997, p. 27.

18 Conservative Party Archive: V.B. Petherick to COO, 6 September 1962, CCO500/31/4, Bodleian Library, Oxford.

19 Birmingham CA: Central Council, 26 September 1947, AQ329.94249CON f. 144, Birmingham Central Library.

# Bibliography

## Archival sources

### Organisations

Britain in Europe, House of Lords Record Office.
Conservative Party Archive, Bodleian Library, Oxford.
Scottish Conservative and Unionist Party Archive, National Library of Scotland.

### Private papers

Avon Mss [Anthony Eden], Birmingham University, Special Collections.
Boyle Mss, Leeds University, Special Collections.
Crookshank Mss, Bodleian Library, Oxford.
Dodds-Parker Mss, Magdalen College, Oxford.
Emmett Mss, Bodleian Library, Oxford.
Headlam Mss, Durham Record Office.
Hinchingbrooke Mss [Victor Montagu], Dorset Record Office.
Legge-Bourke Mss, Leeds University, Special Collections.
Lennox-Boyd Mss, Bodleian Library, Oxford.
Macmillan Mss, Bodleian Library, Oxford.
Marten Mss, Bodleian Library, Oxford.
Rhys-Williams Mss, British Library of Political and Economic Science.
Thorneycroft Mss, Southampton University, Special Collections.
Tuckman Mss, Southampton University, Special Collections.
Tufton Beamish Mss, East Sussex Record Office.
Waterhouse Mss, private possession.

### Conservative constituency associations

Accrington, John Rylands Library, University of Manchester.
Aldershot and North Hampshire, Hampshire Record Office.
Ayrshire Central, National Library of Scotland.
Birmingham, Birmingham Central Library.
Birmingham, All Saints, Birmingham Central Library.
Birmingham, Aston, Birmingham Central Library.
Birmingham, Ladywood, Birmingham Central Library.
Birmingham Young Conservatives, Birmingham Central Library.
Blackpool North, Lancashire Record Office.
Blackpool South, Lancashire Record Office.
Brixton, British Library of Political and Economic Science.
Chelmsford, Essex Record Office.
Chippenham (North Wiltshire), Wiltshire Record Office.

Cornwall North, Cornwall Record Office.
Dorset West, Dorset Record Office.
Easington, Northumberland Record Office.
Edinburgh North, Edinburgh City Archives.
Glasgow, National Library of Scotland.
Harborough, Leicestershire Record Office.
Hartlepool West, Durham Record Office.
Langstone, Portsmouth Record Office.
Louth, Lincolnshire Archives.
Newcastle North, Northumberland Record Office.
Newcastle-upon-Tyne West, Tyne and Wear Archives.
Northampton, Northamptonshire Record Office.
Northern Area, Northumberland Record Office.
Norwood, Lambeth Archives.
Nottingham South, Nottinghamshire Record Office.
Penryn and Falmouth, Cornwall Record Office.
Plymouth Sutton, West Devon Record Office.
Portsmouth South Young Conservatives, Portsmouth Record Office.
Reigate and Banstead, Surrey Record Office.
Rushcliffe, Nottinghamshire Record Office.
Salisbury, Wiltshire Record Office.
Sheffield Central, Sheffield City Archives.
Sheffield Eccleshall, Sheffield City Archives.
Sheffield Park, Sheffield City Archives.
Shoreham, West Sussex Record Office.
South Buckinghamshire, Buckinghamshire Record Office.
Southampton Test, Southampton City Archives.
Swindon, private possession.
Truro, Cornwall Record Office.
Tynemouth, Tyne and Wear Archives.
Vauxhall (Kennington), British Library of Political and Economic Science.
Wansbeck, Tyne and Wear Archives.
Warwick, Leamington and Kenilworth, Warwickshire Record Office.
Waterloo (Crosby), Lancashire Record Office.
West Wiltshire, Wiltshire Record Office.
Winchester, Hampshire Record Office.
Wood Green and Lower Tottenham, Greater London Record Office.

### Interviews

Transcripts held by British Oral Archive of Political and Administrative History, British Library of Political and Economic Science, London School of Economics.
Viscount Amory
Lord Brooke of Cumnor
Lord Butler of Saffron Walden
Lord Carr of Hadley
Lord Inchyra
Viscount Muirshiel
Lord Strathclyde
Lord Boyle of Handsworth

### Newspapers and magazines

*Daily Express*
*Daily Telegraph*
*Hampshire Chronicle*

*Harborough Mail*
*Independent*
*Reformer Magazine*
*The Sunday Times*
*The Times Magazine*
*Warwickshire Advertiser*

## Published and digital resources

*Archives of the British Conservative Party*, microfiche, Harvester/Primary Media Resources.
*The Times Digital On-Line Archive*, Gale Publishing.
*Macmillan Cabinet Papers 1957–63 Online*, Adam Matthew Publishing.
Churchill, R. (ed.) *Europe Unite: Speeches 1947 and 1948 by Winston Churchill* London: Cassell, 1950.
Ritchie, R. *Enoch Powell on 1992* London: Anaya, 1989.
[Thatcher, M.] *Complete Public Statements of Margaret Thatcher, 1945–90* Oxford: Oxford University Press, 1998; CD-ROM.
*Hansard: The Debates of the House of Commons*, 5th and 6th series, London: HMSO.
*Minutes of Evidence to Select Committee on Direct Elections to the European Parliament* London: HMSO, 1976.
*Select Committee on Direct Elections to the European Parliament 2nd Report* London: HMSO, 1976.
O'Neill, C. *Britain's Entry into the European Community: Report on the Negotiations of 1970–72* London: Whitehall History Publishing/Frank Cass, 2000.

## Select bibliography

Alderman, K. 'The Conservative Party Leadership Election of 1995' *Parliamentary Affairs* 49(2), 1996, pp. 316–32.
—— 'The Conservative Party Leadership Election of 1997' *Parliamentary Affairs* 51(1), 1998, pp. 1–17.
Alderman, K. and Carter, N. 'The Conservative Party Leadership Election of 2001' *Parliamentary Affairs* 55(4), 2002, pp. 569–85.
Aldous, R. and Lee, S. (eds) *Harold Macmillan's World Role* Basingstoke: Macmillan, 1996.
Amery, J. *The Life of Joseph Chamberlain*, vol. 6, London: Macmillan, 1951.
—— 'A Conservative view of the Commonwealth' *Political Quarterly* XXIV, 1953 pp. 167–80.
Amery, L. 'The British Empire and the Pan European Idea' *Journal of the Royal Institute of International Affairs*, January, 1930 pp. 1–22.
Ashford, N. 'The European Economic Community' in Layton-Henry, Z. (ed.) *Conservative Party Politics* London: Macmillan, 1980.
—— 'The Political Parties' in George, S. (ed.) *Britain and the European Community: The Politics of Semi-Detachment* Oxford: Oxford University Press, 1992.
Aughey, A. 'The Party and Foreign Policy' in Norton, P. (ed.) *The Conservative Party* London: Prentice Hall, 1996.
Aughey, A. and Norton, P. *Conservatives and Conservatism* London: Temple Smith, 1981.
Baker, D., Gamble, A. and Ludlam, S. 'More "Classless" and Less "Thatcherite"? Conservative MPs after the 1992 Election' *Parliamentary Affairs* 45, 1992, pp. 656–68.
—— '1846 ... 1906 ... 1996? Conservative Splits and European Integration' *Political Quarterly* 64, 1993, pp. 420–34.

—— 'Whips or Scorpions? The Maastricht Vote and the Conservative Party' *Parliamentary Affairs* 46(2), 1993, pp. 151–66.

—— 'Mapping Conservative Fault Lines: Problems of Typology' in P. Dunleavy and G. Stayner (eds) *Contemporary Political Studies 1994* Exeter: Exeter University Press, 1994.

—— 'The Parliamentary Siege of Maastricht' *Parliamentary Affairs* 47(1), 1994, pp. 37–60.

Baker, D., Gamble, A. and Seawright, D. 'MPs and Europe' *British Elections and Parties Review* 9, 1999, pp. 170–85.

Baker, K. *Turbulent Years* London: Faber and Faber, 1993.

Ball, M. *The Conservative Conference and Euro-sceptical Motions* London: Bruges Group Publication, 1996.

Ball, S. *Baldwin and the Conservative Party* London: Yale University Press, 1988.

—— 'Local Conservatism and the Evolution of the Party Organisation' in Ball, S. and Seldon, A. (eds) *Conservative Century* Oxford: Oxford University Press, 1994.

—— 'The National and Regional Party Structure' in Ball, S. and Seldon, A. (eds) *Conservative Century* Oxford: Oxford University Press, 1994.

——'Harold Macmillan and the Politics of Defence' *Twentieth Century British History* 6, 1995, pp. 78–100.

—— *Parliament and Politics in the Age of Churchill and Attlee: The Headlam Diaries 1935–51* Cambridge: Royal Historical Society Camden Series, 1999.

Ball, S. and Holliday, I. (eds) *Mass Conservatism: The Conservatives and the Public since the 1880s* Newbury: Frank Cass, 2002.

Ball, S. and Seldon, A. (eds) *Conservative Century* Oxford: Oxford University Press, 1994.

—— *The Heath Government: A Reappraisal* London: Longman, 1996.

Barnes, J. and Cockett, R. 'Factions and Ideology' in Ball, S. and Seldon, A. (eds) *Conservative Century* Oxford: OUP, 1994.

Barr, J. *The Bow Group: A History* London: Politicos, 2001.

Barty, J. 'Living with the Euro' *Reformer Magazine*, Spring, 1999, http://core2.trg.org.uk/reformer/spring1999.

Baston, L. *Reggie: The Life of Reginald Maudling* Thrupp: Sutton, 2004.

Baylis, J. *The Diplomacy of Pragmatism: Britain and the Formation of NATO* Basingstoke: Macmillan, 1993.

Beamish, T.P.H. and St John Stevas, N. *Sovereignty: Substance or Shadow* London: CPC, 1971.

Beazley, C. 'Blockhead Views on Tory Bloc' *Reformer Magazine*, Autumn, 2001, http://core2.trg.org.uk/reformer/autumn2001.

Beck, P. 'Politicians versus Historians: Lord Avon's "Appeasement Battle" against "Lamentably, Appeasement-Minded" Historians' *Twentieth Century British History* 9(4), 1998, pp. 396–419.

Beichman, A. 'Hugger-Mugger in Old Queen Street: The Origins of the Conservative Research Department' *Journal of Contemporary History* 13(4), 1978, pp. 671–88.

Bellamy, R. (ed.) *Constitutionalism, Democracy and Sovereignty* Aldershot: Avebury, 1996.

Beloff, N. *The General Says No: Britain's Exclusion from Europe* Harmondsworth: Penguin, 1973.

Benn, S. 'The Uses of Sovereignty' *Political Studies* 3(2), 1955, pp. 109–22.

Berrington, H. *Backbench Opinion in the House of Commons* Oxford: Pergamon, 1973.

Birn, D.S. *The League of Nations Union* Oxford: Clarendon Press, 1981.

Blackwell, N. *A Defining Moment?* London: CPS, 2003.

Blondel, J. 'United Kingdom' in Lindsay, K (ed.) *European Assemblies: The Experimental Period 1949–59* London: Stevens and Sons, 1960.

Body, R. *The Breakdown of Europe* London: NEP, 1989.

—— *Europe of Many Circles: Constructing a Wider Europe* London: NEP, 1990.

Boothby, R. *About Western Union* London: CPC, 1949.

—— *Recollections of a Rebel* London: Hutchinson, 1978.

Boyson, R. *Speaking My Mind* London: Peter Owen, 1994.

Brandreth, G. *Breaking the Code: Westminster Diaries 1990–1997* London: Weidenfeld and Nicolson, 1999.

Branston, U. *Britain and European Unity* London: CPC, 1953.

Brittan, L. *Europe: The Europe We Need* London: Hamish Hamilton, 1994.

—— *A Diet of Brussels: The Changing Face of Europe* London: Little Brown, 2000.

Brittan, L., Howe, Lord, Heseltine, Lord, Hurd, Lord, Clarke, K., Gummer, J., Curry, D., Hayhoe, Lord, Garel-Jones, Lord, Taylor, I., Jackson, R., Walter, R., Gent, C., Tugendhat, Lord, Bishop, M., Inglewood, Lord, Bowness, Lord, Marshall, G., Welsh, M. *The Future of the EU: A Positive Conservative Approach* London: Tory Reform Group, 2003.

Broad, R. *Labour's European Dilemma* Basingstoke: Macmillan, 2000.

Broad, R. and Preston, V. (eds) *Moored to the Continent? Britain and European Integration* London: Institute of Historical Research, 2001.

Bromund, T. 'Whitehall, the National Farmers' Union and Plan G, 1956–57' *Contemporary British History* 15(2), 2001, pp. 76–97.

Brunson, M. *A Ringside Seat: The Autobiography* London: Hodder and Stoughton, 2000.

Buller, J. *National Statecraft and European Integration* London: Pinter, 2000.

Bulpitt, J. 'The European Questions: Rules, National Modernisation and the Ambiguities of *Primat der Innenpolitik*' in Marquand, D. and Seldon, A. (eds) *The Ideas that Shaped Post-war Britain* London: Fontana, 1996.

Butler, D. and Butler, G. *Twentieth Century British Political Facts* Basingstoke: Macmillan, 2000.

Butler, D. and Jowett, P. *Party Strategies in Britain: A Study of the 1984 European Elections* Basingstoke: Macmillan, 1985.

Butler, D. and Kavanagh, D. *The British General Election of 1987* Basingstoke: Macmillan, 1988.

—— *The British General Election of 1992* Basingstoke: Macmillan, 1993.

—— *The British General Election of 1997* Basingstoke: Macmillan, 1997.

—— *The British General Election of 2001* Basingstoke: Palgrave, 2002.

Butler, D. and King, A. *The British General Election of 1964* London: Macmillan, 1965.

—— *The British General Election of 1966* London: Macmillan, 1966.

Butler, D. and Kitzinger, U. *The 1975 Referendum* London: Macmillan, 1976.

Butler, D. and Marquand, D. *European Elections and British Politics* London: Longman, 1981.

Butler, D. and Pinto-Duschinsky, M. *The British General Election of 1970* London: Macmillan 1971.

Butler, D. and Rose, R. *The British General Election of 1959* London: Macmillan, 1960.

Butler, D. and Westlake, M. *British Politics and the European Elections 1994* Basingstoke: Macmillan, 1994.

—— *British Politics and the European Elections 1999* Basingstoke: Macmillan, 2000.

Butt, R. 'The Common Market and Conservative Party Politics 1961–62' *Government and Opposition* 2(3), 1967, pp. 372–86.

Campbell, J. *Edward Heath: A Biography* London: Pimlico, 1994.

—— *Margaret Thatcher: Grocers Daughter, Volume One* London: Jonathan Cape, 2000.

—— *Margaret Thatcher: Iron Lady, Volume Two* London: Jonathan Cape, 2002.

Camps, M. *Britain and the European Community 1955–63* London: Oxford University Press, 1964.

Cannadine, D. *In Churchill's Shadow* London: Allen Lane, 2002.

Carlton, D. *Anthony Eden: A Biography* London: Allen Lane, 1981.

Carrington, Lord *Reflect on Things Past* London: Collins, 1988.

Cartledge, B. 'Margaret Thatcher: Personality and Foreign Policy' in Pugliese, S. (ed.) *The Political Legacy of Margaret Thatcher* London: Politicos, 2003.

Cash, B. *Against a Federal Europe: The Battle for Britain* London: Duckworth, 1991.

Castle, B. *The Castle Diaries 1964–70* London: Weidenfeld and Nicolson, 1980.

—— *The Castle Diaries 1974–6* London: Weidenfeld and Nicolson, 1980.

Catterall, P. (ed.) *The Macmillan Diaries 1950–57* London: Macmillan, 2003.

Ceadel, M. 'The First British Referendum: The Peace Ballot, 1934–35' *English Historical Review* 95, 1980, pp. 810–39.

Chamberlain, A. 'Great Britain as a European Power' *Journal of the Royal Institute of International Affairs*, March, 1930 pp. 180–8.

Charlton, D. *The Price of Victory* London: BBC, 1983.

Charmley, J. *Chamberlain and the Lost Peace* London: Hodder and Stoughton, 1989.

—— *Splendid Isolation: Britain and the Balance of Power 1874–1914* London: Hodder and Stoughton, 1999.

Chatham House *Britain in Western Europe: WEU and Atlantic Alliance* London: Royal Institute for International Affairs, 1955.

Chryos, E., Kitromidldes, P. and Svolopoulos, C. (eds) *The Idea of European Community in History* Athens: National University of Athens, 2003.

Clark, A. *Diaries* London: Weidenfeld and Nicolson, 1993.

Cockfield, Lord. *The European Union: Creating the Single Market* London: Wiley Chancery Law, 1994.

Cole J. *As It Seemed to Me* London: Weidenfeld and Nicolson, 1995.

Collings, D. and Seldon, A. 'Conservatives in Opposition' *Parliamentary Affairs* 54, 2001, pp. 624–37.

Conservative Central Office *Conservative Campaign Guide* London: Conservative Central Office, 1964.

—— *Rising Standards in Europe* London: Conservative Central Office, 1971.

—— *The Strong Voice in Europe* London: Conservative Central Office, 1984.

—— *A Strong Britain in a Strong Europe* London: Conservative Central Office, 1994.

—— *In Europe, Not Run by Europe* London: Conservative Central Office, 1999.

—— *Putting Britain First* London: Conservative Central Office, 2004.

Conservative Political Centre *Our Voice in Europe* London: CPC, 1976.

Cook, C. and Ramsden, J. *By-elections in British Politics* London: UCL Press, 1997.

Corbet, R. Hugh (ed.) *Britain Not Europe: Commonwealth before Common Market* London: ACML, 1967.

Cowley, P. 'How Did He Do That? The Second Round of the 1990 Conservative Leadership Election' in Broughton, D. (ed.) *British Elections and Parties Yearbook 1996* London: Frank Cass, 1996.

Cowley, P. and Bailey, M. 'Peasants' Uprising or Religious War? Re-examining the 1975 Conservative Leadership Contest' *British Journal of Political Science* 30, 2000, pp. 599–629.

Cowley, P. and Green, J. 'New Leaders, Same Problems: The Conservatives' in Geddes, A. and Tonge, J. (eds) *Britain Decides: The UK General Election 2005* Basingstoke: Palgrave, 2005.

Cowling, M. *The Impact of Hitler: British Politics and British Policy 1933–40* London: Cambridge University Press, 1975.

Craig, F.W.S. *Europe Votes I: European Parliamentary Results 1979* Chichester: PRS, 1980.

Criddle, B. 'Members of Parliament' in Ball, S. and Seldon, A. (eds) *Conservative Century* Oxford: Oxford University Press, 1994.

Critchley, J. and Halcrow, M. *Collapse of the Stout Party: The Decline and Fall of the Tories* London: Gollancz, 1997.

Crowson, N.J. 'Conservative Parliamentary Dissent over Foreign Policy during the Premiership of Neville Chamberlain: Myth or Reality?' *Parliamentary History* 14(3), 1995, pp. 315–36.

—— *Facing Fascism: The Conservative Party and the European Dictators, 1935–40* London: Routledge, 1997.

—— *The Longman Companion to the Conservative Party since 1830* Harlow: Pearsons, 2001.

—— 'Lord Hinchingbrooke, Europe and the November 1962 South Dorset By-election' *Contemporary British History* 17(4), 2003, pp. 43–64.

Currie, E. *Lifelines* London: Sidgwick and Jackson, 1989.

—— *Diaries 1987–1992* London: Little Brown, 2000.

Curtis, S. (ed.) *Journals of Woodrow Wyatt: Thatcher's Fall and Major's Rise*, vol. 2, London: Macmillan, 1992.

Daddow, O. (ed.) *Harold Wilson and European Integration: Britain's Second Application to Join the EEC* London: Frank Cass, 2003.

—— *Britain and Europe since 1945: Historiographical Perspectives on Integration* Manchester: Manchester University Press, 2004.

Dale, I. (ed.) *Conservative Party Manifestos 1945–2000* London: Routledge, 1999.

Davies, N. *Europe: A History* Oxford: Oxford University Press, 1996.

Deighton, A. *The Impossible Peace: Britain, the Division of Germany, and the Origins of the Cold War* Oxford: Clarendon Press, 1993.

—— 'Last Piece of the Jigsaw: Britain and the Creation of Western European Union 1954' *Contemporary European History* 7(2), 1998, pp. 181–97.

Deighton, A and Ludlow, Piers '"A Conditional Application": British Management of the 1st Attempt to Seek Membership of the EEC, 1961–63' in Deighton, A. (ed.) *Building Postwar Europe* London: Macmillan, 1995, pp. 107–26.

Dell, E. *The Schuman Plan and the British Abdication of Leadership in Europe* Oxford: Oxford University Press, 1995.

Denman, R. *Missed Chances: Britain and Europe in the Twentieth Century* London: Cassell, 1996.

Dickie, J. *Inside the Foreign Office* London: Chapmans, 1992.

Diez, T. 'Europe as a Discursive Battleground' *Nordic Journal of International Studies* 36(1), 2001, pp.5–38.

Dockrill, S. *Britain's Policy for West German Rearmament 1950–55* Cambridge: Cambridge University Press, 1991.

Dudley, N. 'Britain, the Tories and the Euro-Zone' *Reformer Magazine*, Spring, 1999, http://core2.trg.org.uk/reformer/spring1999.

Dutton, D. *Austen Chamberlain: Gentleman in Politics* Bolton: Ross Anderson, 1985.

—— 'Anticipating Maastricht: The Conservative Party and Britain's First Application to Join the European Community' *Contemporary Record* 7(3), 1993, pp. 522–40.

—— *Anthony Eden: A Life and Reputation* London: Arnold, 1997.

—— *History of the Liberal Party in the Twentieth Century* Basingstoke: Palgrave, 2004.

Ellison, J. 'Harold Macmillan's Fear of "Little Europe"' Leicester University Discussion Papers BE95, 5 September 1995.

—— 'Accepting the Inevitable: Britain and European Integration' in Kaiser, W. and Starek, G. (eds) *British Foreign Policy 1955–64* Basingstoke: Macmillan, 1999.

—— *Threatening Europe: Britain and the Creation of the European Community 1955–58* Basingstoke: Macmillan, 2000.

European Movement *European Movement and Council of Europe* London: Hutchinson.

Evans, H. *Downing Street Diary: Macmillan Years 1957–63* London: Hodder and Stoughton, 1981.

Evans J. 'Law and Order: What Is the Role of the EU?' *Reformer Magazine*, Autumn, 2002, http://core2.trg.org.uk/reformer/autumn2002.

Fisher, J. 'Political Donations to the Conservative Party' *Parliamentary Affairs* 47(1), 1994, pp. 61–72.

Foreign and Commonwealth Office *Facts and Fairy Tales Revisited* London: Foreign and Commonwealth Office, 1995.

Forster, A. *Euroscepticism in Contemporary British Politics: Opposition to Europe in the Conservative and Labour Parties* London: Routledge, 2002.

Francis, M. and Zweiniger-Bargielowska, I. *The Conservatives and Society 1880–1990* Cardiff: University of Wales Press, 1996.

Frasure, R. and Kornberg, A. 'Constituency Agents and British Politics' *British Journal of Political Science* 5, 1975, p. 459.

Fursdon, E. *The European Defence Community* London: Macmillan, 1980.

Gambles, A. *Protection and Politics: Conservative Economic Discourse 1815–1852* Woodbridge: Royal Historical Society/Boydell Press, 1999.

Gardiner, G. *A Europe for the Regions* London: Conservative Political Centre, 1971.

Garnett, M. and Aitkens, I. *Splendid! Splendid! The Authorised Biography of Willie Whitelaw* London: Cape, 2002.

Geddes, A. and Tonge, J. (eds) *Britain Decides: The UK General Election 2005* Basingstoke: Palgrave, 2005.

Gehler, M. and Kaiser, W. 'Transnationalism and Early European Integration: The *Nouvelles Equipes Internationales* and the Geneva Circle 1945–57' *Historical Journal* 44(3), 2001, pp. 773–98.

George, S. 'Britain and the European Community' in *Contemporary Britain: An Annual Review 1990* Oxford: Blackwell, 1990, pp. 63–71.

—— *Britain and European Integration since 1945* Oxford: Blackwells, 1991.

—— 'Britain and the European Community' in *Contemporary Britain: An Annual Review 1991* Oxford: Blackwell, 1991, pp. 68–75.

—— 'Britain and the European Community' in *Contemporary Britain: An Annual Review 1993* Oxford: Blackwell, 1993, pp. 87–96.

—— *An Awkward Partner: Britain in the European Community* Oxford: Oxford University Press, 2nd edn, 1994.

Gill, C. *Whips' Nightmare: Diary of a Maastricht Rebel* Spenneymore: Memoir Club, 2003.

Gilmour, I. *Dancing with Dogma* London: Simon and Schuster, 1992.

Gilmour, I. and Garnett, M. *Whatever Happened to the Tories* London: Fourth Estate, 1997.

Girvin, B. *The Right in the Twentieth Century: Conservatism and Democracy* London: Pinter, 1994.

Gowland, D. and Turner, A. *Reluctant Europeans: Britain and European Integration 1945–1988* Harlow: Pearson, 2000.

Grayson, R. *Austen Chamberlain and the Commitment to Europe: British Foreign Policy 1924–29* London: Cass, 1997.

Green, E.H.H. *Ideologies of Conservatism: Conservative Political Ideas in the Twentieth Century* Oxford: Oxford University Press, 2002.

Greenwood, S. *Britain and European Cooperation since 1945* Oxford: Blackwell, 1992.

—— *Britain and European Integration since the End of the Second World War* Manchester: Manchester University Press, 1996.

Hague, R. and Berrington, H. 'Europe, Thatcherism and Traditionalism' in Berrington, H. (ed.) *The Politics of Paradox* Newbury: Frank Cass, 1998.

Hearl, D. 'Britain and Europe since 1945' *Parliamentary Affairs* 47(4), 1994, pp. 516–31.

Heath, A., McLean, I., Taylor, B. and Curtice, J. 'Between First and Second Order: A Comparison of Voting Behaviour in European and Local Elections in Britain' *European Journal of Political Research* 35(3), 1999, pp. 389–414.

Heath, E. *Course of My Life: My Autobiography* London: Hodder and Stoughton, 1998.

Heathcote-Amory, D. *The European Constitution and What It Means for Britain* London: CPS, June 2003.

Heffer, S. *Like a Roman: The Life of Enoch Powell* London: Weidenfeld and Nicolson, 1998.

Hennessy, P. and Seldon, A. (eds) *Ruling Performance: British Governments from Attlee to Thatcher* Oxford: Blackwell, 1987.

Heppell, T. 'The Ideological Composition of the Parliamentary Conservative Party 1992–97' *British Journal of Politics and International Relations* 4(2), 2002, pp. 299–324.

Heseltine, M. *The Challenge of Europe: Can Britain Win?* London: Weidenfeld and Nicolson, 1989.

Hickson, K. (ed.) *The Political Thought of the Conservative Party since 1945* Basingstoke: Palgrave, 2005.

Hinsley, F.H. *Sovereignty* Oxford: Alden Press, 1966.

HMSO *Britain in Europe: The European Community and Your Future* London: HMSO, 1992.

Holmes, M. 'The Conservative Party and Europe' Bruges Group Paper No. 17, 1994.

—— (ed.) *The Eurosceptical Reader* Basingstoke: Macmillan, 1996.

Holroyd-Doveton, J. *Young Conservatives* Edinburgh: Pentland, 1996.

Howard, A. *Rab: The Life of R. A. Butler* London: Macmillan, 1987.

Howe, G. *Conflict of Loyalty* London: Macmillan, 1994.

Hurd, D. *An End to Promises: Sketch of Government 1970–74*, London: Collins, 1979.

—— *Memoirs*, London: Little Brown, 2003.

Jackson, R. *Rebels and Whips* London: Macmillan, 1968.

Jackson, R. *The Powers of the European Parliament* London: CPC, n.d. [1978].

James, A. *Sovereign Statehood* London: Allen and Unwin, 1986.

James, R.R. (ed.) *Complete Speeches of Winston Churchill 1897-1963*, vol. VII, New York: Chelsea House, 1974.

—— *Bob Boothby: A Portrait* London: Hodder and Stoughton, 1991.

Jansen, T. *The European People's Party* Basingstoke: Macmillan, 1998.

Jarvis, M. *Conservative Governments, Morality and Social Change in Affluent Britain 1957–64* Manchester: Manchester University Press, 2005.

Jenkins, R. *Churchill* London: Macmillan, 2001.

Kaiser, W. 'Using Europe and Abusing the Europeans: The Conservatives and the European Community 1957–94' *Contemporary Record* 8(2), 1994, pp. 381–99.

—— *Using Europe, Abusing the Europeans: Britain and European Integration 1945–63* Basingstoke: Macmillan, 1996.

Kaiser, W. and Staerck, G. (eds) *British Foreign Policy 1955–64* Basingstoke: Macmillan, 1999.

Kandiah, M. 'British Domestic Politics, the Conservative Party and Foreign Policy-Making' in Kaiser, W. and Staerck, G. (eds) *British Foreign Policy 1955–64* Basingstoke: Macmillan, 1999, pp. 61–88.

Kavanagh, D. *Thatcherism and British Politics* London: Macmillan, 1990.

Kellas, J. 'The Party in Scotland' in Ball, S. and Seldon, A. (eds) *Conservative Century* Oxford: Oxford University Press, 1994.

Kelly, R. *Conservative Party Conferences: The Hidden System* Manchester: Manchester University Press, 1989.

Kelly, S. and Gorst, A. (eds) *Whitehall and the Suez Crisis* London: Frank Cass, 2000.

Kendrick, S. and McCrone, D. 'Politics in a Cold Climate: The Conservative Decline in Scotland' *Political Studies* 37, 1989.

Kennedy, P. *Realities behind Diplomacy: Background Influences on British External Policy 1865–1980* London: Fontana, 1985.

Kilmuir, Earl of, *Political Adventure: The Memoirs of the Earl of Kilmuir* London: Weidenfeld and Nicolson, 1964.

King, A. *Britain Says Yes: 1975 Referendum on the Common Market* Washington: AEI Press, 1977.

King, A. and Wybrow, R. (eds) *British Political Opinion 1937–2000: The Gallup Polls* London: Politicos, 2001.

King, C. *The Cecil King Diaries, 1965–1970* London: Cape, 1972.
—— *The Cecil King Diaries, 1970–1974* London: Cape, 1975.
Kitzinger, U. *Diplomacy and Persuasion: How Britain Joined the Common Market* London: Thames and Hudson, 1973.
Krasner, S. *Sovereignty: Organised Hypocrisy* Princeton, NJ: Princeton University Press, 1999.
Lamb, R. *The Macmillan Years 1957–63: The Emerging Truth* London: John Murray, 1995.
Lamont, N. *Sovereign Britain* London: Duckworth, 1995.
—— *In Office* London: Little Brown, 1999.
Larres, K. 'Integrating Europe or Ending the Cold War? Churchill's Post-war Foreign Policy' *Journal of European Integration History* 2(1), 1996, pp. 15–49.
Lawson, N. *View from Number 11: Memoirs of a Tory Radical* London: Bantam Press, 1992.
Leiber, R.J. *British Politics and European Unity: Parties, Elites and Pressure Groups* Berkeley: University of California Press, 1970.
Lindsay, K. *European Assemblies: The Experimental Period* London: Stevens and Sons, 1960.
Lloyd, S. *Suez 1956: A Personal Account* London: Jonathan Cape, 1978.
Lodge, J. *The 1994 Elections to the European Parliament* London: Pinter, 1996.
Lord, C. *British Entry to the European Community under the Heath Government* Aldershot: Dartmouth, 1993.
—— *Absent at the Creation: Britain and the Formation of the European Community* Aldershot: Dartmouth, 1996.
Lowe, R. 'Archival Report: Plumbing New Depths: Contemporary Historians and the Public Record Office' *Twentieth Century British History* 8(2), 1997, pp. 239–65.
Lucas, W.S. (ed.) *Divided We Stand: Britain, the US and the Suez Crisis* London: Hodder and Stoughton, 1991.
—— (ed.) *Britain and Suez: The Lion's Last Roar* Manchester: Manchester University Press, 1996.
Ludlam, S. 'The Spectre Haunting Conservatism' in Ludlam, S. and Smith, M.J. (eds) *Contemporary British Conservatism* Basingstoke: Macmillan, 1996.
Ludlow, N. Piers *Dealing with Britain: The Six and the First UK Application to the EEC* Cambridge: Cambridge University Press, 1997.
Lynch, P. 'The Conservatives and Europe, 1997–2001' in Garnett, M. and Lynch, P. (eds) *The Conservatives in Crisis* Manchester: Manchester University Press, 2003.
McCrillis, N. *The British Conservative Party in the Age of Universal Suffrage: Popular Conservatism 1918–29* Columbus, Ohio: Ohio State University Press, 1998.
McKay, D. *Federalism and European Union: A Political Economy Perspective* Oxford: Oxford University Press, 1999.
Macmillan, H. *Britain, the Commonwealth and Europe* London: Britain in Europe, 1961; republished July 2001.
—— *Tides of Fortune 1945–55* London: Macmillan, 1969.
—— *Riding the Storm 1956–59* London: Macmillan, 1971.
—— *Pointing the Way 1959–61* London: Macmillan, 1972.
—— *At the End of the Day 1961–63* London: Macmillan, 1973.
Macmillan-Scott, E. 'Voting the Right Way in Europe' *Reformer Magazine*, Spring, 1999, http://core2.trg.org.uk/reformer/spring1999.
Major, J. *John Major: The Autobiography* London: HarperCollins, 1999.
Mawby, S. *Containing Germany: Britain and the Arming of the Federal Republic* Basingstoke: Macmillan, 1999.
Medlicott, W.N. *British Foreign Policy since Versailles* London: Methuen, 1967.
Mendoza, M. 'Thirty-one Years on: May–August 1961' *Contemporary Record* 6(3), 1992, pp. 166-73.
Meyer, A. *Stand Up and Be Counted* London: Heinemann, 1990.

—— 'What's Wrong with the Tories' *Reformer Magazine*, Winter, 2001, http://core2.trg.org.uk/reformer/winter2001.

Milward, A.S. *The Reconstruction of Western Europe 1945–51* London: Routledge, 1984.

—— *The European Rescue of the Nation-State* London: Routledge, 1992.

—— *The UK and the EC, volume 1: The Rise and Fall of a National Strategy 1945–63* London: Frank Cass, 2002.

Milward, A., Ruggero, R., Lynch, F. and Romero, F. *The Frontier of National Sovereignty: History and Theory* London: Routledge, 1993.

Moon, J. *European Integration in British Politics 1950–63: A Study of Issue Change* Aldershot: Gower, 1985.

Morris, P. 'The British Conservative Party' in Gaffney, J. (ed.) *Political Parties and the European Union* London: Routledge, 1996, pp. 122–38.

Morris, R. *Tories: From Village Hall to Westminster* Edinburgh: Mainstream, 1991.

Newton Dunn, B. 'Letter from Europe' *Reformer Magazine*, Autumn, 2000, http://core2.trg.org.uk/reformer/autumn2000.

Nicolson, N. (ed.) *Diaries and Letters of Harold Nicolson 1945–62* London: Collins, 1968.

Norton, P. *Dissension in the House of Commons 1945–70* London: Macmillan, 1975.

—— *Conservative Dissidents* London: Temple Smith, 1978.

—— 'The Parliamentary Party and Party Committees' in Ball, S. and Seldon, A. (eds) *Conservative Century* Oxford: Oxford University Press, 1994.

—— 'The Conservative Party: In Office but Not in Power' in King, A., Denver, D., McLean, I., Norris, P., Sander, D. and Seyd, P. (eds) *New Labour Triumphs: Britain at the Polls* Chatham NJ: Chatham House, 1998.

—— 'Electing the Leader' *Politics Review* 7(4), 1998, pp. 10–14.

—— 'The Role of the Conservative Political Centre 1945–98' in Ball, S. and Holliday, I. (eds) *Mass Conservatism: The Conservatives and the Public since the 1880s* Newbury: Frank Cass, 2002.

Nott, J. *Here Today Gone Tomorrow: Recollections of an Errant Politician* London: Politicos, 2002.

Nutting, A. *Europe Will Not Wait* London: Hollis and Carter, 1960.

Onslow, S. *Backbench Debate within the Conservative Party and Its Influence on British Foreign Policy 1948–57* Basingstoke: Macmillan, 1997.

Parker, R.A.C. *Chamberlain and Appeasement* Basingstoke: Macmillan, 1994.

Parr, H. *British Policy towards the European Community: Harold Wilson and Britain's World Role 1964–67* London: Routledge, 2005.

Parris, M. *Chance Witness: An Outsider's Life in Politics* London: Viking, 2002.

Patten, C. *Britain, Asia and Europe: A Conservative View* London: Conservative Political Centre, 1995.

—— 'Letter from Europe' *Reformer Magazine*, Winter, 2001, http://core2.trg.org.uk/reformer/winter2001.

Pearce, R. (ed.) *Patrick Gordon Walker: Political Diaries 1932–1971* London: Historians' Press, 1991.

Pegg, C.H. *Evolution of the European Idea 1914–32* Chapel Hill, NC: University of North Carolina Press, 1983.

Perry, R. 'Just How Democratic Is the EU?' *Reformer Magazine*, Spring, 2002, http://core2.trg.org.uk/reformer/spring2002.

Pinder, J. 'Federalism in Britain and Italy: Radicals and the English Liberal Tradition' in Stirk, P.M.R. (ed.) *European Unity in Context: The Interwar Period* London: Pinter, 1989.

Pinto-Duschinsky, M. *British Political Finance 1830–1980* Washington: American Enterprise Institute, 1981.

Pym, F. *The Politics of Consent* London: Hamish Hamilton, 1984.

Ramsden, J. *The Making of Conservative Party Policy: The Conservative Research Department since 1929* London: Longman, 1980.

—— *The Age of Churchill and Eden, 1940–1957* London: Longman, 1995.

—— *Winds of Change: Macmillan to Heath, 1957–75* London: Longman, 1996.

—— *Britain Is a Conservative Country that Occasionally Votes Labour: Conservative Success in Post-war Britain* London: CPC, 1997.

—— *An Appetite for Power: A History of the Conservative Party since 1830* London: HarperCollins, 1998.

Redwood, J. *Our Currency, Our Country: The Dangers of European Monetary Union* Harmondsworth: Penguin, 1997.

—— *Stars and Strife: The Coming Conflict between the USA and European Union* London: Palgrave, 2001.

*Reformer Magazine* 'Britain in Europe', Autumn, 1999, http://core2.trg.org.uk/reformer/autumn1999.

Renton, T. *Chief Whip* London: Politicos, 2004.

Reynolds, D. *Britannia Overruled: British Policy and World Power in the Twentieth Century* Harlow: Longman, 2nd edn, 2000.

Riddell, P. 'Margaret Thatcher: The Lady Who Made the Weather' in Pugliese, S. (ed.) *The Political Legacy of Margaret Thatcher* London: Politicos, 2003.

Ridley, N. *My Style of Government* London: Hutchinson, 1991.

Routledge, P. *Public Servant, Secret Agent: The Elusive Life and Violent Death of Airey Neave* London: Fourth Estate, 2002.

Seldon A. *Churchill's Indian Summer: The Conservative Government 1951–55* London: Hodder and Stoughton, 1981.

—— 'The Churchill Administration 1951–55' in Hennessy, P. and Seldon, A. (eds) *Ruling Performance: British Governments from Attlee to Thatcher* Oxford: Blackwells, 1987, pp. 63–97.

—— *Major: A Political Life* London: Weidenfeld and Nicolson, 1997.

Self, R. (ed.) *The Neville Chamberlain Diary Letters: Volume Three* Aldershot: Ashgate, 2002.

Seyd, P. and Whiteley, P. 'Conservative Grassroots: An Overview' in Ludlam, S. and Smith, M.J. (eds) *Contemporary British Conservatism* Basingstoke: Macmillan, 1996.

Shannon, R. *The Age of Disraeli: The Rise of Tory Democracy* London: Longman, 1992.

—— *The Age of Salisbury 1881–1902: Unionism and Empire* London: Longman, 1996.

Shepherd, G. *Shepherd's Watch* London: Politicos, 2000.

Shepherd, R. *The Power Brokers: The Tory Party and Its Leaders* London: Hutchinson, 1991.

—— *Iain Macleod* London: Hutchinson, 1994.

—— *Enoch Powell: A Biography* London: Pimlico, 1996.

Sowemimo, M. 'The Conservative Party and European Integration 1988–95' *Party Politics* 2(1), 1996, pp. 77–97.

Spaak, P.H. *The Continuing Battle: Memoirs of a European 1936–1966*, trans H. Fox, London: Weidenfeld and Nicolson, 1971.

Spicer, M. *A Treaty Too Far: A New Policy for Europe* London: Fourth Estate, 1992.

Steinnes, K. 'The European Challenge: Britain's EEC Application in 1961' *Contemporary European History* 7(1), 1998, pp. 61–80.

Stephens, P. *Politics and the Pound: The Tories, the Economy and Europe* London: Macmillan, 1996.

Stewart, G. *Burying Caesar: Churchill, Chamberlain and the Battle for the Tory Party* London: Weidenfeld and Nicolson, 1999.

Stewart, R. *The Foundations of the Conservative Party* London: Longman, 1978.

Stuart, M. *Douglas Hurd: The Public Servant: An Authorised Biography* Edinburgh: Mainstream, 1998.

Taylor, J. *Please Stay to the Adjournment* Studley: Brewin Books, 2003.

Tebbit, N. *Upwardly Mobile* London: Weidenfeld and Nicolson, 1988.

Thatcher, M. *Downing Street Years* London: HarperCollins, 1993.

—— *Statecraft: Strategies for a Changing World* London: HarperCollins, 2003.

Thompson, D. *The Rome Treaty and the Law* London: Conservative Political Centre for Bow Group, July–September 1962.

Thompson, H. *British Conservative Government and the European Exchange Rate Mechanism: 1979–94* London: Pinter, 1996.

Thorpe, D.R. *Alec Douglas-Home* London: Sinclair-Stevenson, 1996.

Tory Reform Group 'Lessons from the 2001 General Election: Winning Back the Missing Conservatives' London: Tory Reform Group, 11 June 2001, http://core2.trg. org.uk/publications/missingconservatives.html.

Towler, G. *Bloc Tory* London: CPS, 2001.

Tratt, J. *The Macmillan Government and Europe: A Study in the Process of Policy Development* Basingstoke: Macmillan, 1996.

Turner, J. *Macmillan* Harlow: Longman, 1994.

Turner, J *The Tories and Europe* Manchester: Manchester University Press, 2001.

Walker, P. *The Ascent of Britain* London: Sidgwick and Jackson, 1977.

—— *Staying Power: An Autobiography* London: Bloomsbury, 1991.

Walker-Smith, D. and Walker, P. *A Call to the Commonwealth: The Constructive Case* London: published privately, 1962.

Walters, S. *Tory Wars: Conservatives in Crisis* London: Politicos, 2001.

Westlake, M. *Britain's Emerging Euro-Elites* Aldershot: Dartmouth, 1994.

White, R. 'The Europeanism of Coudenhove-Kalergi' in Stirk, P.M.R. (ed.) *European Unity in Context: The Interwar Period* London: Pinter, 1989.

White, V. 'Voting for the Euro' *Reformer Magazine*, Winter, 2001, http://core2.trg.org. uk/reformer/winter2001.

Whitely, P., Seyd, P. and Richardson, J. *True Blues: The Politics of Conservative Party Membership* Oxford: Oxford University Press, 1994.

Williamson, P. *Stanley Baldwin* Cambridge: Cambridge University Press, 2001.

Wilson, G.K. *Special Interests and Policymaking: Agricultural Policies and Politics in Britain and the United States of America* London: Wiley, 1977.

Windlesham, Lord, *Communication and Political Power* London: Cape, 1966.

Wood, A. (ed.) *The Times' Guide to the European Parliament 1984* London: Times Books, 1984.

Wyatt, W. *Journals of Woodrow Wyatt: Thatcher's Fall and Major's Rise*, vol. 2, ed. S. Curtis London: Macmillan, 1999.

Young, H. *One of Us: Life of Margaret Thatcher* London: Pan, 1990.

—— *This Blessed Plot: Britain and Europe from Churchill to Blair* London: Macmillan, 1998.

Young, J.W. *Britain, France and the Unity of Europe* Leicester: Leicester University Press, 1984.

—— 'Churchill's "No" to Europe: The "Rejection" of European Union by Churchill's Post-war Government' *Historical Journal* 28(4), 1985, pp. 923–37.

—— (ed.) *The Foreign Policy of Churchill's Peacetime Administration 1951–55* Leicester: Leicester University Press, 1988.

—— 'German Rearmament and the European Defence Community' in Young, J.W. (ed.) *The Foreign Policy of Churchill's Peacetime Administration 1951–55* Leicester: Leicester University Press, 1988, pp. 81–108.

—— *Britain and European Unity 1945–1999* Basingstoke: Macmillan, 2nd edn, 2000.

## Media and electronic sources

### *Television and radio broadcasts*

Cockrill, Michael *Westminster's Secret Service: The Whips' Office* BBC 2, 21 May 1995.

Macmillan Scott interview *Today* programme, BBC Radio 4, 30 January 2006

'I Can Remain No Longer' documentary on Howe resignation, *Westminster Hour* BBC Radio 4, 22 February 2004.

### Electronic references

Anti-Common Market League, www.bullen.demon.co.uk/cibacml.htm
Centre for Policy Studies, www.cps.org.uk/
Conservative Party, www.conservative-party.org.uk/
Council of Europe, www.coe.int/
Early Day Motion Database, http://edmi.parliament.uk/edmi/
European Foundation, www.europeanfoundation.org/
European Parliament, www.europarl.eu.int/
Party General Election Manifestos since 1945, www.psr.keele.ac.uk/area/uk/man.htm
The Conservative Group for Europe, www.cge.org.uk
The Thatcher Foundation, www.margaretthatcher.org
Tory Reform Group, http://core2.trg.org.uk/

## Unpublished sources

### Conference and seminar papers

'Britain and Strasbourg' witness seminar held 23 February 1995, ICBH, 2002, www.icbh.ac.uk/icbh/brussels/.
Aspinwall, Mark 'Comparative Party Politics of Euroscepticism' OERN briefing paper No. 4, 2003.
Baker, D., Gamble, A., Ludlam, S. and Seawright, D. 'Backbenchers with Attitude' paper presented to the European Consortium for Political Research Conference, Bordeaux, 1995.
Brittan, L. 'A Pro-European Policy for Conservatives' Tory Reform Group, 1999, International Lecture.
Catterall, P. 'Macmillan and Europe' paper presented to Western Conference on British Studies, Houston, 2000.
Ellison, J. 'A Grand Design? Selwyn Lloyd, the Foreign Office and the Question of Europe 1955–57' paper presented to 20th Century History Seminar, Birmingham University, December 1998.

### PhD/MPhil/BA theses/dissertations

Ashford, N. 'The Conservative Party and European Integration 1945–75' unpublished PhD, University of Warwick, 1983.
Beswick, P. 'The Tory Strasbourgers and the Evolution of Conservative Party Debate over Europe 1945–61' unpublished MPhil, University of Birmingham, 2001.
McKay, J. 'Labour Party Attitudes to European Integration 1945–75' unpublished PhD, University of Birmingham, 2006.
Millsopp, D. 'The Conservative Party and the European Community' unpublished BSc dissertation, Queen's University of Belfast, 1993.
Richardson, D. 'The Macmillan Government and De Gaulle's 1963 Veto' unpublished BA dissertation, University of Birmingham, 2006.
Toomey, J. 'The Velvet Veto: Harold Wilson, Charles de Gaulle and Britain's 2nd EEC Application 1964–1967' unpublished PhD, University College Dublin, 2004.

# Index

1970 Group 154, 156, 158, 173, 176–7
9/11 76
92 Cheyne Walk 175
92 Group 63, 175

*A Call to the Commonwealth* (1962) 154
*A Europe for the Regions* (1971) 162
*About Western Union* (1949) 21
Act of Union 162
Africa 37, 103
air travel 13
All-Party Common Market Safeguards
  Campaign 154, 169, 175
Amery, Julian 25, 107, 108, 120, 121,
  198, 222
Amery, Leo 77, 81, 106, 112, 120
Amsterdam Treaty (1997) 4, 79, 80, 211
Ancram, Michael 12, 67, 68
Andrew, Herbert 28
Anglo-American relations 15, 23, 26, 28,
  32, 72, 75–6, 87, 128, 129, 181
Anglo-French cooperation 33, 75, 87,
  116
animal welfare 206
Anti-Common Market League (ACML)
  30, 63, 83, 95–6, 122, 145–6, 155, 156,
  160, 163, 166, 167–72, 175, 180
Anti-Marketeers 29, 30, 31, 33, 36, 37,
  39, 42, 43, 45, 46, 50, 53, 57, 77, 81,
  86–7, 110, 117, 118, 119, 124, 143,
  144, 152–87, 225; alternatives to EEC
  36, 103, 109, 143, 176, 180–5;
  definition 152, 159; election
  candidates 32, 96, 149, 154, 155,
  170–1; leadership 153–9; motivations
  159–65; propaganda 30, 96, 109, 117,
  135, 145–6, 165, 168, 169, 172, 177;
  on sovereignty 86–7, 118, 153, 155,
  156, 157, 158, 160, 176, 179, 181

appeasement 10–11, 43, 65, 111–12, 219,
  223
asylum 67
Atlantic alliance 22, 72, 73, 108, 222
Atlantic Free Trade Area parliamentary
  group 176, 181, 186
Australia 77, 109, 160
Austria 3, 61
Avon, Lord *see* Eden, Anthony
*Ayrshire Post* 186

Baker, Kenneth 55, 56, 194
Baker, W.H.K. 161
balance of payments 37, 181
Baldwin, Stanley 13, 223
Balkans 112
Ball, Stuart 7, 10
Balneil, Lord 119, 137, 181
Barber, Anthony 38
Barnes, William Gorell 119
Basle agreement (1968) 37
BBC 138, 140, 176, 184, 186, 187
Beamish, Tufton 108, 121, 124–5, 207,
  218
Beaton, Len 123
Beaverbrook, Lord 83, 139–40, 185–6
Beazley, Christoper 196
Beethoven 184
Behrens, Edward Berrington 141
Belgium 21, 111, 192, 211
Bell, Ronald 152, 167
Beloff, Nora 5
Belsen 111
Benn, Tony 41
Bennett, Frederic 199, 202
Bennett, Nicholas 62
Bentwick, Lord George 155
Berlin airlift (1948) 21
Bestremau, Bernard 125

Better Off Out campaign 182
Bevin, Ernest 17
Biffen, John 54, 55, 152, 153, 157–8, 161, 176
Biggs-Davison, John 168, 188
Birkenhead, Lord 198
'Black Wednesday' 4, 71, 101, 151, 159; *see also* European Exchange Rate Mechanism, British withdraw
Black, Conrad 103
Black, Cyril 43, 108
Blackburn, John 164
Blair, Tony 67, 121, 165, 225
Blake, George 32
Blumenfeld, Erik 125
Board of Trade 2
Boardman, Tom 133
Body, Richard 61, 163, 168
Booker, Christoper 185
Boothby, Robert 15, 21, 22, 23, 107, 112, 113, 120, 196, 197, 207, 208, 224
Bow Group 122–3, 171
Boyle, Edward 108, 134
Boyne, H.B. 140
Boyson, Rhodes 91–2, 101, 149, 175
Branston, Ursula 198, 218
Bretherton, Russell 2, 26
Bretton Woods 58, 72, 84, 103
Briand Plan (1929) 11, 107
Briand, A 106
*Britain and Europe* (1962) 123
*Britain in Europe* (1992) 145
Britain in Europe (BIE) 32, 41, 42, 112, 120, 121, 187; co-ordinates 1975; finances 43; re-launch (1999) 121, 134; 'yes' vote 41–3, 121, 140
Britain, agriculture 26, 27, 28, 30, 94–8, 110, 130, 134–5, 142, 160–1, 172, 176, 186, 219, 220
Britain, Commonwealth 15, 17, 18–19, 34, 73, 76–8, 92, 109–10, 114, 130, 142, 143, 154, 156, 160, 168, 172, 176, 179, 180, 200, 220, 223; Empire 7, 15, 21, 34, 72, 76–8, 160, 221–2; trade with 19, 26, 28, 35, 37, 77–8, 93, 109–10, 154
Britain, decline of 115–16, 123
Britain, East of Suez role 12
Britain, economic policy 5, 26–8, 93, 100, 116–17, 163, 223
Britain, frontier 13
Britain, leadership in Europe 20, 23, 25, 26, 28, 50, 51, 54, 73, 78–80, 101, 102, 113–15, 117–18, 131
Britain, trade with America 75–6

Britain, world role 5, 34, 37, 71–8, 115–16
British Army on the Rhine 13, 21, 24, 25, 31
British beef, ban on 94, 184
British Business for World Markets 175
British Chamber of Commerce 38
British Council of the European Movement *see* European Movement
Brittan, Leon 5, 69, 121, 211, 213, 215–16, 216; cabinet resignation 52
Broad, Roger 5
Brown, Gordon 64, 68, 121
Browne, John 151
Bruce-Gardyne, Jock 123
Bruges Group 55, 63
Brussels Treaty (1948) 24
Bryant, Arthur 177
BSE crisis 184
Buchan-Hepburn, Patrick 197
Buck, Anthony 138
Budgen, Nicholas 65, 162
Buller, Jim 7
Bulpitt, Jim 10
Butler, David 208
Butler, Rab 11, 14, 76, 94–5, 134–5, 148, 184

Callaghan, Jim 3, 41, 45, 50, 100
Cameron, David 70, 132, 196, 226
Camps, Miriam 5–6, 118
Canada 109, 182, 183
Carr, Robert 116
Carrington Study Group (1965) 116
Carrington, Peter 49, 193, 201
Carttiss, Michael 133
Cash, Bill 60, 62, 91, 153, 160, 162, 168, 218
Castle, Barbara 41
Caswell, Douglas 182
Catherwood, Fred 199
Caumont Ridge 111
Centre for Policy Studies (CPS) 195–6
Chamberlain, Austen, 12–13, 107, 223
Chamberlain, Joseph 27, 153, 221, 222, 223–4, 225
Chamberlain, Neville 11, 43, 65, 111–12, 114
Channel Tunnel 33, 116
Channon, Paul 202, 205
Chataway, Chris 121
China 138
Christian Democracy 102, 188–9, 190, 191, 192–3, 194
Christian Democrat Congress, Stockholm (1968) 191

Church House, Westminster 136
Churchill, Winston 1, 14, 15, 22, 23, 43,
   65, 78, 107, 112, 120, 207, 218, 224;
   criticism of 18, 113, 120, 154, 160;
   government (1951–55) 16–17, 107–8,
   113; speeches, Llandudno (1948) 17,
   Royal Albert Hall (1947) 15, 120,
   Zurich (1946) 15, 63, 128, 196; state-
   craft 72; 'three circles' 17, 72, 73, 74,
   75, 76, 108; views on Europe 7, 12,
   14–15, 16–17, 21, 31, 62, 72, 75, 82,
   106; wartime government (1940–45) 11
Churchill, Winston Jr 86, 214
City of London 52, 102, 201
Clark, Alan 173, 215
Clark, William 124
Clarke, David 167
Clarke, Kenneth 64, 67, 69, 91, 103, 121,
   126, 132, 163, 185
coal mine closures 165, 226
Cocker, William 27
Cockfield, Arthur 51, 127, 211, 213, 214
Cold War 1, 12, 21, 72, 78–9, 112–13,
   154, 185
Colombo, Emilio 193
Committee on Europe (Policy Making)
   36
Common Agricultural Policy (CAP) 5,
   37, 40, 47, 74, 94, 97, 106, 149, 210,
   219; 1969 crisis 97; Conservative
   views of 97–8, 161, 179, 189; cost to
   Britain 47, 96, 97; creation of (1966)
   5, 30; reform 98, 104
Common currency *see* European Union,
   single currency
Common Market Committee 29, 154,
   176, 177–8
*Common Market Topics* 135, 137
Commonwealth and Europe Committee
   35, 36, 119
Commonwealth Industries Association
   *see* Empire Industries Association
Commonwealth Prime Ministers'
   Conference (1962) 146, 169
Communism 12, 13, 14, 17, 22, 41, 75,
   76, 104, 112, 128, 183, 222
Community Tax 165
computers 116
Concert of Europe 222
Concorde 33, 116
Congress of the European Movement
   (1968) 113
Congress of Vienna 17
Conservative Anti-Common Market
   Information Service 177

Conservative Group for Europe (CGE)
   46, 63, 124–6, 139, 143, 193, 213, 214
Conservative Mainstream 121
Conservative Party Archive (CPA) 8, 9,
   10
Conservative Party, alternative names in
   Europe 189
Conservative Party, archival sources on
   8–10
Conservative Party, *Campaign Guide
   1964* 33, 129
Conservative Party, conference, (1948)
   Llandudno 17; 1949 London 21; 1953
   Margate 17, 73; 1961 Brighton 29, 122,
   160, 166; 1962 Llandudno 29, 39, 136,
   148, 166, 169; 1963 Blackpool 33;
   1965 Brighton 34; 1967 Brighton 35,
   109; 1968 Blackpool 143, 180; 1970
   Blackpool 39; 1971 Brighton 65, 122,
   125, 154, 166; 1972 Brighton 46; 1973
   Blackpool 46; 1975 Blackpool 46,
   192; 1992 Brighton 58, 166; 1996
   Bournemouth 63; conference motions
   20–1, 29, 34, 35, 46, 58, 62, 63, 109,
   135–6, 143, 166–7, 169
Conservative Party, domestic statecraft
   10–11, 14, 44, 52, 68, 71, 104, 220
Conservative Party, economic policy 19,
   26–8, 51, 52, 57–8, 163
Conservative Party, electoral success and
   strategy 6–7, 17, 32, 33, 42, 50, 64,
   66, 94–5, 142, 146–51, 166; rural vote
   94
Conservative Party, European strategy
   18, 26–8, 31, 32, 35–6, 37, 49, 60,
   65–6, 67, 68, 100, 104, 120, 127–51,
   212, 220
Conservative Party, expulsion from 65,
   67, 126, 133, 171
Conservative Party, finances, treasurers
   and donors, 64, 124, 125, 126, 142,
   151, 200, 201
Conservative Party, ideologies 44, 67, 92,
   104, 159, 165, 177, 189, 193, 208–9,
   218, 219, 221–5,
Conservative Party, leadership contests
   (1965) 34, 109; (1975) 40; (1990)
   54–5; (1995) 61, 91, 126; (1997) 64;
   (2001) 67–8, 166; (2003) 69; (2005)
   70; leadership, divisions over Europe
   52, 54, 56, 57–8, 63, 64, 65, 66–7, 68,
   84, 101, 131, 155, 158–9, 219;
   Shadow Cabinet (1945–51) 50;
   (1966–70) 99, 157, 167; (1975–79) 9,
   50; (1997–2001) 64

Conservative Party, links with continental parties 125, 188–96

Conservative Party, manifestos, 1950 general election 147; 1959 general election 136; 1966 general election 147; 1970 general election 38, 90, 130, 147; 1979 European election 50; 1979 general election 100, 149; 1984 European election 149; 1987 general election 54; 1994 European election 150; 1997 general election 64; 1999 European election 66, 150, 214; 2001 general election 150; 2004 European election 150; 2005 general election 150

Conservative Party, Members of European Parliament (MEPs) 70, 109, 126, 149, 163–4, 188, 194, 195, 199, 201–6, 208–9; relations with London 202–3, 204–5, 209, 211

Conservative Party, MP/constituency relations 9, 39, 61, 142, 143, 156, 163, 166, 170–1, 173–4

Conservative Party, nationalism 2, 31, 48, 87, 183–4, 188, 225

Conservative Party, parliamentary party, 132–5, 137–8, 150, 224; 1922 Committee 21, 61, 110, 175, 178, 203; agriculture committee 95, 120; attitudes to Europe 20, 29, 30, 36–7, 41, 43, 52, 53, 56, 57–8, 61, 91, 99, 102, 124, 125, 131, 150–1, 159–65, 196, 200, 211, 218–19; Committee on Europe (Policy Research) 119; Commonwealth Affairs committee 77; European affairs committee 163, 178; foreign affairs committee (FAC) 25, 36, 38, 118–19, 178, 181, 190, 200; parliamentary voting behaviour 8, 19, 29, 39, 40, 41, 43, 46–7, 51, 56–7, 59, 60, 61, 91, 110, 132, 175, 177; political divisions 37, 39, 43, 57–8, 61 –7, 68, 131, 148, 152; Schuman plan response 16–17, 110, 147, 218; whips' office 29, 39, 57, 61, 133, 135, 139, 161, 162, 163, 172–3, 175, 177, 201

Conservative Party, policy making 8, 10, 35, 36–7, 45, 100, 118–20, 127, 134; committee on direct elections to European Parliament 45; *Industrial Policy* 19; Advisory Committee on Policy (ACP) 88, 95, 136

Conservative Party, pro-Europeans 20, 23, 31, 34, 36, 40, 54, 62, 63, 65–6, 67, 71, 77, 88, 105–26, 136–7, 161, 174,

181, 188–209, 211, 222, 226; *see also* Conservative Party, Tory Strasbourgers

Conservative Party, professional organisation 6, 14, 41–2, 46, 134, 135, 220–1; agents, 42, 95–6, 122, 143–4, 146, 171, 172, 186, 220–1; area agents 30, 31, 142, 169, 173, 221; Board of Management 203; Central Office 9, 30, 68, 88, 89, 91, 96, 120, 124, 125, 135, 138, 140, 141, 145, 150, 163, 169, 172–3, 186, 201, 221; Conservative Overseas Bureau (COB) 189–90, 191; Conservative Political Centre (CPC) 9, 21, 91, 117, 138, 142, 143, 146, 173, 182; Conservative Research Department (CRD) 20, 31, 59, 85, 99, 119, 125, 135, 138, 140, 143–4, 147, 181, 193; discussion groups 21, 34, 39, 59, 61, 143, 144; publicity material 42

Conservative party, single currency ballot (1998) 65–6

Conservative Party, tactics 1967 negotiations 35–6

Conservative Party, Tory Strasbourgers 7, 16, 18, 19, 22, 28, 75, 107–8, 114, 196

Conservative Party, views on, anti-Americanism 22, 27, 72, 108

Conservative Party, views on, world view 4, 10–11, 12–13, 17, 18–19, 34, 37, 70–8, 128–32

Conservative Party, voluntary organisation, activists 9, 10, 30, 39, 42, 58, 60, 89, 90, 132, 140, 165–72, 202, 220, 225; activists, views on Empire 18, 26, 27, 77–8, 93, 122, 166, 200, 225; anti-foreignerism 73, 185; views on economics 22, 61, 93, 144; views on Europe 20, 21, 29, 30, 34, 43, 46, 58–9, 61–2, 81, 130, 136, 142, 143–4, 146, 167, 169, 182, 218, 221; views on sovereignty 83–4, 85, 86, 166, 172, 176; views on terms of EEC entry 31, 39, 97, 167

Conservative Party, voluntary organisation, constituency associations, 8–9, 31, 42, 139, 147, 171, 220–1; Accrington 27, 167; Alresford 116; Banbury 167, 173; Birmingham 225; Buckinghamshire South 167; Burton-on-Trent 173; Chelmsford 142; Dorset North 146;

Dorset West 167; East Hertfordshire 173; Edinburgh North 30; Esher 174; Essex North East 205; Falmouth and Camborne 173; Glamorgan 174; Harborough and Blaby 173; Hereford and Worcester 205; Hexham 205; Isle of Ely 167; Liverpool 146; Ludlow 174; Norwood 167; Plymouth Sutton 174; Reigate 163, 174; Rushcliffe 26; Shoreham 116; Weston-super-Mare 173; Worcester 29, 109; Lancashire Central Euro 58; Newcastle West 42; areas, Yorkshire 20–1, 142, 225; National Union 10, 18, 20, 29, 38–9, 136, 142, 145, 169, 174, 203; Young Conservatives, 122, 125, 126, 143, 154, 155, 167–8, 189; Young Conservatives, West Midlands 42, 82
continental commitment 222–3, 225
Cooper, Gordon 167
Co-ordinating Committee on Europe 137
Corn Laws 92, 94, 126, 148, 153, 219, 225
Corrie, John 202
cost of living 95, 96, 117, 139; *see also* food prices
Coudenhove-Kalergi, Count 107
Council of Europe 18, 19, 22, 23, 33, 74, 75, 83, 111, 162, 188, 191, 194, 196–200, 211, 218; British delegation 111, 125, 133, 164, 190–1, 194, 196–200, 206–8; dual mandate 198; foundation 15–16, 196; structure 16, 24, 191
County Councils 212
Cowling, Maurice 10–11
Cran, James 87, 173, 177, 185, 226
Critchley, Julian 63, 67, 87, 114, 126, 133, 198–9
*Crossbow* 122, 123
Cummings, Dominic 68
Cunningham, Knox 118
currency exchange rates 50, 53, 100
Curry, David 65, 126
Curry, Edwina 78, 208, 213
Curtis, Lionel 107
Cyprus 37, 103, 154

d'Ancona, Matthew 185
d'Estaing, Giscard 68
*Daily Express* 83, 121, 185–6, 187
*Daily Mail* 43, 185
*Daily Telegraph* 43, 65, 140, 185, 186, 195

Dalkeith, Lord 114
Danish Conservatives 192, 193
Dankert, Pieter 206
Danube 13
Davies, David 67, 173
Davies, Philip 182
D-Day, 50th anniversary 150
de Chair, Somerset 168, 225
de Gaulle 25, 31, 32, 80, 111, 136, 137, 143, 178, 180, 190
de Zulueta, Philip 115
Dean, Paul 138
Debenham, Piers 140, 154, 187
decolonisation 18, 72, 76–8, 122, 222
Deedes, Bill 137, 176, 186
Dell, Edmund 5
Delors, Jacques 3, 53, 54, 104, 186
democracy, traditions of 184
Denmark 2, 37, 110; Maastricht 'No' vote 57, 133, 178
Derek's Diner *see* 1970 Group
Deutschmark 50, 58
Digby, Simon Wingfield 167, 199
Dilhorne, Reginald 155
Direct European Elections bill (1977) 46
Disraeli, Benjamin 153, 155, 225
Dodds-Parker, Douglas 36, 111, 192, 201, 218
dollar 5, 84
Donnelly, Brendan 126
Dorrell, Stephen 65
Drogheda, Lord 43
du Cann, Edward 43, 52, 162
Duncan, Alan 162
Dunn, Bob 175
Dunn, William 'Bill' Newton 63, 82, 208, 209, 212
Dykes, Hugh 63, 163

early day motions (EDM) 29, 57, 58, 61, 82, 90, 102, 133, 162, 164, 176, 177–8, 180, 196, 197
Eccles, David 15, 19, 20, 74, 95, 196, 198, 208
*Economist* 27
Eden Plan (1952) 23–5
Eden, Anthony 14, 15, 22–3, 26, 83–4, 218; attitude to Europe 24, 31, 83–4, 108, 155–6; as foreign secretary 22–4, 107, 113; speeches, House of Lords (1962) 84, 156, Leamington Spa (1962) 84, 155, Rome (1951) 23
Eden, John 198
education 67, 221

elections, by-elections 32, 170;
  Bromsgrove (1971) 39; Devizes (1964)
  186; Kingston (1971) 171;
  Macclesfield (1971) 39, 162; Norfolk
  South (1962) 96; Orpington (1962)
  32; South Dorset (1962) 96, 140,
  154–5, 170, 187; West Derbyshire
  (1962) 96; Worcester (1961) 109
elections, European (1979) 47; (1984)
  206;(1989) 194; (1994) 195; (1999) 65,
  67, 126, 195; (2004) 70, 150, 196, 209
elections, general elections (1945) 14,
  224; (1951) 16;(1959) 129; (1964) 33,
  34, 129, 147, 170, 176; (1966) 34, 94,
  99, 147, 176; (1970) 38, 94, 147; (Feb.
  1974) 40, 130, 148; (Oct. 1974) 40;
  (1979) 45; (1992) 56, 147; (1997) 63,
  64, 150, 151; (2001) 7, 66, 67, 91, 151;
  (2005) 7, 70, 91; *see also* Conservative
  Party, election manifestos
elections, local 149
Elizabeth I 17
Elles, Diana 218
Elliot, Walter 15
Empire Industries Association (EIA) 77,
  169
English law 216–17
Euro '96 football competition 184
Euro-passport 157
*Europe Will Not Wait* (1960) 113
Europe, 'missed opportunity' 5, 20,
  113–15; British leadership of 16, 21,
  22, 48, 50, 51, 78–80, 98, 110, 113,
  117–18, 196, 197, 200; British trade
  with 19, 20, 27, 37, 47–8, 75–6, 94,
  116–17; British views of 2, 12–13, 17,
  18, 42, 57, 184, 186, 223;
  decision-making 18; defence of 37,
  74, 78–80, 88, 128, 223–4; definition
  1, 4, 11–12, 13, 17, 108, 116, 185, 197;
  eastern 3, 16, 78, 104, 183; economic
  recovery 19; as electoral issue 7, 32;
  harmonisation with 37–8, 40, 84, 98,
  99, 138, 158; views of Britain 26–7,
  33, 92, 128, 189, 208; *see also* Britain,
  leadership of Europe;
  Europeanisation
European 'Tactical' Group 137
European army 78–80, 106
European Atomic Energy Community
  (Euratom) 2, 26, 117
European Coal and Steel Community
  (ECSC) 1–2, 19, 21, 108
European Commission 3, 49, 51, 52, 54,
  84, 98, 99, 101, 106, 124, 150, 184,
  210, 212–14, 215; Commissioners
  213; Conservatives views of 212–14;
  directives 101–2, 213–14
European Communities (Amendment)
  bill (1992–93) 158, 177; *see also*
  Maastricht, ratification of
European Communities (Finance) bill
  (1994) 61
European Conservative Group (ECG)
  192, 193
European Council of Ministers 46, 51,
  60, 104, 188, 210, 213, 214–16, 217;
  Athens (1983) 209; Brussels (2004)
  70; Dublin (1979) 48; Fontainebleau
  (1984) 2, 49, 51; Hague (1969) 84,
  100; Madrid (1989) 53–4; Paris (1974)
  45 Rome (1990) 54
European Courts of Justice (ECJ) 82,
  98, 101, 184, 216–17
European customs union 107
European Defence Community (EDC)
  22–5, 78–80, 117
European Defence Co-operation 70, 75,
  78; *See also* European Union, Rapid
  Reaction Force; Pleven Plan; Western
  European Union
European Democratic Group (EDG)
  193, 206
European Democratic Union (EDU)
  192, 194
European Economic Communities
  (EEC) bill (1971) 38–9, 85, 134, 139,
  154, 156, 157, 164, 165, 170, 178–9
European Economic Communities
  (EEC), Information Office 123, 141
European Economic Community (EEC),
  1961 British application 1, 2, 6, 7, 25,
  28–33, 44, 72, 85, 94–6, 129, 133, 153,
  176, 218; 1967 British
  application 2, 6, 34–7, 129, 154; 1970
  British application 2, 37–40, 116;
  British accession (1973) 2, 14;
  alternatives to 30, 33, 35–6, 38, 103,
  109, 119, 130, 178, 180–5, 225;
  authority 84; British public opinion
  31, 35, 39, 43, 85, 91, 102, 120, 127,
  133–4, 147–8, 149, 155, 170; budget
  2, 40, 45, 47, 98, 100, 179, 209, 210;
  budget, British
  renegotiation 48, 51, 88, 118, 131;
  consequences for Britain 5, 48, 116,
  117–18, 129, 179; creation of 2, 26,
  128; Draft Treaty on European
  Union (1984) 51, 203, 209;
  enlargement 2, 13, 37, 55, 61, 90,

103–4, 116, 131, 150, 209, 212, 214, 125; political unity 30, 80; renegotiation 40, 130, 138; Solemn Declaration on European Union (1983) 50; veto (1963) 25, 32–4, 74, 116, 129, 137, 186; veto (1967) 35, 37, 74, 136, 143, 180
European Exchange Rate Mechanism (ERM) 1, 4, 50, 74, 219; British join 4, 7, 53–4, 58, 100–101, 158; British withdraw 4, 58, 101
European Forum 123–6; *see also* Conservative Group for Europe
European Foundation 63, 168
European Free Trade Area (EFTA) 26–8, 31, 36, 75, 92–3, 95, 104, 109–10, 129, 160, 179, 180, 182, 219, 220
European League for Economic Cooperation (ELEC) 19, 121
European Monetary System (EMS) 3–4, 45, 50–1, 84, 100, 130, 150
European Monetary Union (EMU) *see* European Monetary System
European Movement 42, 63, 81, 120–1, 125, 139, 141, 145, 201
European Parliament 10, 16, 45, 50, 54, 83, 125, 149, 164, 183, 191, 193, 195, 204, 208, 209–12, 213; Conservative delegation 10, 45, 46, 47, 164, 192, 199, 201–2, 206, 208–9; Conservative MEPs *see* Conservative Party, Members of European Parliament; criticisms of 210; direct elections to 34, 45–7, 131, 144, 157, 179, 193, 201, 204, 211–12; dual mandate 201–2, 205
European Peoples' Party (EPP) 192–3, 194, 195, 206, 226; and Conservative Allies 70, 193, 194, 195–6
European Policy (Cabinet) Committee 76
European Referendum (1975) 1, 2, 40–4, 45, 70, 84, 85, 91, 121, 125–6, 130, 139, 148, 152, 174, 187, 218–19
European Representation Fund 201
European Research Group 63, 164
European Union of Women 121, 190, 218
European Union, associate status 103–4; British withdrawal from 55, 70, 103, 180, 182, 226; central bank 61, 164; common foreign policy 3, 51, 55, 79, 80, 83, 112; constitution 4, 68–70, 71, 82, 85, 104, 179, 196, 216; Convention on the Future of Europe 68–9; Dutch rejection 4, 70; economic union 3, 80, 81; French rejection 4, 70; institutions, reform of 54, 69, 84,

104, 106, 130, 150, 205, 210, 212, 213, 214, 215, 216; law 86, 214, 216–17; national veto 34, 66, 81, 85, 211; origins of Euro 53–4, 60; political union 3, 54, 80, 81–3, 129; Rapid Reaction Force 67, 79; single currency (Euro) 3, 4, 53, 57, 60–3, 63–6, British refuse to join Euro 4, 56, Conservative hostility towards Euro 61–2, 63–5, 99–100, 102–3, Conservative support for Euro 62, 63, 114; social chapter 3, 51, 55, 56, 60, 66, 142, 178, 195; social chapter, British opt-out 56, 59, 98; treaty renegotiation 66, 68, 69, 226; workers rights 3, 51, 66
Europeanisation 7, 37, 51, 100, 115, 138, 158, 193, 219
Europhile *see* Pro-Europeans
Euro-ratchet effect 101
Euroscepticism 7, 37, 53, 54, 55, 56, 61–70, 81, 152–87, 196, 219–20, 226; alternatives to EU 182–5, 226; arguments 57, 72, 82, 85, 86–7, 88, 98–9, 101–2, 132, 150, 159–60, 176, 179–80, 183, 184–5, 210, 214, 215; definition 152, 159, 183; leadership 153–9; and the media 185–7, 195; motivations 159–65, 215–16; *see also* Anti-Marketeers
*Evening Standard* 132
Expanding Commonwealth Group 27, 77

*Facts and Fairy Tales Revisited* (1995) 145
Falklands War 131, 155
Farr, John 173
Favell, Tony 91
federalism 4, 34, 55, 58, 65, 68, 80, 81–3, 101, 121, 155, 162, 176, 184, 189, 194, 211, 214, 217, 224
Federation of British Industry (FBI) 32
Feldman, Basil 174
Fell, Anthony 29, 152, 153, 163, 168, 171, 176
Finland 3, 61
Fisher, Nigel 171
fishing 61, 149, 161, 219
Fletcher-Cooke, Charles 202
food prices 37, 43, 83, 96–7, 117, 139, 157, 179
Foot, Michael 151
Foreign Affairs Council 215
Foreign Office 11, 17, 49, 54, 72, 108, 113, 141, 145, 191
Forth, Eric 182, 209

Forward Britain Movement 169
Foster, Arnold 140
Foster, John 108, 198
Fowler, Norman 65
Fox, Marcus 61
Franc 53
France 3, 4, 18, 21, 22, 25, 26, 34, 53, 60,
    72, 117, 148, 184, 193, 207, 220;
    agriculture 74, 97, 98; attitudes towards
    25, 33, 36, 73–4, 79–80, 113, 166, 200,
    223; self-interest 74, 98, 115, 215
Francis, Jeremy 167
Franco-German relations 13, 22, 45, 48,
    50, 74, 75, 80, 98, 113, 128, 130, 223
Fraser, Hugh 108
Fraser, Michael 191, 201
Free French 111
free trade 3, 92–4, 96, 116–17, 138, 158,
    219, 222
Free Trade Area (FTA) 26, 73, 92, 128–9
Freedom Association 182
Freeman, Roger 177
Fresh Start Group 59, 63, 162, 177, 178
Fresh Start petition (1992) 166
functionalists 81, 82

Gaitskell, Hugh 148
Galbraith affair (1962) 32
Gale, George 187
Gardiner, George 63, 124, 125, 162, 163,
    174, 175
General Agreement on Tariffs and Trade
    (GATT) 88, 129
German Christian Democrats (CDU)
    191, 192–3, 194, 206
Germany 3, 18, 21, 22, 24, 50, 60, 72, 97,
    115, 209, 211; economy 53, 58, 62, 73,
    74, 118, 129, 159, 222; fears of 3, 15,
    23, 73–4, 112, 117, 223; military
    defence of 21–2; rearmament 23,
    24–5; reunification 3, 74
Get Britain Out 175
Gill, Ben 98
Gill, Christopher 59, 153, 160, 174, 177
Gilmour, Ian 46, 49, 52, 126
Gladwyn, Lord 120, 141
globalisation 221
Goebbels, Josef 67
gold standard 58, 103
Goldsmith, Lord 63
Good Friday Agreement 90, 179
Goodhart, Philip 144
Gorbachev, Mikhail 3
Gorman, Teresa 152, 153, 177
Goschen, Lord 198

Gould, Brian 156
Graham, Fergus 92
Gramm, Phil 183
Grant, Anthony 167
Greece 2, 37, 103
Green, Ewen 7
Green, Maurice 186
Grieve, Percy 111
Griffith, Eldon 123, 143, 202
*Guardian, The* 140
Gummer, John 122

Hague Congress (1948) 15
Hague, William 13, 63, 99, 196;
    commitment to referendum 91,131;
    as Conservative leader 64–7, 102–3,
    132, 166, 182, 195; criticism of 64,
    65–6, 68; on single currency 64, 66,
    102, 184; single currency ballot 65–6;
    speech, Fontainebleau (1998) 66; wins
    leadership (1997) 64
Hallett, John Hugh 108
Hallstein, 33, 212
Hannan, Daniel 164
Hare, John 191
Harris, John 44
Hart, Michael 170
Hartlepool 88
Hawkins, Nick 183–4
Hay, John 108
H-Block 209
Headlam, Cuthbert 78, 79
Heath, Edward 14, 25, 28, 32, 33, 36, 40,
    46, 48, 50, 62, 84, 88, 104, 112, 113,
    119, 121, 123, 129–30, 133, 136, 156,
    162, 198, 218, 223; 1970 application
    37; conducts 1961–63 entry
    negotiations 30, 32; defeated
    February 1974 election 40; defeated
    in leadership contest (1975) 40;
    elected party leader 34; Europeanism
    34, 82, 87, 108–9, 115–16; on
    federalism 82; on free vote 39–40;
    leadership 109, 143, 144, 148, 180–1;
    maiden speech (1950) 20, 108; on
    referendum 38, 90; on single currency
    62, 65; on sovereignty 39, 86; speech,
    Harvard (1967) 113–14; speech,
    national union central council (1971)
    38–9, 86, 138; speech, Paris (1970) 38;
    speech, to nation (1971) 110, 138
Heathcote-Amory, Derek 63, 69, 173,
    214, 217, 226
Heffer, Simon 156, 185
Helmer, Roger 182

Henry IV 17
Heseltine, Michael 65, 66, 69, 80, 101, 117, 121, 126, 133; cabinet resignation 52, 63; leadership challenge (1990) 54
Hill, Lord 186
Hinchingbrooke, Lord 152, 153, 154–5, 156, 160, 168, 170, 187
historiography 4–8
Holland 55, 192
Hollobone, Phillip 182
Holy Alliance 17
Home, Alec Douglas 25, 33, 34, 76, 81, 84, 123, 125, 191, 212
Hope, Lord John 108
horticulture, *see* Britain, agriculture
*House* 62
House of Commons 28–9, 38–9, 52, 54, 55–6, 60, 69, 81, 85, 86, 89, 91, 109, 132, 138, 143, 153, 168, 201, 202, 208; ministerial questions and answers 133, 134, 137, 170, 178
House of Lords 57, 84
Howard, Michael 56, 64, 69, 132, 150, 184, 196, 216; becomes leader 69; speech, Berlin (2004) 69–70
Howe, Geoffrey 49, 54, 67, 69, 80, 100, 122, 149; on EU 52, 62, 85, 101; resignation from cabinet 54–5, 63; on sovereignty 87, 89
Howell, David 62, 121
Hudson, Miles 125
human rights 208
Hunt, John 202
Hurd, Anthony 120
Hurd, Douglas 39, 44, 47, 55, 57, 59, 62, 67, 69, 84, 91, 114, 117, 121, 138, 145
Hutchinson, John 198
Hynd, Harry 121

immigration 32, 56, 77, 157, 161, 167
imperial preference 18, 72, 77, 92–4, 142, 198, 222, 225
imperialism 18, 225
imperialists 72, 76, 119, 160, 222
*Independent* 65
Independent Broadcast Authority (IBA) 187
Independent Labour Party 29, 176
inflation 40, 58, 163
informed opinion 136–7, 139, 142; *see also* public opinion
Inglewood, Lord 195
Institute of Economic Affairs 102
*International Affairs* 82

internet 13
*Inverness Courier* 186
Ioanninan compromise 60
Iraq, war with 165
Ireland 2, 15, 37, 103, 107, 161
Irish Home Rule 153
*It's Your Line* 140
Italy 4, 15, 24, 26, 27, 50, 192, 211

Jackson, Robert 216
James, David 146
Jansen, Thomas 193, 194
Japan 3, 107, 109, 117, 222, 223
Jay, Douglas 156
Jenkin, Bernard 162
Jenkin, Patrick 123, 138
Jenkins, Roy 44, 48, 178
Johnson, Boris 185

Kavanagh, Dennis 49
Keep Britain In 42
Keep the Pound campaign (2000–2001) 66, 102, 132
Kellett-Bowman, Elaine 202, 212
Kennedy, Paul 224
Kerr, Hamilton 108
King, Tom 62
Kingston Conservatives Against the Common Market 171
Kinnock, Neil 56
Kirk, Peter 113, 123, 198, 201, 204–5
Klepsch, Egon 206
Knapman, Roger 151
Korean War 2, 21, 78
Krushchev 75
Kuwait 131

Labour Party 11, 33, 35, 39, 43, 44, 45, 51, 59, 60, 64, 90, 93, 121, 130, 141, 151, 175, 178, 195, 200; manifesto Feb. 1974 general election 40, 148
Laeken Declaration (2001) 68
Lamont, Norman 56, 62, 83, 99, 103, 162, 163, 171, 182
Lancashire 171
Lancaster House 138
Lawrence, Ivan 162
Lawson, Nigel 50, 53, 54, 63, 100, 101
League of Empire Loyalists 169
League of Nations 107, 224
League of Nations Union 121; Peace Ballot (1935) 42, 89
Lee, Frank 28
Legge-Bourke, Henry 19, 23, 95, 109–10, 111, 160, 161, 167

Leiber, R.J. 169
Leigh, Edward 152
Lewis, Russell 122–3, 138, 144
Liberal Democrats 63, 126
Liberal Party 32, 33, 40, 107
Liberal Unionists 222
Lightbown, David 172
Lilley, Peter 54, 56, 64
limited liability 12, 113, 185, 221, 222–3
little Englander 183–4, 203
Lloyd, Selwyn 27
Longden, Gilbert 108, 125
Luce, Richard 114
Ludlow, Piers 218, 220
Luxembourg 21
Luxembourg Compromise (1965) 34, 85

Maastricht Conference 3, 54, 55–6, 104, 158, 211
Maastricht Treaty 1, 3, 54, 55, 59, 71, 80, 98, 114, 117, 142, 149, 159, 213, 220; British opt-outs 3, 80, 217; Eurosceptic criticisms of 55, 80, 85, 175; ratification of 3, 4, 56–60, 132, 133, 134, 145, 164–5, 172–3, 174, 178–9
MacDonald, Peter 15
MacGregor, John 123
Maclay, John 24, 108, 111
Macleod, Iain 31, 32, 33, 38, 137, 142, 170, 191
Macmillan government, criticisms of 30, 32, 44, 77, 84, 142, 148, 163; ministerial statements 32, 133, 135; preparing for EEC application 95, 109, 117–18, 129, 136
Macmillan, Harold 1, 2, 6, 15, 17, 25, 26, 33, 74, 75, 84, 94, 113, 123, 129, 133, 154, 196, 218, 223; announces 1961 application 28, 136, 176; on anti-marketeers 155; attends Council of Europe 16, 197–8, 207, 208; criticisms of Churchill 17; economic thinking 7; speech, conference (1962) 29; 'Supermac' 32; views on EDC 23, 25, 117; views on Europe 28, 120, 200
Macmillan, Maurice 74, 121
Macmillan-Scott, Edward 195
Maitland, Patrick 77, 198
Major, John 3, 4, 6, 7, 54, 56, 63, 66, 69, 79, 98, 144, 175, 178, 183, 203; cabinet 'bastards' 60, 139, 158; criticism of 55, 59, 60, 61, 62, 63, 80, 91, 114, 151, 158, 163; on Europe 55, 215; on Eurosceptics 153;
government 37, 91, 101, 131, 172, 179, 194, 214, 216; leadership contest (1995) 61, 126, 177; on single currency 62, 102; speech, Bonn (1991) 55; speech, Leiden (1995) 18; on WEU 79
Maples, John 195
Margaret, Princess 33
Marlow, Tony 60, 65, 153
Marquand, David 208
Marshall Plan 75, 108
Marshall, John 209
Marten, Neil 36, 41, 46, 90, 134, 146, 153, 156–7, 160, 167, 168, 172, 174, 177, 186, 210, 218, 226
Martens, Wilfred 194, 195
Mathew, Robert 121
Maude, Angus 46, 154, 170
Maude, Francis 66, 104, 215
Maudling, Reginald 121, 184
Maxse, Marjorse 120
Maxwell-Fyfe, David 15, 22, 81, 113, 198, 208
Mayhew, Christopher 198
McAlpine, Alastair 43, 63, 177
media 139–40, 148, 185–7; views on 42, 103
Messina Negotiations 2, 5, 6, 26, 218
Mexico 183
Meyer, Anthony 33, 82, 125
Mill, J.S. 86
Milward, Alan 5, 13, 103, 128, 220
miners' strike 131
Ministry of Europe 40
Minoprio, Peter 95, 120
Moate, Roger 167, 177
Mollet, Guy 84
Monday Club 169, 171
Monetary union *see* European Union, single currency
Monnet Committee (1969) 84, 100
Monnet, Jean 111, 196
Montagu, Victor *see* Hinchingbrooke, Lord
Montgomery, Lord 31
*Monthly News* 162, 172
More, Jasper 226
*Morning Star* 43
Morris, Peter 10
Morris, Peter Temple 63, 64
Morrison, Charles 186
Morrison, Herbert 207
Mudd, David 173
Munich agreement (1938) 43
Murdock, Rupert 103

Nabarro, Gerald 152
National Archives, Kew 6, 8
National Common Market Petition
    Council 177
National Farmers' Union (NFU) 96, 98,
    171, 206
National Health Service (NHS) 67, 221
National Referendum Campaign (NRC)
    41–4, 156, 168, 173, 175, 178, 182;
    finances 43
nationalisation 19, 22
nationalism 102, 183–4, 225
Neave, Airey 20, 40, 116
Nelson, Anthony 63
Netherlands 21
New Zealand 35, 77–8, 109, 160
newspapers 9, 36, 43, 59, 62, 91, 103,
    135, 170, 185–87
Newton, Tony 57
Nice Treaty (2000) 4, 67, 80, 104
Nicholls, Harmar 163–4, 181, 208, 209
Nicholson, David 199
Nicholson, Emma 63
Nicolson, Harold 207
Nicolson, Nigel 108, 207
Night of the Long Knives (1962) 155
Nixon, Richard 87
*No Tame or Minor Role* (1963) 123
No Turning Back 63
Non-governmental organisations 136,
    141, 206
Nord, Hans 125
Normanton, Tom 201, 202
North Atlantic Free Trade Area
    (NAFTA) 36, 76, 119, 138, 143, 160,
    176, 180–1, 182–3, 225
North Atlantic Treaty Organisation
    (NATO) 4, 12, 17, 21–2, 23, 24, 26,
    36, 55, 70, 74, 75, 78–80, 83, 88, 150,
    188, 224
Northern Ireland 90, 139, 161, 178–9
Norton, Philip 8
Norway 37, 61
Nott Report 102–3
Nott, John 102
*Nottingham Guardian Journal* 186
Nouvelles Equipes Internationales (NEI)
    189, 190
nuclear weapons and deterrence 75, 80, 87
Nutting, Anthony 23–4, 25, 113, 184, 189

O'Neill, Con 41
*Observer* 140
Oder 13
Oil crisis (1979) 3

Onslow, Sue 7
Organisation for European Economic
    co-operation (OEEC) 4, 27
Osborn, John 202
Ottawa Agreement (1932) 92

Page, John 202
Page-Croft, Henry 77
*Panorama* 140, 187
Parkinson, Cecil 54
Parliamentary Common Market
    Committee 176
Parliamentary Group on the Common
    Market 137
Partido Popular 206
patriotism 18, 71, 94, 102, 121, 183, 221
Patten, Chris 104, 117, 193, 194, 213
Paul, John 167–72
Pawsey, James 175
Pears, Gordon 34–5, 88, 143
Petherick, Maurice 168, 225
Pitman, James 108
Pleven Plan (1950) 22
Plumb, Lord Henry 193, 199, 209
Poland, guarantee to (1939) 224
Poll Tax *see* Community Tax
Portillo, Michael 67, 79, 80, 102, 150,
    158
Portugal 2, 3, 37, 103
Positive Europeans 59, 63, 121
Post Office 65, 145, 226
Pounder, Rafton 204
Powell, Enoch 19, 34, 40, 41, 122, 152,
    153, 156, 157, 158, 160, 167, 184, 185
Price, David 186
Price, Peter 149
Primrose League 169
Prior, James 46, 115, 138
Prodi, Romano 214
Pro-European Conservative Party 67,
    126, 134
Pro-Europeans 73, 74, 77, 105–26, 161,
    170, 188–209, 211, 226; case for
    Europe 74–6, 84, 87, 88, 96, 109,
    110–18, 127, 129, 136–7, 147, 163,
    182, 222; converts 109–10; definition
    105–6, 107–8; forums 118–26;
    inter-war champions 106–7, 221–2;
    propaganda 32, 42, 62, 63, 65, 81, 96,
    117, 124, 135,141
proportional representation 46
protection 74, 92, 96, 160, 163
Prout, Christopher 194, 206
public opinion 10, 35, 39, 43, 56, 67, 69,
    72, 78, 80, 89, 90, 133, 136, 137, 137,

138, 165, 221; educating 96, 120, 124, 125, 127–51; *see also* informed opinion
Public Record Office (PRO) *see* National Archives
Pym, Francis 5, 39, 46, 49, 50, 90, 138, 177

Qualified majority voting (QMV) 51, 60–1, 79, 82, 101, 163, 211
Quoddle 163

Radio 4's *Today* programme 131
Ramsden, John 10, 148
Rathbone, Brian 86
Rathbone, Tim 67, 134
Redmayne, Martin 27, 75
Redwood, John 54, 61, 64, 103, 158, 183
Rees-Mogg, Lord William 60, 140
Referendum Party 63, 66, 128, 132, 151, 183
Referendum, Beckenham (1971) 139, 144; calls for 38, 39, 56, 60, 62, 67, 68, 89–92, 125, 132, 144, 166, 179; Conservatives on single currency policy 65, 166; Danish on Maastricht (1992) 57, 133; French on Maastricht (1992) 57, 178; Irish on Maastricht (1992) 57; Isle of Ely on EEC (1971) 110; leadership support for 89
*Reformer* 112
Rhine 13, 223
Rhodesia 161
Rhys-Williams, Brandon 202
Ridley, Nicholas 54, 63, 74, 104, 123, 137, 162, 163, 198, 206, 212
Rifkind, Malcolm 76, 131, 150, 182
*Right Approach* (1976) 193
Rippon, Geoffrey 38, 88, 100, 121, 138, 205
Roberts, Peter 108
Roberts, Shelia 209
Rodger, John 199
Rodgers, Bill 44
Rogers, Adrian 63, 65
Rogers, John 202
Roman Catholicism 161, 186, 189
Ross, Ronald 198
Rossi, Hugh 192
Rotary clubs 141
Royle, Anthony 125, 132, 141
Ruhr, Volker 194
Russell, Ronald 160, 198
Russell, William 123
Russia 3, 12, 17, 72, 104, 116; threat from 21, 27, 78–9, 107, 154, 188, 224

Ryder, Richard 173, 177

Sainsbury, John 43
Salisbury, 4th Marquess 11
Salisbury, 6th Marquess (Bobbety) 26
Sandwich, Earl of *see* Hinchingbrooke, Lord
Sandys, Duncan 15, 16, 21, 29, 77, 108, 120, 121, 137, 196, 197, 224
Santer Commission, resignation 214
Santer, Jacques 194, 214
Schuman Plan (1950) 1–2, 5, 16, 19, 20, 108, 110, 157
Schuman, Robert 19
Scotland 43, 52
Scott, Nicholas 167
Scott-Hopkins, J.S.R. 193, 198, 205, 209
Scruby, Edgar 171
Second World War, impact on European views 110–13, 184
Seldon, Anthony 5
Select Committee, Direct Elections to European Parliament 124
Select Committee, Foreign Affairs 91
Selsdon Group 55
Shaw, Michael 203–4
Shay, Michael 167
Shepherd, Gillian 184
Shepherd, Richard 55, 60, 160
*Shetland News* 186
shoe and boot industry 161
Single European Act (SEA), British parliamentary ratification 51–2, 152, 162; consequences 99, 101, 158–9, 162, 179, 211, 216; creation 3, 51–3, 69, 71, 85, 88; Thatcher government support 3, 51, 131, 152
single market 51–3, 98, 101
Sinn Fein 179
Smith, Dudley 42
Smith, Iain Duncan 67–8, 161, 162, 217; elected leader 68, on Euro 68; 166; as leader 68–9, 132, 151
Smith, John 150
Smith, Tim 59
Smithers, Peter 75, 107, 191
Social Democracy 102
Social Democratic Party (SDP) 43
Southern Television 140, 186
sovereignty 15, 28, 43, 46, 52, 56, 59, 65, 69, 71, 83–9, 90, 99, 101, 104, 118, 123, 153, 154, 156, 157, 160, 161, 176, 179, 181, 184, 210, 215, 217, 220, 224; pooling 79, 83, 86, 87–8, 106, 183, 224

Soviet Union *see* Russia
Spaak, Paul Henri 16, 23, 111, 196
Spain 2, 3, 37, 94, 103
Special Operations Executive (SOE) 111
special relationship *see* Anglo-American relations
*Spectator* 74, 163, 187
Spencer, Tom 66
Spicer, James 103, 124, 202
Spicer, Michael 153, 177
Spinelli Report (1984) 209
Spink, Bob 182
Stalin 78
Stanley, Oliver 199–200
sterling 5, 37, 58, 66, 99, 100–101, 103, 119
Sterling Crisis (1986) 100
Stevas, Norman St John 124, 144, 181
Stevens, John 126, 133
Stormont 90
strikes 40
subsidiarity 55
Suez 26, 28, 72, 85, 87, 113, 115, 128, 154, 155
Suez Group 110
*Sun* 185, 186, 225
*Sunday Express* 163
*Sunday Times* 63, 140
Sweden 3, 61
Sweeney, Walter 80, 174
Swinton, Lord 88
Sykes, Paul 65

Tapsell, Peter 67
tariff reform 7, 94, 148, 153, 158, 219, 221–2
taxation 38, 67, 84, 99, 166, 219, 221
Taylor, A.J.P. 186
Taylor, Ian 59, 65, 174
Taylor, John 195
Taylor, Teddy 84, 161, 183, 226
Tebbit, Norman 54, 57, 58, 99, 216
television 140
*That Was The Week that Was* 32
Thatcher Foundation 9
Thatcher, Margaret 2, 7, 41, 46, 57, 59, 66, 80, 84, 156, 203, 206; on 1975 referendum 40–1; domestic statecraft 7, 97, 130–1, 219; on EDU 192; on Europe 40, 45, 49–50, 51, 53; European budget battle 48–50, 88, 130, 149; Euroscepticism 153, 194; memoirs 48; on NAFTA 183; on proportional representation 46; resigns office 54–5; on sovereignty 87;

speech, Chicago (1991) 55; speech, 'No, No, No' (1990) 54; speech, Bruges (1988) 53, 73, 85, 101, 219; speech, Hanover (1975) 192; speech, on European referendum (1975) 42; *Statecraft* 183; views of 48, 49, 53, 58; views on EMS 51, 100; views on ERM 52, 58; views on Euro 66; views on SEA 101; visits to Europe 49, 216; wins leadership (1975) 40
Thatcherism 44, 51, 54, 85, 92, 102, 159, 179, 213
Thatcherites 55, 57–8, 101, 158–9, 162, 163
*The Challenge from Europe* (1957) 122–3
*The Future of Europe* 69, 213
'there is no alternative' (TINA) 129, 138, 218
thirty-year rule 8, 9
Thomas, Peter 172
Thompson, Helen 7
Thorneycroft, Peter 15, 16, 28, 42, 117, 174, 223
Tilney, John 108
*Times, the* 43, 94, 140, 146, 174, 176, 185, 186
*Tory European* 125
Tory Reform Group 112, 121
Townend, John 175
trade unions 141, 216
'traditional British foreign policy' 224
Treasury 4, 5, 47, 50, 64
Treaties of Rome (1957) 2, 5, 26, 28, 38, 51, 78, 113, 117–18, 122, 128, 158, 161, 209
Tucker, Geoffrey 124
Tuckman, Fred 206
Tugenhat, Christopher 213
Turkey 37, 103
Turner, John 7
Turton, Robin 29, 153, 154, 155, 161, 168, 169, 181, 225

UK Independence Party (UKIP) 63, 65, 128, 150, 196, 226
Ulster Unionists 153, 161, 178–9
unemployment 30, 32, 43, 93, 131
United European Movement (UEM) 15, 113, 120, 190, 199
United Nations 75, 83, 86, 88, 224
United States of America 3, 11, 14, 17, 18, 21, 23, 27, 72, 76, 93, 107, 109, 116, 138, 160, 182, 222; and decolonisation 76–8; isolationism 23,

72, 75, 224; links with Europe 21, 72, 74–6, 117, 180
Upper Clyde shipbuilders 139

Valued Added tax (VAT) 38, 48, 84, 99, 165
Vassall affair (1962) 32
veto 15, 149; *see also* European Union, national veto
Vredleing Proposals (1984) 203

Waldegrave, William 103, 182
Walker, Bill 162
Walker, Peter 29, 46, 77, 109–10, 153, 154, 160, 161, 167–8, 169, 171, 186
Walker-Smith, Derek 29, 122, 153–4, 160, 161, 163, 168, 169, 170, 173, 184, 202, 218, 225
Wall, Patrick 175
Walters, Alan 54
Ward, Irene 19
Warren, Kenneth 202
Warsaw Pact 3, 12, 13
Waterhouse, Charles 77
Wegener, Henrig 193
Welsh Assembly 89
Welsh, Michael 195
Werner Committee (1970–71) 60, 81, 84, 100
West Indies 109
Western European Union (WEU) 4, 17, 23–5, 31, 33, 78–80, 88, 111, 114, 188, 191, 204, 218

*Western Gazette* 186
Westland Affair (1984) 52
*Which?* 206
Whipless Nine 61, 172
White Papers, Defence (1957) 24–5; Direct European Elections (1977) 46; *Europe: The Future* (1984) 51; European Economic Communities (June 1971) 38, 138, 145; European referendum (1975) 40, 41
Whitelaw, William 41, 42, 62, 86, 111, 121, 139, 143, 174
Whittingdale, John 162
Wilkinson, John 162
Williams, Herbert 18, 160
Williams, Robin 123
Wilson, Harold 34, 41, 45, 148
Winterton, Ann 182
Winterton, Nicholas 162, 182
Wistrich, Ernest 120
Women's Institute 141
Wood, David 140
Wood, Richard 119, 181
Woolton, Lord 14, 18, 20
World Trade Center 76
Wright, Michael 181

'Year of Europe' (1967) 143–4
*Yes to Europe* (1975) 139
Young Farmers 141
Young, Hugo 50, 51, 148
Younger, John 46
Yugoslavia, civil war 112

Printed in the United Kingdom by
Lightning Source UK Ltd., Milton Keynes
141276UK00001B/72/P